THE GREAT GAME IN WEST ASIA

MEHRAN KAMRAVA
(*Ed.*)

The Great Game in West Asia

جامعة جورجتاون قطر
GEORGETOWN UNIVERSITY QATAR

Center *for* International *and* Regional Studies

OXFORD
UNIVERSITY PRESS

OXFORD
UNIVERSITY PRESS

Oxford University Press is a department of the
University of Oxford. It furthers the University's objective
of excellence in research, scholarship, and education
by publishing worldwide.

Oxford New York
Auckland Cape Town Dar es Salaam Hong Kong Karachi
Kuala Lumpur Madrid Melbourne Mexico City Nairobi
New Delhi Shanghai Taipei Toronto

With offices in
Argentina Austria Brazil Chile Czech Republic France Greece
Guatemala Hungary Italy Japan Poland Portugal Singapore
South Korea Switzerland Thailand Turkey Ukraine Vietnam

Published in the United States of America by
Oxford University Press
198 Madison Avenue, New York, NY 10016

Library of Congress Cataloging-in-Publication Data is available
Mehran Kamrava.
The Great Game in West Asia.
ISBN: 9780190673604

Printed in India on acid-free paper

CONTENTS

PART III

THE TRAVAILS OF STATE-BUILDING

CONTRIBUTORS

Hamid Ahmadi is Professor of Political Science in Tehran University and a Senior Research Fellow at the Institute for Middle East Strategic Studies. His most recent books include *Ethnicity and Ethnic Politics in Iran: Myth and Reality*, 10th edition (2015, in Farsi); *The Foundations of Iranian National Identity* (2013, in Farsi); and *Political Sociology of the Islamic Movements* (2012, in Farsi). His articles have appeared in a wide array of journals in both English and Farsi.

Meliha Benli Altunışık is Professor in the Department of International Relations and Dean of the Graduate School of Social Sciences at the Middle East Technical University in Ankara, Turkey. In addition to a number of journal articles, she is the author of *Turkey: Challenges of Continuity and Change* (2005, co-authored with Ozlem Tur).

Bayram Balci held positions as a nonresident scholar at the Carnegie Endowment for International Peace, as Director of the French Institute of Central Asian Studies in Tashkent, and Jean Monnet post-doctoral fellow at the European University Institute in Florence. His most recent publications include "Turkey's Religious Outreach and the Turkic World" in *Current Trends in Islamist Ideology* (2014), and *China and India in Central Asia: A New "Great Game"?* (Palgrave-McMillan, 2010), edited with J.F. Huchet, M. Laruelle, and S. Peyrouse.

Richard Giragosian is the Founding Director of the Regional Studies Center, an independent think tank located in Yerevan, Armenia. He also serves as a Visiting Professor and as a Senior Expert at the Yerevan State University's Center for European Studies and is a contributing analyst for *Oxford Analytica*.

Giragosian's writings have appeared in *Jane's Information Group*, *Current History*, *Demokratizatsiya*, and the *China and Eurasia Forum Quarterly*.

Mehran Kamrava is Professor and Director of the Center for International and Regional Studies at Georgetown University's School of Foreign Service in Qatar. He is the author of a number of journal articles and books, including, most recently, *Qatar: Small State, Big Politics* (2015); *The Modern Middle East: A Political History since the First World War*, 3rd edition (2013); and *Iran's Intellectual Revolution* (2008).

Alexander Kupatadze is a Lecturer (Assistant Professor) at the School of International Relations at St Andrews University. His publications include several journal articles as well as *Organized Crime, Political Transitions, and State Formation in Post-Soviet Eurasia* (2012).

Anatol Lieven is Professor in Georgetown University's School of Foreign Service in Qatar. He is also a senior fellow of the New America Foundation in Washington, DC. His books include *Pakistan: A Hard Country* (2011); *Ethical Realism: A Vision for America's Role in the World* (co-authored with John Hulsman, 2006); *America Right or Wrong: An Anatomy of American Nationalism* (2004 and 2012); *Ukraine and Russia: A Fraternal Rivalry* (1999); *Chechnya: Tombstone of Russian Power?* (1998); and *The Baltic Revolution: Estonia, Latvia, Lithuania and the Path to Independence* (1993).

Jeffrey Mankoff is Deputy Director and Senior Fellow with the Center for Strategic and International Studies' Russia and Eurasia Program. He is the author of *Russian Foreign Policy: The Return of Great Power Politics* (2011).

Mahmood Monshipouri is Professor of International Relations at San Francisco State University. His edited books include *Inside the Islamic Republic: Social Change in Post-Khomeini Iran* (2016) and *Information Politics, Protests, and Human Rights in the Digital Age* (2016). Monshipouri is author of *Democratic Uprisings in the Middle East and North Africa: Youth Technology, and Modernization* (2013); and *Terrorism, Security, and Human Rights: Harnessing the Rule of Law* (2012).

Anar Valiyev is Assistant Professor of Political Science and Associate Provost of ADA University in Baku, Azerbaijan. His articles have appeared in a number of peer-reviewed journals such as *Demokratizatsiya*, *Problems of Post-Communism*, *Eurasian Geography and Economics*, and *Cities*.

Gareth Winrow is an independent research analyst and consultant based in Oxford, England. His most recent publications include *Realization of Turkey's*

Energy Aspirations: Pipe Dreams or Real Projects? (2014); *Turkey, Russia and the Caucasus: Common and Diverging Interests* (2009); and *Problems and Prospects for the Fourth Corridor: The Position and Role of Turkey in Gas Transit to Europe* (2009).

ACKNOWLEDGMENTS

This book grew out of one of the research initiatives undertaken by the Center for International and Regional Studies at Georgetown University's School of Foreign Service in Qatar. In addition to the contributors to the volume, the group benefited from the insights and comments of a number of scholars and experts who at various stages took part in the research initiative. Grateful acknowledgment goes to Haya Al Noaimi, Leila Alieva, Zahra Babar, Michael Bushku, Elahe Koolaee, and Suzi Mirgani. All provided invaluable feedback in discussions leading up to the project's crafting and on earlier drafts of the chapters. The volume also benefited from the invaluable research assistance of Tamim Alnuweiri, Umber Latafat, and Erika Thao Nguyen. My colleagues at the Center for International and Regional Studies, where the project was conceived and completed, were instrumental in helping create a most supportive and intellectually stimulating work environment. Their support and assistance with this volume, as with everything else I have written or edited since 2007, is deeply appreciated. Grateful acknowledgment goes also to the Qatar Foundation for its support of research and other scholarly endeavors.

1

THE GREAT GAME IN WEST ASIA

Mehran Kamrava

There is something funny about geography. The importance of certain locations can rise or decline depending on what may be found underneath it or the changing priorities and aspirations of those on or near it. It can shape the fate of empires by facilitating their rise or hastening their demise, and it can become a source of intense competition or neglect by powers near and distant. There is an intimate connection between geography and power, with the geographic dimensions of power being often defined as "geopolitics" and the strategic competition over or acquisition of that geographic power as "geostrategy."[1] These political and strategic competitions over valuable swathes of land may be less frequent now than they were in bygone eras, but they are just as salient in the first decades of the twenty-first century as they were in centuries past.[2] The global powers of the nineteenth and early twentieth centuries played what came to be known as the "great game" over land, influence, and power—games perfected especially by Britain and Russia over what was once the Ottoman Empire.[3]

The games never subsided, and as the decades of the twentieth century wore on the strategic stakes were raised, and the ensuing competition, which involved both the great powers and newer entrants, became more intense in both depth and scale. Almost no region of the world was spared, and the powers competed and fought one another and their proxies in both hot and cold wars in Europe, Asia, Latin America, Africa, and the Middle East. The Second World War and the Cold War were among the most sustained and systematic, as well as bloody and brutal, of the strategic competitions that the world witnessed across continents and regions.

Near the end of the century, once the Soviet Union collapsed, the apparent triumph of the West over the Communist Bloc led to a diminishing of strategic competitions over many familiar territories. But a promised "new world order" of high idealism, trumpeted by politicians and academics alike, was not to be.[4] Old competitions may have died down, but new ones quickly emerged to take their place. Old strategic rivalries gave way to new ones as formerly contested territories and regions ceased to be sites of contestation and competition and were instead replaced by new, emerging fault lines and sources of division. One of these new, emerging regions over which new actors began competing, and still compete, is the South Caucasus. In fact, a new great game has begun, this time over the South Caucasus. And the prime contenders, new entrants into the global power game, are Iran and Turkey.

This is a book about Turkey and Iran's strategic competition over power and influence in the South Caucasus. These two neighboring Middle Eastern powers have vied for supremacy and influence throughout the region and especially in their immediate vicinity, having in the process to contend with ethnic heterogeneity within their own territories and also across the border. Turkey has long conceived of itself as not just a land bridge between Asia and Europe but in more substantive terms as a central player in regional and global affairs.[5] If somewhat more modest in articulation, Iran's parallel ambitions for strategic centrality and influence have only been masked by its own inarticulate foreign policy agendas and the repeated missteps of its revolutionary leaders.[6] But try they both have nonetheless, and in the South Caucasus each has achieved a modicum of success. In fact, as the contributions to this volume demonstrate, as much of the world's attention has been diverted to conflicts and flashpoints near and far, a new great game has been unraveling between Iran and Turkey in the South Caucasus.

Geographers often question the validity of the various shorthand terms that other social scientists and journalists employ as designation for groups of otherwise disparate countries within the same region. Not surprisingly, it is not clear whether the very term "South Caucasus" even refers to a distinctively identifiable region.[7] It is indeed true that the three countries lumped together today as belonging to the South Caucasus share little in common in terms of ethnic, linguistic, or political affinities. They, like much of the rest of the global south, were once forced into neighborly tranquility and cooperation by greater imperial forces. In their case, it was the overwhelming force of the Soviet Union that sought to forge among them a common identity and a shared polity. In the Middle East, starting at about the same time, it was the French and the British who tried to do the same thing in their own respective spheres of influence. Not surprisingly, historians and geographers have also parsed—more often deconstructed—the validity of the very concept of a "Middle East," seeing it as no more valid than such designations as "the Far East" or, for that matter, "the West."[8]

Like it or not, these terms today have become part of the parlance of academic discourse as well as political action. Academics and journalists may stretch the boundaries of the different regions, but there is broad agreement over which countries lie at the core of each. We know, for example, that Iran is part of the Middle East; and so is Turkey—although for the past several decades its leaders have sought consistently, though largely unsuccessfully, to identify themselves and their country as European. From a purely geographic perspective, both countries do lie in Asia—in Turkey's case around 97 percent of the country's landmass is in Asia and the rest in Europe—and both are located in Asia's western half. They are West Asian powers.

Armenia, Azerbaijan, and Georgia, the three countries that make up the South Caucasus, have emerged as prime areas of competition between Iran and Turkey as the two countries seek to expand their spheres of influence economically, politically, and militarily. Iran and Turkey have not been the only countries competing over the South Caucasus. In the early years following the collapse of the Soviet Union, as an "especially complicated and conflict-prone part of the post-Soviet space," the South Caucasus, along with Central Asia, attracted increasing attention from the United States, the European Union, and Russia, as well as Iran and Turkey, becoming the focal point for what one observer called a "New Great Game."[9] Before long, however, it became clear that none of the great powers had a unified strategic vision for the region, and, as such, none of them was willing to deploy resources to the South Caucasus. In fact, by the mid-1990s, the United States, Russia, and the European Union had decided that the region was of little strategic value and not a first-order priority for any of them.[10] But even if they wanted to, as Lieven argues in the following chapter, they would not have succeeded in establishing hegemony over the region. The ensuing space enabled the two nearby regional middle powers, Turkey and Iran, to actively court the emerging republics to align with them and to try to expand the different dimensions of their influence over them.

A somewhat permissive regional context was one factor in creating opportunities for Iran and Turkey to compete for influence in the South Caucasus. Another was the predicament of the three young republics themselves. As brand new states, the South Caucasus republics had to constitute themselves from scratch. They had to create institutions of rule and instruments of power, forge national identities that sustained and reinforced their sovereignty and independence, establish economies that were networked internally and functioned without dependence on what were now other sovereign states, and they had to navigate their international relations in the ominous shadows of a giant former overlord and smaller but no less ambitious middle powers nearby.

For the South Caucasus republics, state-building has been a particularly arduous task, and in many ways it still continues more than a quarter century after independence. For Armenia, Georgia, and Azerbaijan, state-building has meant embarking on three overlapping processes: 1) political institutionalization, which has meant crafting the institutions of the state and outlining the ways in which they interact together and with social actors and social institutions; 2) political consolidation, in the sense of making state institutions operational in relation to society and with other states; and 3) fostering cohesive if not necessarily uniform national identities.[11] In the process, each state has had to contend with what nearly all other newly-established states have faced, namely the intrusions and interference of outside powers in their domestic politics.

In this introductory chapter I examine first the nature and consequences of the attention paid to the South Caucasus, or lack thereof as the case may be, by the United States, the European Union, and Russia. I then analyze ongoing processes of state-building in each of the region's three states and how the attendant domestic and international challenges of such processes have facilitated opportunities for Iran and Turkey to expand their commercial and strategic ties with each. The chapter ends with an examination of relations between Turkey and Iran, uneasy neighbors that compete on several fronts but also cooperate out of need and necessity. It highlights the unfolding of a new game of geostrategic competition and rivalry by these two regional powers over the South Caucasus. In this part of the world, often neglected by the world's major powers, a new great game is unfolding. Turkey's favored tools of competition and rivalry have been its soft power and pipeline politics, and Iran's are commerce and natural resources. The stakes ultimately boil down to power and influence. But they go beyond the centrality of transit routes, access to new and emerging markets, and footholds in countries and cultures that traverse Asia and Europe. They also impact the domestic politics of each of the competitors themselves, their own ethno-linguistic mosaics, and their projection abroad of national identity and sense of place in history.

The South Caucasus and the Great Powers: Russia, the United States, and the European Union

By virtue of its history, cultural and economic connections, and geographic proximity, Russia maintains by far the most extensive ties with the South Caucasus and pays the closest attention to it as compared to either the European Union or the United States. This was not the case in the early post-independence years, as both the Russian Republic and the countries of the South Caucasus devoted much of their attention to domestic issues or, in Russia's case, to their position in the newly emerging global power structure. In many ways, Moscow took for granted that the newly independent states on its expansive borders would always remain within its diplomatic and security orbits, unable to break away their systemic and structural dependence on Russia's economy and military protection. Change to this outlook has been slow in coming, and for many in Moscow it still has yet to come.[12]

It was only in the mid-1990s that Russia began to see the South Caucasus as an area of potential strategic importance and started to expand proactively its military and economic presence in the region. In 1995, Russia acquired a military base in Armenia, followed by a 1997 military cooperation agreement between the two countries.[13] Armenia, as we shall see shortly, has always remained in the Russian security orbit. As the 1990s came to a close, two developments in the South Caucasus added urgency to Russia's security and economic presence in the region. One was Azerbaijan's discovery and export of massive quantities of oil and gas and the increasing importance of the entire region as a resource-rich and key transit route. A second worrying development for Moscow was the trend within the Georgian body politic to pull away from Moscow and instead move closer to the European Union. By the second half of the 2000s, in fact, the Kremlin began to see Western activity in the South Caucasus as an overt attempt to curtail Russian influence in the region.[14]

Moscow's response was multi-pronged. It shored up its economic and security cooperation with Yerevan, all the while ensuring that Azerbaijan did not completely abandon its orbit.[15] A delicate balancing act ensued in which Moscow retains Armenia as a close military ally and Azerbaijan as a close economic partner.[16] Economic partnership with Azerbaijan has taken the form of cooperation in the oil sector, particularly in the transit of oil and gas from the Caspian basin to Europe. Moscow has sought to join Turkey in trying to position Russia as a middleman for European energy buyers.[17] As the Caspian–Black Sea region has assumed greater importance in the first decade of the twenty-first century, Russia has sought to remain a major transit route for energy vis-à-vis the South Caucasus.[18]

In relation to Georgia there was no delicacy. In August 2008, in a punishing war that lasted only six days, Moscow ensured that Georgia's breakaway regions of Abkhazia and South Ossetia, within a stone's throw of Tbilisi, remain Moscow's satellites. Neither the bluster nor the cries of the Georgian president at the time, Mikheil Saakashvili, were enough to lure the US or the EU to his rescue. Ever since, Russia has sanctioned Georgian products, especially hurting the small country's proud and once vibrant wine industry.

Soon after the 2008 war between Georgia and Russia, the global financial crisis hit, and the US and the EU scaled back many of their activities in the South Caucasus, resulting in the emergence of a new status quo in which Russian military presence in Abkhazia and South Ossetia has become part of the long-term landscape of the region.[19] This is likely to continue in the foreseeable future. As the Georgian example has shown, and as both Armenia and Azerbaijan are keenly aware, Russia has demonstrated a willingness to use its hard power to defend its interests. And, moreover, neither the United States nor the European Union have been willing to become militarily involved in the region. As one observer has noted, "countries in Russia's 'near abroad' cannot expect any external help in the event that they encounter security problems with Russia."[20]

Significantly, however, Russia cannot rely too heavily on its hard or even soft powers as effective instruments of influence in the South Caucasus.[21] History has proven long-term military occupations to be untenable. And given its limited financial resources and its "unattractive socio-political model," it will be increasingly difficult for Russia "to rise to the position of the South Caucasus principal partner or to defend its leadership role there."[22] Not surprisingly, therefore, the US and EU's relative absence from the South Caucasus has not necessarily given Moscow a free hand in the region.

Whether out of an awareness of Russia's limitations in the region or its own lack of interest, the EU itself has taken a backseat in the South Caucasus and has adopted what some have called a "Russia-first" approach.[23] The EU's status in the region as a "great absentee" appears rooted in its collective strategic calculations.[24] The EU considers the South Caucasus to be peripheral as compared to the Balkans, Ukraine, and Moldova.[25] This general neglect seemed to come to an end around 2003, as signs appeared that Azerbaijan's natural resources-driven boom may reverberate across the region.[26] But those signs paled in comparison with the growing strategic importance of areas further west and the early-starter advantages of Russia and the United States. From Europe's perspective, chronic regional tensions in the South Caucasus undermine the region's potential as a land bridge linking Europe to Central Asia and the Caspian Sea.[27] Thus, the best that the EU has done is to support various peace-building institutions, the success of which, given the region's many frozen conflicts, is debatable.[28]

The United States, a credible argument may be made, has not fared much better. On the one hand, the US has been seeking a less confrontational approach to Russia, while on the other hand it has been encouraging more European activism in the South Caucasus.[29] Whether the product of a "leading from behind" policy preference or simple disinterest, "there has been a notable lack of coherent and consistent US, and Western, policy for the region."[30] Similar to the European Union, in the years immediately after the collapse of the Soviet Union, the US pursued a policy of strengthening and bolstering statehood in the South Caucasus, coupled with conflict management and mediation. But in many ways until after 9/11 and its ensuing "war on terror," the United States did not see any vital interests in Central Asia or the South Caucasus.[31] Since then, its policies toward the region fall into four broad categories: support for democracy; support for market reforms and privatization; support for counter-terrorism and security; and efforts at conflict management and mediation.[32] Under the Obama administration, these efforts have come to feature deeper support for democratization, more assertive moves to contain Russian influence in the region, and a more pronounced emphasis on security and counter-terrorism.[33]

While Russian activities and presence in the South Caucasus remain robust and multi-dimensional—military, commercial, and cultural—the US and the EU have sidelined themselves from the region, choosing instead to focus their energies on containing Russia's possible strategic gains in the Balkans and in Ukraine. This has created space for new aspiring regional powers, the most significant of which are Turkey and Iran. Turkey views itself as a natural power in the South Caucasus and conceives of the region as an extension of its cultural zone and a ready market for its expansive economic power. For Iran, whose relations with countries to its south, east, and west have always posed challenges, the South Caucasus offers much needed possibilities in international partnerships, markets for its stuttering economy, and perhaps, just perhaps, even a measure of soft power. That these are countries still in the throes of state-building and identity formation, themselves with few friends and tenuous international alliances, makes them the perfect candidates for influence peddling, more likely victims to machinations emanating from Ankara and Tehran. It is to their processes of state-building that the chapter turns next.

State-Building in the South Caucasus

In all three republics of the South Caucasus, state-building has taken place under two ominous shadows, each reinforcing the other. One has been the scourge of ethno-national conflicts, and the other of political elites who put their own interests before those of their country. What has ensued has been an instrumentalization of unresolved territorial and ethnic conflicts for purposes of retaining power.[34] Within the Soviet Union, the South Caucasus was mostly sealed off from the rest of the other Socialist Republics and was presented as a place of ethnic and political harmony.[35] This was hardly the case, with tensions already brewing before the communist system started crumbling. Once the USSR finally collapsed, the floodgates of ethnic hatred blew open. The states of the South Caucasus witnessed the most bloodshed out of all the post-Soviet states.

In ethno-territorial conflicts of the sort that exist in Nagorno-Karabakh, South Ossetia, and Abkhazia, identity assumes a particularly important role, and leaders find that they must appeal more and more to identity as reflected in popular and populist settlements.[36] Today the most intractable of these conflicts is the one between Azerbaijan and Armenia in the Nagorno-Karabakh region, which casts a shadow over the entire South Caucasus. For both Armenia and Azerbaijan, the conflict has come to take on "a central, identity defining role in the political and cultural self-understanding of the two countries."[37] Nagorno-Karabakh now has the dubious distinction of being "the longest running ethno-territorial dispute in the post-Communist world."[38]

Internal displacements, refugees, and the flight abroad of people and capital seem to matter little to those for whom these conflicts have proven politically profitable. On both sides, for example, the Karabakh issue is used by incumbents and the opposition to enhance their own patriotic credentials.[39] The few who have dared to entertain thoughts of solutions or compromise have been repeatedly stymied or kicked out of office. Reportedly, Azerbaijan's President

Heydar Aliyev could not get the endorsement of his inner circle for a peace deal with Armenia in which he would give up Nagorno-Karabakh in return for a land corridor to the Nekhchivan exclave. In Armenia, when President Levon Ter-Petrosian tried to sign off on a peace plan with Azerbaijan in 1998, he was thrown out of office by members of his own inner circle.[40] Such is the intensity of the Nagorno-Karabakh hold on the Armenian psyche that although the population of the region is estimated at no more than 100,000, two Karabakh natives, Robert Kocharyan (1998–2008) and Serzh Sargsyan (2008–), have already served as Armenia's president.[41]

The economies of the three countries of the South Caucasus, meanwhile, remain monopolistic, do not have well-defined property rights, and retain strong clientelistic ties between economics and politics.[42] Markets stagnate and are highly underdeveloped, and are dependent on the export of natural resources and therefore highly susceptible to international pressures and nuances. In all three countries, middle-class consumers can hardly afford many of the basic goods and household durables they need. Those who can afford them leave. Today, approximately 800,000 Georgians, 2.5 million Armenians, and 2 million Azerbaijanis live and work abroad, and send remittances back home.[43] Domestic economies would suffer deeply if these revenue streams dry up.

Let us look more closely at each of the three cases.

Armenia

In many ways, Armenia's post-independence political and economic experiences are reminiscent of that of other post-Soviet republics, its birth the product of a non-violent revolution. And, again not unlike other post-Soviet states, Armenia appears to be in a perpetual state of social, economic, and political crisis.[44] In particular, the Armenian Republic has not yet succeeded in building a set of democratic state institutions and a democratic political culture.[45] Nevertheless, similar to Georgia, Armenia at least has a nominally functioning democratic system, which Azerbaijan does not. Elections, however, do not necessarily make a political system effective or even viable.

Despite major changes to the nature and functions of state institutions as compared to those of the Soviet era, their basic functions, and the basic patterns through which power is distributed and exercised, remain fundamentally the same.[46] As in the Soviet Union's final years, politics remain decidedly non-ideological. The executive also remains dominant and the National Assembly pliant, featuring little debate and all too often approving the executive's bills, frequently through "expedited procedures."[47] Not surprisingly, the legitimacy of elections and their fairness are often contested.[48] The oligarchy, as detailed in Giragosian's chapter in the volume, remains powerful, and the president needs its continued support to stay in power. In fact, the country's lack of a tradition of stateness—of having viable institutions of its own and a history of state–society relations—in part explains its difficulties in post-Soviet state-building.[49] This has helped foster an informal balance between the various centers of power within the country, resulting in a semblance of political stability.

Prevailing patterns in Armenia's politics—or, more accurately, its lack of political development—have not helped government efforts at fostering economic growth. In the first two decades of independence, the life of the Armenian economy can be divided into three stages: disintegration in the early 1990s; reconstruction in the mid to late 1990s; and finally, crisis ever since. Throughout, the country's economy has suffered from a number of "systematic deformations."[50] The Armenian economy today remains uncompetitive, is riddled with monopolies, and is susceptible to external shocks, with high unemployment rates and an inadequate social security system.[51] Remittances and other monies sent from abroad help alleviate some but not all of Armenia's economic difficulties. Nevertheless, continued out-migration from Armenia remains a challenge for the economy.[52]

The country's economy was almost completely destroyed in the early 1990s and was rebuilt only with significant advantages accruing to politically-connected business elites. As in most other post-Soviet states, Armenia has taken many hasty steps toward ushering in capitalism without an adequate understanding of what these steps really entail. Mass privatization of state assets took place, and a romantic and unfounded notion of capitalism emerged. This had the practical effect of de-industrializing the country, facilitating private transfers and capital flight, and facilitating the emergence of an oligarchy.[53] Today, major oligarchs often own monopolistic businesses and occupy important positions in the state.[54] This has helped foster a vibrant shadow economy, comprising an estimated 40 percent of all economic activity in the country,[55] much of it controlled by powerful neighborhood bosses. No administration has been able to reduce the pervasiveness of the shadow economy or the role of neighborhood bosses, many of whom have acquired and consolidated their positions in army command or in other high-ranking government positions.

Economic difficulties have not prompted political leaders in Yerevan to ease up on the country's hold on Nagorno-Karabakh. This is largely because the Karabakh movement plays a foundational myth for the Armenian state.[56] As one observer has noted, "a nation obsessed with loss of land throughout its history is finding it very difficult to give up the land it now occupies."[57] In some respects, this is as much due to the influence of the powerful Armenian diaspora as it is a product of the preferences of the country's political leaders themselves.[58]

The diaspora is similarly opposed to any compromises with Turkey over the question of the 1915 genocide of Turkish Armenians—all three of Armenia's traditional parties represented among the diaspora have rejected the idea of a "historical commission" to determine whether the events of 1915 indeed constituted a genocide—thereby hampering any meaningful prospects for a Turkish–Armenian rapprochement.[59] Ironically, there is a similar lack of enthusiasm on the other side. Perceiving Turkey to be in a position of strength, Turkish political elites are less interested in establishing relations with Armenia than Armenia is in normalizing relations with Turkey.[60] Although improvements in Turkish–Armenian relations could lead to significant changes in the geopolitical realities of the region, for now such a possibility remains highly unlikely.

Yerevan's icy relations with Ankara stand in sharp contrast to its warm economic and military ties with Moscow. Armenia remains perhaps "one of the most loyal members of the Commonwealth of Independent States."[61] Armenia's National Security Strategy document, drafted in 2007, stipulates that the country is in a "strategic partnership" with Russia. The document calls for "complementarity" in foreign and security policy, "aimed at maintaining an overall balance in the region." In reality, however, Armenia has much closer ties to Russia than to the EU or the US.[62] In fact, Yerevan's continued strategic reliance on Russia has so far precluded it from receiving greater US military assistance and the "train and equip" missions sent by the US to both Georgia and Azerbaijan.[63]

The challenges in Armenian–Turkish relations and in Armenia's less than cordial relations with the US and the EU have also opened up opportunities for Iran, which has long viewed close relations with Armenia as a way to break out of its isolation and develop a potential transit route to Europe.[64] This relationship has been more economic and diplomatic, and, in many ways, is more symbolic than substantive. Iran's trade with Armenia, for example, stood at slightly more than $290 million in 2014, up from $183.3 million in 2004. Given the state of Turkish–Armenian relations, this is actually not much more than the amount of Turkish–Armenian trade. Turkey's trade with Armenia rose from only $39 million in 2004 to $234 million in 2014.[65] Whatever gains

Iran has had in relation to Armenia appear to have been rooted less in material gains and more in diplomatic niceties and symbolism.

Georgia

Not unlike other post-Soviet states, Georgia is currently undergoing "a process of deep restructuring" in multiple arenas of its macro-economy, political culture, state institutions, state–society relations, self-identification, and social peace-building.[66] The country's initial years of independence, in the early 1990s, were characterized by considerable political instability and turmoil. It was only with the 1995 election and subsequent consolidation of power of Eduard Shevardnadze, who had previously served as foreign minister of the Soviet Union under President Gorbachev, that the country's politics assumed a semblance of stability. Shevardnadze created a hybrid political system with some space for political freedom but few conditions for meaningful political competition, instead concentrating power within the hands of a narrow elite. Once power was consolidated, in the second half of the 1990s an ambitious reform agenda was pursued in which the legal and institutional foundations of the new regime were established and strengthened. By the late 1990s, however, the president and his inner circle had grown wary of reforms, and the system became increasingly less tolerant of dissent and featured fraudulent elections and rampant corruption.[67] Kupatzade's contribution in this volume offers an in-depth examination of the problem of corruption in Georgia.

The 2003 "Rose Revolution" ushered in an era of excitement, optimism, institutional reform, and economic investments. After the revolution, when Shevardnadze was forced to step down, the constitution was amended to strengthen and further centralize executive power.[68] Saakashvili introduced a number of reforms—to the state administration, the police force, tax collection, combatting corruption, and combatting smuggling—while at the same time building up a clientelistic network for himself.[69] The new government soon began to cut corners and bulldoze perceived obstacles. Judges were ridiculed, procedures violated, media repressed, and decisions centralized. While unemployment rose, reforms were implemented with "excessive arrogance and self-confidence" though with little benefit to the public.[70] President Saakashvili and his entourage became increasingly arrogant and impulsive. By 2008–9, the Rose Revolution of 2003 had come to a screeching halt.

Like Armenia and Azerbaijan, Georgia inherited entho-territorial conflicts and secessionist movements from the USSR.[71] In the late 1980s, communist authorities sought to create a distinctively Georgian identity by playing up ethnic divisions within the country, especially insofar as Abkhazia and South Ossetia were concerned. In turn, in the early 1990s, political consolidation meant emphasizing Georgian ethnic identity and further alienating Abkhazia and South Ossetia.[72] This did not bode well for subsequent processes of state- and nation-building and the integration of regions such as Abkhazia and South Ossetia into the new republic. Conflicts erupted soon after independence in 1991, resulting in some 8,000 casualties and 250,000 internally displaced persons. Russia's mediation in 1992 helped freeze the conflicts for some time, though their underlying dynamics remained unaddressed. They flared up once again in August 2008, settled this time through Russian intervention in favor of the two regions.[73] Today, the South Ossetia and Abkhazia conflicts have once again become frozen, similar to Nagorno-Karabakh, and constitute perhaps the single most important factors in Georgia's domestic and foreign policies.[74]

Civil wars brought Georgia to the verge of being a failed state.[75] But Georgia has persevered and the country has on occasion demonstrated impressive spurts of economic growth. In the late 2000s, in fact, Singapore, the UAE, and New Zealand were frequently mentioned as models for Georgia to emulate. Although the Saakashvili interregnum saw a proliferation of state institutions and emphasis on their efficacy, processes of political institutionalization and state-building were undermined by their very rapid pace. Today, the country is far from the risk of becoming a failed state. But it also has some way to go in its effort toward political institutionalization and consolidation. Georgian politics remains zero-sum in nature, and the country's main challenge has been to take concrete steps toward institutionalizing democracy.[76]

The Georgian system may be best described as an example of "competitive authoritarianism."[77] There is, for example, little media freedom in Georgia today.[78] In Azerbaijan and Armenia, the state has been "de-ideologized" in the service of power concentration. Georgia is not too different, though this was not always the case. Under Saakashvili, libertarianism increasingly became the mantra of the state and the economic and political blueprints it was following. Saakashvili's libertarianism meant dismantling many of the regulatory powers of the state, which in 2006 adopted a Labor Code hostile to employees, instead giving much leeway and latitude to corporations.[79] Along the same lines, in 2009 the president announced the enactment of the Law on Economic Freedom, Opportunity and Dignity that banned the establishment of regulatory bodies and made future tax increases subject to approval by popular referendums.[80]

Similar to Armenia, Georgia's turbulent politics has not helped its economic growth and development. During the first decade after independence in Georgia, the goal was to build the basic mechanisms for a market economy, including introducing a new currency in 1995, achieving market stabilization, and improving the business and investment environments. There was mixed success in achieving these goals. While the mid-1990s saw improved levels of economic growth in Georgia, with an annual growth rate of around 10 to 11 percent, the late 1990s saw a deterioration of the economy and marked rise in corruption and absence of rule of law.[81]

Also mixed was the economic legacy that Saakashvili left behind. The president's ambitious efforts at streamlining state institutions to improve their performance and efficiency, and the introduction of e-government in a variety of areas, continue to have positive results in helping the state improve its management of incoming revenues and its services to the public. The economic costs of Georgia's short war with Russia in 2008, for which Saakashvili was generally blamed, are estimated at $4.5 billion.[82] The Georgian economy has yet to recover from the consequences of the war. Particularly hard hit have been the urban middle classes, many of whom have seen precipitous declines in their relative income and their purchasing power. Over the last two decades, up to 1.5 million Georgians have emigrated from their country in search of better employment opportunities abroad.[83]

Perhaps the single most important factor in Georgia's international relations is its relations with Russia in general and the South Ossetia and Abkhazia issue in particular. Keenly aware of its power and position as a small state bordering a giant, global power, Georgia's self-perception and its conduct of foreign relations are deeply informed by its tormented relationship with Russia. In fact, defining an independent identity vis-à-vis Russia remains a fundamental challenge for Georgia.[84]

Needless to say, South Ossetia and Abkhazia could not exist and are not viable on their own without Russian aid.[85] Today both Abkhazia and South Ossetia exist as Russian protectorates whose security is guaranteed by Russia. By the same token, a settlement of Georgia's conflict with these two regions will not be possible without Russian involvement.[86] Yet, there appears to be no end in sight, nor any prospects for ending Georgia's conflicts with Russia as far as Abkhazia and South Ossetia are concerned.[87]

The Russian factor has prompted Georgia to try to draw itself ever closer to NATO and the European Union. Georgia's National Security Concept, drafted in 2011, is explicit on this point: "As a Black Sea and Southeastern

European country, Georgia is part of Europe geographically, politically, and culturally; yet it was cut off from its natural course of development by historical cataclysms. Integration into NATO and the EU is Georgia's sovereign choice, one which will strengthen Georgia's security and ensure its stable development."[88] This effort led to the signing of the Association Agreement with the EU in 2014, through which Georgia has sought to position itself as "the center of gravity" of Western engagement with the South Caucasus.[89] An Association Agreement is the most that the EU has so far been willing to grant to Georgia. And, so far at least, the country's constant efforts to gain membership in NATO have been met with only a lukewarm reception.[90] While NATO has been reluctant to embrace Georgia's bid for membership, it has, however, helped the country establish a "defense capacity building mission" by providing a "substantial package" of assistance.[91]

Azerbaijan

On the surface, Azerbaijan differs from Armenia and Georgia in a number of important respects. Politically, whereas Armenia and Georgia have held relatively meaningful elections and have witnessed a rotation of elites in and out of elected office, Azerbaijan's political system, dominated by a single family, the Aliyevs, has been alternatively described as "sultanistic semi-authoritarian" or as a "neo-monarchy."[92] Economically, Azerbaijan's natural resources have enabled it to embark on massive infrastructural development over the last decade and a half and have given it a strategic importance that the two other countries lack. This has had consequences for the small state's geopolitical and foreign policy calculations, prompting its leaders to engage in a carefully crafted balancing act between the European Union, the US, Russia, Turkey, and Iran. This stands in sharp contrast to Georgia's pro-Western and Armenia's pro-Russian tilts in the region.

Despite these differences, Azerbaijan's political history and its overall national trajectory since independence have not been that fundamentally different from its South Caucasus neighbors. Since independence, three overall stages in Azerbaijan's political development may be identified: the period immediately after independence, which witnessed less than a year of revolutionary democracy; the ten-year period of Heydar Aliyev's rule, when the institutional foundations of the new republic were laid; and the rule of his son Ilham since 2003, which has so far resulted in a steady increase in the control of the state over Azerbaijani society.[93] Similar to both Armenia and Georgia, many of the institutional features of the Soviet Union persevere in Azerbaijan, including present-day incarnations of the Central Committee of the Communist Party, which now exists in the form of the president's administration.[94]

Similar to other post-Soviet states, Azerbaijan's early days of independence witnessed great turmoil and political instability. The country's first post-Soviet president, the populist Abulfaz Elchibey, was overthrown in June 1993 and Heydar Aliyev, who had been leader of the Azerbaijan Soviet Socialist Republic from 1968 to 1982, returned to power. Almost overnight, Aliyev went from being a member of the Soviet Communist Party's Central Committee to becoming "the presidential Olympus of Azerbaijan."[95] Over time, the Azerbaijani public came to accept many of the myths that the president created about himself as he methodically went about establishing the new institutions of the state and at the same time consolidating power. From the start, Aliyev was focused on creating a family dynasty. In the process, he created a highly centralized political system with many democratic trappings.[96] Especially in the early 1990s, the country witnessed a period of feverish state-building, during which a national army, a central bank, and a national currency (the manat) were established, and the Cyrillic alphabet was replaced by the Latin alphabet.[97]

The president died in 2003 and was succeeded in office by his son Ilham in questionable presidential elections. Expectations that the new president would launch political reforms were soon dashed. In fact, with Ilham Aliyev's consolidation of power there has been a clamping down on the media, with many journalists arrested and imprisoned, while the personal powers of the president have been significantly enhanced.[98] Ilham proceeded to dispense with even the pretense of democracy. The following observations, by a scholar of the country, are worth quoting at length:

> Ilham Aliyev's regime of personal authority rests upon a rigid vertical administrative apparatus, with a repressive police force, special services, prosecutor's office and courts, as well as a monopolised economy. Vast information resources—eight national television channels, 11 radio stations, numerous printed and Internet publications—serve the power as well. The ruling system is governed by its unwritten laws, which is a characteristic of authoritarian regimes.[99]

There is a narrow circle of the president's entourage that follow him unquestionably and submit to his power. Not surprisingly, promotions are invariably based on loyalty, and many cabinet ministers with proven allegiance have tenures reaching into decades. A number of wealthy oligarchs are closely affiliated either with the president or with his wife's family. Meriban Aliyev, the president's wife, has emerged as one of the country's most powerful figures, and her humanitarian projects and charity enterprises receive about as much media coverage as do the president's initiatives.[100] Many independent-minded politicians have either been sidelined or arrested and imprisoned. Abbasov notes:

> The constitution is not operational, the principal of the separation of powers is not working, civil society institutes are underdeveloped, and market economy does not exist. Power structures, which should enhance the country's security, are corrupt and politicised, and their main task is to protect the narrow elite circles.[101]

In 2008, the government even used the Russian–Georgian war as a further excuse to restrict political space and weaken civil society.[102]

As with other authoritarian states that like to adopt the pretense of democracy, sometimes the outcome is farcical comedy. During the 2013 presidential elections, for example, the results were accidentally released earlier than the polls closed, showing the incumbent president winning re-election by 72.76 percent of the votes cast. When the ballots did actually close, the president had actually won 84.5 percent of the votes, about 3 percentage points lower than the votes he had garnered in the 2008 elections.[103]

The state also maintains the charade of parliamentary politics. The country's constitution, originally passed in 1995, was amended in 2002 and again in 2012 in order to strengthen the office of the presidency and to weaken parliament further. The Azerbaijani parliament has unofficial "factions," but all are "utterly loyal to the President."[104] Most Azerbaijanis view the "opposition" to be as corrupt and tainted as those already in office.[105] The office of the president dominates the entire political landscape.

This very centralization of power within a narrow, authoritarian presidency, and the increasing contraction of permissible political space, have left Azerbaijan open to the possibility of extremism and outbursts of violent political protests. The fear in Azerbaijan that government policy and local conditions would give rise to religious extremism and other terrorist groups is not new. A combination of poverty, refugees from the Nagorno-Karabakh conflict, and Salafi influences from the North Caucasus, especially Chechnya and Dagestan, could give rise to Islamic extremism in Azerbaijan.[106] By the mid-2000s, in fact, Islam had become a sufficiently consequential force in Azerbaijani society as to provoke a sharp clampdown on religious activists by the state. The political vacuum created by the state has resulted in the emergence of political Islam and has enabled the "mosque (to become) a kind of political club."[107]

What legitimacy the state does have rests on its ability to maintain the "Azerbaijan miracle" by trying to emulate the Asian Tigers through the continued export of oil and gas.[108] The miracle appeared to have fizzled out in dramatic fashion in late 2015 and early 2016 as the price of oil plummeted on the global market, and the manat fell precipitously against the dollar and the euro. Rising unemployment and inflation throughout 2015, coupled with drastic increases in the price of essential goods such as wheat and flour, resulted in nationwide, and at times violent, protests in January 2016, quelled only after mass arrests and police crackdown. For now, the Aliyev family dynasty does not appear to be facing the danger of collapse. But the façade of political stability appears to have been cracked.

The January 2016 protests notwithstanding, beginning in the early 2000s and lasting for nearly a decade and a half, Azerbaijan's economy experienced persistent growth.[109] In the early years of post-independence, similar to both Armenia and Georgia, in Azerbaijan the various sectors of the economy collapsed following the disintegration of the Soviet Union. By the late 1990s, as oil revenues began to trickle in, the economy started its upward ascent, with a boom starting in 2003. Incoming state revenues went toward the construction of infrastructure, especially roads and bridges, and city beautification campaigns. As Valiyev's contribution in this volume shows, the state hoped to turn Baku into "the Dubai of the Caspian." The oil and gas sector, the country's economic lifeline, was especially targeted for infrastructural growth, and before long Azerbaijan became the only country in the region able to extract, refine, transport, and negotiate its natural resources to European markets.[110] Not surprisingly, the European Union remains interested in a secure and diversified energy supply from Azerbaijan.[111]

Despite rapid infrastructural growth, systemic problems continue to plague Azerbaijan's economy, not least of which is over-dependence on a single, albeit sought-after, natural resource. Despite the growth of the oil sector, many of Azerbaijan's most labor-intensive industries remain the least efficient.[112] Corruption, perpetuated by a powerful oligarchy, remains an endemic problem across the board.[113] There are very close connections between those who have economic resources and those with political power, and the pervasive powers of oligarchs result in very closely protected monopolies that keep commodity prices higher in Azerbaijan than in most other places in the South Caucasus.[114] Tax collection, meanwhile, remains a major problem, with an estimated 1.3 million workers out of a labor force of four million not paying taxes.[115] All the while, as the state's coffers swell and its affiliated oligarchy benefit, people's real economy does not. This has prompted many Azerbaijanis to seek better lives abroad. Similar to Armenia, immigration by Azerbaijanis out of the country, especially to Russia, remains a major problem and a big drain on the country's economy.

Azerbaijan's overwhelming reliance on the exploitation and export of natural resources has had direct effects on its international relations. One of the central pillars of the country's foreign policy, in fact, has been "pipeline diversity," whereby Azerbaijan has positioned itself to become an "enabler" for the EU's Southern Gas Corridor.[116] Throughout the 2000s, this centrality was reinforced by the West's desire to develop the regional energy sector while bypassing Iran and Russia.[117] At the same time, however, Azerbaijan has discovered the prudence of a foreign policy that treads a middle line between the West on one side, as represented especially by the European Union and Turkey, and Russia and Iran on another.[118] The result has been a comparatively more balanced foreign policy of "careful pragmatism."[119]

The need for a more even-handed and pragmatic foreign policy was driven home by the relatively mild response of the US and the EU to the 2008 war between Russia and Georgia. The war was seen by many Azerbaijanis as a sign that they should be more attentive to Russian priorities and needs and that Russia's special position in the South Caucasus cannot be completely ignored.[120] This trend has been reinforced by the relative inattention of the US to Azerbaijan as a potential security partner of any kind. Largely influenced by the powerful Armenian lobby in Washington, US policy toward Azerbaijan has instead focused on humanitarian aid, democratization assistance, and efforts to manage and mediate the Nagorno-Karabakh conflict.[121] Azerbaijan has therefore moved away from a consistently pro-Western policy to one that is more nuanced and is in line with the Non-Aligned Movement.[122]

The United States may not perceive Azerbaijan as a valuable security partner, but Israel does. In recent years, perceived security threats emanating from Iran have resulted in an expression of economic, cultural, developmental, and more recently military cooperation between Azerbaijan and Israel.[123] These relations deepened at a time when Turkish–Israeli strategic cooperation was also at its peak, the two relationships synergistically complementing one another.[124] Besides Azerbaijan–Iranian tensions, Azerbaijan–Israeli relations are a product of mutually beneficial cooperation in a variety of economic fields, especially the energy sector. By the 2010s, for example, Israeli–Azerbaijani trade was put at $46 billion annually, making Azerbaijan Israel's main trading partner in the Muslim world.[125] Many Israeli companies have been active in the Azerbaijani energy sector, and by 2013 oil from Azerbaijan accounted for 40 percent of all the oil consumed in Israel.[126] Azerbaijan has also purchased billions of dollars' worth of military equipment from Israel, including drones and advanced anti-aircraft missile defense systems.

While maintaining relatively close ties to Israel, Azerbaijan has sought to avoid direct confrontation with Iran. At any rate, Azerbaijan's strategic cooperation with Israel cannot all be attributed to Iran and is in large measure a product of Baku's countering at times tense relationships with Russia and with other South Caucasus states.[127] Relations with Israel would also help Azerbaijan's image as a "pro-Western, progressive" republic.[128]

Azerbaijan's relationship with Israel and its delicate balancing act in relation to Iran, as well as with Russia, Turkey, the EU, and the US, exemplify the dilemmas faced by small states in general and the three countries of the South Caucasus in particular in furthering their foreign policy objectives. Georgia and Armenia have chosen to bandwagon with bigger patrons and protectors, the former with the West and the latter mostly with Russia. Azerbaijan has opted for a more nuanced positioning of itself, pursuing a foreign policy that is proactive and—albeit more in style than in substance—is more even-handed and balanced. That each of the three countries has chosen separate geostrategic paths has not stopped Iran and Turkey from competing over them, a rivalry that goes beyond the South Caucasus and involves state and non-state actors close and far.

In each of the three countries of the South Caucasus, a combination of developments has facilitated the opening of space for competition between the two aspiring regional powers of Iran and Turkey. Ongoing processes of state-building and political consolidation have increased the likelihood of political elites to look for outside allies and patrons (in Georgia and Armenia) or to try and hedge their bets in order to maximize available options and potential friends (Azerbaijan). Ethno-linguistic conflicts and their attendant economic difficulties have increased the need for regional allies and partners. At the same time, a lack of strategic attention to the region and therefore appetite for in-depth involvement by the EU and the US have increased the regional shadow of Russia and the available space for Iran and Turkey. The South Caucasus provides a corridor to Russia in the north, Iran and Turkey to the south, and the Caspian basin to the east.[129] The two aspiring regional powers, therefore, have come to see the South Caucasus as a significant region ripe for furthering their diplomatic influence, their economic presence, and their soft power.

Turkish-Iranian rivalry

Turkey and Iran have been uneasy neighbors with begrudging respect and tolerance for each other.[130] The two countries are both regional middle-level powers, and as such are central to the balance of power in the Middle East and especially West Asia, have their own regional spheres of influence, and have the ability to resist and deter a coalition of other regional states against them. And although they are economically and technologically dependent on other core states, and need to diversify their economies out of necessity, they can on their own resist intervention by the great global powers.[131]

Middle range powers may be defined as those countries:

> that are neither at the apex nor the bottom of the international power structure. They are not so powerful as to be able to exert decisive influence on major issues or international security and economy. Nor are they so powerless as to be unable to protect themselves from the undesirable impacts of other countries' actions. They have considerable resources and capabilities, but are not dominant in international relations.[132]

Much of the literature on "rising" or regional middle powers has focused on their role in and relationship with global governance institutions.[133] But the greatest significance of middle powers is at the regional level and is often felt within their immediate vicinity. Middle powers often explicitly challenge the hegemony of established great powers, not so much at the global level but more specifically, and more immediately, within the regions in which they are located.[134] As such, the South Caucasus is an area of considerable strategic importance for both Iran and Turkey, where they can expand their own influence and, potentially, even challenge Russian interests.[135]

For some time now, Iran and Turkey have aspired to be regional heavyweights in West Asia. These aspirations have met with measured success on the one hand and with the fear and trepidation of other regional actors on the other.[136] As early as 2011, veteran Middle East observer Mohammed Ayoob predicted that in the post-Arab Spring Middle East there will be a "shift in the center of political gravity" away from Egypt and toward Iran and Turkey.[137] The "Turko-Persian future" that Ayoob predicted may not necessarily come to pass, but Iran and Turkey will continue to remain pivotal regional powers for the foreseeable future.

While Iran and Turkey compete with one another in multiple areas, necessity and interest have also forced them to cooperate in a number of other areas. The contributions in this volume by Ahmadi, Monshipouri, and Winrow examine the multiple areas of direct competition between the two countries. But there are also a number of areas in which the two have had to cooperate and collaborate. Neither Tehran nor Ankara, for example, want to see an independent Kurdistan emerge. At the same time, a convergence of three goals prompts the two countries to cooperate over the Kurdish question: both are interested in participating in the oil and gas resources of northern Iraq and their distributive networks; the need to agree on respective spheres of influence in northern Iraq; and their need not to interfere in each other's policies with regards to issues that can have domestic repercussions for both.[138]

As outlined in Monshipouri's chapter in this volume, there has also been an "evolving energy interdependency" between Iran and Turkey that, at one level at least, has drawn the two powers closer.[139] The two countries are aware that energy cooperation between them is a win–win proposition. The two neighbors also have robust trade between them. By the end of 2015, Iranian–Turkish trade was estimated at around $30 billion a year.[140] This interdependency has not been lost on the politicians. In the words of Iranian President Hassan Rouhani, Turkey and Iran need one another, each serving as a bridge for the other.[141]

Cooperation in specific matters notwithstanding, the relationship between Iran and Turkey has been characterized more by competition in a whole host of issues and areas. One of these areas, where competition has been the most intense but paradoxically largely unnoticed, is in the South Caucasus. At the dawn of independence in 1991, for all three countries of the South Caucasus, Iran and Turkey offered two very different models of governance. The model that has emerged has been considerably closer to Turkey than to Iran. Moreover, common ethno-linguistic bonds have drawn Azerbaijan much closer to Turkey than to Iran, at least at the level of official state ties. Between the two regional powers, competition over Azerbaijan, by far the most prosperous and powerful of the three South Caucasus states, has been the most intense.[142] Closer Turkish–Azerbaijani relations have drawn Armenia closer to Iran, whereas Georgia, though ideologically and economically closer to Turkey, has maintained warm relations with both. A complex web of overlapping and competing relationships has emerged as a result, through which each country tries to maximize its own interests, deepen alliances and partnerships with friends, and undermine its foes and competitors.

Today, a multi-polar system appears to have emerged in the South Caucasus with three separate but interconnected vectors. One vector is the Turkey–Azerbaijan alliance, cemented by the 2010 signing of the Strategic Partnership and Mutual Aid Agreement. A second vector is a Russian–Armenian alliance, also signed as an agreement in 2010, through which there is increased Russian military and political presence in Armenia.[143] The third vector revolves around Iran and centers on Iranian–Georgian and Iranian–Armenian economic ties.

For its part, Iran sees the South Caucasus as both an opportunity and a threat.[144] Due to its diplomatic isolation from the West and the diplomatic and military pressures it faces, Iran has been forced to pay greater attention to the South Caucasus.[145] The Islamic Republic has four main interests in the South Caucasus. They include reducing the influence of outside powers; continuing to neutralize possible security threats; obtaining a bigger economic and cultural foothold; and setting the legal regime of the Caspian Sea.[146] At the same time, principally for trade and commercial reasons as well as possibilities of spillover, Iran has been interested in stability in the South Caucasus. In 2003, therefore, it proposed the so-called 3+3 regional security system that would be comprised of Iran–Turkey–Russia plus the three South Caucasus states. The proposal was not met with enthusiasm by the other states—and neither did the US or the EU have any appetite for it—so it fell by the wayside.[147]

Within the South Caucasus region, Iran's principal relationship is with Armenia, based on a shared sense of isolation and common strategic interests. Not surprisingly, Armenia is an important trading partner for Iran and biggest direct purchaser of its natural gas.[148] Iran has also repeatedly offered to mediate in the Nagorno-Karabakh conflict.[149] The Islamic Republic's relationship with Georgia has also deepened in recent years. After visa requirements were waived in 2010, the number of Iranian tourists to Georgia increased substantially, as did levels of Iranian investment in the country, which has emerged as one of Georgia's most important trading partners.[150] As far as Azerbaijan is concerned, its dealings with Israel (and Turkey), as well as the Azeri factor in Iranian domestic politics (discussed in Ahmadi's chapter), have often made its relations with Iran somewhat complicated.

Comparatively, Turkey has had greater success in pursuing its interests in the South Caucasus region. With US approval, following the break-up of the Soviet Union, Turkey proactively sought to increase its economic and political influence in the South Caucasus and Central Asia, steadily coming to be seen as a model for the new republics to follow.[151] Since the early 1990s, the country has also been at the center of global energy politics, even exploring the "Turkish stream" of having Russian gas piped from the Russian coastal town of Anapa all the way to Ipsala, located on Turkey's border with Greece. As one observer has noted in relation to Turkey, "the country is moving to become a neo-Ottoman powerhouse and the center if Eurasia's energy structure."[152] One of the centerpieces of this effort has been the Baku–Tbilisi–Ceyhan pipeline project.[153]

Because it has so much vested in the Baku–Tbilisi–Ceyhan pipeline project, Turkey prefers regional stability and security in the South Caucasus region, resulting in a "deep freeze" of regional conflicts such as the Nagorno-Karabakh conflict.[154] The process of normalization between Turkey and Armenia, started in 2009, today appears to be on standby, partly because Turkey does not want to antagonize Azerbaijan.[155] In itself, the economic significance of the South Caucasus for Turkey is rather limited. Nevertheless, Turkey sees the region more as an important transit route to the Caspian Sea and Central Asia. At the same time, as Altunışık and Balci's contributions to this volume make clear, Turkey exerts considerable soft power in the South Caucasus, and many from the region routinely travel to Turkey for work, tourism, and shopping.

There is a new great game afoot. The contenders are Iran and Turkey, and the South Caucasus is their arena of competition. In many ways the game has not yet really commenced and is today only in its beginning phases. How the outcome will turn out, and how the game itself will affect each country's internal dynamics, only time will tell. For now, what we know is that the two regional middle powers are in competition with one another for greater influence and power in the three countries immediately to their north.

This volume

The volume begins with Anatol Lieven's sweeping history of the demise of empires and the region's historical and geographic hostility to imperial hegemony. The politics of the South Caucasus is too perilous and complex, Lieven argues, and the depth of its internal conflicts and rivalries so intense that no outside power, no matter how proximate, will be able to establish a successful hegemony over it. Lieven is equally pessimistic in his prognosis of the current and future state of the greater Middle East. The savagery of the conflicts marking it, he argues, show no signs of abating, nor do they necessarily make it easier for any one power to cast a shadow of any kind over the region.

Imperial hegemony in the South Caucasus may well be a thing of the past, but geopolitics is alive and well there, and in many ways it takes the form of energy and specifically pipeline politics. This is the subject of Mahmood Monshipouri's chapter, focusing on the wide array of geopolitical, strategic, and economic factors that influence Iranian and Turkish approaches to energy and pipeline politics in the region. Competition between the two powers for access to the South Caucasus energy routes have become impossible to avoid, and neither Iran nor Russia has been able to forge a meaningful partnership that would block American energy giants from exploiting the ensuing vacuum. It is in the South Caucasus that Europe and Asia intersect, and despite the region's access to enormous energy resources and its significance as a transit route, it remains victim to a "new great game."

Gareth Winrow zeroes in on Turkey's energy policy, which has emerged as one of the central pillars of the country's drive for regional power and influence. Over the last decade or so, Turkey has sought to become a key energy transit state for gas to Europe from Azerbaijan and also from Russia, Turkmenistan, Iran, and the Kurdish Regional Government. This is in addition to ensuring ample supplies for its own growing domestic market. In the process, for Turkey as well as for the many other actors involved, energy has become politicized and securitized. But securitization does not necessarily mean security. In fact, it often undermines security in the long term. Winrow points to a number of such potential pitfalls that Turkey faces in achieving its goals, not least of which include the deteriorating security situation around Turkey, as well as the changing position of Iran in the regional security framework.

Turkey's efforts at becoming, or remaining, a key regional energy hub may face difficulties, but Iranian ambitions are not without obstacles either. Hamid Ahmadi draws our attention to the salience of ethnicity as perhaps the single most important factor in shaping Iranian–Azerbaijani relations during the last century. Ahmadi focuses on clashing Iranian and Azerbaijani nationalisms, each rich in their own nuances and histories. He examines the role of ethnic identity in the foreign policies of the two countries, and how each side views the other through its own multi-dimensional and ethnically-layered lens. Ultimately, Ahmadi concludes, political pragmatism appears to trump ethnic populism.

Common ethno-linguistic bonds across national borders may pose threats to the central government, but they can also provide opportunities for the projection of soft power by others. In relation to the South Caucasus, this is especially the case in relation to Russia's position in the region, where we see the continued existence of a post-Soviet political culture. Somewhat belatedly, Moscow has discovered the utility of soft power in maintaining semblances of linkages with the newly established states of the Commonwealth of Independent States in general and those of the South Caucasus in particular. By far the biggest manifestation of soft power has been the cultivation of civil society organizations, many of which promote aspects of Russian culture and generally seek to give currency to a narrative that is in sync with Russian strategic objectives. These pro-Russian civil society organizations are the subject of Jeffrey Mankoff's chapter.

Mankoff outlines the subtle, and at times blatant, competition for constituents and influence by civil society organizations supportive of Russia and the United States. The "Russian variant," he argues, is far more pronounced in pro-Russian civil society organizations as compared to those set up by Western entities and governments. Because of its historical bonds and its geographic proximity, Russia's soft power holds more sway in the South Caucasus than does the soft power of the West.

Russia is not alone in its attempts to project soft power across the new states of the South Caucasus. Turkey has sought to do so as well. For Turkey, the employment of soft power has evolved to become one of the central objectives of the foreign policy of the Justice and Development Party (Adalet ve Kalkınma Partisi, or AKP), which has been in power since 2002. This is the focus of Meliha Benli Altunışık's contribution, which provides a comparative analysis of how Turkish soft power is projected and received in the South Caucasus and in the Middle East. According to Altunışık, Turkish soft power began to expand starting in the 1990s, before the country's political elites were actually aware of it. By the time they tried proactively to capitalize on its various dimensions in the 2000s, their efforts fell victim to changing geopolitical realities in both the South Caucasus and the Middle East. Soft power is perceived differently across regions and even among different actors within the same country. Turkey's employment of foreign policy, culture, and political ideology for purposes of soft power projection, Altunışık concludes, has met with only measured success in the South Caucasus.

Bayram Balci contextualizes this measured success. Whatever success Turkey initially had in soft power projection owed largely, though by no means entirely, to the growth of the Gülen movement across the South Caucasus and Central Asia. Balci examines the evolution and spread of the Gülen movement, named after its founder Fethullah Gülen (b.1938), first with the tacit support of the ruling Justice and Development Party and then as its informal opposition. The Gülen movement's fraught relationship with the AKP, Balci argues, has done much to tarnish the image of the AKP outside Turkey. The outcome is likely to cause more difficulty for the Turkish state in its efforts to portray itself as an ideological model to be emulated. Nevertheless, as a fundamentally Turkish phenomenon, the Gülen movement itself is likely to continue to serve as a source of appeal for aspects of Turkish culture.

The volume's final three chapters turn our attention back to the South Caucasus and the travails of state-building and development. Anar Valiyev's contribution focuses on the Azerbaijani state's efforts to turn the capital city, Baku, into the Dubai of the Caspian. The Azerbaijani state has sought to place the country on the global map through what Valiyev calls "post-political urban boosterism." In the last decade or so, Baku has undergone a remarkable transformation into an aspiring global city and a business center for the South Caucasus. Many of Baku's newer buildings—such as the iconic Flame Towers or the Haydar Aliyev Cultural Center—have been designed with an eye toward crafting a new Azerbaijani national identity.

The travails of statehood go beyond the construction of impressive buildings and iconic structures. New states invariably suffer from institutional weaknesses, and such political exigencies provide space and opportunities for economic mismanagement, wealth accumulation, and widespread corruption. Richard Giragosian focuses on the emergence and powers of oligarchs in Armenia and how the predominance of "strongmen over statesmen" continues to hamper the country's political development. Alexander Kupatadze explores the dynamics of corruption and white-collar crime in Armenia and Georgia, pointing to both political elite dispositions as well as the importance of ethnic conflict as contributing factors. More specifically, Kupatadze points to a correlation between the prevalence of corruption and the degree to which each of the countries has been able to depart from the orbit of their former colonial overlord. Georgia, with its efforts to draw itself closer to the West, exhibits less corruption and white-collar crime, while Armenia, still firmly in the Russian orbit, tends to have more of the two plagues.

With the tragic turn of events in Syria and Iraq over the last several years, and the plague of Da'esh-type extremism, today the Middle East is demanding much of the world's attention. Both Turkey and Iran are involved—some would say complicit—in the tragedies unfolding near their borders, and each is supporting its own proxies in civil conflicts with seemingly no end. But they are also involved in a far less noticed and much more subtle game of geostrategy, each trying to enhance power and influence in an area of the world largely neglected by the US and the EU. The South Caucasus is now emerging as a new arena of competition between Iran and Turkey.

Together, the chapters in this volume paint an enormously complicated picture of a region that is at once in flux and yet the subject of competition by rising regional powers. The degree to which Georgia, Armenia, and Azerbaijan are equipped to deal with the domestic and international challenges of independence remains questionable some quarter-century after the collapse of the Soviet Union. Russia remains a formidable presence in the region, at least economically and culturally if no longer politically. But there is still considerable room for influence-peddling through soft-power projection, playing on ethno-linguistic bonds, and ensuring economic connectivity and dependence. As the world's attention is diverted toward real-life tragedies elsewhere, Iran and Turkey are locked in a new great game, with the South Caucasus as the prize. Who will ultimately come out on top, and whether the prize is worth all that it is thought to be, will only be answered with time. For now, what is certain is that the South Caucasus remains at the center of West Asia's latest geostrategic rivalry.

PART I

COMPETING INTERESTS

2

WEST ASIA SINCE 1900

LIVING THROUGH THE WRECK OF EMPIRES

Anatol Lieven

The history of West Asia over the past century has been defined by the collapse of three great empires. The contemporary history of the region is being defined by the decay of a fourth, informal empire—that of the USA—and the appearance of a new local power, the Islamic State (IS) or Da'esh, which is radically hostile not just to US hegemony and to all local regimes but to the very existence of the states of the region.[1] All of these ruins of empire have been preceded, accompanied and to a considerable extent caused by the decay of the civilizational ideologies, which had legitimized imperial rule.

The ideological project under threat today is Western-led modernization in its broadest sense. In the past, this included socialist–nationalist programs inspired by the USSR—but these collapsed because of their own internal flaws or were destroyed by the USA and Israel between 1967 and 1973. At present, US-backed modernization is also paralyzed and in danger of destruction, while due to the rise of sectarian conflict the region itself is in some respects more bitterly divided than it has been since the Ottoman–Safavid wars of the seventeenth century.

Drawing on the history of liberal modernization in nineteenth-century Catholic Europe and Latin America, and the experience of Meiji Japan, this chapter will argue that while internal cultural, social, and economic factors have been crucial barriers to modernization, so too has been the dependence of would-be modernizing Middle Eastern states on the US imperial hegemon. This dependency has stripped these states of the nationalist legitimacy which elsewhere has been vital to the introduction of necessary but highly painful and contested reforms.

To understand the need for this legitimacy in order to carry out successful modernization, it is necessary to transcend the happy fairy tale of Western-led modernization that Western governments and Western-dominated NGOs and international financial institutions have narrated to themselves and the world over the past decades, and to understand fully not just how deeply painful this modernization has been for most societies that have undergone it, but also how closely it has been associated with state strength and state coercion—including, in previous centuries, in the West itself.[2]

Both domestic and international developments in West Asia (embracing former Soviet Central Asia as well as the Greater Middle East) are therefore a product of the interaction of a range of local factors—cultural, historical, social, economic, and political—impacted by the outside great powers.

One of the foremost scholars of the modern history of the region, Leon Carl Brown, sees that history overwhelmingly in terms of the penetration of the Middle East by outside powers. Brown describes the Middle East as "the most penetrated political sub-system in today's world," in the sense of a system "that is neither absorbed by the outside challenger [in the sense of full imperial control] nor later released from the outsider's smothering embrace. A penetrated system exists in continuous confrontation with a dominant outside political system."[3]

Writing during the Cold War, Brown described the recent geopolitics of the region as a direct continuity from the nineteenth-century Eastern Question and the various European powers' "slow sundering of the Ottoman Empire." Since the fall of the USSR, however, the United States has in effect been the sole outside great power to play a truly important role in the region, aspiring to and even to some degree achieving a kind of imperial hegemony (as opposed to a direct imperial role). Outside the Caucasus, Russia has been only a limited challenger, Britain and France have been subordinate US allies, and China—as yet—has not sought to play a great power role in the Middle East

One reason for China's reticence in this regard may be that despite the fact that (contrary to Brown's historical model) the US has enjoyed a near-monopoly of outside geopolitical influence in the region since 1991, this has not allowed the USA to stabilize the region, end local conflicts, develop local economies, or defeat local enemies. The greatest apparent US victory, that over Iraq in 2003, only led to a chaotic and bloody civil war which eventually spawned the Islamic State, or Da'esh—the greatest threat to successful modernization that the Middle East has ever seen.

Brown therefore was partially correct at the time when he wrote that:

> The intensive interrelatedness of politics at all levels produces homeostasis. Diplomatic folk wisdom about the Middle East has it that "things are never so good or so bad as they seem." Rarely does a single political actor—whether outside great power or regional power—have the ability to impose its will or even to set in motion major new orientations.[4]

Today, the limits on the power of a single political actor—even one as apparently powerful as the USA—have been starkly revealed by US travails since 2003. However, the decay of the entire modernizing project in the region has produced a situation where homeostasis no longer exists, and the appearance of Da'esh means that things are indeed just exactly as bad as they seem, or possibly even worse.

A secondary thesis of this essay will therefore be that the local conflicts and rivalries of the Middle East, both between and within states, are so deep that no stable outside hegemony is in fact possible, at least without the introduction of massive numbers of outside troops over several generations and the imposition of direct empire. A parallel will be made in this regard with the experience of Russia's attempt to create hegemony over the South Caucasus in the mid-1990s.

In the past, these outside powers included a range of actors, but since the fall of the USSR the only really important one has been the USA, which has sought and to some extent achieved a kind of imperial hegemony (as opposed to direct empire) over the region.

As a result of these tendencies, the territorial, the political, and the ideological orders of the region are all being stretched to the point of collapse. At the very least, we are witnessing a shift of equivalent importance to the wars and revolutions that accompanied the decline of the British Empire after 1945. We may even be in an era comparable to that of the decline of the

Ottoman Empire, in which an entire moral and political world is shifted on its foundations.

Until the revolt of IS in 2014, with the exception of Israel, the states and their borders in the Middle East remained those created by the British and French empires after the defeat of the Ottoman Empire. In the Gulf and Jordan, the regimes in 2015 remain those created under British sponsorship. Elsewhere, until recently the regimes in place remained essentially those that emerged from the collapse of the French and British empires from the mid-1940s to the mid-1950s.

In the former Soviet Caucasus, the state order remains the same as under the Soviet Union, though with modifications as a result of the wars that followed that empire's collapse. In Azerbaijan, a renamed faction of the local former Soviet Communist Party remains in power, under the son and heir of the old Communist strongman. Other countries are ruled by a variety of different post-Soviet regimes. Internally, these post-Soviet countries have proved relatively stable, after the civil wars that accompanied the Soviet collapse ended or were suspended. However, neither the traditional regional hegemon, Russia, nor the would-be new hegemon, the USA, have been able to suppress or resolve these conflicts and create a new regional order.

Among the most important reasons for these successive failures of empire in the region have been contradictions in the imperial ideology. These contradictions have been produced either by internal tensions, or by the impossibility of finding an ideology that could appeal to enough elements in an extremely varied and bitterly divided region, or provide a cultural and intellectual order through which to overcome those divisions. Even on the much smaller stage of the Caucasus, Soviet Communist ideology and Stalin's monstrous repression were only able to suspend and cover over—but not reconcile or end—the ethnic and religious conflicts of the region. As the memories of that repression faded, especially in the late 1980s when it became apparent that Gorbachev would not employ anything as ferocious in defense of Communist rule, these conflicts re-emerged and helped destroy the Soviet empire.

The last Muslim Great Power: the end of the Ottomans

In many ways, the most disastrous imperial collapse of all in the modern history of the region remains that of the Ottoman Empire and Caliphate in the period before, during, and after the First World War. Of all the Middle Eastern states of the early modern and modern periods, only the one created by Mehmet Ali in Egypt had any real chance of providing a convincing replacement. Even so, Egypt was still invaded by Britain and reduced to a protectorate in 1881, a blow from which Egypt has still not recovered.

The end of the Ottoman Empire therefore deprived the Middle East, and the Muslim world as a whole, of the only state that had a chance of emerging as a modern great power capable of resisting the domination of Western powers and maintaining something of the historic grandeur of Islam. The end of the Caliphate left a sense of moral, cultural, and political loss that haunts not just the region but the entire Muslim world to this day; a loss that combines geopolitical humiliation and dependence with cultural orphanhood.

None of the states that have succeeded the Ottomans has been able to reproduce anything like the power, cultural achievements, or universal claims of the Ottoman Empire at its height. All have been more or less crippled by some combination of dependence on outside powers, lack of domestic legitimacy, reliance on a narrow sectarian base at home, and reliance on modernizing ideologies more or less at odds with the cultural traditions of a majority of their populations.

Of course the economic, military, and ideological decline of the Ottoman Empire long pre-dated its final collapse. Militarily, the empire had suffered a long series of defeats and losses of territory dating back to the failed siege of Vienna in 1682. Although as the tremendous fight put up by the Ottoman armies against the British and French in the First World War demonstrated, even at the end of its strength the Ottoman military tradition was still very strong.

The modernization efforts embarked upon from the mid-nineteenth century on to strengthen the empire against its Russian and European foes had however involved it in an insoluble contradiction, which was later to contribute decisively to the fall of another great empire founded on ideology, the USSR. This was the contradiction between the Universalist ideology necessary to hold together the multinational empire and the nationalist sentiments and forces produced in response to economic change, and as a result of the influx of Western ideological influences due to modernization.[5]

The turmoil of Universalist, nationalist, and religious ideologies that emerged from the fall of the Ottoman Empire continues both to roil the Middle East as a whole and to divide individual states of the region to this day. Despite real development during the last fifty years before 1914, like the USSR in its last twenty years, the Ottoman Empire was also unable to generate a level of economic growth that would have helped legitimize it in the eyes of its own elites. This was all the more so because so much Western-driven economic development actually worsened the lives of ordinary people, and even the elites that benefited were too often drawn from the empire's Christian minorities, increasingly under the protection of Western powers.

Thus the last but one Ottoman Sultan, Abdul Hamid II (r.1876–1909), attempted to hold the Muslim provinces of his empire together by emphasizing—to a greater degree than for several centuries—his symbolic role as universal Muslim Caliph. This had the added advantage of appealing to Muslims outside the empire who in the course of the nineteenth century had become horrified by the inexorable conquest of Muslims lands by the British, French, Dutch, and Russian empires.[6]

But the Universalist ideology of the Caliphate came into direct conflict with the nationalism of the empire's Christian minorities and the embryonic nationalism of some of its Arab subjects. That in itself was not catastrophic; after all, to resist these challenges was the point of Abdul Hamid's strategy. Much more dangerous, and ultimately fatal, was this old–new ideology which clashed with a wholly new ideology generated in an effort to strengthen the Ottoman state, namely modern Turkish nationalism.

It was the triumph of this ideology in the Ottoman officer corps that was to lead to the revolution of the Young Turks, the deposition of Abdul Hamid, and the final Ottoman catastrophe between 1911 and 1918.[7] Young Turkish nationalism precipitated the empire's demise by involving it in the First World War; but even if this had not been the case, the Young Turks' Turkish ethnic nationalism (which in the form of Kemalism was to pass after 1922 into the official founding ideology of the new Turkish Republic) would in the long run have proved radically incompatible with the maintenance of a multinational empire.

Nationalism was absolutely central to the ideology and the legitimacy of the new Turkish republic, and to its ability to impose radical Westernizing reforms on an overwhelmingly rural, deeply religious, and conservative Turkish population. The anti-religious aspect of these reforms, intended to break the power of the clergy and establish the dominance of a new education system, was of an almost Communist radicalism and ferocity.[8]

Only the power of Turkish nationalism allowed Kemal Ataturk's regime to impose such changes. Ideologically, Kemalism was built on several generations of Westernizing reform under the Ottomans. The difference in terms of both radicalism and success can be explained by the facts that the series of wars from 1911 on, and the loss of territory, colossal refugee movements, and social upheaval that they produced had led to a spread of nationalism from the elites into the masses; and that unlike the later Ottomans, Kemalism had achieved military victories over Turkey's enemies: the Armenians, Greeks, and French. In the words of Hugh Poulton:

> [Kemal] strongly embodied many traditional characteristics held in high esteem by Turks—for example, military prowess, organisation and respect for law—*and had also succeeded against outside forces after a century and a half of failed attempts*. He was the Ghazi. Reforms introduced by him were not seen as forced under duress by the outside. They could be accepted with pride rather than shame.[9]

These nationalist victories gave Kemalist nationalism its prestige, its legitimacy, and its consequent ability to establish hegemony in Turkish society. It is precisely such victory that has been denied to modernizing nationalist forces in the Arab world. As with many such nationalist triumphs, this came at immense cost. The Turkish republic was in many ways a magnificently successful creation, but establishing it involved the massacre or deportation of the Christian (and later Jewish) minorities of Constantinople, in the Aegean and Pontic provinces and Anatolia, and the systematic suppression of any claims to ethnic identity of the Kurds and other Muslim minorities.

The Turkish military establishment's abandonment of Ottoman multiethnicity therefore set a pattern of national homogenization and consolidation with sinister precedents for what is happening in parts of the Middle East today, and perhaps for the future of Russia. For as I remarked in a book written soon after the USSR's collapse, given the fact that, like Turkey, the Russian successor state of the USSR itself still contained huge national minorities, those Westerners who expressed wishes that Russia should become a "normal" national state should have been careful what they wished for.[10]

Later in this chapter I shall draw certain parallels between this aspect of the Ottoman collapse and the way in which after 1989 sections of the Russian elites and peoples abandoned the Soviet Union in an effort to consolidate a Russian national state, with extremely mixed consequences.

The British Empire in the Middle East and the contradictions of liberalism

The move of the British and French empires into the former Ottoman Arab and Kurdish territories after 1918 presents the interesting spectacle of a great imperial expansion carried out by empires that were themselves mortally wounded, though they did not know it. The French Empire was never to recover from its appalling casualties in the First World War, a rate of loss that contributed directly to the French defeat by Nazi Germany in 1940 and the final agony of the French Empire over the following twenty-two years.

The British Empire had not suffered so badly, but nonetheless the unprecedented casualties produced a public sense of shock and disillusionment that contributed greatly to the empire's decline. In both Ireland and India, the war helped to drive a new wave of nationalist mobilization to which—after relatively brief attempts at ferocious repression—Britain was forced to make a series of concessions. Even as the British were establishing an indirect or informal empire in the Middle East through League of Nations-sanctioned "mandates" and the creation of client states, Great Britain in the old sense was ceasing to exist at home, with the establishment of the Irish Free State.

As the adoption of the "mandate" system indicates, the decline of the old imperial ideology in the face of Woodrow Wilson's rhetoric of freedom and national self-determination was also of great importance (at least in the case of Britain). These were the values for which the First World War had supposedly been fought. The resulting ideological confusion in the British imperial mind led to a situation in which, as David Fromkin writes, "having destroyed the old order in the region, and having deployed troops, armored cars, and military aircraft everywhere from Egypt to Iraq, British policy-makers imposed a settlement upon the Middle East in 1922 in which, for the most part, they themselves no longer believed."[11]

The final collapse of imperial ideology within Britain itself was not to come to full fruition until the Suez Crisis almost forty years after the end of the First World War, but it was already visible in the 1920s, with the growth of the Labour Party and strong criticism by the left-wing and liberal press in Britain of imperial actions, like the use of the Royal Air Force to bomb civilian targets in Iraq and on the North West Frontier of India.

Of even greater significance for the Middle East was, and has always been, the inherent contradiction between the imperial projects of Britain and the USA and the quasi-liberal regimes and programs that they have ostensibly been committed to promoting in the region as part of their "*missions civilisatrices*." The British and French imperial projects shattered the religious basis of legitimacy for the new states that they created; and it is very important to remember in this context that rather than having been the absolutist despots portrayed in Western propaganda, the Ottoman state like most Muslim rulers had most of the time neither the power nor the will to interfere in the sphere of religion and religious norms, which remained independent of the state. At the same time, the belief in a religion shared by rulers and ruled was a powerful source of state legitimacy.

Its destruction by the Western irruption into the region left a vacuum of legitimacy that in most countries has never really been filled.[12]

In Fromkin's words:

> The European powers at that time believed that they could change Moslem Asia in the very fundamentals of its political existence, and in their attempt to do so introduced an artificial state system into the Middle East that made it a region of countries that have not become nations even today. The basis of political life in the Middle East—religion—was called into question by the Russians, who proposed communism, and by the British, who proposed nationalism or dynastic loyalty, in its place.[13]

But the very nature of British, or any other, imperial domination meant that it was in practice impossible for the British to promote nationalism, or to allow their client regimes to establish real nationalist legitimacy—since this could only have come from nationalist defiance of the British. The British and French (and later the Americans) therefore deprived their client states of the nationalist legitimacy that they needed to place themselves and their modernizing programs on a secure footing.[14]

The chief contradiction here is not, as has widely been assumed, with the authoritarian character of the regimes concerned. Much of nineteenth-century European and Latin American liberalism had a markedly authoritarian and even military cast—necessarily so, both as the civic religion of self-appointed progressive elites frequently faced with the opposition of conservative Catholic peasant majorities of their own populations, and as the progressive justification for European imperial rule over "backward" non-European peoples.[15]

This was also true of the alliance between liberal ideas of progress and semi-authoritarian British rule in mid-nineteenth-century Ireland, whose Catholic majority population was assumed to be incapable of self-rule and of spontaneous progress unless guided firmly by liberal British elites. In the words of an Italian liberal nationalist intellectual (though himself from southern Italy), writing of the conservative, Catholic, and economically backward rural population of southern Italy:

> It does not take much intelligence or insight to understand that a people that is profoundly degraded and filled with misconceptions and gross prejudices, that believes in the evil eye, in spiritual possession, magic and magicians, dreams, the liquefaction of St Gennaro's blood, hair miraculously growing on the crucifix, and a thousand other crazy and absurd things, cannot think seriously about freedom, cannot understand it, want it, die for it.[16]

These sentiments are very close to those of a great many liberal modernizers in the Arab Middle East today concerning the conservative and religious majorities of their countries' populations.

In Germany, Max Weber's *The Protestant Ethic and the Spirit of Capitalism* is in part a veiled polemic justifying the continued domination of (allegedly Protestant-derived) capitalist elite dominance in Germany against the rise of political Catholicism.

Entirely characteristic in this regard was the repeated use of troops by liberal regimes to suppress peasant uprisings (the pattern being set by Garibaldi's own use of force against peasant protesters on the estate of the Duke of Bronte in Sicily in 1860) and the determination of most continental European and South American liberal parties to limit the vote to the propertied and educated classes.[17] In view of this tradition, there is nothing at all contradictory about contemporary Arab liberals supporting authoritarian regimes like that of Egypt out of hostility to conservative Muslim majorities of their own populations.

The real contradiction that has undermined liberal (or rather, mostly semi-liberal) regimes in the Middle East from the 1920s to the present day lies in the area not of authoritarianism but of nationalism. For liberalism as it grew up in early and mid-nineteenth-century Europe was closely associated with movements of national "liberation" and/or reform for the sake of national strength in the face of imperial domination or other states.[18]

The astonishingly radical reforms carried out under the Meiji regime in Japan from the 1860s on were explicitly justified and legitimized by the need to strengthen the nation and avoid the fate of other Asian countries at the hands of European imperialism. "Each modernization effort was clearly related to the central problem of increasing the wealth and power of the nation, and almost every major move was initiated and pushed by the national state in order to serve clearly defined national aims."[19] At the core of these reforms and their legitimization was the spread of a new Japanese nationalism through a new mass education system.[20] The legitimacy of the new regime and its reforms was then cemented by military victory over China in 1894 and Russia in 1904–5.

Indeed, it was this association of liberalism with nationalism, more than the liberal reform agendas in themselves, which often provided the chief source of legitimacy for liberal regimes; and as the Socialist challenge grew toward the nineteenth century, parties like the National Liberals in Germany came to rely more and more on nationalism for support. Nationalism also consolidated the alliance between political liberals and the armed forces, and thereby gave the liberals the muscle necessary to push through their agenda against popular resistance.

Nationalism was at the heart of what Antonio Gramsci later called the "hegemony" of bourgeois liberal ideas in late-nineteenth-century Italy: their acceptance by much of the population as a form of "common sense" leading to the consent of a majority of the population, most of the time, to elite rule and elite policies—though just as elite rule rests on the ever-present possibility of intermittent coercion as well as the regular pattern of mass consent, so that consent is liable to be interrupted by periodical protests and upheavals. As described by Eugen Weber, Barrington Moore, and others, nationalism was inculcated in the masses above all through newly-created state school systems:

> Still another aspect of the rationalization of the political order has to do with the making of citizens in a new type of society. Literacy and rudimentary technical skills are necessary for the masses. Setting up a national system of education is very likely to bring on a conflict with religious authorities. Loyalty to a new abstraction, the state, must also replace religious loyalties if they transcend national boundaries or compete with each other so vigorously as to destroy internal peace... In overcoming such difficulties, the existence of a foreign enemy can be quite useful.[21]

In the words of Heinz Ziegler:

> The idea of the nation forms the philosophical foundation for the legitimacy of bourgeois society. It guarantees ... the legitimacy of modern structures of government. It implies the consent of the masses to the new state, and is one of the basic factors governing the process whereby the masses are incorporated into the political constellation.[22]

Thus there is an inherent historical contradiction in a liberal regime effectively abandoning nationalism and acting as the client state of an alien empire, for such a status strips the liberals of their greatest claim to the allegiance of the mass of the population. The only successful compensating factor can be very successful and sustained economic growth, which both legitimizes the state and ultimately creates a measure of social and cultural integration of society; but that has not been achieved anywhere in the Arab world outside the oil-rich states of the Gulf.

To put it another way, European liberalism during its period of decisive struggle was an ideology of the military and economic victory. No ideology can be expected to retain its prestige in the face of repeated defeat and humiliation. Open subjugation to British imperial goals was to hollow out the monarchies and regimes in both Egypt and Iraq, and lead to their fall once British power declined after the Second World War.

Britain's hegemony in the region, like that of the USA later, was also gravely undermined by the Zionist project, which by introducing Western settlers into Arab lands (as the French had done in Algeria, but the British had been careful to avoid doing elsewhere in their Muslim possessions) revealed the impotence and dependency of the Arab client regimes in the starkest light, and continues to do so.[23]

British problems were further complicated by the Hashemite dynasty's loss of the Hejaz to the House of Saud in 1925. Thereafter, Britain's Hashemite allies in Transjordan and Iraq would lack the immense prestige that stemmed from the protection of Mecca and Medina. In the longer run, a combination of Saudi Arabia's oil wealth with the control of the Holy Places would mean that the most important and permanent US client state in the Middle East has been ruled by a regime whose ideological agenda is radically opposed to the liberal ideological underpinnings and professed progressive mission of the US empire.[24]

Even when most closely allied to the USA—as in funding and supplying the Afghan Mujahedin fighting Soviet occupation in the 1980s—the Saudis have supported their own program of ideological indoctrination through the funding of Wahhabi madrasahs and clerics. In Afghanistan and Pakistan, Riyadh helped thereby to lay part of the foundation for the Taliban and al-Qaeda.[25] This is a contradiction that continues to haunt US policy to this day, and came into sharp focus after the rise of the Saudi dissident Osama bin Laden and al-Qaeda, whose theology is derived from and shared with that of Saudi Arabia.

The Cold War: progress divided

The growth of Soviet influence in the Middle East after 1945 coincided with the replacement of British hegemony in the region with that of the USA. The result was to embroil the region in the Cold War rivalry of the two superpowers. At the time—and in much Western writing to this day—this was cast as an existential struggle between two rival ideologies, one rooted in Western capitalist democracy, the other in Soviet Communist dictatorship. With hindsight, however, the Cold War in West Asia may be more accurately seen as a fratricidal and mutually disastrous struggle between two branches of European modernizing ideology, the result of which was to open the way for the rise of a third force implacably hostile to both of them: Islamist radicalism.

This has long been apparent in Afghanistan, where the USA has come to rely heavily on Soviet-trained officers and technocrats (like General Sher Mohammad Karimi and General Sayed Malouk) from the 1980s to staff its own Afghan client regime, in order to fight Taliban enemies whose ideology and support base is often substantially the same as that of the US-backed Afghan Mujahedin of the 1980s. I have interviewed former Communist officers now with the Afghan National Army, and they are quite convinced that the war they are fighting today against the Taliban is the same as that which they waged in the 1980s against the Mujahedin: a struggle for a modern, progressive Afghan state against the forces of rural obscurantism and tribalism.[26]

In Afghanistan, US support for the Mujahedin destroyed the Soviet-backed regime and helped undermine the USSR itself, but in the process (together with Saudi finance and ideological influence) created the conditions for the rise of the Taliban and al-Qaeda, and for 9/11 and the catastrophes that followed.

In the Middle East, the USA and Israel over time defeated the USSR and subverted or destroyed its client states, but in the process severely damaged America's own position and the whole Western modernization effort in the region. The ultimate consequence has been the rise of the Islamic State (IS) and the challenge it now poses to all the states of the region and the entire regional order.

The ultimate reason for this self-destructive US course was that the real or perceived needs of the struggle with the USSR and "Communism" led the United States into a far more intense and militarized presence in the region than US energy interests and even sympathy with Israel would have required. The result was to draw the USA into conflict with local nationalist forces that were not originally hostile to the USA and whose agendas were modernizing ones.

This disastrous process began with the US overthrow of the (originally pro-American) Iranian liberal nationalist Prime Minister Mohamad Mossadeq in 1953, due to a perception that he and other local nationalists must inevitably be Soviet stooges. This US perception stemmed from the Cold War but was assiduously fostered by the British in order to gain US support for their continued imperial hegemony in Iran: not the last time that US force and subversion in the Middle East were to be deployed as a result of manipulation by a third party.

The result of the CIA-orchestrated coup against Mossadeq was to restore the rule of the Shah, but also—by turning the Shah into an obvious US client—to hollow out the nationalist legitimacy of his regime and to open the way twenty-five years later for the overthrow of the Shah and his replacement by an Islamic nationalist state order, which for thirty years or so was far more hostile to the USA than Mossadeq was or indeed could have been given his underlying modernizing ideology. The Pahlavi dynasty's nationalist credentials had already been undermined by the ease with which the British and Soviets invaded Iran and deposed Reza Shah in 1941, leading to his son's accession. Reza Shah, like Ataturk, had laid a firm basis for Iranian nationalism, but it was chiefly to mitigate the opposition and especially those parts of the opposition led by the Shia clergy.[27]

Even more disastrous for US long-term goals was US backing for Israel's repeated victories over its Arab neighbors. During the 1956 war with Egypt and the Suez Crisis, President Eisenhower's administration resisted pressure to support Israel, and by pressure on Britain and France not only ended their Suez adventure but helped to finish off what remained of the British Empire in the Middle East. This was, however, to be the last time until the Obama administration's Iran initiative almost sixty years later that a US administration proved able to oppose Israeli actions significantly.

Israeli victory in 1948 and the Israeli, French, and British Suez aggression of 1956 dealt a severe blow to the British-backed royal regimes in the Middle East and paved the way for the collapse of the monarchies in Egypt, Iraq, and Libya. Israeli victories in 1967 and (in a more qualified way) 1973 played a central and disastrous role in mortally wounding their progressive nationalist successors—most immediately by leading to President Sadat's decision to make peace with Israel and make Egypt a client state of the USA.[28] Thereafter, only Iraq was left as a major state representing progressive Arab nationalism in the Middle East—and Iraq was finished off between 1980 and 2003 by a combination of Saddam Hussein's crimes and US actions.[29]

With the effective demise of the Libyan and Syrian states after 2011, there is now no state at all credibly representing Arab nationalism in the region.[30] Hopes of the unification of the Arab Middle East have therefore long since collapsed. Thanks to US and Israeli power, no state was permitted to play the role of Prussia in unifying mid-nineteenth-century Germany, even had any state been strong enough to do so. Nor was an outside great power—which in this case would have been the USSR—permitted to play the part of France in unifying through war as in mid-nineteenth-century Italy. Apart from overall US power in the region, the ultimate sanction of the US nuclear deterrent made sure that it was never remotely in Moscow's interest to run the risks involved in such an attempt, even if the USSR had been sincerely interested in the triumph of Arab nationalism.

Of course, to portray the demise of Arab progressive nationalism as only the result of US and Israeli actions would be to miss half the story. As already stated, European liberalism triumphed on the strength of a combination of victorious nationalism and capitalist economic growth in response to liberal economic policies. If this growth did not always or quickly benefit the mass of the population, it nonetheless created bourgeois classes that supported the national states, drove further economic growth, and above all achieved a cultural hegemony which persuaded sufficient parts of the population of the legitimacy of liberal nationalism, its program, and its institutions. Economic growth in turn allowed national states to raise enough money in taxes to pay for universal and compulsory school systems, which as noted were crucial to inculcating nationalism in the masses. There is therefore a reciprocal effect between lack of successful economic reform and lack of the nationalist legitimacy necessary to make that reform possible.

The need for such bourgeois nationalist hegemony in order to shape national consciousness has been all the greater in the Arab world, where—to an even greater degree than in Germany, Italy, or Eastern Europe—new states lacked real historical and cultural depth. In the partisan but also prophetic words of the Algerian Francophile liberal Ferhat Abbas in 1936, "If I had discovered the Arab nation, I would have become a nationalist ... I did not discover it. I looked to history, I questioned the living and dead, I could not find it."[31] According to Michael Hudson:

> The central problem of government in the Arab world today is political legitimacy. The shortage of this indispensable political resource largely accounts for the volatile nature of Arab politics and the autocratic, unstable character of all the present Arab governments.[32]

Hudson was writing in 1977, but—except that in recent years several autocracies have been destroyed and replaced by anarchy—the same is true thirty-eight years later.

Most unfortunately, with the exception of the Gulf states (with their abundant oil wealth and small populations) no Arab state has been able to achieve the kind of economic success that would either allow the creation of really effective nationalist indoctrination through mass education, or provide a partial alternative to nationalism in consolidating society, legitimizing the state and giving the state the educational tools to indoctrinate the population in state loyalty. Whether they have pursued ostensibly socialist or ostensibly free market economic policies, all have found themselves hampered and even crippled by traditions of patrimonialism, kinship loyalty, patronage, and corruption.[33]

Instead of generating entrepreneurial bourgeois classes like those that underpinned the victories of nineteenth-century European liberalism, all have tended to develop clientelistic groups dependent on links to the state for patronage and protection, and in no position to push their own agendas, whether economic or political. Dependence on factions within the state has also critically undermined the bourgeoisie's ability to develop autonomous judicial systems and codes to regulate and encourage business. Instead, business advantage is sought through political favoritism.[34] In Turkey, as in other parts of Asia, nationalism has been absolutely critical to breaking down such traditional obstacles to modernization.

The weakness of nationalism in the Arab Middle East is therefore inextricably linked to the region's failure to develop.[35] This feature of the Arab Middle East is especially striking when contrasted with Iran, where nationalism remains central to the strength and cohesion of the clerical-led state and to its achievements in the areas of education and various forms of social progress (including, most unusually for the region, in family planning).[36]

The failure to develop modern structures extends even more strikingly to Arab states themselves, and especially the persistence (albeit in new forms) of kinship as the basis for regime solidarity and longevity.[37] Here, there is an especially sharp contrast with Western modernization in both its capitalist and its socialist forms. To overcome kinship as the primary focus of loyalty and solidarity (and even of effective sovereignty) has been perhaps the single greatest goal and challenge for states ever since their first appearance.[38] It is a goal that most Arab states have yet to achieve. According to Hisham Sharabi, writing in the 1990s:

> In contemporary Arab society ... the individual has no individuality. He/she is lost if he breaks with the family, tribe or sect. The modern state is not only incapable of replicating such primary groups for him but is also usually regarded by the individual as a source of oppression and persecution.[39]

In the Gulf states, hereditary monarchies not only rule but create and personify their kingdoms. Saudi Arabia is that portion of Arabia that is ruled by the House of Saud. Qatar is the creation of the house of Al Thani. The Hashemite Kingdom of Jordan (an artificial British creation) is the portion of Arabia that is ruled by the House of Hashem, and so on.

But even where regimes have been explicitly modeled on the totalitarian parties of Europe, kinship allegiances came to dominate the inner circle of the state, and heredity to determine the actual or planned succession. Thus in both Iraq and Syria, the Ba'ath party came under the domination of particular clans: in Iraq, the Tikriti clan of Saddam Hussein centered on his immediate family; and in Syria, the house of Assad based on the Alawite ethno-religious group. Until 2003 and 2011 or so, one could therefore to a degree (and with all due reference to old regional identities) talk of Syria as the Alawite Kingdom of Syria and Iraq as Tikriti Arabia. Libya under Moamer Ghaddafi also moved in the direction of dynastic rule.

Only in Egypt, thanks to the strong military tradition established by Gamal Abdel Nasser and his associates, has a strong, meritocratic (within its own terms of reference) national military established a military–bureaucratic rather than kinship-based government—albeit one devoted not to national development but to the closely linked goals of collective enrichment and state stability. The officer corps has also to a considerable extent merged with the state-sponsored business classes and with whatever Egypt possesses of a technocracy—which helps to explain their backing for General el-Sisi's coup against the Muslim Brotherhood government. Nasser too, however, wholly failed to found a political movement with the discipline, organization, and longevity of the European totalitarian parties, and with a real capacity for effective reform and development.[40]

In the words of Bassam Tibi from 1997 (adapted by Paul Glass for the title of his book *Tribes With Flags*):

> The Middle East continues to be formally a regional system of states. These states are however tribes with national flags, i.e. nominal nation states ... Once, Arab nationalism served equally as a hope and a legitimacy. The de-legitimisation process deprived the Arab states of both. It is not the bond of Arab nationalism, but rather the Mukhabarat [secret police] that keeps Middle Eastern nation states as entities on the political map. Political Islam is a challenge to these states, but the most it can deliver is not the promised new order but rather chaos and disorder.[41]

Arguing along the same lines, Nazih Ayubi describes Arab states as not "strong" but "fierce" (in other words ferociously repressive) precisely to make up for their lack of underlying ideological hegemony and consequent legitimacy and political strength.[42]

A combination of military defeat, economic failure, and political stagnation therefore deprived both the liberal–capitalist and the socialist–nationalist versions of modernization of the prestige necessary to consolidate legitimacy in their populations. Even before the Iraqi state was destroyed by the USA in 2003, and Syria and Libya destroyed by uprisings (in the latter case, with Western support) after 2011, the European-inspired modernization programs in the region were effectively dead on their feet.

Despite their immense wealth, the Gulf states for their part have been unable to give leadership for development in the region as a whole due to a combination of religious, cultural, political, and demographic limitations.[43] Saudi prestige among the Sunni Arab masses of the region has also been badly damaged by dependence on the USA.

The Wahhabi religious ideology of Saudi Arabia is however of inherently limited appeal; and, very dangerously for the Kingdom, the House of Saud has to some extent been supplanted by the Islamic State as Wahhabism's—and even embattled Sunnism's—most prominent and radical exponent. The especially ferocious and reckless Saudi response to Houthi Shia successes in Yemen may be in part an attempt to claw back some legitimacy for the Kingdom as the defender of the Sunni regional community.

Equally important is the predominance of kinship and local identities and allegiances over pan-Arab ones, a factor that has played a key part in frustrating every attempt at pan-Arab unity and even cooperation. In the case of the Gulf states, this takes the form of a conjoined determination of the monarchies to retain full control of government, and of the indigenous, formerly tribal populations to retain near-exclusive possession of citizenship and all the immense state benefits that citizenship brings.

Hence the inherent and insoluble tension between, on the one hand, the desire of Kuwait, the UAE, and Qatar to become great cultural and economic centers of the Arab and Muslim worlds, and on the other, their policy of recruiting non-Arab labor and thereby remaining tribal oligarchies ruling over transient populations, rather than established pan-Arab metropolises. A Peter the Great of Russia or a Sultan Muhammad bin Tughluq of Hindustan would not have allowed their grand imperial designs to be thwarted by such considerations; but these were genuine autocrats, not tribal chieftains dependent in the end on maintaining consensuses within the leaderships of their tribal federations.

The Caucasus

The Caucasus has experienced only one and a half collapses of empire over the past century, unlike the repeated convulsions of the Middle East. Unlike the Ottoman Empire, which outside its Anatolian core collapsed completely, the Russian Empire that collapsed as a result of the First World War was put back together again, albeit in a radically new form. The consequences of the second collapse, that of the USSR, are however still very much present, and—just as in the Middle East—are very far from having reached any kind of conclusion. Like the Middle East, the Caucasus exemplifies the difficulty of maintaining imperial hegemony over bitterly divided regions, especially when the population of the imperial power is uncertain about making major sacrifices for the sake of that hegemony. Russians have been willing to undergo very considerable sacrifices both to defend the territorial integrity of Russia itself (in the Chechen wars) and to defend Russia's hold on what are seen as historically and ethnically Russian territories beyond Russia's borders (in Ukraine). A purely imperial war for the domination of non-Russian countries in the South Caucasus would most probably be a very different matter.

Like the Ottoman Empire, the USSR collapsed in large part because of the collapse of the ideology (virtually a state religion) that underpinned it. In a mainly national state like China, the ideology was reformed and the imperial state continued. In the multinational USSR, a combination of loss of legitimacy among the core Russian elites and national upheaval in some of the union republics brought about the system's doom.

As with the reappearance of ethnic, tribal, and sectarian tensions in the Middle East in the first part of the twenty-first century, the eruption of nationalism in parts of the USSR took most observers by surprise. Focusing on the official modernizing ideology of the state, they missed the degree to which older loyalties and animosities (albeit shaped by modern change) had continued to flow under the ice of Soviet power.

It is very important to note, however, that as in the Middle East, national and ethnic conflict in the Caucasus has been only in part to do with revolt against imperial rule or imperial hegemony. Of even greater importance both in undermining direct imperial rule and frustrating quasi-imperial hegemony has been conflict between the Caucasian peoples themselves, along lines which in some cases long pre-date the establishment of imperial rule.

Thus in the USSR, the first major sign of national unrest and the weakening of the central state came in 1987 when the Armenians raised the issue of transferring the Armenian-majority autonomous region of Nagorno-Karabakh from the Soviet republic of Azerbaijan to Armenia. This was not a new issue. In the years between the collapse of the Russian Empire and the Soviet conquest of the South Caucasus, Armenia and Azerbaijan fought over the region, and its incorporation into Azerbaijan was never accepted by most Armenians.[44]

Intermittently throughout Soviet rule, discreet attempts were made by governments of Soviet Armenia to have the territory transferred, but these were always brushed off by the center. When Mikhail Gorbachev began his attempts to reform and loosen Communist rule in the late 1980s, Armenians inevitably raised this issue again—and inevitably met fierce opposition from Azerbaijan.

Although in the course of this gathering conflict nationalists on both sides also adopted anti-Soviet and pro-independence positions, these were not in fact at the core of either movement. Due to the need for imperial protection from much stronger Turkic Muslim neighbors, Armenians have throughout modern history been the most pro-Russian of the major nationalities of the

Caucasus (and indeed of the former USSR as a whole). Since the fall of the USSR, Armenia has therefore been unusual among former Soviet republics in continuing voluntarily to host a Russian military force. Like France and the USA, Russia is also home to a very large and influential Armenian diaspora, which has grown still further as a result of labor migration since the fall of the USSR and its attendant economic crises.

Azerbaijan for its part is very much less inherently pro-Russian than Armenia. On the other hand, Azerbaijan has resembled most of the former Soviet republics of Central Asia in the persistence of rule by leaders of the former Communist parties under new names. After a brief interlude of rule by the nationalist opposition in 1992–3 caused by the Karabakh conflict, a coup brought the Nakhichevan faction of the Communist Party to power, led by former Party First Secretary and KGB chief Heidar Aliyev, whose dynasty rules Azerbaijan to this day. Aliyev broke sharply with the policies of the previous nationalist government in seeking good relations with Moscow—though without compromising on the issue of Azerbaijan's sovereignty over Nagorno-Karabakh.[45]

Even in the case of Georgia, whose nationalism has the most anti-Russian coloring of all those of the South Caucasus, the origins of this lie to a considerable extent in local ethnic conflicts—albeit ones assiduously played on by Moscow. Thus a key moment in the growth and radicalization of Georgian nationalism under Gorbachev was the bloody suppression by Soviet troops of the nationalist demonstrations in Tbilisi in April 1989. These demonstrations were however organized not to demand Georgian independence, but to protest against a mass meeting in the Georgian autonomous republic of Abkhazia calling for separation from Georgia and the establishment of Abkhazia as a union republic of the USSR, as it had been briefly in the 1920s. The origins of the Georgian national revolution and subsequent civil wars were therefore directly parallel to what happened in Azerbaijan over the separation of Nagorno-Karabakh.[46]

In Georgia and to a lesser extent in Azerbaijan, Soviet and then Russian backing for the ethnic separatist regions (including in the case of Georgia that of South Ossetia) led by 1994 to their military victory and de facto separation, though this was not officially recognized even by Russia, let alone the international community.[47] As in Azerbaijan, the period of nationalist rule in Georgia was ended in December 1991 by a coup which brought back to power Georgia's former Communist leader—former First Secretary and Soviet Foreign Minister Eduard Shevardnadze—and his faction of the old Communist Party.[48]

The civil wars of the early 1990s also meant that the economic collapse of the South Caucasus was even more savage than that which affected the former USSR as a whole. By 1994, with former Communists ruling in Georgia and Azerbaijan, anti-Russian nationalists defeated, Abkhazia and South Ossetia under Moscow's military protection, a pro-Russian nationalist regime ruling in Armenia, and millions of people from all the countries of the region seeking work in Russia (poor, but a great deal richer than the South Caucasus of the 1990s), it seemed to many observers that the region had in effect fallen back under a looser form of hegemonic rule from Moscow, a variant of *Pax Russica.* It also seemed that this outcome was at least as much due to the conflicts among the peoples of the region as it was to Moscow's own strategy and actions.

That this outcome did not in fact come to pass was due to a number of factors. Imperial competition from the United States and the European Union was one of them, although (by contrast with Central Europe and the Baltic States) this was relatively slow to develop in the South Caucasus. As outlined in Meliha Benli Altunışık's chapter in this volume, Turkey's initial hopes of establishing a sphere of influence in the region after the Soviet collapse were disappointed and had to be drastically scaled back. However, Turkish soft power was of some significance, and Turkey also provided a trade and energy route for Azerbaijan and Georgia to the West; but not for Armenia, because of tensions with Ankara over the Karabakh War and demands for recognition of the Armenian genocide.

Russia's own economic resources were limited, and Azerbaijan could look to the West for the development of new oil fields below the Caspian Sea. The humiliation of the Russian army in the first Chechen War of 1994–6 did much to undermine Russia's military prestige in the region and the world—though this outcome was reversed by the renewed Russian military intervention launched by the new Russian government of Vladimir Putin in 1999.

Perhaps the most important factor in limiting Russian hegemony, however—and with the closest analogies to US hegemonic dilemmas in the Middle East—was Moscow's inability to solve the ethnic and national conflicts of the region on terms acceptable to the main parties. A strong impression exists that Heidar Aliyev, given his background and his desire for Russian support to consolidate his dynastic rule, would have been entirely willing to take Azerbaijan into a Russian-dominated military and economic alliance. He could only have done so, however, if by accepting Russian hegemony he could have recovered Nagorno-Karabakh. To enter such an alliance without achieving this would have led to an upsurge of nationalist fury in Azerbaijan that would have threatened the survival of his regime.

But the Armenians refused categorically to return Karabakh even to a highly qualified form of Azerbaijani rule, and given the historical, cultural, and geopolitical importance of Armenia to Russia, Moscow was never prepared to put the necessary pressure on Yerevan to force the Armenian government to surrender. Attempts by the European Union and the USA to bring about a settlement, along very similar lines to the compromise proposed by Russia, subsequently also failed in the face of Armenian resistance to Azeri demands. The USA and France in particular were gravely hampered in their ability to put pressure on Armenia by the presence of powerful Armenian diasporas within these countries.

Similarly in the case of Georgia, Eduard Shevardnadze during his time in power there from 1992 to 2003 actively sought better relations with Moscow. But neither could he have agreed to entry into a Russian-led alliance if Moscow had been prepared to sacrifice Abkhazia and South Ossetia. This Moscow was not prepared to do, partly because of military and cultural ties to the Ossetes dating back to the eighteenth century, and partly because this would have involved Russia sacrificing small but concrete and permanent regional assets in return for a Georgian submission to Russian hegemony that might be reversed by a new Georgian regime.

As demonstrated by the Georgian "Rose Revolution" of 2003 that overthrew Shevardnadze and replaced him with the radical nationalist Mikheil Saakashvili, this was probably a correct calculation from Moscow's point of view, on the old principle of a bird in hand being worth two in the bush. With Georgian hopes of a peaceful return of Abkhazia and South Ossetia at an end, and the USA now appearing to offer Georgia the prospect of military support, Saakashvili in August 2008 launched an attempt to recover South Ossetia by force. The result was a crushing Georgian defeat (made inevitable by the US refusal to intervene), Russian recognition of Abkhaz and Southern Ossete independence, and a geopolitical break between Georgia and Russia that will remain for the foreseeable future, and has wrecked any remaining Russian hope of keeping hegemony over the South Caucasus as a whole.

On the other hand, the US failure to give military support to Georgia (and, in 2014, Ukraine), after all the US promises of future NATO membership, also indicates the severe limits on US power in the region, and on Washington's hopes of establishing a new US hegemony to replace that of Russia. A close parallel therefore exists with these Russian dilemmas in trying to establish a stable hegemony in the Caucasus and the repeated US failures to help stabilize the Middle East and US hegemony there by bringing about a peace settlement between Israel and Palestine. A looser parallel also exists between the situation in the Caucasus and US inability to reconcile Shia, Sunni, and Kurds in Iraq after the US conquest, or the warring groups in Syria, Libya, and Yemen after the revolutions there.

In other words, such are the divisions and tensions in these regions that any outside power will face extreme difficulties in maintaining hegemony—at least, without the deployment of huge numbers of its own troops over a period of decades. After the disastrous experience of the occupations of Iraq and Afghanistan, no will exists in the American public for more wars of occupation in the Middle East. Nor, after viewing US travails in the region, does China seem to have any desire to imitate the USSR and challenge the USA for hegemony in the Middle East. As a Chinese diplomat put it to the author of this chapter, "Why would we want to get involved in that mess? Do you think we could sort it out?"

Russia too, though it fought back against Georgian attack in 2008, and has deployed proxy forces in Ukraine, is not willing to make the huge long-term commitment of forces (and loss of international prestige) necessary to impose military hegemony on the Caucasus or actually conquer the Russian-speaking areas of Ukraine. The Putin administration must have serious concerns whether nationalist support in Russia for government would hold up in the face of the kind of sacrifices that such a strategy would require.

Conclusion

In the South Caucasus, the ideological foundations of Russian hegemony collapsed a generation ago in the face of the twin appeals of nationalism and Western liberal capitalism. However, the US and EU agendas in turn have found themselves paralyzed by a combination of Russian military power, local national conflicts, and their own weaknesses of resources and will.

Without US military backing, Georgia and Azerbaijan cannot defeat their local enemies and create a basis for US regional hegemony; and that military backing will not be forthcoming, both because of US commitments elsewhere and because the power of the Armenian lobby in the USA would prevent any such commitment to Azerbaijan. Meanwhile, the West in the Caucasus also lacks the supreme inducements which helped (to a degree) consolidate democracy and the free market in Eastern Europe, namely the credible promise of membership of the EU and NATO as a reward for reforms. The South Caucasus therefore seems set for a very prolonged period of frozen conflict in a form of geopolitical no-man's land.

In the Middle East, by contrast, the conflicts are anything but frozen and the situation is very much more volatile. Unlike in the Caucasus, one great power—the USA—retains overall dominance, but that dominance appears to be crumbling under the combined pressure of its own internal contradictions and those of the region itself.

The ideological foundations of US hegemony have collapsed, as have hopes that any US-backed agenda can lead to real progress. With the USA now backing a mixture of Sunni autocrats and Shia militias in a frantic effort to contain the Islamic State, the US "Freedom Agenda" for the region proclaimed as the centerpiece of Bush administration strategy now looks like a fantastically bad joke. None of the forces now being backed by the USA have any serious agenda for modernization. Indeed, all have proved repeatedly their incapacity for any such program. This is especially stark in the case of Egypt, the most populous and important state of the region, where the military-based regime of President Abdel Fattah el-Sisi is simply continuing the failed structures and policies of the Mubarak regime that led in the end to revolution.[49]

Military pressure from the US and Iran has led to the containment of IS, but it is extremely difficult to imagine how the Iraqi and Syrian states can be put together again in any meaningful way. The frontier between Syria and northern Iraq, which survived the coming to power of supposedly pan-Arabist parties in both countries, has effectively been abolished, with other frontiers perhaps to follow. The territorial terms of the Sykes–Picot partition have therefore been radically undermined: not, as everyone expected, by Pan-Arab nationalism, but by jihadi Islamism with a program demanding the abolition of all nation states in the name of a restored Caliphate.

When it comes to international relations in the region, the Obama administration distanced itself from Israel, but not to the extent of bringing serious pressure to bear for a peace settlement with the Palestinians. Moreover, none of the leading candidates for president in 2016 (Democrat or Republican) have followed Obama's lead. What if anything the future Trump administration will do is at the time of writing impossible to predict.

Some two decades after this should have occurred, the USA under Obama finally made a serious—and at the time of writing, apparently successful—attempt at an agreement with Iran on the nuclear issue, leading to the possibility of détente between the two countries. In the past, there might have been hope that a new accord between the USA and the only (relatively) modern nation state of the region would lead to a peaceful and consensual regional order under a looser US hegemony. In the meantime, however, the spread of

Sunni–Shia conflict in the region has meant that the USA has gained at best somewhat more freedom of maneuver—as long as the Trump administration permits this to continue.

With the regional hegemon internally divided, militarily weakened, and ideologically bankrupt, the region itself split by savage and apparently irreconcilable conflicts, and states and state borders collapsing over wide areas, the Middle East seems set for a long period of violent instability, the outcome of which cannot be foreseen.

3

PIPELINE POLITICS IN IRAN, TURKEY, AND THE SOUTH CAUCASUS

Mahmood Monshipouri

The South Caucasus region—comprising Armenia, Azerbaijan, and Georgia—is a crucial region known for its vast hydrocarbon deposits and geopolitical position, largely as a crossing point between the Middle East, Europe, and Asia. In terms of energy security, the South Caucasus is a region where interests pursued by local, regional, and global actors are linked in complex and often contradictory ways. The region will continue to hold crucial geopolitical importance, where many countries' interests—including the United States, the EU, Russia, and some key regional players, such as Iran and Turkey—intersect.

While Armenia, Azerbaijan, and Georgia have been preoccupied with their political survival and viability, cooperation and competition in economic and energy areas have provided a major impetus for the relationships among large regional players such as Russia, Iran, and Turkey over the past decade. The relationships among these three countries are best described as difficult and volatile, and often their interests clash pointedly in the Caucasus.[1] Turkey and Russia appear likely to manage their differences in the Caucasus and Caspian

Basin in the short term, but competing and conflicting energy and political interests, as well as lingering cultural and religious suspicions, seem likely to rekindle historical rivalries, also involving Iran, over the longer term.[2]

Iran and Russia hold differing positions on the boundary demarcation of the Caspian Sea. Russian support for a median-line solution would sharply limit Iran's share of Caspian energy resources. The two countries see themselves as long-term competitors in the European energy market. Despite these differences, both governments oppose the development of the trans-Caspian pipeline. Moreover, they have tacitly agreed to avoid confrontations in the Caucasus and to support mutual goals with regard to Caspian energy routes.[3] For the South Caucasus region, seven decades of Soviet rule have proven to be an onerous legacy, worsened by fragile economies, interminable conflicts, and a lack of democratic legitimacy. It is a region where Russia, Turkey, and Iran have competed for influence over much of the past two centuries.[4] Yet there can be no doubt that Russia is still the most important external player in the South Caucasus region.[5]

The relationships between Iran, Turkey, and the South Caucasus states have arguably been influenced by a wide array of geopolitical, strategic, cultural, and economic factors. The competition between Iran and Turkey and their roles in the South Caucasus are best defined by traditional balance-of-power relations, as well as the broader context of the post-Soviet era. The multiple energy routes that connect these countries with the Caspian Sea energy supplies take on an added significance. It is very important to acknowledge that Russia's control of Caspian energy reserves has drastically diminished since the opening of the Southern Corridor's Baku–Tbilisi–Ceyhan (BTC) oil line in 2005 and the South Caucasus Pipeline (SCP) gas line, also known as the Baku–Tbilisi–Erzurum (BTE) pipeline, or the Shah Deniz pipeline in 2006.[6]

Competition between Iran and Turkey to get access to the South Caucasus energy routes has become increasingly impossible to avoid. Turkey has seen its role in Eurasia expand from that of a major transit country into a fully-fledged regional energy hub. Turkey and the Caucasus region, according to one source, can also develop a similarly entwined relationship by 2021.[7] This, however, requires that various streams of natural gas be traded far more flexibly than is possible today. If Caspian gas, Iraqi gas, Egyptian gas, and Iranian gas (including in the form of swaps with Iranian gas delivered in the Persian Gulf), and Turkey's off-shore gas could be traded, the South Caucasus would truly become an energy hub for Eurasia.[8] This scenario requires a full normalization of the political and economic relations between all countries in the broader region, including Syria and Iran.[9]

Iran's border with the South Caucasus's two key countries—Azerbaijan and Armenia—affords it a great advantage. However, Iran's close relationship with Armenia has entailed a geopolitically important cost, including further intensifying pan-Turkish contentions in neighboring Azerbaijan. Iran's position in the South Caucasus is not only challenged by Turkey, but also by Russia. The latter seeks to dominate the region's oil and gas pipeline politics to increase its geostrategic depth in times of crisis, and appears keen to keep an energy-hungry Europe dependent on its resources.[10] While Iran and Russia are potentially the two great powers in the field of energy reserves in the world, they have yet to make successful joint investments in the fields of exploitation and transportation of energy and in the formation of a strong partnership in global energy markets.[11]

Although Turkey has cultivated good relations with Azerbaijan and Georgia, its relations with Armenia continue to be problematic, in part because of Turkey's refusal to acknowledge that an Armenian genocide occurred between 1915 and 1923, and in part due to the fact that Turkey favors Azerbaijan in the Nagorno-Karabakh conflict. Azerbaijan has long viewed Turkey as an ally that could potentially serve as a balance to Armenia's ties with Russia and Iran. Georgia has an enduring interest in ties with the approximately 1 million Georgians residing in Turkey and the approximately 50,000 residing in Iran, and as a result they have signed multiple friendship treaties with both countries.[12] Turkey is one of Georgia's primary trade partners. The existing east–west oil and gas pipeline (BTC) reflects the basis for most of the cooperation between Azerbaijan, Georgia, and Turkey.

This chapter seeks to unpack the complex dynamics of pipeline politics in the South Caucasus region by underlining the need to understand the "Great Power Game" involving geostrategic and geo-economic interests of local governments, regional actors, global powers, and international oil companies. Our larger focus turns on underscoring the importance of the region's large oil and gas reserves, its land connection between the Caspian Sea, South Caucasus, and Europe, and its long-standing territorial conflicts in the post-Soviet era, namely Abkhazia and South Ossetia in Georgia and Nagorno-Karabakh in Azerbaijan.[13] Iran and Turkey have fought for influence in the South Caucasus while maintaining relatively good bilateral relationships in the region. The relationship between Iran and Turkey is best described as important but ambivalent, given that hydrocarbon resources and the need for their transportation to Western markets keep Turkey and Iran in a tight but considered competition and collaboration.

Beyond these geopolitical reasons, the discovery of new oil and gas deposits in the Caspian Basin has led to an increase in the stakes for both regional and extra-regional powers. This chapter's central argument is that while oil and gas pipelines facilitate economic growth and ensure the energy security of the region, they are likely to intensify competition among key regional actors, such as Iran, Turkey, and Russia, on one hand, and extra-regional players, such as the United States and the EU, on the other. Without regional cooperation, such competition could evolve into new geopolitical conflicts that are by their nature difficult to curb. The consequences for the region's stability are arguably so high that the rivalry between the key regional players is unlikely to lead to violent conflicts.

Iran's strategy toward the South Caucasus

Iran's connection with the South Caucasus reflects a long history of cultural, ideological, and economic ties. In 1813 and 1828, Iran failed to repel invading Russian armies, and subsequently the Persian Qajar Dynasty signed the treaties of Gulistan and Turkmenchay respectively. With these two agreements, Persia relinquished to the Russian Empire its territorial claims on the South Caucasus states. The independence of the newly emerged states since the early 1990s led to the conflict between Armenia and Azerbaijan, revealing deep contradictions—or better yet, trade-offs—in the foreign policy strategy of the Islamic Republic, as Iran chose to support Armenia in this conflict. Clearly, the adoption of this foreign policy position by Iran went to show that it was economics—not politics or religious factors—that seemed to have dominated this mutually beneficial relationship. This suggests that when geopolitical interests conflict with commitments of Islamic ideology, beliefs, and solidarity, Tehran almost always prioritizes its security and economic considerations above others.[14]

Iranian leaders regard Armenia as a buffer to Turkish influence on the north-west borders of their country, and despite their religious and ideological differences, Iran and Armenia have managed to develop closer bilateral economic cooperation in recent years. With Iran exporting consumer goods to Armenia and both countries engaging in complex interrelated energy transfers, the dynamics of relationship between the two countries have taken new turns. Armenia and Iran also share an interest in building a north–south pipeline running from Russia to Iran, which would likely play a much more significant part in determining Iran's regional role in the future.[15]

The countries of the South Caucasus, especially Armenia and Azerbaijan, have relied on Iranian gas exports, although these imports have failed to prompt a significant expansion of Iran's natural gas exports. Armenia receives approximately 20 percent of its natural gas imports from Iran, using the great bulk of this natural gas to generate electricity at the Hrazden power plant. In exchange, the Armenia Nuclear Power Plant (ANPP) exports electricity generated from this plant to Iran. It is estimated that Armenia supplies 3 kilowatt-hours of electricity for every cubic meter of natural gas it receives from Iran.[16] The latter also exports natural gas to the isolated Azerbaijani exclave of Nakhchivan via the Salmas–Nakhchivan pipeline. Azerbaijan repays Iran by exporting natural gas to Iran's northern provinces in exchange for electricity. This gas deal has been possible via the Astara–Kazi–Magomed pipeline. Nakhchivan's sole supply source of natural gas is Iran.[17] Azerbaijan and Iran also maintain their cooperation in the transport of Caspian Sea oil as well as Iranian oil to the Turkish port by using the Tabriz–Ankara pipeline.[18]

To fulfill these commitments, as well as to meet its domestic natural gas consumption, Iran imports natural gas from Turkmenistan. In 2012, Iran imported 9 billion cubic meters (BCM) of natural gas from Turkmenistan, accounting for about 30 percent of all Turkmen natural gas exports. This economic relationship was reinforced by the completion of the Dauletabad–Hasheminejad pipeline. These imports are currently integral to Iran's ability to meet both season peak demand and industrial demand in northern Iran.[19] Turkmenistan's pace in supplying gas to Iran and China has risen dramatically in recent years. Iran has become heavily dependent on Turkmen gas imports until 2015, given that all new Iranian gas projects, especially those in the South Pars field, have been delayed. This situation has allowed Turkmenistan to set a price in line with European market prices for these countries.[20]

In general, as one expert points out, Iranian foreign policy toward the South Caucasus has proven remarkably durable. Three key aspects have characterized this policy: 1) a concern over the emergence of the independent state of Azerbaijan; 2) a strategic partnership with Russia; and 3) an increasing desire to control the development of petroleum resources in the Caspian Basin, while seeking to restrain Turkish influence over pipeline routes.[21]

Azerbaijan: conflicts and emerging opportunities

Since Ilham Aliyev became president of Azerbaijan in 2003, Baku has grown both economically stronger—thanks to revenues from energy exports—and notable for taking a bolder foreign policy approach of forging closer ties with Israel, knowing full well that this approach would cause resentment in Iran. In February 2012, Azerbaijan signed a $1.6 billion defense deal with Israel that included air defense systems, intelligence equipment, and unmanned aerial vehicles. Azerbaijani leaders have been adamant that Iran has no basis to criticize its ties with the Jewish state, given that Tehran has long overlooked Baku's pleas to ostracize Christian Armenia.[22] These closer ties between Israel and Azerbaijan have come to mirror the tumultuous relations between Iranian and Azerbaijani leaders. From Tehran's standpoint, Azerbaijani ties with Turkey, Israel, NATO, and the United States will decrease Iranian influence in the region.[23] Azerbaijanis should take careful note of the larger factor at play here: that any attempt to isolate Iran could further push Tehran toward cultivating enhanced rapprochement with Moscow and Yerevan—an eventuality that would entail negative consequences for Azerbaijan.[24]

Since the fall of the Soviet Union in the late 1980s, US strategic and economic interests in the South Caucasus have revolved around containing Iran and Russia, as well as securing the transit of oil and gas exports from the Caspian Basin—a region surrounded by the five countries of Azerbaijan, Iran, Kazakhstan, Russia, and Turkmenistan. By shoring up Georgia and Azerbaijan with their direct involvement in the BTC pipeline and by maintaining friendly relations with Kazakhstan and Kyrgyzstan, the United States has attempted to isolate Russia from its natural sphere of influence.[25] In the case of Iran, however, such an isolationist approach may not be prudent or even practical, given Iran's geographical proximity and historical presence there. One of the central reasons for Iran's increased interest in the South Caucasus region has been that the Caucasus has historically been known as a crossroads of trade from the Mediterranean to China and from the Baltic Sea to the Arabian Peninsula. Because of its strategic location, the Caucasus was regularly viewed as the reason for territorial contests between the Persian, Ottoman, and Russian empires. On balance, established and durable ties and infrastructure links in the Caucasus region tend to tip the regional balance of influence in Moscow's direction.[26]

Beyond the geopolitical reasons, as some experts have argued, the existence of oil and gas reserves were the main reason for attracting outside actors such as Iran, Turkey, Russia, the United States, NATO, and the European Union (EU).[27] Another view holds that the United States aims to enhance the energy independence of the Caspian Basin by guaranteeing the free flow of petroleum resources to the international markets. As such, the principal goal of US policy in the region is not merely to build oil and gas pipelines, but rather to use those pipelines as instruments for establishing a political and economic framework that will advance US influence throughout the South Caucasus.[28] Likewise, Iranian leaders view pipeline networks through the Caucasus as a way to gain access to European energy markets. Any normalization of the relations between Iran and the United States resulting from settling the nuclear dispute is likely to facilitate this connection. Tehran seeks to become a transit route for Caspian Sea oil resources to the Persian Gulf.[29]

These developments have come to shape Iran's main strategy in the South Caucasus. Some experts have noted that Iran's entry into Caucasian affairs has thus far had little impact on its broader competition with the West. Despite the South Caucasus's proximity to Iran, small economies, limited openness to Iranian ideological and political propaganda, and deep-rooted local divisions and grievances have all served to confine Tehran's reach. Viewed as one of the few geographic regions where strategic overreach threatens the stability of the Iranian state, Tehran's pragmatism and emphasis on stability are likely to continue.[30]

Following the pressure from the United States, Azerbaijani authorities refused to give a 5 percent share to Iran at the International Oil Consortium. As a result, the Iranian State Oil Company was denied the opportunity to explore the oil and gas reserves in the territory of Azerbaijan, including the Caspian Sea sector.[31] This was a major blow to Iran's interests in the region, especially its desire to gain access to the Caspian Sea oil and gas resources by becoming the main transit country. Acutely aware of such economic rivalries in the Caucasus and Caspian regions, Iran has always found itself in the middle of power struggles to control transport corridors.

In 2001, Russia began to sign bilateral demarcation agreements with Azerbaijan and Kazakhstan. In response, in July 2001, Iran instigated a crisis over Caspian Sea demarcation, by sending gunboats to threaten a BP explorer vessel surveying in a disputed area of the sea. The deadlock over the Caspian demarcation has continued.[32] In a meeting in Astrakhan, Russia, on 29 September 2014, the leaders of the five littoral states of the Caspian Sea signed a new agreement on cooperation in hydrometeorology of the sea, an agreement on cooperation in warning and liquidating emergencies in the sea as well as an agreement on the preservation and rational use of the sea's biological resources. Leaders of these five countries also adopted a policy statement on the principles of national sovereignty of each country over the coastal maritime space in the range of fifteen miles and ten "fishing" miles. They also agreed on the principles of the right to free access from the Caspian Sea to other seas and back on the basis of international law, taking into account the interests of the transit parties.[33]

In the meantime, the leading US oil companies have attempted to contain Russian and Iranian oil activities in the region. The BTC pipeline project has broken Russia's monopoly on oil exports and circumvented Iran.[34] Over time, however, the relations between Iran and Azerbaijan have improved. The two countries have signed an agreement disallowing the use of their respective territories for launching an attack on the other. The Azerbaijani exclave of Nakhchivan is entirely dependent on Iranian natural gas. Tehran plans to trade 500 megawatts (MW) of electricity with Russia that will be transferred through Azerbaijan, with which Iran plans to trade about 200 MW of electricity.[35] The transfer capacity of electricity between Iran and Azerbaijan is expected to increase from 200 to 600 MW.[36]

From Iran's standpoint, the most politically sensitive issue in the region is ethnic tension with Azerbaijan. Indeed, Iran's relations with Azerbaijan could deteriorate rapidly if there is any Azerbaijani involvement in supporting nationalist and secessionist feelings among ethnic Azeris in Iran who make up nearly 16 percent of the population.[37] This fear of nationalistic backlash has confined Iran's ability to involve itself aggressively in the Caucasus region. Increased Azerbaijani–Armenian enmity has historically provoked nationalist attitudes on both sides, arousing the sentiment that Iran seeks to avoid. As Iran's influence over the peace process between the two countries has proven ineffective, its strategy in the region has underscored the importance of trade, energy, and other non-controversial topics.[38]

In addition, Iran and Azerbaijan have experienced further tensions, including conflicting claims on maritime and seabed boundaries in the Caspian Sea and Iran's support for Armenia's position in the Nagorno-Karabakh conflict.[39] It should be noted that in 1991, when nearly 130,000 Armenians living in Nagorno-Karabakh claimed a self-declared republic, a bloody war broke out between Azerbaijan and Armenia. Since 2009 the ceasefire agreement between the two has been breached on a regular basis by both sides.[40]

Another major dispute between Iran and Azerbaijan concerns their drastically different interpretations of the legal regime of the Caspian Sea. Azerbaijan's understanding of sharing the Caspian Sea reflects control of the sea from the coast of each country to the middle point of the sea—a point equal to all coastlines. Iran's interpretation, by contrast, relies on the principle of fair use, emphasizing the seabed and the special characteristics of the sea, such as the shape of the sea, length of the sea, and the distribution of energy sources.[41] It is worth noting that the Caspian region has the third largest oil and gas reserves after the Persian Gulf and Siberia, with its estimated energy sources being about 4 percent of global reserves.[42] The US Energy Information Administration (EIA) estimates that the Caspian Sea region holds nearly 48 billion barrels of oil and 292 trillion cubic feet of natural gas, and each of the coastal countries has announced discoveries of large natural gas fields, suggesting that natural gas will soon become the main form of hydrocarbon exported from the region.[43]

Relations between Armenia and Iran have also strengthened since the fall of the Soviet Union. Iran established diplomatic relations with Armenia in February 1992, and signed several economic agreements with Armenia in the midst of a major war between Azerbaijan and Armenia. Iran served as Yerevan's main route for supplies and energy, providing an outlet for its trade. In the ensuing months, at one of the most crucial points in the confrontation between Azerbaijan and Armenia over Nagorno-Karabakh, Iran agreed to supply natural gas and fuel to Armenia as well as improving transportation links. Also, fuel from Russia was often delivered to Armenia by way of Iran. The then Armenian Prime Minister and Vice President Gagik Harutyunyan remarked at a ceremony commemorating the opening of a bridge over the Aras River linking Armenia and Iran that the bridge will help stabilize the economic situation that Armenia has encountered as a result of a blockade.[44]

Despite Iran's deepened engagement with Armenia, Tehran has approached Nagorno-Karabakh cautiously. Iran favors less Russian involvement in the South Caucasus, but has thus far avoided confronting Moscow and has benefited from a distrust of Turkey in the region. Despite pursuing divergent interests in the region, Turkey, Iran, Russia, and the United States have all agreed on one common interest in Central Asia and the Caucasus region—that is, preventing instability following the 2014 withdrawal of NATO and partner forces from Afghanistan.

Critics of Iranian foreign policy toward the South Caucasus states argue that the main success of Tehran's South Caucasus diplomacy is the rapprochement with Armenia, because this policy does not conflict with Moscow's interests. Iran's foreign policy of pragmatism as such, some experts have observed, has often fallen short of implementing a regional policy independently of Moscow. Tehran's emphasis on Moscow's diplomatic protection at the UN Security Council, especially in the wake of the nuclear dispute with the West, has clearly prevented an independent Iranian regional policy in the

Caucasus region. The Iranian ambition to appear as an independent actor in the Caucasus region in particular and in the former Soviet space more generally remains, therefore, largely a failed objective.[45] Others have noted that Iran's foreign policy in the region could be described as "primarily reactive" in the sense that it has had to cope with what Russia, the United States, Turkey, and Eurasian countries have chosen to do in the region.[46]

Conflict and geopolitics in Armenia

Landlocked between Turkey, Azerbaijan, and Georgia, Armenia has always relied on Russia and Iran to break from its enclave, to bypass sanctions imposed by Turkey, and to win the war with Azerbaijan. Armenia's increasing dependence on Russia has at times proven problematic. Although it is believed that strong ties with Russia are crucial for Armenia over the long term, the so-called "strategic partnership" with Moscow has frequently become one-sided, marked by Russian control over key sectors of the Armenian economy, including much of the energy sector and the rail network, as well as an expanding hold over the mining, construction, and telecommunications sectors. On balance, however, Armenia has maintained its security relationship with Moscow, in large part because Russia has indeed offered a security umbrella for Armenia given the tacit state of war with Azerbaijan over Nagorno-Karabakh. Today, Armenia is the only country in the region to host a Russian military base.[47] It has frequently ruled out any aspirations for full NATO membership and reinforced its commitment to the Russian strategic relationship.[48]

To diversify its dependency on outsiders, Armenia has often turned to Iran. A gas pipeline from Iran to Armenia, which was completed in 2007, has played an important role in ending the country's blockade and strengthening their mutual relations. Iran is the only country that could help Armenia break its economic and energy dependence on Russia.[49] Yet Armenia's energy policy entails a balancing act between Iran and Russia. It relies on Russia for the majority of its oil and gas, as well as technical expertise to run its power plants. At the same time, however, Armenia needs Iran to keep Russia's price monopoly in check and as a direct source of energy when hydroelectric supplies fall short. This means that Armenia relies heavily on Iran for its energy production. Any US efforts to reduce cross-border trade in electricity and hydrocarbon are bound to encounter substantial opposition in Yerevan.[50]

Still, a contrasting view points out that since the early 2000s Russian–Iranian relations have gained new momentum. Trying to neutralize the US influence in the South Caucasus, Russia has intensified its ties with Iran, and Armenia has become number three in this anti-Western coalition, while the Azerbaijan–Georgia–Turkey coalition has emerged as a pro-Western regional grouping.[51] It should be noted that Armenia relies on Iran for some gas imports, yet due to Russia's control over Armenia's gas network, these imports too often end up being burned for electricity and exported back to Iran. The gas pipeline currently moves around 24 million cubic feet per day, all of which is used in the thermal plants that provide roughly a quarter of Armenia's total power. Armenia also receives oil shipments from Iran via truck.

Armenia and Iran are currently negotiating to construct a Tabriz–Yeraskh pipeline to decrease oil transportation costs. The total cost and carrying capacity of this pipeline are not yet known.[52] Since 2012, the two countries have announced that they will jointly produce and manage a hydroelectric station on their Aras River border. The planned line can carry up to 400 kilovolts (KV), allowing Iran and Armenia to enhance their energy trade at peak demand from 350 MW to 1400 MW.[53] While Iran's energy infrastructure is likely to disintegrate further until sanctions are removed, the small scale of this project and its seasonal nature will do little to address with any urgency Iran's long-term energy security.[54] For its part, Iran regards Armenia as a key gateway for accessing South Caucasus and European countries. Azerbaijanis take a dim view of Iran's ties with Armenia, considering the closer relationship between these two countries detrimental to their interests.[55]

Caught in the middle of the Russia–Georgia conflict

Some analysts have asserted that Russia's foreign policy strategy appears to consider the current status quo regarding Nagorno-Karabakh convenient, and thus Moscow is less keen on seeking a quick or sustainable resolution to this conflict. The Kremlin, they note, seems to fear that a possible Armenian–Azerbaijani peace deal would decrease Armenia's security dependency on Russia.[56] A key obsession of post-Soviet Russia's foreign policy has been the full control of energy export routes to Europe. To that end, Russian authorities have exerted a great deal of control over the exports of rival Turkmen gas, Azerbaijani oil, and Kazakh oil to the European markets by ensuring that these energy resources are carried through pipelines that run across Russian territory rather than along routes that circumvent Russia.[57]

Of all the South Caucasus states, Georgia has the least developed relations with Iran and shares no common border with that country. Historically,

Georgia has fallen into the Soviet sphere of influence. In 1801, following the annexation of Georgia by the Russian Empire, Iran lost control over Georgia. Since the break-up of the Soviet Union, however, the Iranians have seriously considered bilateral relations between the two countries. Georgia was seen by Tehran as a country with necessary infrastructure and ports to boost Iran's foreign trade operations and Iranian exports abroad.[58] While Russia failed to retain post-Soviet Georgia within its sphere of influence, the United States had a major role in Georgia's stability, having invested heavily in the pipeline that would deliver Caspian Sea oil to Western markets. The development of Georgia as an energy corridor for the Caspian Basin became a vital element of US policy in the region. The main export pipeline of the Baku–Tbilisi–Ceyhan (BTC) route and the Baku–Tbilisi–Erzurum (BTE) gas pipelines, which became operative in 2005 and 2006 respectively, have turned Georgia into a pivotal country in the East–West energy corridor.[59]

The Russian invasion of Georgia in 2008 compelled the latter to make a drastic reassessment of its relations with Iran. Understandably, this war opened a new chapter of bilateral cooperation between Tehran and Tbilisi. In 2006, Moscow imposed heavy economic sanctions on Georgia, by cutting transport links and announcing that it would increase the gas price for Georgia from $110 to $230 per thousand cubic meters. Georgia has since desperately sought a way out of its political dependence on Russia. Stronger economic ties with Iran, Georgian authorities have concluded, could assist Tbilisi to diversify its foreign policy portfolio and trade.[60] Tehran has the necessary energy reserves to supply Georgia with gas and subsequently break Georgia's dependence on Russia. Iran and Georgia have also agreed to swap electricity via Armenia.[61] The two countries have since cooperated in many fields, including energy, transport, trade, education, and science. Iran has become one of Georgia's most important trading partners, and the Intergovernmental Joint Economic Commission is currently functioning between the two countries.[62] And yet, as some experts note, Georgia and Iran are still marginal trading partners, and while the gains from trade for Georgia could be moderate to substantial, they are unlikely to improve Iran's economy significantly.[63]

In short, Iran's relations with the three South Caucasus states will continue to be influenced by political and strategic considerations. Armenia's relations with Turkey continue to be murky, making Iran a good alternative in coming years. Iran perceives its Azeri minority and their irredentist sentiments as unsettling at best and an existential threat at worst. For Georgia, which seeks to eliminate or minimize its energy dependence on Russia, Iran could be an alternative market.

The South Caucasus has become increasingly entangled in the stand-off between Iran and its allies—Russia and Armenia—and the West and its allies—Azerbaijan and Turkey. These factors tend to complicate any potential peace-building operations that the Iranian Rouhani administration could have otherwise pursued.[64] For now, Iran's regional policy continues to be low-profile, cautious, balanced, and largely shaped by a desire to maintain a balance of power vis-à-vis other regional actors, such as Russia and Turkey, in the South Caucasus while accommodating their interests in the region as necessary.[65]

Turkey's energy strategy and the South Caucasus

Since the end of the Cold War, Turkey has worked toward a policy of rapprochement with the three new republics in the Caucasus. "For Turkey," one expert has noted, "the Caucasus, especially Azerbaijan, was a gateway to the Caspian Sea, and the rest of Central Asia."[66] Of all the newly independent Muslim states of the post-Soviet era, Azerbaijan was culturally, linguistically, and ethnically the closest country to Turkey. Additionally, the Azeris were locked in a conflict with Armenia—Turkey's age-old foe.

Much of Turkey's efforts in the South Caucasus have focused on becoming a regional energy hub by establishing transit infrastructure projects linking Azerbaijan and Georgia and transportation routes to and from the Caspian Sea. Azerbaijan's oil and gas reserves as well as its potential transit through Turkey promised to be economically very rewarding for Ankara.[67] Notwithstanding Turkey's 2008–9 efforts to normalize relations with Armenia, Ankara and Baku signed a strategic partnership and security cooperation—known as the Agreement on Strategic Partnership and Mutual Support—on 16 August 2010.[68]

Several Turkish diplomatic efforts have aimed to promote stability and security in the region, including the Caucasus Stability and Cooperation Platform announced in 2008, the Protocol on the Establishment of Diplomatic Relations, and the Protocol on the Development of Relations signed with Armenia in Zürich in 2009.[69] However, Turkey has never actively pursued peace-building policies toward the Nagorno-Karabakh stalemate, and its position has all along been known to be pro-Azerbaijan. In fact, since 2009 Turkey has closed its borders with Armenia. Turkey's denial that the mass killings of Ottoman Armenians in 1915 constituted an act of genocide and Turkey's support for Azerbaijan regarding the Nagorno-Karabakh dispute continue to lock the two countries into poor diplomatic relations.[70]

Turkey's relations with Azerbaijan and Georgia, by contrast, remain strong and steady. Several energy and communication projects tie these countries to Turkey. As noted above, these include the Baku–Tbilisi–Ceyhan (BTC) crude oil pipeline, the Baku–Tbilisi–Erzurum (BTE) natural gas pipeline, and the Baku–Tbilisi–Kars railway. Turkey sees its role not only as a transit country but also as central to the US foreign policy-driven East–West energy corridor. In addition to political benefits, the revenue generated from transit fees is considerable.[71] In 2006, Turkey anticipated $200 million per year in transit fees from BTC.[72] Some experts have observed that Turkey's ambition to become an energy corridor between the Caspian Sea and Europe has led to increased attention to Georgia, which serves as a geographical link between Turkey, Azerbaijan, and Central Asia.[73] Turkey has established good relations with Georgia and supported the peaceful resolution of its internal conflicts—not to mention the fact that it has provided substantial humanitarian aid to independent Georgia since the 1990s.[74]

Additionally, Turkey is one of the main suppliers of arms to Azerbaijan and Georgia, and maintains military facilities in both states. Both Azerbaijan and Georgia view Turkey as a link to the West and particularly to Western international security structures such as NATO. Experts underscored the significance of the role that Turkey can play in bringing Georgia closer to NATO.[75] While Turkey's strategic role in promoting stability and peace in the South Caucasus, especially in the aftermath of the Arab Spring, cannot be underestimated, most analysts underline the fact that "energy policy and the influence associated with it will continue to determine Turkish choices in the region case by case."[76]

On energy matters, Turkey's policy toward Russia and Iran is strikingly similar. Both common economic and commercial interests on the one hand and geopolitical and ideological differences on the other have characterized Turkey's policy in the past. Despite the regional rivalries for Caspian oil resources, Turkey's need to meet its growing demand for natural gas and petroleum is a central motive for continued partnership and cooperation with both Iran and Russia.[77] Although on several occasions competition rather than cooperation with Russia characterized Turkish policy, Ankara has in general taken a drastically different attitude toward Moscow. The recent rapid expansion of trade and economic ties between the two countries has underlined this trend. Furthermore, Turkish private firms and trading companies, which have strong ties with their Russian counterparts, have become a leading impulse in shaping Ankara's policies toward Moscow. With Turkish business circles developing a great stake in the improved political and economic relations with their Russian partners, geopolitical rivalries between the two regional powers in the South Caucasus have noticeably receded. The question persists, however, whether Turkey's policies vis-à-vis Russia will be driven solely by geopolitical concerns, or by geo-economic expectations.[78]

Russian Eurasianism and Turkey's pragmatism

The Iran–Turkey competition over the South Caucasus states has softened since the 1990s for several reasons. First, Russia's continued exercise of influence in the region—economically as well as militarily—has deterred both Turkey and Iran from playing more active roles in the South Caucasus and Central Asia. Neo-Eurasianism, which has become an important tenet of the new Russian doctrine and ideology after the breakdown of the Soviet Union, proceeds from the assumption that the "origins of the Russian state are found in Asia rather than in Europe; that the encounter with Mongols, Tatars, and Asian tribes largely shaped Russia; and that, rejected by the West, Russia should look for its future in Asia."[79] Today, as experts argue, insofar as the foreign policy of the new Russia is concerned, the appearance of Russia as a Eurasian power could expedite closer relations with Turkic people, perhaps also with the Far East. This also means that Russia could serve as one of several powers in a grand coalition based on close economic and political collaborations among several key Asian and Middle Eastern states.[80]

The rise of Eurasianism in Turkey since 1988, however, can be attributed to a two-pronged strategy: (a) it serves to present Turkey as a bridge between Asia and the West, a message aimed at Brussels and Europe more broadly; and (b) it may also be used to pressurize the EU or even take revenge if they should reject Turkey's membership bid.[81] Throughout the 1990s, pan-Turkism in Central Asia was taken up by an increasingly pragmatic private sector, including tourism and transportation firms, as well as multinationals working with former Soviet countries.[82] Today, nationalists, Islamists, and radical secularists look to a Eurasian alternative to Europe with a different focus and yet share several overlapping tendencies. All these groups, as one analyst observes, at least share a distrust of the West as well as a staunch loyalty to Turkey based on its history and cultural traditions, while simultaneously pursuing an increasingly independent Turkish foreign policy.[83]

Another factor contributing to the reduction of tensions between Ankara and Tehran is Turkey's dependence on Iran in order to have access to the

South Caucasus states. This is so because Turkey lacks a direct land corridor to Baku. Still, another reason is that Turkey serves as a portal to the West for Iran as well. As a result, Iran and Turkey have refrained from alienating each other and escalating the conflicts between them. Lastly, Iran and Turkey have become cognizant of the fact that neither one has enough capacity individually to fill the vacuum in the Caucasus and Central Asia left in the aftermath of the breakdown of the Soviet Union and that rigid competition for this purpose was detrimental to both countries.[84]

And perhaps far more important is the fact that regional rival Turkey also depends on Iran's energy. A new electricity transfer line in northern Iran boosted exports to Turkey to 400 MW per hour. Iran is the top supplier of Turkey's petroleum and natural gas.[85] According to a recent report on Iran's energy production, Iran could provide more than 15 percent of total electricity needed in the Middle East and North Africa within a few years. During the 2000–10 decade, the overall electricity generation capacity in Iran increased at an average annual growth rate of 7 percent. Iran seeks to become a major exporter of electricity. In 2013, Iran annually exported 8 billion kilowatt of electricity to neighboring countries, which was about 3 percent of the country's total output.[86]

In 2008, the Russian Federation attacked Georgia, and in 2014 it interfered in the Crimea in response to explicit outside meddling by the EU in support of the Ukraine's potential political membership. The collapse of the pro-Russia government in Ukraine and the West's continued support for the incoming government in Ukraine led to the upsurge of nationalist sentiments among the Russian residents of Crimea. The subsequent Russian intervention in Crimea, followed by the 16 March 2014 popular referendum in Crimea, resulted in the annexation of Crimea by Russia. In this regard, a key question arises: What explains Turkey's lack of interest in Ukraine and Crimea?

Turkey's then prime minister, Ahmet Davutoğlu, the architect and chief exponent of Ankara's activist foreign policy, has noted that Turkey "will not fall into a trap" and will not allow others to "turn the Crimea problem into a Turkish-Russian crisis."[87] Despite its aspirations to become an EU member and its already strong NATO ties, Turkey enjoys excellent relations with Russia, its second-largest trading partner, and is also a partner of the Sino-Russian Shanghai Cooperation Organization. To alienate Russia for the sake of establishing new ties with Europe, Davutoğlu has emphatically pointed out, would be a colossal mistake. Turkey is bound to live alongside Russia.[88]

Perhaps one of the most direct effects from this crisis and the lingering tension over Ukraine could be in reshaping Europe's energy policy. It is in this context that the EU's awakened interest in reducing its problematic dependence on Russian gas needs to be understood. Over the years, Europe has moved toward diversifying its energy sources. This crisis has underscored the need to resume that process in earnest.[89] The continuation of the tensions between Russia and European countries over Ukraine could fundamentally alter the dynamics of global energy markets, holding serious ramifications for global energy security. It is worth noting that Russia exported 86.1 BCM of gas to fifteen European countries through Ukraine in 2013. During that period, Italy was the largest recipient of the Russian gas that accounted for 25.3 BCM of gas, or about 30 percent of the total gas imported to Europe from Russia. Italy was followed by Turkey and Germany, which imported 13 BCM and 11.7 BCM of gas from Russia respectively.[90]

Thus far, EU member states have been reluctant to consider Iran as an alternative supply source to their heavy dependence upon Russia's natural gas and oil, because of pressure applied by the US and the UN sanctions regime imposed on Iran. Emphasizing the need for Iranian oil and gas in international markets, some experts have noted that the sanctions against Iran have minimized the West's leverage against Russia's Vladimir Putin.[91] Others see the possibility for exporting gas to Europe as an immensely valuable and unique opportunity to enhance Iran's bargaining power within the context of the "P5+1" negotiations with the West. They argue that Iran, given its massive natural gas reserves, appears to be in a good position to export gas and liquefied natural gas (LNG) to Europe via pipeline. As such, they note, the Islamic Republic will be able to serve as part of the EU's solution for the diversification of its gas supply sources. If this scenario unfolds, Turkey can serve as the transit route to take Iran's gas to Europe and, at the same time, supply part of the gas that Ankara needs to meet the country's domestic demand.[92]

It is worth noting that Russia and Turkey, which have grown economically and politically interdependent since 1997 when the Black Sea Trade and Development Bank (BSTDB) was created, have become important foreign trading partners. The announcement of the Turkish Stream Project in December 2014 by Vladimir Putin followed the cancellation of the South Stream Project (with Ukraine), marking a new era toward promoting Eurasianism.[93] This pattern of foreign policy behavior became the most visible feature of the Turkish government's outlook under the AK Party leadership. Ankara has frequently replaced its traditional security-driven objectives of foreign policy with those that are decidedly economic-oriented and pragmatic.[94]

Some experts have even suggested that Turkey appears to be changing its position regarding Russia's expansionist tendencies in the Black Sea region.

Moscow has increasingly become Ankara's major trading partner and key energy supplier. Furthermore, the continuing tension between Russia and the EU over Ukraine is likely to create enticing opportunities for Turkey as a substitute for European suppliers. The West's coercive sanctions have pushed Moscow to seek alternative trading partners. Not surprisingly, Turkey, Iran, and China come to mind. Turkish companies have been invited to play an important role in Moscow's plans to reconstruct its Crimean interests and invest in the fields of agriculture and tourism.[95]

However, following the shooting down of a Russian fighter jet in November 2015 by the Turkish army, claiming that the airplane had violated its airspace from Syria, the so-called "peace era" that had for so long characterized Eurasia came to an abrupt end. The foreign policy differences between the two grew larger over the Syrian civil war. Both sides began severing strong economic ties worth about $30 billion annually in trade—a figure that the two countries had previously pledged to increase to $100 billion in 2020.[96] The two crucial energy projects sought by Russia—the Akkuyu nuclear power plant which Moscow was building for Turkey and the Turkish Stream pipeline seen as an alternative route to similar proposals blocked by Europe—were suspended.[97] Russia's main gas industry, Gazprom, is keen to get the Turkish Stream back on track, in large part because other routes to Europe have been blocked, and Turkey is just as eager to become a hub for gas distribution.[98]

A failed coup attempt in Turkey (15 July 2016) accelerated the rise of anti-Americanism in Turkey, as well as a renewal of ties between Ankara and Moscow. President Putin has tended in the past to pursue policies that both exploit opportunities to weaken NATO and drive a wedge into the European unity of purpose in foreign and domestic policy, and now seeks to forge a new, closer relationship with Turkey. Russia expects Turkey to seal its borders with Syria and stem the flow of fighters and weapons to the insurgents, as well as to reverse its demand that Mr Assad must resign. Ankara, in turn, would like Moscow to stop bombing its insurgent allies; to eschew support for the Kurds; and to halt the bombing of civilian populations, which pushes refugees into Turkey.[99]

Iran and Turkey: collaboration and competition

Historically, bilateral trade ties between Iran and Turkey have been grounded in practical necessities. The two countries have been at peace since 1639, when Safavid Iran and the Ottoman Empire signed the Treaty of Zuhab, which recognized and subsequently placed what is known as present-day Iraq under the sovereignty of the Turkish Ottomans.[100] Since the dissolution of the Ottoman Empire in the early twentieth century, Iran and Turkey have had stable and cordial relations. The founding of the modern Turkish Republic (1923) coincided with the establishment of the Pahlavi dynasty (1925), followed by the fairly predictable diplomatic, economic, and cultural ties between the two countries. The attempt to spread the ideology of the 1979 Iranian Revolution, however, strained the country's relations with Turkey, as Iran embraced a revolutionary foreign policy that posed serious threats to the status quo in the region. Since the 1990s, when Iran's post-revolutionary foreign policy took a pragmatic turn and Turkey's domestic politics reflected their own democratic changes and trajectory, the relations between the two countries have steadily grown.[101]

Iran and Turkey have since become important economic partners and have made long-standing economic deals in gas, oil, and trade. There are strong cultural identity ties between them. On most foreign policy issues regarding the region, they both support diplomacy and regional détente. There is a substantial level of common interest between the two countries on regional and international issues. For example, both states are against separatism in their Kurdish regions and oppose the establishment of an independent Kurdish state. They are also both cooperating to export gas to Europe, working with Turkmenistan as a conduit for the transfer of the Central Asian energy resources. They are both members of the Organization of Islamic Cooperation (OIC), as well as the Developing Eight (D-8) group of countries: Bangladesh, Egypt, Indonesia, Iran, Malaysia, Nigeria, Pakistan, and Turkey—a group that was created by Turkey in 1997. Turkey has in the past played a constructive role in mediating nuclear talks within the context of the IAEA–Iran negotiations. In 2010, Turkey and Brazil took the initiative to defuse the nuclear dispute, only to be disregarded by the United States, which was intent on imposing further sanctions on Iran.

This section seeks to examine the impact of the potential longer-term agreement between Iran and Turkey at a time when the United States is withdrawing from the Middle East region, while paying increased attention to Asia (like the Obama administration's declared "pivot to Asia"). Despite competition and occasional frictions, cooperation between these two countries could foster a balance of power necessary for enduring stability in the region. US regional security concerns in the Middle East will be positively impacted by an offshore balancing strategy that renders such cooperation between the region's two middle powers sustainable.

This new strategic vision can be formed around the export of Iran's natural gas to Europe via Turkey. The latter has sought to become the region's natural gas export hub, holding great potential as a transit nation for Iran's natural gas bound for southern and eastern Europe. Since the interim agreement between Iran and the "P5+1" group on the former's nuclear program, the Turkish government has intensified its efforts to reach an agreement with Iran to build the Iran–Turkey–Europe (ITE) Natural Gas Pipeline Project. If implemented, this vision will hold important implications for the security and stability of the Middle East region at large.

Iran–Turkey relations in the new century

The closer relations between Iran and Turkey came about in 2003 with the US invasion of Iraq. The two countries have shown common interest in the stability and territorial integrity of Iraq.[102] The resurgence of a call for autonomy in the Iraqi Kurdish autonomous region has renewed the rivalry between Tehran and Ankara. The rise to power of the Justice and Development Party (AKP) has led to a subtle shift in Turkey's policy toward the Kurds, both internally as well as with regard to the Kurdish Regional Government (KRG) in northern Iraq. The Ankara and Erbil rapprochement has since pointed toward Turkish–Kurdish reconciliation.[103]

The energy nexus is indeed the most significant parameter that will determine the future of not only the Erbil–Baghdad relationship but also that of Erbil and Ankara. In May 2012, Ankara and Erbil announced their plan to construct oil and gas pipelines from the KRG into Turkey. From Turkey's perspective, such an arrangement serves to pressure Baghdad, offers a counterbalancing act against Baghdad in the longer term, renders Turkey as an energy hub, provides some relief to Turkey's current over-reliance on Iran and Russia, and affords it a means to control Erbil.[104] The KRG is increasingly seen as a major trade outlet for Turkey, a potential source of energy, and the least hostile Middle Eastern neighbor that Turkey has. Likewise, Iraqi Kurdistan cannot avert dependence upon Turkey, for both trade and security matters.[105]

The rapprochement between Turkey and the Iraqi KRG is driven primarily by geo-economic logic, but it has its own geopolitical limits. To counterbalance the growing Iranian influence in Baghdad and the tightening of economic bonds between Iran and Iraq, Turkey has made significant progress toward improving its position in Iraq and strengthening its economic and political ties with the KRG. The KRG is likely to become Turkey's principal source of gas and oil, as the latter could become the main route for the former's energy exports to markets worldwide.[106] In 2014, Ankara and the KRG inaugurated a new oil pipeline to the Turkish port of Ceyhan. Yet Turkey continues to oppose Kurdish secession from Iraq and considers the establishment of a Kurdish state inconsistent with its strategic interests. The KRG leaders, in contrast, regard these growing economic ties with Turkey as reinforcing their autonomy as well as paving the way for the notion of independence.[107]

Beyond pursuing such competing goals, Iran and Turkey share a common interest in avoiding the disintegration of Iraq that could, among other things, lead to the creation of an independent Kurdish state—an outcome least welcomed by both countries.[108] Turkey's domestic and regional interests dictate adopting a pragmatic and prudent approach toward Iran. These include the country's growing interests in gas/oil, expanding its reach in the Caspian region through Iran, and containing separatist tendencies among its Kurdish population. With Iran and Turkey being central Eurasia's most populous and oldest republics, they have forged a tacit alliance that promises to bring stability and development to the region.[109]

The 2011 Arab uprisings introduced new complications in Iran–Turkey relations, however. Among the more obvious areas of potential friction between the two is Syria, as Tehran and Ankara find themselves on opposite sides of the Syrian crisis. While Tehran supports the Assad regime, Turkey is bent on toppling it. The relationship between the two countries has come to be aptly described as "cooperative rivalry."[110] It is thus wrong, some experts explain, to construe the current disagreement between the two countries over Syria as "an expansion of the Ottoman–Safavid rivalry or as a struggle for primacy in the Fertile Crescent."[111] The significance of the bilateral relationship between Iran and Turkey is likely to overshadow their frictions on Syria and other regional issues.

Iran–Turkey pipeline

Turkey is a large importer of Iranian natural gas and presently one of Iran's most important trading partners. In the past, the energy deals between Iran and Turkey have not been prevented by US sanction policies, most notably the Iran and Libya Sanctions Act of 1996. In fact, Turkish Prime Minister Necmettin Erbakan's first foreign visit to Iran in August 1996 resulted in the signing of a $23 billion natural gas deal and an agreement for the construction of a pipeline.[112] This contract was accepted by Washington, because the deal involved no direct investments in Iran by either Turkey or other Western countries.[113]

In July 2007, Iran and Turkey signed a memorandum of understanding that would pave the way for $3.5 billion worth of Turkish investment in Iran's South Pars gas field on a buyback basis.[114] In 2008, Iran exported only 4.2 BCM of gas to Turkey. Gas supply shortages within Iran prevented further exports.[115] It is worth noting that the Iran–Turkey pipeline has at times been sabotaged by Kurdish PKK terrorists.[116] The Iran–Turkey natural gas pipeline can be extended to the Caspian Sea shore. Without Iran, however, Turkey's access to Caspian natural gas will be limited. The Iran–Turkey pipeline can arguably be a reliable transportation route insofar as EU energy security is concerned. The fact remains that the only way that Turkmenistan natural gas can reach Europe is via the Russia, Iran–Turkey, or Azerbaijan–Georgia–Turkey routes.[117]

Since the interim agreement between Iran and the "P5+1" group on the former's nuclear program, the Turkish government has quietly intensified its efforts to reach an agreement with Iran to build the Iran–Turkey–Europe (ITE) Natural Gas Pipeline Project in an attempt to convey Iranian natural gas to Europe via Turkey. The history of the pipeline can be traced back to an agreement protocol signed on 17 November 2008 between the Iranian Ministry of Oil and the Turkish Energy and Natural Resources Ministry for transit passage of the natural gas from the source in Iran through Turkey. The total length of the ITE pipeline is about 5,000 kilometers (3,107 miles), approximately 1,750 kilometers (1,087 miles) of which will be in Turkey.[118]

Furthermore, Caspian Sea hydrocarbon sources have the necessary capacity—especially if they include Iran's natural gas—to provide Europe, Russia, China, and Iran with gas. Europe's main obstacle is the lack of a reliable transportation route. Given Turkey's unique location between the countries that hold over 70 percent of the world's oil and gas reserves to its east, north, and south, it can develop to become a major European energy hub. The search for oil and gas resources in the Caspian and their transportation to Europe has come to be known as the "Great Game." Turkey's leaders intend to play a crucial role in transferring these resources to Europe, attempting to reduce the Turkish dependence on Russian energy sources.[119]

Some experts have defined Turkey's role as an "interconnector" and bridge between the region and Europe.[120] It is in this context that the importance of the ITE pipeline is underscored. Turkey is fully aware of the significance of its trade ties with Iran. In 2008, as Suleyman Elik observes, Turkey effectively dealt with the global financial crash by structurally changing its strategic economic opening toward the Middle East, especially Iran. Iran's economy has also become heavily dependent on the trade with Turkey, especially in the wake of sanctions on Iran's energy sector. The alternative to the ITE pipeline is one that passes through Iraq, Syria, Lebanon, and eventually the Mediterranean Sea. The undersea route passing beneath the Mediterranean presents yet another alternative, but none is as cost-effective as the ITE pipeline.

Iranian president Rouhani's visit to Ankara (9–10 June 2014) demonstrated that despite some ideological differences and regional competition, economic relations (energy and trade) continue to be a key priority for both countries, as they want to double the value of bilateral trade to $30 billion by 2015 in the near future.[121] Iran seeks a conduit to engage in trade with the outside world, and Turkey serves as such a channel. The extent to which both sides have curbed their dispute over Syria is remarkable, and is underpinned by vital economic and infrastructure ties.[122] In the long term, however, experts argue that perhaps the most important spot for Iran–Turkey competition will prove to be post-Saddam Iraq. With the US exit from Iraq and the increasingly visible role that the independent Kurdistan Regional Government (KRG) plays in northern Iraq, the Turkish–Iranian competition will likely intensify.[123]

Finding an effective way to deal with the complexities of Syria's political situation poses the most difficult challenge for Turkey since the 2011 Arab uprisings.[124] The rise of the Islamic State in Iraq and Syria (ISIS) is blamed partially on Turkey. By allowing thousands of jihadists from Libya and Chechnya to flood into Syria to combat Syrian president Bashar al-Assad, Ankara has played a crucial role in ISIS's operations there. In his rush to topple the Assad regime, Turkey's then prime minister (now president), Erdoğan, actually empowered ISIS and Al Nusra to spread the fight inside Syria, a development that undermined the activities of the opposition group on the ground known as the Free Syrian Army (FSA).[125] While the ruling AKP continues to deny helping ISIS, the evidence for the key role that AKP has played by providing arms, logistics, training, and funds to ISIS is undeniable. The 500-mile border with Syria, including the Rojava region controlled by the Kurds, has also served as a staging area for groups including ISIS to launch attacks in Syria. Moreover, there are reports that Turkey has become a market for smuggled oil and that ISIS thrives on the revenue made from the sale of oil from the captured oil fields in Syria and Iraq that is ultimately smuggled to Turkey.[126]

Conclusion

The collapse of the Soviet Union in 1991 opened up new possibilities for both Iran and Turkey in the South Caucasus region. However, these opportunities were complicated by numerous factors, including the region's protracted conflicts as well as oil and gas pipeline rivalries among Iran, Turkey, Russia, and the United States more generally. No less significant was Russian resolve to deny external actors' access to its sphere of influence, and Moscow's ability to maintain its dominance over the supply of natural gas to Europe. That may explain why the South Caucasus region's stability and development have almost always depended not only on the domestic politics of Armenia, Azerbaijan, and Georgia, but also on whether key regional and global powers can reach a consensus on geopolitical issues.[127] Today it is not so much the volume of trade, hard currency, and market size of these small states of the Caucasus region that matter the most. Rather, it is their hydrocarbon reserves and geopolitical location that offer an infrastructure corridor to transfer such reserves from Central Asia to Turkey and the West. One of the primary geopolitical objectives of the United States in the region has been to gain economic access to the Caspian Sea's underutilized natural resources.[128]

Iran and Turkey appear to have been locked in geopolitical competition over influence and access to the South Caucasus region's strategic resources as well as its transportation routes, while at the same time taking a restrained approach in the face of the Russian presence and influence there—an approach that has given them a relatively small measure of leverage. A quarter century after the disintegration of the Soviet Union, it can be argued that some things have not changed in the South Caucasus region. Chief among these is the Russian domination of the region. Russia's willingness to block the Turkish–NATO nexus throughout the South Caucasus region has afforded Iran a unique opportunity to spread its influence there.

Turkey has nonetheless maintained close energy and trade ties with Iran, has defended Iran's right to possess peaceful nuclear technology, and has helped sustain stable economic and diplomatic relations with Iran. In recent years, both countries' leaders have become fully cognizant of their respective abilities to ease tensions in the South Caucasus region through influence and diplomacy.[129] Some experts have noted that the only country capable of being a counterbalance to Iran and its potential long-term power in the region is Turkey. Iranian domination in the region as such is not in Turkey's interest because Ankara needs regional dominance to increase their access to regional energy.

Meanwhile, the Arab world tends to view Sunni Turkey as its best bet against a resurgent Shiite Iran.[130] Others have argued that Iran and Turkey, so-called "middle-power" states, are likely to negate each other's power and influence in the region, while at the same time they are considered a major deterrent against superpower penetration into the region. Although middle-power and outside superpower interests will be in conflict over some regional politics, such conflicts are less likely to lead to any military confrontations.[131]

The potential rapprochement between Iran and the United States that could result from the Framework Agreement within the 5+1 negotiations on Iran's nuclear program would likely drastically alter the political dynamics in the South Caucasus region. This development, if it comes to pass, would render Iran less subservience to Russian interests in the region and would afford Iran a chance to implement a bona fide policy of mediation between Armenia and Azerbaijan. Until the current stand-off between Iran and the West is resolved, Iran's leverage in the South Caucasus remains stalemated.

4

TURKEY'S ENERGY POLICY IN THE MIDDLE EAST AND SOUTH CAUCASUS

Gareth M. Winrow

While much has been written on Turkey's energy policy and on Turkey's attempts to become a significant regional power, less attention has been focused on how Ankara has sought to combine foreign policy goals and energy policy objectives. For example, concerning the Middle East, Han noted that energy "has the potential to strengthen Turkey's aspirations to become a regional geopolitical force."[1] Likewise, Babalı asserted: "Energy is one of the pillars of Turkey's re-emergence as a regional political force."[2] However, neither Han nor Babalı explored in detail how energy could be exploited to boost Turkey's credentials as a major regional actor. This chapter addresses this issue by examining Turkey's role in the Middle East and South Caucasus, where energy policy will be considered with reference to debates on regional hegemony.

The priority of Turkey's energy policy has been to meet the energy needs of a growing economy. Becoming an important energy transit state and leading energy hub were secondary objectives. The impact of these concerns and ambitions on Turkey's efforts to become a "regional geopolitical force" will be discussed in this chapter. For example, could over-dependence on gas imports from Russia hinder Turkey's regional policy? And how may officials in Ankara play the energy card in their foreign policy, given that Turkey is an insignificant producer of hydrocarbons?

This chapter is organized as follows. An introductory section discusses the linkages between energy policy and foreign policy with regard to Turkey. The significance of Turkey as a major energy consumer especially dependent on crude oil and gas imports is then examined. Turkey's ambitions are to become an energy transit state and hub with a particular focus on gas. Specific attention is given to Turkey's energy policy in the Middle East and South Caucasus. Possible complicating factors are considered, including the role of Russia. Although the importance of energy in Turkey's regional policy should not be over-stated, it is evident that energy has been used to further foreign policy objectives.

Energy and Turkish foreign policy

In a landmark study, Correlje and Van der Linde explained how in international politics and economics, energy and foreign policy could be considered within two storylines.[3] In the "markets and institutions" storyline, a neo-liberal perspective prevails in which the global energy system is an integrated one with principal roles for markets and effective institutions and where energy companies seek to secure profits. In the "empires and regions" storyline, a neo-realist outlook predominates in which geopolitics is at the fore, states are leading actors, and energy companies champion national interests. In this second storyline, there is more scope for energy to be used as an instrument of foreign policy.

The empires and regions storyline can accommodate the concepts of "securitization" and "politicization" as depicted by the Copenhagen School. The "securitization" of energy occurs when an energy issue is perceived as urgent and extraordinary measures may be taken to tackle what is regarded as an existential threat. The "politicization" of energy involves an energy issue that is seen as important but not posing an existential threat and so can be addressed through normal political procedures.[4] In the case of Turkey, over-dependence on Russian gas imports resulted in the securitization of energy in the Russo-Georgian War in August 2008 and in late 2014 before the announcement of the Turkish Stream project. Attempts by Ankara to exploit Turkey's location to control energy flows to bolster regional influence may be perceived by other states as the politicization of energy. The establishment of a genuine commercial energy hub in Turkey would be a feature of the markets and institutions storyline. Instead of threats and politics, the focus would be on matters of energy governance, transparency and the rule of law, and energy issues would be desecuritized and depoliticized.

Under the government of the Justice and Development Party (AKP), expectations were raised that Turkey could play an influential role in its neighborhood. Prime Minister Ahmet Davutoğlu referred to Turkey as a "central country" with multiple regional identities, where its location and common history with nearby states are utilized to further its foreign policy objectives.[5] In the immediate aftermath of the Arab Spring in 2011, there was much discussion about the relevance of the current Turkish model for the Arab world. This model, stressing the roles of Islam, democracy, and market forces, differed from the one promoted in the 1990s when secularism and Turkic identity, in addition to democracy and capitalism, were underlined to enhance Turkey's presence in the Caucasus and Central Asia. However, Turkey's potential role in its neighborhood must be re-assessed in the light of the deteriorating security situation in the Middle East, with civil war in Syria, growing sectarianism, and the rise of Islamic State (IS). The unexpected and ongoing turns and twists of the Arab Spring led to the overthrow of the Turkish-backed Moslem Brotherhood regime in Egypt.

Turkish commentators have contended that as a rising regional actor Turkey has made effective use of soft power through such instruments as trade, aid and investment, public and cultural diplomacy, and high-level political dialogue.[6] Turkey has been depicted as a "trading state" in which foreign policy was increasingly shaped by commercial considerations.[7] In line with the markets and institutions storyline, companies and business associations in Turkey apparently acted as autonomous actors, and their interest in making profits and striking trade deals molded foreign policy and bolstered regional cooperation. However, given the recent turmoil in the Middle East in which Turkey's access to markets has suffered following events in Egypt and Syria, the notion of Turkey as a trading state can be challenged. The importance of soft power can also be reconsidered after the attraction of the Turkish model diminished, given the negative publicity following the violent clampdown on protesters at Istanbul's Gezi Park in summer 2013.

The empires and regions storyline has had more bearing on Turkey's foreign policy and energy policy. The Turkish Energy Ministry stated that in addition to becoming a transit state and commercial hub, Turkey aimed to be "a strong regional actor bringing together the West and the East with its multi-directional energy policies."[8] Rather than acting autonomously, private Turkish energy companies tended to follow the policies laid down by the AKP government. Atlı has argued that Turkey functions within a "corporatist setting," where a powerful state bureaucracy exercises control over the business community.[9] With regard to energy, only tentative steps have been taken toward the liberalization of the gas market in Turkey. A dominant role is still played by the State Pipeline Corporation, BOTAŞ, which controls most of the gas import contracts. Neither a member of the European Union (EU) nor the Energy Community Treaty—in which the EU's energy *acquis* operates in most of south-eastern Europe—Turkey is not bound by the rules and regulations of energy governance prescribed by Brussels. This provides opportunities for Turkey as an energy transit state to politicize the role of energy.

Malik argued that under the AKP government Turkey has aspired to become a regional hegemon. Much like the Ottoman Empire, Turkey was striving to establish a sphere of influence in its neighborhood. Through this more assertive policy, Turkey would compete with other regional players such as Russia and Iran.[10] Hegemons often depicted themselves as providers of public goods and services.[11] In reality, however, rather than acting altruistically, they invariably seek to strengthen their presence in a region.[12] Through this lens, Turkey's moves to project itself as a provider of services by being an energy transit state and hub is an attempt by government officials to use energy as a tool to further ambitions of becoming a regional hegemon.

The authorities in Ankara also seek to ensure that Turkey's energy demand is satisfied. But dependence on gas imports may negatively impact on Turkey's foreign policy. The use of energy as a foreign policy instrument is usually examined with reference to major energy producers threatening to turn off the tap to downstream customers in order to secure political and economic gains. However, as an importer of substantial volumes of Russian gas, Ankara is instead obliged to remain on good terms with Moscow.

Turkey as an energy consumer

Growth in the Turkish economy slowed from over 4 percent in 2013 to less than 3 percent in 2014.[13] Officials in Ankara remain confident that growth will recover in spite of problems in markets in Europe, instability in Turkey's neighborhood, and the likely reduction of vital capital inflows from the United States (US). Turkey purchases approximately 75 percent of its energy requirements, and energy imports have traditionally accounted for about two-thirds of the country's current account deficit.

Gas is a crucial component in Turkey's energy mix. As of September 2014, gas accounted for 47.8 percent of electricity generation. Coal and renewables were responsible for 29 percent and 21.8 percent of power output respectively.[14] The AKP government declared that by 2023, gas coal, and renewables will each provide 30 percent of electricity generation, and 10 percent would come from nuclear power. Oil is an important source of fuel for the transportation sector, but Turkey has insubstantial oil reserves. In 2014, 17.5 million tonnes (mt) of oil were imported, with Iraq (5.5 mt) and Iran (5.2 mt) being the main suppliers.[15]

Despite these goals, in practice gas may still account for more than 30 per cent of power output in Turkey by 2023. Domestically produced coal is highly polluting, and more incentives will be required and bureaucratic hurdles removed for further investment to be made in renewables. Delays are likely in the development of nuclear power. The first of four nuclear reactors to be built by the Russian company Rosatom for Turkey's inaugural nuclear power plant may only be ready in 2022, three years behind schedule, because of technical problems and Russia's financial difficulties.[16] In June 2015 Turkey's Energy Minister, Taner Yıldız, criticized a report of the European Parliament which ruled that Rosatom's plans to construct the plant at Akkuyu on the Mediterranean coast were unsafe because the facility would be located in an area prone to earthquakes.[17]

Gas is not a globally traded commodity in spite of the increased use of liquefied natural gas (LNG), which is shipped by tanker. Most gas is transported by pipeline and is traded in regional markets. In the case of Turkey, much of its gas is imported from Russia along two networks running across the Black Sea and through south-eastern Europe via Ukraine. In 2014, Turkey produced only 0.479 million cubic meters (mcm) of gas and imported over 49 billion cubic meters (bcm).[18] Exploration for hydrocarbons off Turkey's Black Sea and eastern Mediterranean coasts does not look promising. Shale gas may be discovered and recoverable in Thrace and in south-eastern Turkey, but these reserves may not be commercially viable. As such, Turkey will still need to import much gas for the foreseeable future.

The extent of Turkey's dependence on gas imports from Russia is illustrated in Table 1. Although the AKP government had aimed by 2020 not to be dependent on one country for more than 50 percent of gas imports,[19] this will still be difficult to achieve in spite of plans to purchase more Azerbaijani gas and import volumes from the Kurdistan Regional Government (KRG) in northern Iraq. Additional LNG could also be procured from the spot market, given the spare capacity in Turkey's two receiving terminals. BOTAŞ has estimated that Turkey will consume 70 bcm by 2020.[20] By 2017 gas demand could outstrip contracted import volumes as additional purchases of gas from Azerbaijan as well as from the KRG would not yet have come on stream.[21] Hence, it is difficult to imagine how Turkey may reduce its dependence on Russian gas. Nevertheless, Turkish officials could still secure advantage from Turkey's geographical location.

Table 1: Turkey's Gas Imports by Source Country (in billion cubic meters)

	2005	*2010*	*2012*	*2013*	*2014*
Russia	17.524	17.576	26.491	26.212	26.975
Iran	4.248	7.765	8.215	8.730	8.932
Azerbaijan	0	4.521	3.354	4.245	6.074
Algeria	3.786	3.906	4.076	3.917	4.179
Nigeria	1.013	1.189	1.322	1.274	1.414
Spot LNG	0	3.079	2.464	0.892	1.689
Total	26.571	38.036	45.922	45.269	49.262

Source: T. C. Enerji Piyasası Düzenleme Kurumu, *Doğal Gaz Piyasası 2014 Yılı Sektör Raporu* (2015), p. 7.

Turkey: energy transit and regional influence

Producers in the Middle East and South Caucasus are keen to transport their gas via Turkish territory to profitable markets in Europe. Turkey would benefit from transit revenues. In conjunction with the lack of effective regulation on energy transit issues, energy transit could facilitate Turkey's quest to become an influential regional power. The markets and institutions storyline is not appropriate for energy transit matters. Because energy transit may become a highly politicized issue, officials in Ankara should be careful about not overplaying their hand in their effort to make Turkey a regional hegemon. However, it is important to note that Turkey may face constraints because of Azerbaijan's ownership of a planned key gas pipeline that will run across Turkish territory.

In force since 1998, the Energy Charter Treaty (ECT) refers to the principles of freedom of transit and non-discrimination and has provision for a dispute settlement mechanism for issues over transit. Russia blocked negotiations on a Draft Transit Protocol within the framework of the ECT, which had aimed to ensure that transit tariffs would be objective, reasonable, and transparent. The EU *acquis*, in spite of its references to non-discrimination and third-party access to pipeline networks, also fails to set clear rules on tariff rates for energy transit. Turkey has signed and ratified the ECT, but is not subject to the EU *acquis* in the energy sphere.

It has been suggested that in practice there are so-called "good" and "bad" transit states.[22] The focus when determining the quality of a transit state is on the smooth flow or possible disruption of hydrocarbons transported from a producer to a consumer by pipelines across the territory of a transit state. "Bad" transit states illegally tap into the pipeline to meet their own energy needs. They may also seek to change agreements to secure more preferential terms: for instance, with regard to transit fees, price discounts for volumes delivered by the producer to the transit state itself, and rights to re-export and sell gas or oil at a higher price to make profits. After the large sunk costs of construction, suppliers and customers "are increasingly vulnerable to the incentives for discretionary renegotiation when confronted by opportunistic transit governments."[23]

Less attention has been given to the control of energy transportation routes by transit states for regional power play ambitions. Various factors may be relevant here, including the extent to which transit states themselves are dependent on supplies from key producers to meet their own energy needs. Transit states may have less influence if there are alternative routes for the transportation of energy from producer to customer. The transportation of considerable volumes of oil or gas from one or more producers across the territory of a transit state could give more opportunities to the transit state to exert leverage. Generally, however, officials in the energy transit state would not want to damage their international reputation and threaten possible foreign direct investment by being perceived as abusing their control of transportation routes. In the case of Turkey, significant gas volumes from several energy producers may be conveyed across Turkish territory.

In practice, Turkey is already an energy transit state. Up to 40 mt of crude are carried annually via the Baku–Tbilisi–Ceyhan (BTC) pipeline. Operational since 2006, substantial volumes from Azerbaijan and smaller quantities from Kazakhstan and Turkmenistan are delivered to the Turkish Mediterranean coast to be shipped to outside markets. Up to 25 mt per annum of Iraqi oil have been transported across Turkey through the Kirkuk–Ceyhan network. This system has been out of service following repeated attacks by IS, but oil from Kurdish northern Iraq and from Kirkuk continues to reach Ceyhan through new infrastructure. Many tankers carry crude oil and petroleum products from Russia, Azerbaijan, and Kazakhstan through the Turkish Straits. According to contracts, as much as 0.75 bcm each year of gas from Azerbaijan may be re-exported to Greece. In 2014, Turkey re-exported over 0.63 bcm along the Interconnector Turkey–Greece pipeline.[24]

EU member states are endeavoring to reduce dependence on Russian gas by developing the Southern Gas Corridor (SGC). This would entail a network bypassing Russia and connecting the Middle East and the Caspian region with Europe. The SGC could meet 20 percent of the EU's future energy needs. The realization of the SGC would make Turkey an important energy transit state, but concerns have been voiced about Turkey's reliability. The now abandoned Nabucco pipeline project would have formed an essential component of the SGC. However, officials in Ankara had demanded that Turkey should have the right to consume 15 percent of gas delivered along the pipeline, which should be sold at a "reasonable price." They had also argued that Turkey had the right to tax the gas in transit and that Ankara could act as an intermediary in gas trade.[25] The AKP government later backed down on these demands, but doubts had been raised about whether Turkey could be depended upon to act as a "good" transit state.

According to Wigen, to be perceived as a viable partner to provide the EU's future energy needs, Turkey should downplay the potential to use pipelines as a foreign policy tool, and instead integrate with the European energy market.[26] However, while Cyprus blocks the opening of the energy chapter in Turkey's accession negotiations with the EU, the Turkish government will not assume the obligations of the EU *acquis* with regard to energy by joining, for example, the Energy Community Treaty. Turkey, therefore, will have an opportunity to exploit its location to seek strategic as well as economic benefits from being an energy transit state, but at the same time should be careful not to abuse these benefits and risk being perceived as an "opportunistic transit government." Aspiring to make Turkey a regional hegemon, Turkish policy-makers will continue to emphasize how Turkey, as an energy transit state and hub, would ostensibly be providing public goods and services for states in its neighborhood.

Turkey: regional influence as an energy hub?

The term "energy hub," when applied to gas, is often used misleadingly and sometimes interchangeably with that of an energy transit state. In practice, there are various types of energy hubs, but it is usual to separate them into two categories, physical and virtual.[27] Hubs deal with energy trading. Unlike transit states, therefore, they do not refer simply to territory in which pipelines and other energy-related infrastructure are in place.

With physical hubs, pipelines are connected but only gas actually passing a precise location may be traded. Virtual hubs, in contrast, are more flexible as physical access is not always required. Virtual hubs refer to trading platforms in which many participants may have entry. More mature virtual hubs could set benchmark prices for the region. However, for extensive gas trading the necessary infrastructure must be in place—pipeline networks, terminals, storage facilities etc.—and the rule of law, transparency, mechanisms to resolve contract disputes, and a balancing and settlement system are essential.

In the case of Turkey, a limited virtual hub is in place with the Ulusal Dengeleme Noktası (UDN)—the national balancing point.[28] Shippers trade relatively small volumes through this mechanism. Turkish officials intend to build more infrastructure and establish new institutions, ostensibly to provide the services of a fully functioning virtual gas hub. Moves are underway to create a hub for the trading of electricity to be followed by a more developed commercial gas hub. Trade in standardized gas markets will be provided by Borsa Istanbul, the Turkish stock exchange. An Energy Markets Operating Company (EPİAŞ) is being set up to handle gas trade on the spot market. These initiatives are in line with the intention to liberalize the gas market by curtailing the role of BOTAŞ. The aim is for the state-owned company to have only a 20 percent share of gas import contracts. For a successful virtual gas hub, price subsidies must also be eliminated as they distort the market. A reliable price index would encourage more investment by providing a predictable pricing mechanism for banks and other financial bodies.

The establishment of a fully functioning virtual gas hub in Turkey will not be easy. In 2013, Turkey had the capacity to store only 2.6 bcm of gas annually, but there are plans to increase storage capacity to 5.3 bcm by 2019.[29] Disagreements over the allocation of shares delayed the formation of EPİAŞ. BOTAŞ has been slow to hand over gas import contracts to private companies, and it still needs to be replaced by an independent operator to run the gas transmission network in Turkey. Moreover, the removal of price subsidies for households and industry could be politically damaging. There are also serious doubts about transparency and the rule of law in Turkey, given investors' concerns over corruption allegations against leading AKP politicians.

A genuine commercial trading gas hub in which suppliers, consumers, and middlemen trade in an open, transparent, and well-regulated market would be in line with the notion of Turkey as a "trading state." In practice, though, officials in Ankara may seek to control rather than facilitate gas trading through an energy hub, for example through acquiring re-export rights and thereby making profits by re-selling gas at a higher price. Currently, Turkey only has re-export rights for gas from Azerbaijan. In the Intergovernmental Agreement for the proposed Interconnector Turkey–Greece–Italy pipeline—effectively an extension of the connection linking Turkey and Greece—there is a clause giving Turkey the right to re-export 15 percent of Azerbaijani gas.[30] Turkish officials have pressed to secure re-export rights for Iranian and Russian gas delivered to Turkey and could seek the same from Turkmenistan and the KRG. Given how the AKP administration has linked Turkey's potential as a gas transit state with Turkey's ambitions to become a major regional player, and bearing in mind its hands-on control of energy policy, it is difficult to imagine how any government in Ankara will merely seek to benefit from the prestige of establishing an effective gas hub. As in the case of energy transit, and in line with the practice of regional hegemons, the Turkish authorities would likely aim to secure economic and political advantage as an energy hub, while declaring that their policy was one of providing public goods and services.

Turkey's energy policy in the Middle East

The post-Arab Spring upheavals in the Middle East had an immediate impact on Turkey's energy policy. The Arab Gas Pipeline which aimed to deliver Egyptian gas to customers in Turkey and Europe, was a victim of the crisis in Syria as work could not be carried out to extend the pipeline across the Syrian–Turkish border. All in all, Turkey's energy policy in the area in recent years has had its ups and downs.

Iraqi Kurdistan has considerable oil and gas reserves. The Anglo-Turkish company Genel Energy is heavily involved in exploration and production. The relationship between Turkey and the KRG has been largely a success story in which Ankara's energy interests and regional and domestic policy concerns have coincided. Closer ties with the regime in Erbil have enabled Ankara to check possible Iraqi Kurdish support for the Kurdistan Workers' Party (PKK) in Turkey. Ankara is also hoping that the KRG will restrain the ambitions of the Syrian Kurds. At the same time, mindful of the dispute between Erbil and Baghdad over the right to develop oil and gas fields and export hydrocarbons, Turkey is determined to maintain simultaneous working ties with the central Iraqi authorities.

In the face of opposition from Baghdad, in 2009 Ankara allowed oil to be trucked from the KRG to Ceyhan, from where it was exported. In May 2014, oil was exported from a new pipeline connecting the KRG with Ceyhan, prompting Baghdad then to suspend budget payments to Erbil. This pipeline was connected to the large Kirkuk oil field after IS attacks seriously damaged the original Kirkuk–Ceyhan pipeline network. Much to the anger of the central Iraqi authorities, the Turkish bank Halkbank managed the revenues from oil sales from the KRG, and some of this money was used to pay the salaries of civil servants in Iraqi Kurdistan.[31] Tensions between Ankara and Baghdad eased after a provisional deal was struck between the KRG and the central Iraqi government in December 2014, which allowed for 550,000 barrels of oil per day (bpd) to be exported by the KRG from Kirkuk and from fields in northern Iraq. This oil would be marketed by Baghdad, and in return the KRG would start to receive monthly budget payments from the central government. Plans of the KRG to construct a second oil pipeline to Ceyhan could lead to further disputes between Baghdad and Erbil, and, at the time of writing, the provisional agreement of December 2014 is in danger of collapsing with both sides accusing the other of violating its terms.

A gas sales agreement concluded between Ankara and Erbil in November 2013 envisioned the export of 4 bcm to Turkey by 2017, increasing to 10 bcm by 2020 and possibly rising to 20 bcm by 2025.[32] Genel Energy is developing fields at Miran and Bina Bawi to supply gas for export. Turkey has started to construct a network to hook up with the KRG. The authorities in Baghdad will most probably not export gas from fields elsewhere in Iraq, given security concerns and the central government's interest in prioritizing domestic energy needs.

Substantial volumes of gas from the KRG, therefore, may reach markets in Turkey and possibly in Europe in the near future. Ankara could reduce its dependence on Russian gas by importing much cheaper gas from the KRG. Turkey is already a transit state for the passage of crude oil from the KRG. Gas volumes from the KRG could also boost Turkey's ambitions to become a leading energy hub. The dependence of the KRG on Turkey for the export and sale of its oil and gas will provide the Turkish government with an opportunity to bolster its influence in the Middle East.

In stark contrast to Iraqi Kurdistan, Turkey's potential energy ties with Israel have been the victim of Turkish domestic politics and tensions in the Middle East. Prominent Turkish energy companies have lobbied to construct a pipeline to connect Israel's Leviathan gas field in the eastern Mediterranean with Turkey.

One of these businesses, the Zorlu Group, which has stakes in Israel's power sector, had close ties with the AKP government. In March 2014, Zorlu Group and Turcas Energy Holding participated in a preliminary tender for the laying of a pipeline linking Leviathan with the Turkish mainland, which would have an annual capacity of 7–10 bcm.[33] Turcas Energy Holding had commenced negotiations with Enerjisa (a joint venture of the Turkish conglomerate Sabancı and E.ON) to work together to sell gas from Leviathan on the Turkish market.[34] The proposed pipeline was deemed commercially viable and offered Turkey the opportunity to diversify its sources of gas imports.

However, after Turkish–Israeli relations further deteriorated with the conflict in Gaza, in August 2014 Turkey's Energy Minister Yıldız declared that the AKP opposed the construction of the gas pipeline because "the blood of innocent infants and mothers" would flow through it.[35] Viewing energy as a strategic good, the Israeli authorities were not enthusiastic about being dependent on Turkey for gas exports from Leviathan. Moreover, the Greek Cypriot authorities in Nicosia opposed the laying of the pipeline in the exclusive economic zone of Cyprus. The case of Leviathan revealed that the interests of Turkish energy companies could not prevail over the concerns of the AKP government when important principles of foreign policy were perceived to be at stake. AKP officials did not wish to alienate the support of their key domestic constituents who had backed the government's anti-Israeli policy. Gas imports from Israel were not seen as crucial to Turkey's future energy needs. However, the AKP's policy had threatened to isolate Turkey in the eastern Mediterranean with Israel, Cyprus, Greece, and Egypt moving to coordinate their energy policies.

Relations between Turkey and Iran are complex and multi-faceted. The two are traditional regional rivals and on opposite sides of the Sunni–Shi'a divide. However, at the same time, commercial ties are important with oil and gas composing most of Iran's exports to Turkey. Delivering gas since 2001, Iran is Turkey's second largest supplier. Iran has expressed an interest in exporting gas to Europe via Turkey along the SGC, and initially it was presumed that the Nabucco pipeline would transport Iranian gas. The lifting of economic sanctions against Tehran could then resurrect the possibility of Iranian gas exports to Europe. The Turkish company Turang Transit hopes to carry annually 35 bcm of Iranian and Turkmen gas along a proposed pipeline which would extend across Turkey and reach Germany. In January 2014, Turkey's Economy Ministry announced that the project had been granted $6.2 billion USD in investment incentives.[36] It is highly unlikely, though, that in the near future

Iranian gas will reach European markets via Turkey. Iran is a substantial gas consumer, and even if sanctions were swiftly removed it would probably not be until the mid-2020s that Iran would produce enough gas to export to outside markets in significant volumes.[37] Gas is expected to be delivered first to customers in the Gulf in line with agreements that have already been signed.

The possibility of Iranian gas transiting through Turkey would have given Ankara leverage in talks with Tehran on technical energy issues, which have historically been contentious. Turkish officials have complained about the price of Iranian gas, onerous take-or-pay obligations, and Iran's practice of prioritizing the needs of Iranian consumers and reducing gas deliveries to Turkey in winter months. In fact, Ankara has taken Tehran to the international court of arbitration to seek a reduction in the gas price. In April 2015, the Turkish authorities rejected an offer from Iran to double gas imports in return for receiving a discount on the additional volumes.[38]

Turkey's energy policy in the Middle East has had its successes and failures. Still dependent on Iran for its energy needs, Ankara failed to gain the upper hand in negotiations over gas pricing. In the case of the KRG, there appears to be a win–win situation for Turkey. The possibility of gas from Iraqi Kurdistan reaching Turkish and European customers would diversify Turkey's gas imports and enhance the prospects for Turkey to become a key energy transit state and gas hub. In turn, this could enable Turkey to pursue a more assertive policy in accordance with that of a regional hegemon and have a decisive say over the political ambitions of Kurds in Turkey, northern Iraq, and Syria. But irreconcilable political differences between the AKP government and the Israeli authorities hinder Turkey's energy policy in the eastern Mediterranean.

Turkey's energy policy in the South Caucasus

Turkey has initiated trilateral cooperation mechanisms with Azerbaijan and Georgia and with Azerbaijan and Turkmenistan to bolster political ties and strengthen energy relations. However, Turkey's influence in the South Caucasus has been constrained by Russia and by a policy which has been indexed to that of Azerbaijan. Over-dependent on Russia for gas imports, the issue of energy was securitized at the time of the Russo-Georgian War in August 2008, when the then Prime Minister Recep Tayyip Erdoğan acknowledged that there was little Turkey could do against Russia given its need for Russian gas to meet its electricity needs.[39] Likewise, Turkey was forced on 1 December 2014 to sign a non-binding memorandum of understanding on

Turkish Stream after Gazprom had reduced deliveries to Turkey along the overland Trans-Balkan pipeline network by more than half.[40]

In the case of Azerbaijan and Turkey, energy policy has become politicized. For one thing, Turkey could not normalize relations with Armenia because of Azerbaijan's insistence that progress should first be made on resolving the Nagorno-Karabakh dispute. Baku has appealed to common Turkic ties to secure backing from Ankara, and gas deliveries from Azerbaijan to Turkey have also reinforced the hand of the Azerbaijani government. One key question, though, is whether Turkey as an energy transit state may still have leverage over Baku, given Azerbaijan's interest in delivering gas to Europe.

Despite the politicization of the relationship, the Turkish–Azerbaijani energy relationship is becoming increasingly important. Significant quantities of crude are carried along the BTC pipeline for export to markets such as Israel. Gas from Azerbaijan's Shah Deniz field has been delivered to Turkey since 2007, and moreover it is cheaper than Russian and Iranian gas. A further 6 bcm is planned to be exported to Turkey by 2019 once production at the field is expanded and the Trans-Anatolian Gas Pipeline (TANAP) is constructed. The first Azerbaijani gas should reach Europe by 2020 along the SGC by means of TANAP, which will be built across Turkey to connect Azerbaijan with Greece. TANAP will hook up with the planned Trans Adriatic Pipeline (TAP), which will deliver gas to Italy via Greece and Albania. The initial annual capacity of TANAP will be 16 bcm, but this may be increased to 31 bcm by 2026 and possibly to as much as 60 bcm eventually.[41]

The State Oil Company of Azerbaijan (SOCAR) has a majority ownership of the TANAP company with a 58 percent stake. BOTAŞ and BP hold the remaining shares, with 30 and 12 percent respectively. According to Article 7.4 of the Intergovernmental Agreement on TANAP of June 2012, the TANAP company has jurisdiction over third-party access and tariffs.[42] SOCAR's control of the pipeline could negate Turkey's role as an energy transit state, with Azerbaijan deciding what gas should be carried along TANAP. This may have serious wider repercussions in the Middle East, for example for the KRG, which is hoping to transport gas to Europe via Turkey. Other Azerbaijani gas fields in the Caspian Sea are being developed, and presumably Baku would want to ensure that these fields have priority access to TANAP. Turkish officials will also be reluctant to alienate their counterparts in Baku, given the power of the SOCAR lobby with the Azerbaijani company intending to invest $20 billion USD in energy infrastructure in Turkey by 2020.[43] Arguably, the prospects of Turkmen gas accessing TANAP for delivery to Europe will be a test case for whether Turkey can use energy as a tool of foreign policy, given SOCAR's control over the TANAP company.

AKP officials have lobbied for Turkmen gas to secure access to TANAP to feed both the Turkish and European markets. Earlier deals concluded in 1998 and 1999 made provisions for 14 bcm of Turkmen gas to be transported annually to Europe via Turkey, and 16 bcm to be delivered each year to Turkey for a 30-year period.[44] These agreements have not been realized because of the failure to construct a Trans-Caspian Gas Pipeline (TCGP) to connect Turkmen gas fields in the Caspian with the Azerbaijani mainland. Both Turkey and the European Commission are pushing for the TCGP to be built. When President Erdoğan visited Ashgabat in November 2014, a preliminary sales and purchase agreement was negotiated between the Turkish company Atagas and the state-owned Turkmengaz.[45]

Disputes between Azerbaijan and Turkmenistan over the ownership of oil and gas fields in the Caspian, as well as opposition from Russia and Iran, prevented any movement on plans to build the TCGP. Additionally, it is not clear who would finance and operate the pipeline. Although Moscow and Tehran cite legal (the status of the Caspian Sea) and environmental arguments to block the laying of a subsea pipeline, the debate over the TCGP is highly politicized. Russia and Iran are concerned that Turkmenistan should not benefit economically and politically from exporting gas to markets in Europe at their expense.

Eager to secure more gas and boost the prospects for Turkey to be a key energy transit state and gas hub, Ankara has continued to lobby for the TCGP. When Turkmen President Gurbanguly Berdymukhammedov was received in Ankara in March 2015, Erdoğan announced that Turkey, Azerbaijan, and Turkmenistan would establish a trilateral mechanism to handle energy issues.[46] A scaled down version of the TCGP, carrying 10 bcm annually rather than the 30 bcm initially proposed, could be realized. The Malaysian company Petronas is producing about 10 bcm annually from an offshore block in the Turkmen part of the Caspian Sea. Significantly, in October 2014, Petronas bought Statoil's 15.5 percent stake in the Shah Deniz consortium.[47] Presumably, Azerbaijan would look more favorably on a TCGP carrying reduced Turkmen volumes, as this could provide spare capacity for more Azerbaijani gas to be transported via TANAP.

TANAP will have an important bearing on Turkey's energy interests in the South Caucasus and in the Middle East. For the foreseeable future, it will be the only major gas pipeline running across Turkey that will form a part of the

SGC. The relationship between Turkey and Azerbaijan is therefore critical. In spite of Turkey's attempts to act as an assertive regional power, Azerbaijan has actually maintained leverage over Turkish foreign policy. On the other hand, given the lack of alternative routes, Azerbaijan is dependent on Turkey for the export of oil and gas to outside markets. In spite of SOCAR's majority ownership of the TANAP company, Turkey may still have freedom of manoeuvre because of the interdependent nature of the relationship between Ankara and Baku. Issues of sequencing and third-party access also need consideration. Gas from Turkmenistan and the KRG could help fill an expanding TANAP until gas from other Azerbaijani fields is ready for export, possibly in the late 2020s. According to EU regulations, discussed in more detail below, Azerbaijan will not have the exclusive right to transport gas on an enlarged TAP. Moreover, the EU has expressed renewed interest in the TCGP and has agreed to work on a legal framework agreement for the supply of Turkmen gas to Europe.[48] Turkey could impress upon Brussels the need to lobby for the TCGP to ensure that gas volumes from various sources flow along TANAP. However, questions over the funding of the proposed TCGP are unresolved. Moscow's moves to promote Turkish Stream is a further complication.

The possible impact of Turkish Stream

Relations between Ankara and Moscow could have a direct impact on Turkey's foreign and energy policy in the South Caucasus. The two are long-standing rivals, and although commercial ties have dramatically expanded, as recently as 2008 Moscow was at loggerheads with Ankara. Turkey was accused of violating the provisions of the Montreux Convention by supposedly allowing the unauthorized entry of US warships to the Black Sea at the time of the Russo-Georgian War.[49] Turkey's increasing energy dependency on Russia has been encouraged by the so-called Russian lobby. This lobby includes major Turkish construction companies which have invested in power plants fed by Russian gas. As such, Turkish Stream would further solidify Turkish–Russian ties while posing a threat to the SGC and to Turkey's regional power play ambitions.

The Turkish Stream project was surprisingly announced by Russian President Vladimir Putin when visiting Ankara in December 2014.[50] The EU had opposed the planned South Stream, which had aimed to deliver annually 63 bcm of Russian gas to central Europe via the Black Sea. South Stream violated the provisions of the EU's Third Energy Package, due to Gazprom's ownership of the pipeline and control over gas transmission. Turkish Stream may encounter similar problems. The route for South Stream had envisioned a system running across Bulgaria. Planned to have the same capacity as South Stream, Turkish Stream would transit Turkish Thrace. One string of the new network would deliver 15.75 bcm annually to Turkey. The remaining volumes may be collected at what was referred to as a "hub" on the Turkish–Greek border before onward delivery to Europe.

According to Ankara, Turkish Stream will not threaten the prospects for TANAP but will provide healthy competition.[51] The AKP government attempted to use Turkish Stream as leverage to secure a price discount for Russian gas. In December 2014, Putin had proposed a 6 percent price reduction. Weeks later, Yıldız was speaking of a possible 10.25 percent discount.[52] One complication, though, was that Gazprom charged different prices for gas supplied to BOTAŞ and to private Turkish energy firms. Disagreements over gas pricing led to Turkey delaying approval for the construction of the offshore section of Turkish Stream in its exclusive economic zone on the Black Sea.

Ankara has to steer carefully to ensure that support for Turkish Stream will not alarm Brussels and Baku and have negative impact on TANAP. Russian backing for South Stream contributed to the collapse of Nabucco and caused an initial setback for the SGC. If the proposed timetable is met, the first gas will flow along Turkish Stream to Turkey three years prior to the launch of TANAP. However, Turkish Stream would not markedly increase Turkey's dependence on Russian gas imports. Moscow has indicated that it may not renew its contract with Ukraine for gas transit in 2019. Turkey concluded contracts with Russia to import up to 14 bcm of gas annually via the network crossing Ukraine. The first string of Turkish Stream would enable Russia to bypass Ukraine to deliver significant gas volumes to Turkey.

Turkey's general reputation as a "good" energy transit state would be irreparably tarnished if the promotion of Turkish Stream leads to the abandoning of TANAP. Turkey's ambitions to become a leading gas hub would also be shattered. The proposed "hub" for Turkish Stream on the Turkish–Greek border would then likely become a simple delivery point where gas is aggregated and then traded. Presumably, this would not have negative impact on Turkey's efforts to develop a form of virtual trading hub. But it is unclear how collected gas at the Turkish–Greek border would be exported, given that the provisions of the Third Energy Package would also apply to Greece as an EU member. In June 2015, Greece signed a non-binding memorandum of understanding with Russia for the construction of a 47-bcm capacity pipeline across its territory.[53]

In reality, EU opposition and prohibitive costs may result in the construction of only two of the four planned strings of Turkish Stream. The first link would feed the Turkish market. A second link may hook up to interconnector lines in south-eastern Europe where gas flows could be reversed, which may not run counter to the provisions of the Third Energy Package.[54] Alternatively, Gazprom could exploit EU regulations on third-party access by pushing to export 10 bcm along TAP after this pipeline doubles its annual capacity to 20 bcm. Gazprom has already spent $4.7 billion USD on building offshore and onshore sections for South Stream, and the realization of Turkish Stream in some form could use much of this infrastructure and help offset any financial losses.[55]

Continued dependence on Russian gas does make Ankara vulnerable to pressure from Moscow. As such, Turkey will probably not block Turkish Stream. Russia might then seek to secure access to TAP if Turkish Stream expands to include more than one string. The role of the SGC as an avenue for the delivery of non-Russian gas to Europe might then be compromised. Gazprom's use of TAP could block the export potential of Azerbaijan and thereby make TANAP less commercially attractive.[56] EU rules on third-party access mean that Baku would have to find alternative routes for exports to Europe once additional volumes of Azerbaijani gas were transported to the Turkish–Greek border along TANAP. There would only be an exemption from third-party access for the initial 10 bcm flowing annually through TAP. Gazprom's possible use of TAP could also make it more difficult for gas from the KRG and Turkmenistan to access TANAP and the SGC. This would have serious negative repercussions on Turkey's aims to become a major energy transit state and leading gas hub, and would be a major setback for Turkey's hopes of becoming a key regional power. However, difficulties with the EU may lead to Russia scaling down its plans for Turkish Stream, and in that eventuality Gazprom may not attempt to secure access to TAP.

Other possible complications

Future EU gas needs, the increasing use of LNG, and security concerns could impact the SGC and thus Turkey's energy and foreign policy ambitions. There are different projections of the EU's future gas demand. This is because geopolitics, questions over the energy mix for individual states, the impact of reduced oil prices, the future for shale gas, and declining North Sea gas production should be considered. According to Eurogas, EU gas consumption amounted to 409 bcm in 2014, which was a decrease of 11.2 percent from the previous year.[57] In the EU's European Energy Security Strategy, published in 2014, it was noted that member states would remain dependent on imports for 66 percent of gas consumption until 2020, after which dependence on imported gas would slightly increase.[58] The European Commission remains committed to reducing dependence on Russian gas, and Turkey could thus play an important role as an energy transit state and gas hub.

A dramatic expansion in the use of LNG in Europe could result in less piped gas. More LNG-receiving terminals are being built, and Brussels has spoken of the importance of LNG imports as part of its policy to diversify gas suppliers. Volumes of US LNG may reach European markets in the immediate future, but the importance of this should not be exaggerated. It will take time for a number of proposed LNG export projects to receive the necessary regulatory approval. Much of the future US LNG exports may be destined for markets in Asia, where gas prices are traditionally higher than those in Europe. The increased role of LNG on world energy markets may therefore not have a negative impact on the prospects for the SGC.

In an increasingly volatile Middle East and South Caucasus, security issues with regard to pipeline projects need to be considered. The Russo-Georgian War in 2008 resulted in the temporary closure of pipelines. Tensions may yet escalate over the unresolved Nagorno-Karabakh dispute. The contested enclave lies close to the BTC oil pipeline and the South Caucasus Pipeline which transports gas from Shah Deniz. In August 2008, the BTC pipeline was shut down for two weeks after an explosion at an above-ground valve in Erzincan province in north-eastern Turkey. While the PKK claimed responsibility for the attack, later reports suggested that the incident may have been caused by a Russian-led cyber-attack.[59] In May and September 2012, gas flows along the South Caucasus Pipeline between Kars and Erzurum were disrupted by what seemed to have been PKK attacks.[60] In the Middle East, as was previously noted, repeated attacks by IS forced the closure of the original Kirkuk–Ceyhan oil pipeline network. If progress is made toward resolving the Kurdish question in Turkey, attacks on pipelines crossing Turkish territory will probably cease. However, a possible serious deterioration in the security situation in either the South Caucasus or in northern Iraq could have damaging consequences for Turkey's hopes of becoming a key energy transit state and gas hub.

Conclusion

There are differences and similarities between Turkey's energy policy in the Middle East and the South Caucasus. In both regions, energy and foreign policy interests overlap. The AKP government has sought to pursue a policy of assertive regionalism to make Turkey a regional hegemon by attempting to use energy as a foreign policy instrument in line with the empires and regions storyline. Turkey's possible role as a trading state in which business groups, rather than government officials, have an impact on foreign policy and energy policy must be seriously questioned, especially following recent geopolitical developments. Oil exports and the prospects for gas from the KRG reaching markets in Turkey and Europe have enabled Ankara to act as a powerbroker in northern Iraq, which could have wider repercussions for Kurds in Syria and Turkey. Turkey has been unable to use the energy card to influence relations with Israel, while the relationship between Turkey and Iran is a complicated one in which technical energy issues also come into play. In the South Caucasus, Ankara's attempts to exert regional influence through exploiting Turkey's potential role as a major energy transit state may only have limited success. Turkey's policy in the region remains indexed to that of Azerbaijan, while an increasingly emboldened Russia could seek to expand its role in the region following the annexation of Crimea.

Turkey will continue to import significant volumes of gas from the Middle East and the South Caucasus to satisfy its growing energy demand and possibly reduce dependence on Russian gas imports. For the foreseeable future, though, Turkey's vulnerability to Russia will mean that the energy issue may pose a serious threat to Ankara's security concerns. Nevertheless, in the cases of Azerbaijan, Iran, and also Russia, Turkey is seeking to obtain preferential terms for gas imports by negotiating price discounts.

Turkey's ambitions to become a major transit state and commercial gas hub are interlinked. Here, in practice, energy issues are politicized. Officials in Ankara have argued that Turkey would provide services for states in its neighborhood by functioning as an energy transit state and hub, although in reality the Turkish authorities are seeking to secure political and economic advantage. Gas volumes from Azerbaijan, and possibly from Turkmenistan, the KRG, and even Iran, transported via Turkey to Europe, would make Turkey a key energy transit state. Here, though, the issue of SOCAR's majority ownership of the TANAP company needs to be considered. This movement of gas would also bolster the prospects for Turkey to become a leading gas hub, although it is not clear if Turkish officials will carry out the reforms required to liberalize the gas market. The Turkish authorities, however, do not appear to have abandoned their goal of re-exporting gas from Russia and Iran, and possibly also from the KRG and Turkmenistan. Nevertheless, Turkish Stream may cause complications for TANAP and thereby damage the prospects for Turkey to become a leading energy transit state and gas hub.

Following the elections held in Turkey in June 2015, the AKP lost considerable votes and could no longer form a single-party government. A new coalition government could lead to a re-assessment of foreign policy, which may have ramifications for energy policy. For example, shortly after the elections it was reported that Turkish and Israeli officials met secretly in Rome to discuss possible reconciliation.[61] A rapprochement might lead to the revival of plans to connect Israel's Leviathan gas field with the Turkish mainland.

Given the changing geopolitical situation in the Middle East and the South Caucasus, and the uncertainties with regard to whether a coalition government may be formed or new elections called in Turkey, it is difficult to predict how Turkey's energy and foreign policy may be affected. However, Turkey's geographical location will not change, and with neighboring states endowed with considerable amounts of hydrocarbons, and states in Europe keen to import gas in the foreseeable future, officials in Ankara will continue to have the opportunity to use energy as a foreign policy instrument and simultaneously pursue the policy of a more assertive regional power.

5

THE CLASH OF NATIONALISMS

IRANIAN RESPONSE TO BAKU'S IRREDENTISM

Hamid Ahmadi

The ethnic factor has been the most salient one determining Iran–Azerbaijan Republic relations during the last century. While the ethnic dimension of Iranian studies is a relatively underdeveloped area, it also suffers general methodological and epistemological problems plaguing the whole sub-discipline of ethnic studies in social science. Specifically, the literature on ethnicity and ethnic nationalism tends to be the most overgeneralized arena in contemporary social science. While the post-positivist tradition of historical sociology has addressed most areas of social studies by differentiating among cases in a time–space spectrum, it has touched less upon ethnicity and ethnic politics.[1] As such, it then appears that the same general and universal concepts and theoretical–conceptual frameworks can overcome the historical specialties of all cases across time and space and explain the bulk of problems with which they are confronted. Consequently, the general trend in the literature assumes that all countries composed of multiple religious, linguistic, or racial groups suffer the same problems.

Iranian studies, as far as the issue of ethnicity is considered, bears this tendency. Most works discussing ethnicity and ethnic groups in Iran, either those ideological works written by members of Iranian ethnic minorities or the more academic-oriented ones, disregard the importance of historical sociology and are influenced by the generalist trend in ethnic theoretical studies.[2] Such works tend to express the perspective that Iran is composed of different politically-oriented ethnic groups all struggling for independence or political autonomy, thus depicting Iran as an ethnic conflict-laden society lacking the elements of nationhood and national identity.

While it is true that Iran is composed of various religious–linguistic minority groups making ethnicity an issue worth studying, Iran has specific features that differentiate it from other societies that have more recent experience in political heritage and the nation-state-building process. Bearing the characteristics of *ancient nations*, as some theorists of ethnicity and nationalism have elaborated,[3] Iran represents a specific historical case in which the saliency of nationalism and an Iranian national identity is more remarkable than that of ethnicity and ethnic nationalism. While I have elaborated on this issue elsewhere,[4] the present study on the case of Iranian Azeris in general and Iran–Azerbaijan Republic relations in particular can shed more light on this fact. Although some students of Iranian studies consider the case of Iranian Azeris and Iran–Azerbaijan Republic relations a challenge for Iran and its future as a nation-state,[5] the present study will show that Iranian national identity and nationalism have had the upper hand in the almost one century of ongoing clashes of nationalisms between Baku and Tehran over the issue of Azerbaijan. While the pan-Turkist-oriented political elites in the Azerbaijan Republic have relied on the idea of ethnic nationalism to invoke an anti-Iranian sense of ethnicity among Iranian Azeris since 1918 and onwards, Iranian nationalism has successfully responded to the military, political, and discursive challenges targeting Iranian Azerbaijan during the last one hundred years. This study also explains how, in challenging Baku's claims to Iranian Azerbaijan and its former Soviet supporters' irredentist policies, two broad strategies have been used. Both Iranian Azeris and Iranian nationalists have used elements of Iranian national identity and Iranian nationalism to address Baku's claims. On the other hand, the Islamic Republic in Iran has used its own specific notion of Islamic and Shiite nationalism as a counter-strategy against Baku's strategy of promoting ethnic nationalism among Iranian Azeris.

This study is divided into three general sections. The first section covers the role of ethno-politics and ethnic nationalism in Azerbaijani foreign policy toward Iran. The second section concentrates on the Iranian reaction to Azerbaijan's irredentist policies regarding Iranian Azerbaijan. This section itself is divided into three sub-sections, the first of which examines Tehran's formal reaction to the Azerbaijani Republic's ethnic nationalist approach, which manifests itself in the form of a religious Islamic and Shiite nationalism. The next two sub-sections focus on the role of Iranian non-state actors approaching the issue: first, the reaction of Iranian nationalists to irredentist policy of the state of Azerbaijan and its non- or semi-state circles will be explained; secondly, the next sub-section will focus on a reflection of Baku's ethnic nationalist policies and views on Iranian Azerbaijan, which has never previously been the subject of research in Iranian studies in general and Iran–Azerbaijan relations in particular. This last sub-section will analyze the response of Iranian Azerbaijanis: both the Iranian nationalist-oriented Azeris and those affiliated with Tehran's Islamic ruling elites' Islamic nationalism.

The third section specifically explains how Baku's irredentist idea of a "united Azerbaijan" and the concept of "southern Azerbaijan" have produced counter-claims from Iranian Azerbaijanis. This chapter argues that Iranian Azeris have produced the most enduring and systematic response to the Azerbaijan Republic's pan-Turkist irredentist and ethnic nationalist claims, and that ultimately contemporary Iranian studies, particularly in the realm of ethnicity, identity, and nationality, have underestimated and disregarded the salience of Iranian nationalism and the central role of Iranian Azeris in the promotion of contemporary Iranian national awakening.

Ethnic nationalism of the Azerbaijan Republic and the question of Iranian Azerbaijan

The salience of the ethnic issue in Iran–Azerbaijan relations is not restricted to the post-Soviet era; it has a longer history going back to the birth of the Azerbaijan Republic in the late 1910s. In fact the ethno-political dimension of Iran–Azerbaijan relations has expressed itself in three specific historical periods, the last one beginning in the aftermath of the end of Soviet control in the Caucasus. The first signs of the ethnic challenge emerged at the end of the Perso-Russian wars of 1811–12 and 1826–8 from the formation of a republic in the Muslim part of the former Iranian territories separated by the Russian Empire

The problem between Iran and Azerbaijan developed more fully in 1918, when the ruling elites of the Muslim Caucasus, gathered around the Musavat

Party, decided to establish their own independent states in order to prevent the Russian revolutionaries from retaking their territory. The name chosen for the Muslim part—the Republic of Azerbaijan—became problematic to the Iranian state. Though the weak Iranian state was in a transitional period, struggling with foreign domination, the Iranian political and intellectual elites in Tehran and Tabriz, the capital of Iranian Azerbaijan, soon protested against such naming. For almost a year, the printed media in Tehran, Tabriz, and other big Iranian cities on the one side, and the media in Baku, the capital of the newly independent Republic of Azerbaijan, on the other side, presented their arguments to prove that such naming was wrong or right.[6] Iranians were generally suspicious of Baku's choice and regarded confiscating the historical name of Iran's north-eastern province as a pan-Turkist conspiracy planned by the Ottoman Young Turks, then active in Baku, for their ultimate goal of establishing a pan-Turk entity (Turan) from Central Asia to Europe.[7] By calling the real historical Azerbaijan located in Iran "southern Azerbaijan", the pan-Turkists could claim the necessity of unifying the Republic of Azerbaijan and "southern Azerbaijan" in their future "Turan." Fearing such threats, Shaikh Mohammad Khiabani, a popular member of the political elite in Iranian Azerbaijan and the leader of the Democratic Party (*Firqhe Democrat*), changed the name of the province to *Azadistan* (land of freedom).[8] According to Ahmad Kasravi, Khiabani's deputy at the time, the main reason for such a change was to prevent any future claim by the pan-Turkist Ottomans to Iranian Azerbaijan on the basis of the similarity of the names.[9]

Alongside this naming controversy, the newly established Republic of Azerbaijan also faced a threat from the overspreading domination of the Soviet communists in Moscow. To avoid the threat of Soviet invasion and the more important threat of an Armenian invasion, the Muslim enclave of Nakhichevan proposed annexing to Iran.[10] The new pro-British Iranian government under Vosough al Dowleh tried to encourage the leaders of the new Republic in Baku to join Iran. To promote this idea, al Dowleh sent two separate delegations, one to Baku and one to the Paris Peace Conference in 1919. The Baku delegation, then under the leadership of Seyyed Zia Tabatabai, went through intensive negotiations with Musavat party leaders amid the increasing instability and chaos in Baku. At the final stage, an agreement was reached between them, but before presenting the idea to Vosough in Tehran,[11] the communists took over Baku and ended the Musavat–Ottoman rule. The Paris delegation, headed by Nosrat al Dowleh Firuz, the Iranian foreign minister, was successful in a unity negotiation with the Baku delegation, and the two signed a confederation agreement.[12] The Soviet control and the annexation of the Muslim territory of the Caucasus thus ended the first ethnic controversy between Tehran and Baku.

The second and more challenging conflict with ethnic underpinnings emerged during the occupation of Iranian Azerbaijan by the Soviet Army in World War II. At the peak of the crisis over the evacuation of the Soviet Red Army from Iran, a separatist party (*Frigha Democrat Azerbaijan*) claimed autonomy over Iranian Azerbaijan on the basis of the common ethnic characteristics of Azeris. Although it was clear from the beginning, and especially after the disclosure of the Soviet secret documents, particularly the three famous Stalin commands of 1945,[13] that the Soviets were behind the crisis, the role of the Soviet Azerbaijan Republic has been remarkable in the whole episode. The post-Soviet released documents emphasize the role of Mir Ja'far Baghirov, leader of the Soviet Azerbaijan Republic and Baku branch of the Soviet communist party.[14] Jamil Hasanli, a professor of history at Baku University, and before him several Iranian Azeri researchers[15] who collected documents and memories of those involved in the crisis, have highlighted the role of Baghirov and other Soviet Azeris in promoting ethnic political awareness among Iranian Azeris. In fact, Stalin pursued his own policy of Sovietizing Iran through Baghirov and his men, who themselves looked for the realization of a united Azerbaijan. Although the crisis ended with the Soviet forces withdrawing in 1946, the nostalgic view of Iranian Azerbaijan continued throughout the Soviet era through the "literature of longing." This was true even during the 1980s when the Pahlavi dynasty was replaced by the Islamic Republic. One example of the "literature of longing" was the poetry of Kamran Mehdi about the Arax river: "True, the Araz divides a nation / But the earth underneath is one!"[16] Another example was Baku's map of the Azerbaijan Republic that contained the Iranian Azerbaijan and its cities, "as if they were both part of the same Azerbaijan."[17]

Considering these two periods, the salience of the ethnic dimension of Iran–Azerbaijan relations in post-Soviet era should not be unexpected. Nevertheless, the core pan-Turkist vision of a united Azerbaijan has played a key role in the further ethnicization of the relations between Iran and Azerbaijan. This ideal, although of Ottoman or Young Turk heritage, was also cherished during the Soviet era by the political elites loyal to the communist party, and was institutionalized through the formal educational system from one generation to the next. Using Eric Hobsbawm's[18] theoretical concept, the pan-Turkist elites in Baku "invented the tradition" of a national history based on the existence of an Azeri nation-state that dominated the northern and southern parts of the Aras river, which was torn apart by a Perso-Russian conspiracy in the Turkmanchai Agreement of 1828. This "imagined community," using Benedict Anderson's framework,[19] was then cherished and institutionalized in formal history books of the educational system during the Soviet and post-Soviet era.

Living in a closed society such as the Soviet Union, thus not knowing the realities of Iran and its Azeri population, the cultural and political elites in Soviet Azerbaijan continued to cherish and promote the idea of a united Azerbaijan in their socio-political and cultural activities. The products of such romantic thought were nostalgic literary works, known as the "literature of longing," which included novels such as *Tabriz meh alood* (Foggy Tabriz) by Mohammad Said Urdubadi, *The Coming Day* (Gelecek üçün, 1951) by Mirza Ibrahimov, and other books in which the life of Iranian Azeris were depicted as a misery imposed by the Fars suppression, therefore waiting for the day when their brothers from the "north" would come and liberate them.[20]

Having inherited such a nostalgic mentality regarding Iran and its Azerbaijan province, the post-independence nationalist political elites in Baku put the historical mission for achieving a "united Azerbaijan" as top priority on their political agenda. Consolidated in the nationalist parties such as *Qizilbash* and *Birlik* (Unity) and especially the Popular Front of Azerbaijan (*Azerbaijan Khalq Jebhesi*), led by Abulfaz Elchibey who had devoted his life to unification,[21] pan-Turkist elites started their campaign for the ethnic awakening of Iranian Azeris. Among others, Elchibey, a professor of history in the former Soviet Azerbaijan, was the most eager and mobilized support for this mission of reunification. Perhaps due to these ideas, Elchibey managed to win newly independent Azerbaijan's first presidential elections in June 1992. In addition to these political parties and their leadership, nationalist intellectuals and Azerbaijani media also included the question of "southern Azerbaijan" in their main political agendas. According to one survey of the Azerbaijani press in 1995–6, both state-dependent and independent outlets covered the question of Iranian Azeris more than any other issue.[22]

The most ardent among all was, however, the Popular Front and its leader Elchibey. The issue was considered their most important political program: "PFA support the restoration of the ethnic unity of Azerbaijanis living on both sides of the border. The Azerbaijani people should be recognized as a united whole. Economic, cultural and social ties between our divided nation should be restored."[23] From the early days of his presidency, Elchibey not only explicitly had a hostile and irredentist tone regarding Iran, but also went so far as to organize a group named the United Azerbaijan Movement. During his presidency "on several occasions, he blasted Iran as a doomed state and predicted that within five years, Azerbaijan would be united."[24] In a conference on "the Iranian factor in Azerbaijan politics" in 1999, he declared that "the problem of a divided Azerbaijan exists and it is our historical task to solve the problem."[25] Before that, at the annual congress of PFA, he more bluntly stated: "The creation of an independent state in Azerbaijan was a great victory of that movement and the beginning of a new stage. This new stage will end with the creation and (or) the restoration of a united Azerbaijan statehood."[26]

Elchibey and his followers went even further and supported the formation of an organization called the Council to Protect the Right of Azerbaijanis of the World (CPRAW) in 1999 and declared that "the establishment of CPRAW is an integral part of the struggle for a united Azerbaijan."[27] Another irredentist step included the formation of the World Azerbaijanis Congress (WAC) in Baku in 2001, following a presidential order by Heydar Aliyev in which the unity of Azerbaijan was also proclaimed to be the main goal.

In addition to the ruling political elites and political parties, some Azeri intellectuals and academics have played an active role in maintaining the ethnic dimension as a dynamic factor in Iran–Azerbaijan relations. One of the most active among these intellectuals has been Nasib Nasibli, a university professor and member of Azerbaijani parliament, who has been the most ardent proponent of the idea of a united Azerbaijan. Perhaps because of his radical views, he was appointed ambassador to Iran during Elchibey's rule. His career as an ambassador did not last long, ending in 1994, possibly because of Tehran's dissatisfaction with his explicit anti-Iranian stance. He even tried to organize ethnic cells among Iranian Azeris students in Tehran.[28] In his writings and lectures, Nasibli considers the ethnic Azeri factor the most important one in Baku–Tehran relations. According to him: "The divided Azerbaijani factor is the most influential factor in relation between the two countries... The Azerbaijani Turks in Iran constitute a significant part of the population of that country but are deprived of their national rights. This factor is central in understanding the relations between Azerbaijan and Iran."[29]

In his politically-oriented academic activities in both Azerbaijan and the United States in the late 1990s and early 2000s he tried to convince the Western states that Iranian Azerbaijan represented a big challenge for Iran and that "the future of Iranian statehood itself could be problematic."[30] In general, Nasibli's lectures and writings on the issue emphasize these familiar notions, and as Brown puts it, "share basically the same views and often repeat the same facts."[31] Beside such academic activities, Nasibli played a continuous role in promoting the idea of a national awakening among Iranian Azeris through organizing opposition figures, such as Mahmoud Ali Chehregani and others, in conferences and occasional gatherings in the Azerbaijan Republic, the United States or Turkey. He has also been an omnipresent figure on GunAz TV programs (south Azerbaijan TV) since its inception in 2005 in Chicago by Ahmad Obali. This TV station has become the main instrument for encouraging dissatisfaction and instigating ethnic strife among Iranian Azeris. Most of its programs contain news, analysis, interviews, and roundtables on Iran. A content analysis of GunAz TV, done in 2014 by an Iranian Azeri, indicates that 86.64 percent of its programs have been negative toward Iran, with not a single positive program.[32]

In contrast to the 1990s, the Azerbaijani government, or as figures such as Nasibli call it, "official Baku,"[33] did not directly involve themselves in overtly anti-Iranian ethnic jargon; but this does not mean that the issue has no impact on bilateral relations. Besides the continuous activities of non-governmental circles, including the media, the government officials and institutions have only lowered their tone regarding the issue. Tehran's sensitivities to the policies and tenure of the Elchibey government have led Heydar Aliyev and his son Ilham to be more cautious in taking positions to which Iran might object. However, besides the activities of independent intellectual and media circles, the governments of Heydar and Ilham from time to time have still engaged, directly or indirectly, in initiatives that Tehran has found objectionable. In other words, the post-Elchibey governments have changed their method of involvement in the issue. Despite Heydar Aliyev's earlier active role in encouraging ethnic national awakening in Iranian Azerbaijan in Soviet era,[34] he preferred not to mention Iranian Azerbaijan specifically per se, but instead focused on Azerbaijanis outside the republic in general. In alignment with this strategy, Heydar ordered the organization of the World Azerbaijanis Congress (WAC) in order to represent the Azerbaijan Republic as the motherland of all Azeri diaspora around the world. Although Ilham's approach tended to take a more cautious stance on Iran by emphasizing good neighborhood relations, thus preferring to refer to world Azerbaijanis instead of "south Azerbaijan," the occasional meeting of WAC and Iranian separatist groups such as the South Azerbaijan National Liberation Movement (SANLM) in Baku, or the anti-Iranian tone of formal and informal media, indicate that the irredentist ideal has not been omitted from the political agenda of the Azerbaijan Republic.

Another factor that has increased the level of Iranian concern over Baku policies relates to its relations with Israel. Iran and Azerbaijan signed a pact of non-aggression in 2005, according to which signatories would not allow a third country to build military bases to be used for military attack on the other.[35] However, there have been reports in subsequent years that the Israelis were "developing a 'secret staging ground' in Azerbaijan for a possible air attack on Iran's nuclear facilities."[36] Not surprisingly, such rumors have made Tehran more suspicious of Aliyev's policies toward Iran.

The Iranian response: from Islamic to Iranian nationalism

It is noteworthy that in the post-Soviet era ethnically motivated quarrels between Tehran and Baku, as in the two other cases in 1918–20 and 1941–6, it was the newly independent state of Azerbaijan that triggered the animosity between the two countries by again raising the issue of a united Azerbaijan and the so-called southern question. Iran intended to have a good relationship with the newly independent state and was among the first countries to start full diplomatic relations in October 1991: Iranian Foreign Minister Ali Akbar Velayati paid a formal visit to Baku in early November of that year. Given these diplomatic intentions, it was a shock for the Islamic Republic then to see the irredentist and pan-Turkist claims raised by Azerbaijani political elites, Azeri political parties, and the formal media. In fact, the Muslim elites in Tehran did not have enough historical awareness of the issue to be prepared for or properly react to Azerbaijan's irredentist policies.

It is worth mentioning that Iran's reaction and response to Baku's stance regarding Iranian Azerbaijan came from two directions, and any real understanding of the problem requires a distinction between them. One was the formal reaction and response of the Islamic Republic, its political elites in state institutions, non-state religious elites, and the formal media affiliated with them. The second and more systemic reaction came from Iranian nationalist circles, intellectuals, university professors and students who cared more about Iranian national interests, identity, and Iran's cultural and civilizational heritage than those of the transnational Islamic world. Subsequently, the nature of their response to pan-Turkist claims of the Azerbaijan Republic also differed. While the state political and religious elites either disregarded such claims or resorted to pan-Islamic, particularly Shiite, values to challenge Baku's policies, the nationalist response mostly concentrated on historical, cultural, and political discourse. The most important factor has been the role of Iranian Azeris, either on the pro-state religious side or in the Iranian nationalist camp. In fact, Iranian Azeris have been at the forefront of the discursive war against the ethnic challenge coming from the Azerbaijan Republic. In this section, the Iranian response will be discussed in three sub-sections: first, the formal state reaction and policies; secondly, the Iranian nationalist non-state reaction; and finally, the Iranian Azeris' response to Baku politics regarding Iranian Azerbaijan.

The Islamic Republic's formal reaction

As mentioned earlier, the political ruling elites in Iran, because of their lack of historical knowledge of the Iran Caucus and Iran–Russia–Soviet relations, did not expect that the newly independent state of Azerbaijan would assume anti-Iranian policies. Consequently, their early reaction was some kind of shock, especially for the religious elites who had expected that the Shiite identity of the new state would result in close and warm bilateral relations. Therefore, both state-related institutions, such as the Ministry of Foreign Affairs and its staff, and the religious elites, such as Friday prayer imams, condemned and protested against Baku's ethnic and irredentist-oriented positions. These occasional protests, however, gradually grew into a bitter sense of their northern neighbor's intentions with respect to what Svante Cornell accurately perceived as the anti-Iranian positions of the "ultra-nationalist pan-Turk, the historian Abulfaz Elchibey."[37]

Iran's resentment toward Elchibey's irredentist policy was reflected during the Nagorno-Karabakh conflict in the early 1990s, when Azerbaijan and Armenia entered a bloody war over the region of Karabakh. Instead of supporting the similarly Shiite Muslim Azerbaijan Republic, Iran preferred to remain neutral, assuming a mediatory policy to end the conflict and restricting its support of humanitarian aid to Azerbaijan. Baku did not welcome Tehran's peace plans and instead accused Tehran of supporting Armenia. The idea that Iran helped Armenia occupy Karabakh gradually became a view held by many observers and analysts. Azerbaijani elites and media have steadily used this claim as an instrument to convince Iranian Azeris of what Baku considers Tehran's betrayal of Islamic commitments. Iranian Azeris, especially those close to and familiar with the subject (as I will discuss later), reject such accusations and argue a counter-claim.

One important dimension of Iran's formal reaction toward Azerbaijan's positions relates to the use of the common religious Shiite factor between the two countries. One effective instrument in this has been the radio and TV channels which broadcast religious teachings and instigate political Islam in opposition to the Azerbaijani state's secular identity and policies. Baku is especially concerned about what it considers to be provocative broadcasts by Sahar 2 Television, and on many occasions Baku has objected to Tehran with regard to the station's programming.[38] Sahar 2 has especially targeted the southern part of Azerbaijan in cities such as Masalli, where populations have been more receptive to religious propaganda.[39] With its Talyshi language program, Sahar 2 has also targeted the Talyshi ethnic population in the Lankaran region in apparent efforts to convince the Talyshi population that they have more cultural affinity with Iran.[40] The promotion of the Grand Ayatollah Fazel Lankarani as *Marja'e Taghlid* of Shiites was also a successful move and made him popular in the southern part of the Azerbaijan Republic where his ancestors were from. Some of his *fatwas* (religious orders) have been particularly directed at the Shiites of the Azerbaijan Republic and their problems.[41] After his death in 2007, other Iranian grand ayatollahs like Naser Makarem Shirazi, and particularly Ayatollah Ali Khamenei, the Iranian Supreme Leader, have also found many followers among the Azerbaijan Republic's Shiite population.[42] Other strategies directed at highlighting the common Shiite factor include Iran actively building dozens of mosques and madrasas in the Azerbaijan Republic during the 1990s. Additionally, Iranian mullahs (religious preachers) have been training young Shiite mullahs, especially in the southern cities of Massali and Jalalabad.[43]

Iranian formal media have also used the Azerbaijani state's ban on the hijab in schools as a symbol of what they call Baku's anti-Islamic nature.[44] Along the same lines, the Iranian media and religious elites began a huge campaign against the Eurovision song contest, which took place in Baku in 2012, calling it an overt anti-Islamic action.[45] While claiming Baku was hosting a "gay parade," which was denied strongly by state authorities in Baku,[46] Tehran recalled its ambassador from Baku, followed by Azerbaijan recalling its ambassador back to Baku.[47] Iran also supported the activities of Islamic elites, such as non-state and opposition imams,[48] and Islamic political parties in Azerbaijan, and has also condemned mosque closures[49] and crackdowns on Islamic literature.[50] It appears that the Islamic Republic's religious elites, both state and non-state-dependent ones, believe that an important part of the population supports ideas such as the application of Shari'a law and Islamic governance, particularly, as Nasib Nasibli has said, in the southern part of the country close to Iran,[51] and that religion is an effective means of leverage to use against Baku's ethno-politics toward Iran.

Iran has also supported religious political groups and their leaders in the Republic of Azerbaijan. In the early years of independence, the leader of the Muslim Spiritual Board, the formal religious establishment of the Soviet era, Allahshukur Pashazadeh, a strong opponent of Elchibey, was supported by Iranian formal media. In the new nationalist and secular political milieu of the post-Soviet era, Pashazadeh was more oriented toward Iran. According to one report, "Pashazade ultimately tried to persuade Shias to accept the political (*velayat-e-faqih*, or the "rule of the jurisprudent") and the spiritual (*marja-al-taqlid*, or "source of emulation") leadership of Iran's Supreme Leader, Ayatollah Khamenei."[52] While supporting and promoting other Shiite religious leaders such as Haji Ilgar, the imam of Baku Jum'a mosque, and Haji Shahin, the former leader of the youth movement Ikmal,[53] the Islamic Republic has supported the development of Islamist political movements, such as the Islamic Party of Azerbaijan. Founded in 1992 in Nardaran, a small town near Baku, the leaders of the party, Alikram Aliyev and Haci Movsum Samadov, have been the most active proponents of Islamic law application in Azerbaijan; and conversely, the strongest adherents of Baku's secular policies. It is said that Alikram called Nardaran "the heart of Shiism and the Qom (the holy city of Shi'ism in Iran) of the Azerbaijan Republic."[54] Nardaran has witnessed several periods of political turmoil,[55] during some of which[56] several protesters were killed by security forces in 2002 and 2006. Iranian media widely conveyed the events in Nardaran as a sign of Muslim suppression in the Azerbaijan Republic.[57]

A political party established by the religious followers of the Iranian Supreme Leader Ayatollah Khamenei, the Islamic Party of Azerbaijan, has advocated the application of Shari'a law and has overtly supported Iran.[58] News of the arrest and jailing of its leaders, Alikram and Samadov, was fully covered by the media in Iran. In an interview with *Bizim Yol*, the provisional leader of the party, Elcin Manafov, who met Iranian Supreme Leader Ayatollah Ali Khamenei in 2013 in Tehran,[59] emphasized that he follows Ayatollah Khamenei in religious matters and not Ilham Aliyev, whom he deemed unknowledgeable of religious issues.[60]

Iranian nationalists' response[61]

While Iran's ruling elites and their proponents have refrained from being involved in actively advocating nationalist sentiments, the nationalist trends around the country and outside Iran have taken a nationalistic position toward the issue. Among other factors, Azerbaijan's irredentist policies toward Iran in the post-Soviet era, as during the crisis of 1945–6 in Iranian Azerbaijan and Kurdistan, aroused a national awakening in Iran in the twentieth century as well. Some prominent figures of the Iranian Marxist left, such as Khalil Maleki, Rahim Namvar, Jalal Al-e-Ahmad, Mostafa Rahimi, M. Makan and others split from the pro-Soviet communist Tudeh Party over Moscow's and Baku's policy in 1945–6, unintentionally establishing the Iranian Nationalist left school.[62]

In the early months of 1991, when Azerbaijan became independent and the early signs of irredentist views of pan-Turkist figures and circles merged toward Iran, Iranian nationalists were among the first who reacted to it. A special issue of the then famous monthly journal *Negahe Now* (January 1992) concentrated on the issues of Iranian nationalism, ethnicity, pan-Turkism, and pan-Arabism. Nationalist-oriented researchers such as Morteza Saghebfar,[63] Kaveh Bayat,[64] Mostafa Rahimi,[65] and others contributed articles. During the presidency of Mohammad Khatami (1997–2005), when WAC and other irredentist trends in the Republic of Azerbaijan, Turkey, and the United States became more active, Parviz Varjavand, a university professor and secretary general of the Iranian National Front (*Jebhe-ye Melli Iran*) inside Iran, wrote an open letter to Mohammad Khatami warning him of the anti-Iranian activities by followers of Elchibey and other pan-Turkist organizations and media, demanding that Khatami take proper decisions to confront them.[66] Outside Iran, the Iranian students studying in Western universities opted to confront the challenge of pan-Turkism by writing their dissertations on the issue of ethnicity and nationalism in Iran.[67] Later on, nationalist-oriented Iranian researchers and university professors touched on the issue in reaction to anti-Iranian claims of pan-Turkist groups and activists such as Elchibey, his Popular Front, or their Iranian pan-Turkist followers.[68] Among such researchers were Mohammad Reza Khubrooye Pak in Paris, who wrote critical works on federalism,[69] and Kaveh Farrokh, a professor of history at the University of British Columbia. Farrokh's English website was among the first, and for a time the only website to concentrate on promoting Iranian national identity and responding to Elchibey and other pan-Turkist supporters. Farrokh also wrote the first long analytical article in English on pan-Turkism's goals regarding Iranian Azerbaijan.[70]

As the availability of social networks and virtual media increased the level of irredentist claims toward Iran, either by the Azerbaijan Republic or by some pan-Arabist circles in the Arab World, more circles in civil society, especially in Iranian universities, gradually took issue against the irredentist claims. Irredentist claims from the outside world on the one hand, and the passive position of Islamic Republic with respect to the national dimension of Iranian identity on the other, encouraged nationalist groups to undertake the responsibility of confronting the anti-Iranian ethnic and irredentist claims. Individual students and later student groups, especially at undergraduate level, became active in the universities. Some of them, such as Tirdad Bonakdar,[71] Nargeskhatoon Barahui,[72] Sadegh Jowkar, Habibolah Fazeli,[73] Bahmani Ghajar,[74] Mas'aud Loghman,[75] Oghab Ali Ahmadi,[76] and Musawi Ghuhe,[77] began to write on pan-Turkism and its goals with regard to Iran, or other historical and theoretical subjects around the issue of ethnicity and nationality.[78] Such students later went beyond individual activities and organized student groups with their own student media. One among many of such nationalist student circles was *Pasargaad* in the University of Tehran's faculty of law and political science, organized by students coming from different parts of Iran, such as Iranian Azerbaijan, Kurdistan, Khuzestan, Khorasan, Kerman, and Fars.[79] *Pasargaad* was active during the late 1990s and early 2000s and was in contact with other nationalist student circles in other faculties. *Pasargaad* published a monthly journal of the same name, in which articles appeared on Iranian national identity, Iranian history, especially ancient Iran, and issues related to Iranian Azerbaijan, Kurdistan, Khuzestan, Baluchistan, and Turkaman Sahra. Similar student papers with nationalistic themes were also published in other universities by student associations (*Kanoon Haye Daneshjuee*). Gradually an institution called the Iranology Center (*Kanoon e Iran Shenasi*) was established in many universities around the country with the goal of spreading a national awakening and identity among the students.

A notable example of a nationalist society outside the universities was *Afra* Society (*Anjoman Afra*) founded in the mid-1990s by Alireza Afshari, a young dedicated Iranian nationalist who arranged meetings and conferences that were attended by university professors, researchers, and poets. *Afra* gradually became a widely recognized circle for other young Iranians in other provinces. In 2014 Afshari founded a still-active social network group in Viber named *Ghowm Shenakht* (ethnology), through which dozens of members discuss issues related to Iranian identity, national interests, irredentist claims of pan-Turkism and pan-Arabism.[80] Among other non-governmental nationalist associations, the following groups stand out: *Kanoone Gostareshe Farhange Irane Bozorg* in Isfahan,[81] *Anjomane Kaveye Ahangar* and *Anjomane Kohan Dej* in Hamadan, *Anjomane Tufah* in Shushtar in Khuzestan province,

Anjomane Kardavan in Sanandaj in Kurdistan province, *Jamiyyate Talaye Darane Andishehaye Now* in Fariman, Khorasan province, *Moaseseye Mizan*, *Kanoone Andisheye Sepid*, and *Moaseseye Nowavaran* in Tabriz in Azerbaijan province, and *Mehraain* (*Moassesey e Ghayre Dowlati Mehraain*)[82] in Ramhormoz in Khuzestan.[83] These nationalist associations, some of which were NGOs, were coordinated through *Showraye Hamahangie Anjomanhaye Melli Iran* (the coordinative council of national associations of Iran), which used to organize annual meetings of nationalist groups throughout the province as well as annual gatherings of the heads of all circles around the country.[84] The city of Ramhormoz in Khuzestan province hosted the fifth gathering of Iran's national groupings [*panjomin neshaste tashakkol haaye Melli Iran Zamin*] in May 2005.[85] One of the most important issues being discussed in these circles was the threat of pan-Turkism, especially Azerbaijan Republic's irredentist claims regarding Iranian Azerbaijan.

The nationalist response to ethnic challenges has touched upon many issues related to Iranian Azerbaijan and pan-Turkist discourse and has tried to shed light on the realities of Iran and the role of the Iranian ethnic groups such as Azeris, Kurds, Baluchis, and others in promoting a cohesive Iranian national identity, solidarity, and unity. The literature produced by them raises counter-claims, which tend to neutralize irredentist discourse regarding Iranian Azerbaijan. Some of such counter-claims include:

- That historical Azerbaijan is located in Iran, and what was established in 1918 as the Azerbaijan Republic was historically known as Aran or the Caucasus Albania;
- The historical name of Azerbaijan was fabricated: using the name Aran was the Ottoman Young Turks pan-Turkist strategy for the future annexation of Iranian Azerbaijan to a pan-Turkist entity;[86]
- Farsi (Persian) and its close dialect Azeri have been the dominant written and oral languages of Azerbaijan. The present-day Azerbaijani Turkish is the result of the gradual immigration of Turkish tribes to Azerbaijan and Caucasus since the Seljuq era (eleventh century). Though Turkish gradually became the spoken language of Azerbaijan, Farsi has remained the dominant language of education, poetry, history writing, and journalism. Farsi, with its ancient roots, plays the role of national language for Iran;[87]
- International politics have had a dominant role in politicizing ethnicity in Azerbaijan, Kurdistan, and Baluchistan;[88]
- An important part of national awareness is to understand the foundations, the goals, and the results of pan-Turkism and pan-Azerism in Iran and the

region,[89] the Iranian historical and cultural identity of Azerbaijan, and how the Turkish language replaced Farsi in Azerbaijan in recent centuries;[90]

- Azeri intellectuals have played a leading role in promoting Iranian national identity,[91] and Azeri figures such as Sattar Khan and Sheikh Mohammad Khiabani loved Iran and are seen as Iranian national heroes. Contrary to the narrative promoted by Baku, they were neither separatists nor pan-Turkist;[92]
- What is called the Azerbaijan Republic as of 1918 was part of Iran, and was separated by the Russian empire in 1828. Thus what pan-Turkists refer to as "united Azerbaijan" is nothing more than an imagined community and its propagation is an effort at forging a kind of nationalism without a nation;[93]
- Post-Soviet Baku elites have used the educational system to create the image of an ancient, independent Azeri state by rewriting history and revising historical texts, through which they portray Azerbaijan as a Turkish entity and demonize the Persians and Iran as the "other";[94]
- The historical data and documents deconstruct the prevalent, ethnic-oriented discourses about the ethnic nature of the Iranian state, Farsi as an imposed language, ethnic cleansing, and genocide in Iran;[95]
- Disclosure of historical documents regarding the role of the Soviets and Baku pan-Turkist ruling elites in manipulating ethnic resurgence in Iranian Azerbaijan from 1941–6.[96]

Iranian Azeris' reaction: the endorsement of Iranian identity

Comparing the state's religious and non-state nationalist reaction to Baku's ethnic nationalist and pan-Turkist discourse toward Iran, the Iranian Azeri elites' reaction has been the most organized and enduring response. This might be a surprising and unconventional phenomenon compared to other ethnically populated countries. Except for those familiar with Iranian national history, most observers may believe that the majority of Iranian Azeris, as is the case of other Middle Eastern, Asian, European, or African ethnic communities, have politically ethnic-oriented minds and are looking for autonomy or independence from Iran. The conventional literature dominating ethnic studies reinforces such beliefs. Therefore, the role of Iranian Azeris in the national life of Iran has been disregarded or underestimated by many students of Iranian and Azerbaijani studies. Compared to other Iranians, however, Azeris have been the most ardent proponents of Iranian nationalism. In fact, Iranian nationalism as a discourse and a theoretical framework has been promoted by Azeris rather than Farsi (Persian)-speaking Iranians. The early theorists, activists, and proponents of Iranian nationalism have been Azeri figures, such as Fath Ali Khan Akhundzade,[97] Ahmad Kasravi,[98] Kazemzadeh Iranshahr,[99] Hassan Taqizadeh,[100] Mahmoud Afshar,[101] and Taqi Arani.[102] The next generation of Azeri academicians, such as Yahya Zoka,[103] Rezazadeh Shafagh,[104] Mohammad Amin Riahi,[105] Salim Naysari,[106] Hasan Anvari,[107] Manuchehr Mortazavi,[108] and educationalists such as Ebrahim Nasehi[109] and Ali Dehghan,[110] have made a significant contribution to the promotion of Iranian cultural and national identity and have engaged in reacting to the pro-Soviet, pan-Turkist discourse of *Firghe Democrat* of 1945–6. Ahmad Kasravi was the first Iranian Azeri intellectual to take a strong position against Ottoman pan-Turkists and wrote the most significant work on the Iranian identity of Azerbaijan and its Old Iranian language, *Azari*.[111] Some of these Iranian Azeris reacted to early pan-Turkist claims over Iranian Azerbaijan, and many of them have been harshly criticized as traitors to the "Azerbaijani nation" in the pan-Turkist media of the post-Soviet Azerbaijan Republic.[112]

In the post-Soviet era, when Elchibey, his Popular Front, and other political elites and printed media initially launched their irredentist claims toward Iranian Azerbaijan by raising ideas such as "united Azerbaijan" or "the question of southern Azerbaijan," Iranian Azeris were among the first to refute the historicity of such claims, beginning their historical, political and cultural research to launch an Iranian counter-argument. Kaveh Bayat, the contemporary Iranian historical researcher, wrote the first articles on pan-Turkism.[113] In his other works, he presented documentary analysis of the early pan-Turkist claims against Iran in Turkey of the 1920s, and showed how Iranian Azeri intellectuals and activists, such as Ali Sadeghi Tabrizi, Habibollah Nobakht, Taqi Arani, Moghaddam Bayat, and Rezazadeh Shafagh, were at the forefront of the fight for the defense of the Iranian identity of Azerbaijan and the Persian language.[114] It was also Bayat who, for the first time, collected and analyzed all the documents relating to the Iranian protests about the confiscation of the name "Azerbaijan" for the Muslim part of the Caucasus historically recognized as Aran. His book, *Azerbaijan Dar Mowj Khize Tarikh: Negahi be Mabahese Mellion Iran va Jarayede Baku Dar Taghire name Aran be Azerbaijan 1296–98*, demonstrates how Iranian Azeris during 1918–19 were concerned with the misuse of the name for future pan-Turkist claims against Iran.[115] In his introductory remarks to the book, Bayat wrote:

> It is surprising that today they call Aran "Azerbaijan", while Azarbaijan or "Azerbaijan" is another land beside Aran, bigger and more easily recognized. For some time, these two territories have been separated from each other and never has

> the name "Azerbaijan" been used for Aran. We have never understood why our Arani brothers who established a free government for their territory and wanted to choose a name for it, put aside their historical name and resorted to pilfering the name Azerbaijan? What kind of benefits did they hope to accrue as a result of their surprising act?[116]

Firuz Mansuri, another Iranian Azeri, has concentrated on the cultural side of the pan-Turkist challenge and has been active in publishing about the Azerbaijan Republic's claims to it. In his two-volume book on Iranian Azerbaijan,[117] Mansuri studied the historical conflict between Iran and the Ottoman Turks, describing how the Ottomans, who used to insult and humiliate the Turks,[118] and in their invasions of Iranian Azerbaijan killed its inhabitants from throughout the Safavid dynasty in 1501 to the Qajar era of the mid nineteenth century,[119] had suddenly changed to become ardent pro-Turkic elites during the Young Turk era of the late nineteenth and early twentieth centuries. His most recent work on the Azeri Turkic language in Iran,[120] which is the result of fifteen years of research and travels around the country,[121] is a comparative work showing how the 5,000 Azeri Turkish words and terms used in Iranian Azerbaijan are also used in other parts of Iran to indicate the same meaning. He argues that the Azeri Turkish language in Iran is not in fact Turkish and shares surprising similarities with Persian words and terms. He concludes by warning that the pan-Turkist circles outside and inside Iran are trying to purify Azeri from Persian influence by importing pure Turkish words and terms from Baku and Istanbul through the media and broadcasting.[122]

Outside Iran, Iranian Azeri academics have also focused their attention on the problems in the early years of Azerbaijani independence. Shireen Hunter and Touraj Atabaki are two examples of academics who have written books and articles on this issue. Hunter, a native Iranian Azeri from Tabriz, wrote one of the first articles on the question of identity in the newly independent republic.[123] When referring to the pan-Turkist irredentist trends of Azerbaijan's political elites toward Iran, Hunter's field research article emphasizes how such elites hate Iranian Azeri nationalists and how the ruling elites in Baku were worried about a possible irredentist counter-claim by Iran and its Azeri elites.[124] According to her, the existence of pro-Iranian trends among the residents of the southern part of the Azerbaijan Republic indicates that such concerns may be justified.[125] Touraj Atabaki, a native Iranian Azeri, is another example of a writer focusing on Iranian Azeris' concerns with regard to the irredentist policies of pan-Turkist groups who ruled Baku in the early 1990s and later. While writing on the roots and causes of pan-Turkism,

Atabaki explains how this irredentist trend has faced the resistance and challenge of Iranian nationalism.[126] His earlier book on the roots of the Iranian Azerbaijan crisis of 1945 was a timely work published in 1993. Relying on primary and secondary sources, Atabaki explained the internal and external causes of it.[127] He continues to be one of the most active Iranian Azeris to write about the question of ethnicity, as well as Iranian national identity and its regional challenges.[128]

Inside Iran, the Iranian Azeri academics have also focused on this issue. Javad Tabatabai, a political scientist and distinguished writer of contemporary Iranian political thought,[129] has taken issue against anti-Iranian irredentist trends and warned about the dangers facing Iran from the challenge of pan-Turkism. He has defended Persian as the national language of Iran[130] and also argued that Turkish and Azerbaijani history has been forged and fabricated. Tabatabai, during a lecture in Tabriz, emphasized that the history of the "Baku Republic" is at the heart of Iranian history.[131] Rajab Izadi, another Iranian Azeri political scientist at the University of Tabriz, was among the early Azeri students in Iran in the 1990s who warned the ruling authorities of the irredentist policies of the pan-Turkist ruling elite in Azerbaijan, as well as their small circle of proponents inside Iranian universities.[132] Coming from Ardabil, he used to publish a weekly journal, *Hafte Nameh Ardabil*, containing articles on Iranian national identity and unity.[133] While locating the history and the identity of historical Azerbaijan in Iranian history and civilization in his long analytical article on identity of Iranian Azerbaijan, he explained a century of foreign challenges coming from Russia, the Soviet Union, the Azerbaijan Republic, and Turkey, as well as the decade of internal efforts at spreading ethnic identity in Iran.[134] As a professor and dean of the faculty of political science at the University of Tabriz, he has also promoted the Iranian identity of Azerbaijan by organizing academic seminars and conferences.[135] Ja'far Jamishi Raad, another Azeri political scientist in the Azad Islamic University, the Tabriz branch, has been ardent in his anti-pan-Turkist positions in his writings, lectures, and organization of student media and conferences.[136]

Bahram Amir Ahmadian, a native of Tabriz, used his book to analyze relations between Iran and the Azerbaijan Republic.[137] While emphasizing the Iranian identity of Iranian Azerbaijan, Ahmadian presented a detailed narrative of pan-Turkist efforts and warned of the irredentist views of the ruling elites in the Republic of Azerbaijan and the manifestation of these irredentist views in the historical texts written for Azerbaijan's schools.[138] *Ata Yordu* (Fatherland), a book of the history of Azerbaijan for grade 5 students, is provided as an example. The cover of the book shows a map of Azerbaijan in which Iranian Azerbaijan and the territories beyond are considered parts of the Azerbaijan Republic.[139] According to Ahmadian, the historical narratives of such books teach irredentism to Azerbaijani students by presenting fabricated and imagined stories of the existence of a united Azerbaijan before 1828.[140] This kind of historical discussion on the Iranian identity of Azerbaijan, as opposed to the narrative of the united Azerbaijan espoused by Baku, is also reflected in the works of a young Azeri academic and political geographer, Ataollah Abdi, who researched old historical names of places in Azerbaijan to prove their Iranian identity.[141] Abdi and his colleagues, such as Mojtaba Maghsoudi, a non-Azeri Iranian professor of ethnic studies in contemporary Iran, have written critical works on the political use of ethnicity in presidential elections and its dysfunctions,[142] and Iranian Azerbaijan's integration into Iran's identity, socio-political, and economic-cultural life.[143]

The performance of the Soviet-dependent *Firghe Democrat Azerbaijan* in Iranian Azerbaijan during 1945–6 has been a point of controversy. While ethnic-oriented media, especially the Baku-based proponents of *Firghe*, used to write on the atrocities of the Iranian army against the Azerbaijani people.[144] Iranian Azeri researchers and journalists, more than others, have also contributed to the subject and have tried to shed light on the realities of those days. Rahim Nikbakht, an Iranian Azeri from Tabriz, has used historical archives and documents, including the local media of the 1940s, to disclose what he calls the atrocities of *Firghe Democrat* and its military forces during 1945–6 against the majority of Azeris who were against the pro-Moscow and pro-Baku local government.[145] He has also shown how Iranian national identity has historically had a strong place among Iranian Azeris.[146] Nikbakht presented documentary analysis of the Iranian Azeri clergy, who were against pan-Turkist and pro-*Firghe* policies.[147]

During the last fifteen years, a younger generation of Iranian Azeri students and graduates has tried to respond to irredentist views toward Iranian Azerbaijan by organizing student circles that publish pro-Iranian nationalist materials in quarterly, monthly, or weekly bilingual journals inside universities. Several of these have been published by Azeri students at Tehran University. *Vatan Yoli* has been noticeably more successful than the others in terms of the form and quality. Davood Dashtbani, the founder and chief editor of *Vatan Yoli*, has been active in giving lectures and organizing conferences related to Iranian Azerbaijan and Iranian identity and nationality.[148] *Vatan Yoli* has covered a wide variety of subjects dealing with the situation of Iranian

Azerbaijan, the foreign policies of Turkey and the Azerbaijan Republic, the Persian language, Iranian history, and Azeri Turkish poetry. Issue no. 19 of August 2012, for example, contained articles on the following subjects: Turkey's Ottomanism, an anti-Iranian book by pan-Turkist activists, a new search done in Cambridge showing that most ethnic groups in Iran have Iranian roots, a new computer game about Turkemanchai (Treaty of 1828), Persian and Turkish literature in Azerbaijan, and the life of Cyrus the Great. The journal also contains a poetry section with poems in both Azeri Turkish and Farsi, the main subject of which is patriotism and ethics.[149] *Vatan Yoli* had a special section on the importance of the discovery of *Safine Tabriz* for Azerbaijan identity and culture. *Safine* [the vessel of] *Tabriz* is an important encyclopedic manuscript from fourteenth-century Ilkhanid Iran compiled by Abu'l Majd Muhammad B. Mas'ud Tabrizi between 1321 and 1323.[150] *Safine Tabriz* contains 209 works on a wide range of subjects in both Persian and Arabic, as well as some poetry denoted by Fahlaviyat and the Iranian language of Tabriz.[151] According to its editor, this manuscript shows that at that time, Fahlawi, or Azeri Persian, was the language of Azerbaijan and had not been replaced by Turkish yet.[152]

Iran Zamin was another student journal published by a group of Azeri students whose chief editor, Payman Asadzade, was a student of theology who switched to political science. Its second issue (January 2009) contained pictures of Iranian Azeri activists and intellectuals known for their love for Iran. This included figures such as Shahriar the poet; Ahmad Kasravi the historian; Sattar Khan and Baqir Khan, two leaders of the Constitutional Revolution of 1906; Shaykh Mohammad Khiabani, an opponent of the establishment of a Turkish Republic by the Ottoman army in Tabriz (1918);[153] and Taqi Arani, an early ardent Iranian nationalist and one of the founding fathers of the Iranian Marxist left. Issues covered in the journal included the Soviet occupation of Iranian Azerbaijan, the Persian language, and Iranian nationalism.[154] Similar student journals have been published in the universities in Iranian Azerbaijan, among them *Sas* (voice) and *Azar* published at Tabriz University, and *Teribune* by Shahid Madani University of Azerbaijan in Azar Shahr and *Hoviyyat* (identity) in Ardabil University. Some of these Azeri students are also active in non-student weekly and daily printed media, such as *Navay-e Azarbaijan* in Marand and other cities in eastern and western Iranian Azerbaijan and the Ardabil provinces.[155]

Both student and non-student media have highlighted what they consider to be Baku's efforts at removing any signs of Iranian identity in the former territories of Iran. The most recent controversy emerged when the cultural authorities in the Azerbaijan Republic decided to replace the Farsi poems of Nizami Ganjavi with Turkish narratives. Khalil Yusifli, the director of the Nizami Ganjavi Centre of the Azerbaijan National Academy of Sciences, said that the Farsi poems had been put there in 1997 and had no historical value.[156] The Iranian cultural authorities, including Mohammad Ali Njafai, director of the organization for the cultural heritage of Iran, claimed that the plate with Farsi poems was hundreds of years old, and when protesting to UNESCO for replacement of the original plates, he characterized Yusifli's decision as an attempt to distort the true identity of Nizami Ganjavi as a poet who wrote in the Farsi language.[157] Iranian Azeris, when protesting against the decision, emphasized the Iranian identity of Nizami and his love for Iran.[158] They then formed a campaign for more organized efforts at defending Nizami's heritage and identity.[159]

Young Iranian Azeris' nationalist activities against what they consider to be the pan-Turkist conspiracy against Iran have been more remarkable outside the universities. Examples include their publications, in print, online, and on social media. They have also been active in organizing academic meetings and conferences on issues related to Iranian Azerbaijan, such as the crisis of 1945–6.[160] Some of these young Azeris are active in different cities of Iranian Azerbaijan, especially Tabriz, and some are established in Tehran. Salar Seifoddini, whose writings have appeared in both local Azeri media in Azerbaijan and in Tehran, started his work in Tabriz, where he wrote for local papers such as *Tarhe Now* and *Misaagh*.[161] He then moved to Tehran, becoming one of the most dynamic young nationalist Iranian Azeris. His writings on the role of Persian language and issues related to the use of local languages in the Iranian educational system have been published in the Iranian media. He along with his friends, including nationalist-oriented Iranian Kurds such as Ehsan Hushmand[162] and Habibollah Fazeli,[163] have argued that "the teaching of local languages" is different from "teaching in local languages," favoring the former at the expense of the latter.[164] In recent years he has organized an annual conference on 12 December, known in Iran as the "salvation day of Azerbaijan" (*Ruze Nejate Azarbaijan*) from the Soviet occupation in 1946. Both the Baku-based *Express* newspaper and GunAz TV have reacted negatively to the annual conference, viewing it as a forum for anti-Azerbaijani Iranian nationalist chauvenists.[165] Less than a decade ago, Salar and a number of other Azeris founded a website called *Azariha* (Azeris), which is considered the most active and effective site in defending Iranian identity and territorial integrity vis-à-vis the pan-Turkist media in the Azerbaijan Republic and the West. On several occasions, *Azariha* has faced reactions from the pan-Turkist circles in Turkey and the Azerbaijan Republic.[166] Subsequently, other Iranian Azeris started using the virtual world to establish similar anti-pan-Turkist internet sites: such as *Hoveyyat* by Laila Hosaynian, based in Meshkin Shahr, and *Vatan Khahan* by Abdol Abdolizadeh, run out of Tabriz. Salar has written in most daily newspapers in Tehran and some academic quarterly journals, using conceptual and theoretical frameworks to explain Iranian national identity and ethnic issues of contemporary Iran.[167]

Among the younger generation of Azeri activists who have Iranian nationalist tendencies, it is worth mentioning Hojjat Kalashi, a graduate of political science. Originally from Ardabil, the capital of Ardabil province, Kalashi has perhaps more radical Iranian nationalist-oriented views on the question of Iran–Azerbaijan relations. In some respects he is different from other Iranian Azeris because of his engagement in Iranian nationalist political parties. Kalashi is the chair of the youth organization of the pan-Iranist party and has a popular image among the present Iranian nationalist political groupings. As an Azeri, Kalashi has explicitly expressed his views on the irredentist trends reflected in the Republic of Azerbaijan and Turkey. In an interview at the last meeting of SANLM in Baku in April 2013, at which members of the Azerbaijan parliament, including Nasib Nasibli, took part, Kalashi rejected the idea of neutrality by the Azeri government regarding the issue. From his perspective, "Iran in general and Azerbaijan in particular are not mouthfuls to be digested in the stomach of a pan-Turkist identity,"[168] and that "at the same time that the state of Azerbaijan is a forged construct, the concept of south Azerbaijan [also] does not have a real and historical embodiment."[169]

Outside the universities, as has been mentioned, young Iranian Azeris have been active in publishing. Such activities are more concentrated in Iranian Azerbaijan than outside it and the role of its capital, Tabriz, is remarkable in this regard. One circle organized around Jalal Mohammadi has been especially active. For over a decade, his weekly publication of *Misaagh* played a vanguard role in confronting the challenge of pan-Turkism to Iranian Azerbaijan. Established in late 2000, the main goal of *Misaagh* was to pinpoint the role and position of Azerbaijan in Iranian history, culture, and political life, thus countering the pan-Turkist propaganda about the alleged Turkish identity of Azerbaijan. One important theme of *Misaagh* articles and reports was that the Azerbaijan Republic has its roots in the history, culture, and civilization of Iran. The emphasis in this regard was on the omnipresent place of the Farsi (Persian) language in Azerbaijan and the historic role of Azerbaijanis in promoting Farsi and Persian literature.[170] Criticizing the pan-Turkist characterizations of Farsi as an imposed language in Azerbaijan and considering it the national language of all Iranians,[171] *Misaagh* emphasized the historical presence of the Farsi language in the Azerbaijan Republic too.[172] *Misaagh* directed its attention to *Shahnameh*, the Iranian national epic poem, and its author Ferdowsi.[173] *Misaagh* published articles and news on Islamic activists, such as the Islamic Party of Azerbaijan.[174] *Misaagh* had good connections with non-pan-Turkist elites of the Azerbaijan Republic, such as Zartosht Alizadeh, leader of the Social Democratic Party of Azerbaijan, and would reflect its positive views on Iran.[175] The weekly included many documentary articles written on the nature and the policies of *Firghe Democrat* of 1945–6, especially its dependence on Moscow and Baku.[176] One specific feature of the weekly was the many reports of trips made by its chief editor and other staff to the Azerbaijan Republic in order to provide a different picture to that offered by pan-Turkist and anti-Iranian elites and media. The general message of these reports was that many ordinary people and socio-cultural and political elites[177] have a positive view of Iran and Iranian culture and civilization.[178] Nasser Hamrang, an Iranian Azeri author and journalist close to *Misaagh*, published reports of his trips to Azerbaijan in which a different picture of Azerbaijan, its ruling family, its socio-political corruption, and its people was depicted.[179]

Jalal Mohammadi and his team, who published *Misaagh*, also established *Jamiyyate Vatan* (Homeland Association), an NGO concentrating on Iranian Azerbaijan and the Caucasus. *Jamiyyate Vatan* organized conferences and published volumes of an occasional bilingual Farsi and Azeri Turkish language journal, called *Vatan*. In its first volume, one article designated Iran the spiritual center of Azeris worldwide, which seemed to be a counter-claim by Iranian Azeris in response to the formation of the World Azerbaijani Congress (WAK) by Heydar Aliyev several months earlier, prior to the establishment of *Jamiyyate Vatan*.[180] The second issue of *Vatan* published an article on the responsibility of Iranian Azeris toward Azeri minorities outside Iran. It conveyed the message that for Iranian Azeris, the Azerbaijan Republic comprises Azeri minorities outside Iran.[181] After *Misaagh* stopped publication in 2007, Mohammadi started publishing *Azarbaijan*, a daily in Tabriz that continued his anti pan-Turkist line of thought and his defense of Persian language,[182] Iranian culture, and civilization.

While both *Misaagh* and *Vatan* were active in the first half of the 2000s, another institution called *Moasseseye Frhangi va Motaleate Baynolmelali Aran* (Aran Cultural and International Studies Institution) emerged in Tabriz. Still continuing its work, the Aran Institution (using the historical name of the Azerbaijan Republic, Aran) gradually increased its activities using more modern social media and virtual networks. It started publishing the occasional journal *Aran*, which later became a quarterly covering news, reports, and analytical articles about the Caucasus, particularly the Azerbaijan Republic. Its first issue published in 2002 covered subjects such as Aran or Azerbaijan,[183] Stalin and *Firghe Democrat Azarbaijan*, Nardaran events, Golestan and Turkmanchai treaties from a different perspective, amongst others. The journal changed its name to *Azar-Aran* in 2013. The Aran Institution has held regular conferences on Caucasus affairs, including the Karabakh crisis,[184] the life and the struggles of Alikram Aliyev, the founder of the Islamic Party of Azerbaijan,[185] the Golestan Treaty of 1812 and its consequences,[186] and the Turkamanchai Treaty of 1828, which led to the separation of the southern Caucasus from Iran.[187] The quarterly also covered various historical and contemporary subjects, such as the Karabakh crisis, Islamic movements in the Azerbaijan Republic,[188] Iranian culture and civilization in the Caucasus,[189] Armenian affairs,[190] anti-Islamic policies of the political ruling elites in Baku,[191] and Azerbaijan–Israel relations,[192] amongst others. The Aran Institution established its special news agency, Aran News (*Khabargozary-e Araan*), covering different socio-political and cultural-economic news, reports, and articles about the daily events in the Azerbaijan Republic and the Caucasus in general, available in three languages (Farsi, Azeri Turkish, and Turkey's Turkish). While presenting a moderate stance regarding Iran–Azerbaijan relations and its promotion, Aran News did not hesitate to criticize the Baku government for its anti-Islamic and anti-Iranian positions in domestic and foreign policy.[193]

The daily newspapers, weekly journals, and magazines in Tabriz and other big cities in Iranian Azerbaijan such as Ardabil or Ourumiyeh have touched on political or cultural issues regarding Iran–Azerbaijan relations or criticized the irredentist pan-Turkist view.[194] A newspaper with more nationalist tendencies appeared in Tabriz called *Tarhe Now* (New Plan), founded by Reza Rabbani, as a student-run semi-monthly newspaper in 2006, before it was turned into a weekly and used to cover news and articles about Iranian national identity and heritage.[195] Later, in the second half of 2014, it became a daily, maintaining the same content intentions. *Tarhe Now* more than any other daily newspaper in Iranian Azerbaijan has focused on subjects such as the role of foreign secret services in instigating ethnic problems in Iran,[196] pan-Turkism in the Caucasus,[197] and Persian language and national unity.[198]

Part of the reaction to the Azerbaijan Republic and its irredentist policies toward Iran also comes from Iranian Azeri religious and political elites. In fact, the Shiite clergies played a notable role in confronting the Soviet policies in Iranian Azerbaijan during 1941–6. In addition to protesting against the Soviets and Baku pan-Turkist policies of that time, they also wrote down their daily memories.[199] Representatives of the Islamic Republic's supreme leader in the Azeri provinces, the highest ranking of whom are mostly in the position of imams of Friday prayers (*imam jom'e*), have during the past two decades criticized what they call the interventionist policies of the Baku government. Ayatollah Mojtahed Shabestari, the Imam Jom'e of Tabriz, raised his voice on several occasions. The most controversial incident was at the Second World Azerbaijani Congress meeting held in Baku in June 2006.[200] Shabestari also criticized the 2012 Eurovision song contest in Azerbaijan and asked the Baku authorities to stop what he considered the "gay parade" in a Muslim country.[201] The Imam Jom'e of Ardabil, Ayatollah Ameli, has also reacted on several occasions. In one case, on 29 May 2010, Ameli criticized pan-Turkist figures such as Abulfaz Elchibey and claimed that he had a hand in the massacre of the Azeri Shiites in Khojali.[202] Ali Akbar Akrami, Imam Jom'e of Sarab, has accused pan-Turkist groups of trying to misuse the earthquake of Azerbaijan in August 2012.[203]

Beside Azeri clergies, Iranian Azeris in state institutions have also taken issue with respect to the ethnic problems between Iran and the Azerbaijan Republic. On several occasions, the Azeri members of the Iranian parliament (*Majles Showraye Eslami*) have reacted to developments in the Azerbaijan Republic. Mir Tajeddini, a representative of Tabriz, has been very active in this respect. In addition to his critical reaction to what was considered the insulting of high-ranking Iranian leaders by Baku-based newspapers, *Gun* and *New Fact*,[204] he bitterly criticized the views of two members of the Azerbaijan parliament, Asim Mollazadeh and Sabir Rustam Khanli, who had expressed irredentist views about Iranian Azerbaijan in a round table called "European values and the Great Azerbaijan," on 16 June 2007 in Baku. Tajeddini also asked the Iranian parliament to scrutinize more precisely what happened when "the former Iranian land was separated from us by the Russians as the result of Golestan and Turkamachai treaties."[205] Some Iranian Azeri members of parliament protested at what they called "anti-Islamic" media in Baku. One example was when all the Azeri members of parliament protested against what they perceived as the Baku-based newspaper *San'at*'s insult against the Prophet Mohammad.[206] On another occasion, 209 members of parliament, including all Azeri members, harshly criticized the Turkish publication of the book *The Satanic Verses* by Salman Rushdie.[207]

A more active member of parliament from Ardabil, and the deputy of the National Security Committee of the Parliament, Mansour Haghighat Pour, has been sensitive to what he considers the anti-Iranian policies of Baku's ruling and political elites and their media. In response to the question of local languages in Iran frequently raised by GunAz TV, he emphasized the role of Farsi as both the national language of Iran and the mother tongue of Azerbaijan too.[208] He emphasized that the present Turkish language of Azerbaijan replaced the historical, native Iranian language after the arrival of the Seljuk Turkish tribes in the region.[209] On the controversy over the establishment of an academy of Turkish language in Iranian Azerbaijan, Haghighat Pour rejected the establishment of the academy by arguing that it was a political matter and that Azersis were originally Iranian but speak Turkish.[210] As a former member of the Revolutionary Guards who had closely followed the Nagorno-Karabakh war of 1993, Haghighat Pour reacted to the Azerbaijan Republic's widespread claim that Iran sided with Armenia and helped them against Azerbaijan.[211] He used his personal experience from when he was a member of the Revolutionary Guard and engaged in the Karabakh war to reject the aforementioned claim. According to him, Iran not only gave Azerbaijan humanitarian assistance, but also military equipment.[212] In a message to the people of Azerbaijan Republic on the occasion of Nowruz 1392 (March 2013), he referred to such help. Later, when Haghiaghat Pour's claims were refuted by a member of parliament in Baku, Siyavush Novruzov, and executive director of the Yeni Azerbaijan Party, Haghighat Pour wrote a letter directed to the people of Azerbaijan in which he disclosed more facts about the Iranian support of Azeris. Haghighat Pour claimed that he was a special adviser to Heydar Aliyev, the acting Minister of Defense and Chair of the Azerbaijan parliament. As he put it, Aliyev was going to give him "the Merit Medal of Azerbaijan," but Haghighat Pour rejected this because of political concerns.[213] Haghighat Pour has gone so far as to allege that "I have several thousand pages of written reports and pictures and more than one hundred hours of video that confirm our help to Azerbaijanis in the Karabakh war."[214] Other Iranian Azeri elites familiar with the conflict expressed similar views.[215]

Irredentism may backfire: Iranian nationalism versus ethnic nationalistic intrigues

Southern Azerbaijan or Northern Iran?

There are essentially two discursive wars being fought over competing nationalist narratives. As discussed previously, the first is between Azerbaijan's ruling elites and political parties on the one hand, and Iran's ruling religious elites on the other. The second is between pan-Turkist state institutions and non-state actors in Baku against Iranian Azeri elites over concepts such as "united Azerbaijan" and "south Azerbaijan." This discursive war has subsequently produced counter-narratives and claims raised by Iranian Azeris. In response to the idea of a united Azerbaijan and claims that the two lands around the Aras river had been one united Azerbaijani state, the Iranian Azeris argue that the so-called united entity never existed and the whole region was part of greater Iran up to the Russo-Persian wars of 1801–28. With respect to the more important idea of a future united Azerbaijan, Iranian Azeris then propose that it is better for the Azerbaijan Republic to join Iran, and not the other way around. Although this issue has not been studied independently, there are signs that most Iranian Azeris share the view.[216] As Brown writes:

> In private conversation, Azeri students from northwestern Iran scoffed at the idea of being part of the local Azerbaijani independence movement. In contrast, they cited the leading role many Azeris play in the Iranian economy and politics. The most important figure in Iran, the Supreme Leader 'Ali Khamenei, is Azeri, as are several government ministers.[217]

In comparison to the Azerbaijan Republic, the political and cultural elites in Turkey are more familiar with the general stance of Iranian Azeris on the idea of a united Azerbaijan. In a roundtable on Iranian Azerbaijan on Saman Yolu, a TV channel affiliated with the Fethullah Gülen movement, in response to a suggestion that Iranian Azerbaijan is welcoming Turkey's call for separating from Iran, Fehim Tastekin, the Turkish researcher and journalist, said: "When we approach Iranian Azeri and raise the issue [of united Azerbaijan], the first thing they say is that it is better that upper Azerbaijan joins us; it means not the separation of Iranian Azerbaijan but the annexation of Azerbaijan Republic to Iran."[218] This view has been raised especially by active Iranian Azeris who monitor the irredentist moves of pan-Turkist institutions such as the World Azerbaijani Congress. In reaction to WAC's claim, also challenging Ilham Aliyev's ambition that "I am the president of all Azerbaijani people,"[219] *Vatan*, the formal organ of *Anjomane Vatan* in Tabriz, raised a counter-argument claiming that Iran is the fatherland of all Azeris around the world:

> We, the Azeris of Iran, have a historical responsibility for the formation of the present and future history of diversified Azeri minorities dispersed around the world and the consolidation of their spiritual, cultural, historical and religious ties to Iran. If we fail to take this responsibility, our sons and the future generations will not forgive us. The foundation of "the center for world Muslim Azeris" by active

cultural elites and intellectuals of Iran's Azeris would be an important step toward the realization of such responsibility.[220]

Ayatollah Shabestari, the most powerful representative of Ayatollah Khamenei, the supreme leader of the Islamic Republic, in Iranian Azerbaijan, once criticized the irredentist idea of a united Azerbaijan and announced: "If it is supposed to talk about the question of annexation, it is they who should join us, and in that time we will demand that our former cities return to us again ... our Iranian identity will never be distorted."[221] This announcement followed Shabestari's remarks that demonstrations against the Azerbaijan Republic began in Tabriz. During these demonstrations, some of the protesters held banners depicting the annulment of the Golestan and Turkamanchai treaties of 1812 and 1828 respectively, which separated the present Azerbaijan Republic from Iran. Local media in Iranian Azerbaijan have also published articles written by Iranian Azeris in which the annulment of the two treaties was discussed.[222] Two weeks later, another demonstration erupted in Tabriz and other cities in protest over what was considered an insult to the Prophet Muhammad in Baku-based media.[223] In April 2013, the reaction of the Azeri media in Iranian Azerbaijan to the meeting of SANLM likely encouraged the chief editor of the radical newspaper *Kayhan*, Hossein Shariatmadari, to write about proposing to Ilham Aliyev the idea of a referendum to be held in the Azerbaijan Republic about annexation to Iran, as was similarly done in Bahrain in 1970.[224]

The concept of a "southern Azerbaijan" has also drawn its own counterclaim from Iranian Azeri elites. In late 2002, the concept of "*Irane Shomali*" (northern Iran), referring to the Azerbaijan Republic, appeared in the Azeri media in Iran. The weekly *Misaagh* in Tabriz then popularized the concept in mid-2006. Later, two Iranian Azeri authors from Tabriz[225] and Ardabil[226] elaborated on the concept and its connotations. From then on, other printed media in Iranian Azerbaijan began using the term "northern Iran" instead of "Azerbaijan." It is even said that Ayatollah Shabestari used those words on several occasions during Friday prayers in Tabriz.[227] At the same time, news came on air that a magazine called *Irane Shomali* was being published in Ardabil, and that "hundreds" of its first issue had been sold in a few days in other Iranian Azerbaijani cities. According to the report:

> The magazine of *Irane Shomali* has the aim of disclosing the anti-Iranian policies of the regime ruling over Irane Shomali (Republic of Azerbaijan) and reflects the ideas of those who support the annexation of this region to Iran. ... the magazine is a common work by a group of authors in Iran and Baku ... it can be said that it is a

limited reaction of Ardabil and Baku intellectuals to the anti-Iranian actions of Baku regime and its widespread distortion of history.[228]

Before the magazine was published, a series of reports about a group called the Movement for the Liberation of Northern Iran (*Harkate Azadibakhshe Irane Shomali*) appeared in the Tabriz media, followed by more reports in mid-2006.[229] The article concluded with the following claim: "the Movement for the Liberation of Northern Iran is a cultural and political trend and movement to which all people, particularly the elites, authors, artists and political activists can join."[230] When the magazine was published in Ardabil and distributed in Iranian Azerbaijan and Tehran, the authorities in Baku reacted sharply to it. Although the printed version of the magazine was discontinued after nine issues, a website carrying the same name continued the magazine's work on the internet,[231] publishing news, articles, and reports about the Republic of Azerbaijan, or what it calls *Irane Shomali*.

In recent years, one aspect of the pro-Iranian orientation of Iranian Azeris has manifested itself in the form of collective actions and petitions with respect to the goals they seek to achieve. In protest to the annual WAC meeting in Baku, more than a hundred Azeri intellectuals, students, and cultural elites directed a letter to the Iranian Foreign Ministry and the Iranian ambassador in Baku, asking for a more definite stance toward the anti-Iranian policies of the Azerbaijan Republic. The signatories specifically asked the Iranian government to include special subjects in school and university textbooks about the Perso-Russian wars of 1801–28, which resulted in the present Republic of Azerbaijan being taken from Iran. They also asked President Rouhani to withdraw its full recognition of the Baku regime and change it to *de facto* recognition.[232] Dozens of Azeri activists signed the most recent petition, which was focused on cultural and political issues, and criticized the controversial removal of the Ferdowsi statue from a circle in Salmas in western Iranian Azerbaijan. The municipality of Salmas justified the removal by saying that the statue was not a good one and they were going to replace the name of the circle Ferdowsi with *Enghelab* (revolution). However, many Iranian nationalists argued that the decision was part of a pan-Turkist policy by those who infiltrated the city council of Salmas. Dozens of Iranian Azeris, among them political elites, students, authors, and poets, signed this petition asking for the return of the statue.[233] While the statue was returned to its original place on 27 February 2015, its removal had initiated a widespread nationalist campaign and protests throughout Iran in early 2015.

Conclusion

As Iran–Azerbaijan Republic relations continue, signs indicate a trend in which the ruling elites in both Tehran and Baku would prefer good neighborhood ties over continued tensions, which do not benefit either side. This stance has been demonstrated on different occasions, including the 20 April 2015 visit of Iranian Defense Minister Hossein Dehghan and his counterpart Zakir Hasanov, at which both emphasized defense and security cooperation.[234] Another sign was the Azerbaijani Foreign Ministry's positive remarks regarding the Iranian nuclear negotiations, saying that "this political framework will provide an opportunity to further peace, security, and stability in the region and beyond."[235] Despite these signs of goodwill, however, the factors behind these tensions still persist and make the future of relations contentious.

Although the Islamic Republic of Iran with its Islamic–Shiite nationalism has also engaged in supporting anti-state forces such as the Islamists against the Republic of Azerbaijan, the historical reading of Tehran's policies indicates that it is more of a retaliatory action than a real irredentist claim over Azerbaijan. This is also true regarding the non-state Iranian nationalist forces, either Azeri or non-Azeri, inside Iran. Although Ilham Aliyev has tried to avoid accusations against his government of taking any directly anti-Iranian ethnic nationalist positions, the continued activities of irredentist elements such as WAC or SANLM and the support given to them by Azerbaijani authorities, whether state or non-state, in conjunction with the continued contradictory reports on the US or Israeli use of territory in the Azerbaijan Republic for military action against Iran,[236] all make Tehran and non-state actors such as Iranian nationalist circles, particularly Iranian Azeris, skeptical about Baku's intentions. However, the recent absence of any state or parliament representatives at the WAC congress of 18 April 2015 in Istanbul was a positive indication to Iran of improved intentions for goodwill.[237] But more important than the issue of WAC or groups such as SANLM is the issue of the continuous institutionalization of ethnic nationalist irredentism in Azerbaijan Republic's media and its educational system. The Islamic Republic and Iranian nationalists are not satisfied with Baku's intentions. As one analyst has put it: "In spite of Azerbaijan disclaimers that it did not support the Azeri nationalist activities of NLMSA or MUN, feathers fly in Tehran when maps are published showing the Azeri flag fluttering over both Azerbaijan and Azerbaijan–Iran on the cover of the 5th grade primary school textbooks."[238]

As I have tried to show here, most literature on Iran's experience of ethnicity, particularly with respect to Iranian Azerbaijan, has relied on conventional readings of ethnic studies that consider the phenomenon to be universal. On the other hand, most of them have used either secondary sources or the literature produced by the Iranian opposition. Few studies have tried to do field research based on primary and original sources in order to see the other side of the picture. As I have tried to explain in other works,[239] the experience of Iran in ethnicity and nationality is different from other cases. Students of Iranian Azerbaijan studies mostly rely on the over-exaggerated dichotomy of Fars–Turk conflict which has deeper roots in abstract theoretical literature, such as Marxist–Leninist works and modernization paradigms, or in pan-Turkist dogmas. The past experience of Iran–Azerbaijan Republic relations shows that the latter's elites have been under the influence of both sources and that their ultimate hope is that the vision of a united Azerbaijan will be realized. For nearly a quarter of a century the idea of Azerbaijani reunification has been raised in the Azerbaijan Republic, but without much success. Here, the role of Iranian Azeris in the promotion of Iranian nationalism, Shiite Islam, and the Farsi language and Iranian cultural heritage has been widely underestimated. As Abrahamian maintains, "The Azeri issue is not a typical 'nationality problem.' It is much more complex and nuanced. Most Azeris identify themselves as Iranians and not just because of Shi'ism. There is a strong Iranian identity."[240]

On the other hand, the Azerbaijan Republic itself is not a monolithic society in terms of ethnicity and identity. It suffers from the same problems it believes Iran is struggling with. As Safizadeh's personal observations suggest, the people in the Azerbaijan Republic "are more sympathetic to the Iranian heritage"[241] than Turkey's. Moreover, as discussions among Azerbaijan Republic elites tend to indicate, Azerbaijani society itself is not accustomed to the idea of a Turkish identity, since elements of Islam and Iran continue to bear their own seals on Azerbaijani identity.[242] This of course does not mean that Tehran's religious rulers wish to install a religious government in Azerbaijan. The more serious challenge for the Azerbaijan Republic would be Iranian nationalism backed by a would-be future state of Iran as a strong regional power tired of the ethnic nationalist irredentist intrigues of Baku. As Shireen Hunter has written, the Azerbaijani ruling elites fear that ethnic nationalist irredentism will fight back,[243] and that in this clash of nationalisms between the ethnic nationalism of the Azerbaijan Republic and Iranian nationalism, the Iranian state and its Azeri and non-Azeri Iranianist elites demand the Azerbaijan Republic's return to Iran. This, of course, is a futuristic vision; and ultimately a more rational, realistic, and beneficial choice would be the promotion of bilateral interests based on their common heritage, devoid of any irredentist ambitions.

PART II

SOFT POWER AT WORK

6

"UN-CIVIL SOCIETY" AND THE SOURCES OF RUSSIAN INFLUENCE IN WEST ASIA

THE SOUTH CAUCASUS

Jeffrey Mankoff

The conflict in Ukraine has focused attention on many post-Soviet states' efforts to maintain a strategic balance between Moscow and the West at a time of deepening confrontation. Even before the conflict, the post-Soviet region comprising Eastern Europe, the South Caucasus, and (to a lesser degree) Central Asia had emerged as both one of the principal sources of estrangement between Russia and the West, as well as the chessboard on which the resulting competition has played out. Russia and the West are each seeking in their own ways to influence the strategic orientation as well as the internal political and economic make-up of these post-Soviet states, but their approaches and the range of hard and soft power tools available to them diverge in several ways.[1]

Compared to the United States or the European Union, the effectiveness of Russian soft power is enhanced by the enduring political, economic, and social linkages between Moscow and its former dependencies. Russian soft power in the region includes both the passive force of a shared culture, including the role of Russian as a post-Soviet *lingua franca*, similarities in the political and social make-up of all the post-Soviet countries including Russia, and large flows of migrants from the smaller states to Russia—as well as the active deployment of financial, informational, and mobilization tools to influence political outcomes in neighboring states.

Despite the extensive levers of control that Russia has available to it in its neighborhood, many officials believe that the West has outmaneuvered Russia in the employment of soft power, particularly through the proliferation of civil society and non-governmental organizations throughout the former Soviet Union over the past two decades. As corrupt regimes in Georgia, Ukraine (twice), and Kyrgyzstan (twice) have fallen under rising pressure from civil society, Russia has grown increasingly alarmed. The Kremlin has come to see "colored revolutions," as well as the activities of anti-government protesters in Russia itself, as the consequences of a deliberate Western campaign to promote regime change and the curtailment of Russian influence. Moscow has focused in particular on the range of civil society groups: anti-corruption campaigners, pro-democracy activists, journalists, human rights defenders, and others, as part of a Western-backed fifth column whose *raison d'être* is less the promotion of good governance, and more the advancement of Western strategic interests at Russian expense.

In response, Moscow has increasingly cracked down on civil society groups at home—especially those that receive foreign funding—while seeking to match what it sees as the West's cultivation of civil society as a tool of diplomatic influence.[2] Partially in response to the West's open support for civil society groups (including through government bodies like the US Agency for International Development and the National Endowment for Democracy), Moscow now actively cultivates parallel groups that mirror such bodies, but which promote illiberal values and actively support Russian foreign policy objectives.

Such organizations typically emphasize promotion of Russian culture and collaboration with ethnic Russians and other groups ("compatriots") which Moscow sees as maintaining a special tie to Russia. What distinguishes them from outwardly similar organizations backed by Western governments is the extent to which they are closely integrated with the state's official diplomatic and political establishment and are responsive to Kremlin direction, as well as the typically conservative and openly pro-Russian ideology they support. They generally seek to establish a narrative favorable to Russian strategic objectives and, in times of crisis, to obfuscate and sow uncertainty.[3] Long-established institutions like the Russian Orthodox Church, associations of Russian "compatriots," as well as newly created activist groups (quasi non-governmental organizations, or QUANGOs) are all important components of Moscow's influence operations.

Such organizations generally operate within the confines of host countries' laws, but despite efforts to portray themselves as grass-roots organizations operating on the basis of local considerations, they are primarily responsive to Russian direction, and often receive funding from official or semi-official Russian sources. As Moscow's aim with these organizations is typically the opposite of what Western-funded civil society groups seek, that is, transparency, representative democratization, and a free press, they are in some sense a simulacrum of civil society rather than the genuine article, a kind of "uncivil society" whose principal aims are not the betterment of local inhabitants but support for Russian foreign policy objectives.[4]

This Russian-backed "uncivil society" operates in the West through entities like the RT media group, not to mention the range of populist parties of the Left and Right that receive Russian funds, but its effects are greater in the post-Soviet region due to the inherited linkages tying these states to Russia. The operation of Russian soft power in the South Caucasus has received less attention compared to Ukraine or the Baltic states. In the South Caucasus, Russia faces less external scrutiny, but also a more complex regional environment, which includes serious fragmentation within and among the states of the South Caucasus, as well as the competing ambitions of other regional powers such as Turkey, Iran, and the EU.

Armenia faces comparatively limited pressure from Russian-sponsored uncivil society, since Moscow already exerts a high degree of control over Armenia's economic and security environment through more direct means. Azerbaijan, with a highly centralized government and significant restrictions on the operations of civil society, faces pressure in particular via Russian involvement with its ethnic minority communities. It is Georgia, though, with a comparatively open political system and strong orientation towards Europe, that faces the widest range of challenges from such organizations, including Russian-backed QUANGOs, politicized religious institutions, and mobilization of ethnic minorities.

South Caucasus: the regional context

Russian diplomacy regards the former Soviet Union as Moscow's top foreign policy priority. The post-Soviet region is still unofficially described by many

Russians as the "near abroad," and Moscow considers it a region where Russia maintains "privileged interests."[5]

Within this framework, the South Caucasus occupies a unique place, in that it remains both deeply fragmented internally and a zone of confrontation among a range of outside powers.[6] Moscow faces a multi-sided competition for influence in the region that involves not only the EU (with backing from the United States) but also major regional powers like Turkey and Iran. Turkey is a strategic ally of Azerbaijan, and facilitates Georgia's ability to resist Russian influence by providing access to energy and global markets. Turkish support for Azerbaijan stems from a shared cultural heritage, but more importantly from Azerbaijan's conflict with Armenia over Nagorno-Karabakh.[7] Iran, meanwhile, has long supported Armenia, while pursuing a more complex relationship with Azerbaijan, colored by concern about irredentism among the tens of millions of ethnic Azeris living in northern Iran. China is increasingly interested in the South Caucasus as well, seeing it as an important transportation corridor for the planned Silk Road Economic Belt and a target for foreign investment.

The strategic significance of the South Caucasus for Russia is also connected to the region's location astride the principal route by which oil and gas from the Caspian Sea region reach markets in Europe. Since the collapse of the Soviet Union, the US and its European allies have sought, with mixed success, to reduce Europe's dependence on Russian hydrocarbons by developing new sources of production in the Caspian waters off Azerbaijan, Kazakhstan, and Turkmenistan. Bringing this Caspian energy to Europe without transiting the territory of Russia (or Iran) requires pipelines through the South Caucasus. Pipelines outside Russian control, such as the Baku–Tbilisi–Ceyhan oil pipeline, have played a critical role in allowing Azerbaijan and Georgia to reduce their economic, and hence political, dependence on Moscow, leaving Russia to search for other means of asserting its influence in these states.

Russia is also interested in the South Caucasus because it borders the increasingly unstable Russian North Caucasus, which has seen two major wars in Chechnya and a spiraling jihadist insurgency in the decades since the Soviet collapse. Ethnic and economic ties between the North and South Caucasus also represent an important tie between the region and Russia (although also a source of Russian vulnerability, since North Caucasus militants have at times found refuge across the border in areas such as Georgia's remote Pankisi Gorge).[8]

The tools available to Moscow in its efforts to maintain the South Caucasus as a zone where Russian influence is paramount are considerable. Hard military power plays a role, especially in Armenia, which hosts around 5,000 Russian troops at a military base in Gyumri along with a considerable number of Russian security forces. This Russian military contingent was initially deployed ostensibly to defend Armenia against Azerbaijan (and Turkey) in the context of the struggle for control of Nagorno-Karabakh, one of a series of "frozen conflicts" dotting the post-Soviet region that Moscow uses to manipulate relations among its neighbors and exert influence over their politics.[9] As Armenia's borders with Azerbaijan and Turkey have been closed since the height of the Karabakh conflict in the early 1990s, Armenia is also dependent on Russia, and to a lesser degree Iran, for its access to the global economy. Armenia is one of Russia's closest allies among the post-Soviet states, participating in Russian-sponsored multilateral organizations like the Eurasian Economic Union and the Collective Security Treaty Organization.

Russian hard power plays a somewhat different role in Moscow's relations with both Azerbaijan and Georgia. Neither is formally allied with Russia and, to a considerable degree, both have succeeded in extricating themselves from direct Russian control over the past two decades, largely thanks to their energy connections with Europe. Nonetheless, both Azerbaijan and Georgia are vulnerable to Russian hard power. Georgia felt the impact of Russian hard power directly in 2008, when Russian military forces seized the break-away regions of South Ossetia and Abkhazia, which Moscow then recognized as independent states, following Georgian President Mikheil Saakashvili's ill-advised attempt to recover South Ossetia by force. Since 2008, the Russian military has tightened its grip on both South Ossetia and Abkhazia, including a 2014 security pact that gives Moscow direct control over Abkhazia's military and foreign affairs.[10] Both break-away regions now host Russian bases, whose garrisons can continue to threaten military operations against Georgia should Tbilisi, for instance, proceed with its ambitions to join NATO.[11]

Unlike its South Caucasus neighbors, Azerbaijan hosts no Russian troops on its territory, but its security environment remains heavily shaped by Russian military power. Azerbaijan's primary foreign policy objective is the reintegration of Nagorno-Karabakh, which was occupied by Russian-backed Armenian forces during the 1992–4 conflict. Given Azerbaijan's energy wealth, it spends vastly more on its military than does Armenia (Azerbaijani military spending is estimated to be greater than Armenia's entire state budget). These spending figures do not entirely reflect the balance of power on the ground; foreign observers generally rate Azerbaijan's military capability as inferior to that of Armenia, which inherited a greater share of Soviet equipment and personnel, while Nagorno-Karabakh's mountainous geography works to the advantage of the defending side, although Baku's successful offensive in April 2016 called some of these assumptions into question.[12] Nonetheless, the presence of Russian forces next door in Armenia remains critical to the overall balance, especially given the close ties between Azerbaijan and Turkey, and Armenian fears about possible Turkish intervention in any renewed conflict with Baku. Of course, Russia's role is somewhat ambiguous, insofar as it provides Armenia with security guarantees both bilaterally and through the CSTO, but also supplies arms to both sides.

Russian soft power tools

While Russian hard power looms in the background of the various rivalries dotting the South Caucasus, soft power plays an important role too. Russia understands the concept of soft power somewhat differently from how Western states do. For one, the Kremlin views soft power as a tool of coercion more than of persuasion. Moscow uses tactics like bribery, blackmail, collusion, control of strategic infrastructure, and the mobilization or "securitization" of identity as normal elements of its foreign policy.[13] Russia's understanding of soft power is also closely tied to what it considers humanitarian diplomacy.[14] In other words, activities that most states see as falling purely in the humanitarian sphere are for Russia explicitly linked to the pursuit of diplomatic and strategic aims. This duality is especially pronounced with regard to Russian support for ethnic Russians, Russian speakers, and "compatriots" throughout the former Soviet Union, and beyond in some cases.

Drawing on the Soviet legacy of support for cultural and humanitarian organizations as tools of Cold War diplomacy, Russia's contemporary use of soft power aims at shaping a narrative within targeted states and populations about the legitimacy of Russian objectives, or at least the acceptance of multiple truths, something the historian Timothy Snyder has called "applied post-modernism."[15]

Rather than a teleological belief in the triumph of liberal democracy, the narrative that Russian soft power promotes owes much to the concept of "sovereign democracy" developed by Kremlin ideologist (and now architect of the conflict in Ukraine) Vladislav Surkov in the mid-2000s.[16] According to Surkov's vision, each state has the right to determine its own form of government and social organization. A corollary to this concept is the assertion that Russia and its post-Soviet neighbors (at a minimum) stand apart from the

West by virtue of their historical and cultural peculiarities, and therefore are by their very nature not suited for Western-style democracy and liberalism. This conceptual framework also retains appeal in much of the post-Soviet region where elites have come out of the same intellectual and social milieu as their Russian counterparts, and where public perceptions continue to diverge in important ways from those in the West.

Russia's active employment of soft power in the post-Soviet states thus encompasses a range of tools. These include institutional links, for instance between security forces and religious institutions; dominance of Kremlin-controlled media (including increasingly effective use of cyberspace and social networks); support for political parties and activist groups; and the mobilization of "compatriot" organizations.

The post-Soviet states are particularly susceptible to the operation of Russian soft power, not only because of their continued economic and political dependence on Moscow, but also because they inherited a common institutional framework, along with a common political culture and set of symbols, which made it easy for Moscow to embed its own people deep within its neighbors' state institutions.[17] Police and other security forces, in particular, remain heavily penetrated by Russian agents across much of the former Soviet Union; Russia's military intervention in Ukraine was greatly aided by the long-standing presence of Russian intelligence officers throughout the Ukrainian government and bureaucracy.[18] Likewise, the key concepts of the Russian world (*russkii mir*) and compatriots (*sootechestvenniki*) are most relevant with regard to Moscow's former dependencies in Eastern Europe, the South Caucasus, and Central Asia.

Moreover, all three South Caucasus states have large diaspora populations in Russia, mostly comprising labor migrants.[19] These migrants are a pressure point, in that Moscow can tighten regulations on visas and work permits (as it has done for citizens of non-Eurasian Economic Union member states) and threaten to expel migrants in the event of crisis in relations. During the run-up to the war with Georgia in 2008, Moscow expelled several hundred Georgians for alleged criminal activity, a move widely interpreted as a warning to Tbilisi.[20]

Underpinning many of the linkages between Russia and its post-Soviet neighbors is the institutional heritage common throughout the former USSR. Politics throughout the former Soviet region operate according to a common code. Power is inextricable from patronage, which leaders distribute as a reward for loyalty. Political change, where it happens by other than revolutionary means, frequently involves the transfer of power from one patronage network to another, even if the transition is dressed up in the guise of democratization. Such was the experience of Ukraine in both 2004 and 2010, in Kyrgyzstan in 2005, and indeed in Russia in 1999–2000 when Vladimir Putin replaced Boris Yeltsin.[21] Even when elections occur, they are more about legitimating intra-elite shifts and allocating control over sources of revenue than exercises in popular sovereignty.[22]

This inherited institutional isomorphism works to Moscow's advantage by perpetuating structures susceptible to Russian penetration and influence. The widely remarked upon presence of Russian intelligence officers within the Ukrainian military and security services is the most prominent example, but hardly the only one, and Russian agents appear to have similarly penetrated state agencies across the South Caucasus as well. From Moscow's perspective, perhaps the most threatening aspect of the association agreement that Ukraine negotiated with the EU was the commitment on the part of Kiev to adopt a significant amount of EU regulations into its body of domestic law. Transforming its institutions along EU lines would have broken many of the institutional links tying Ukraine to Russia and rooted out at least some of the corruption that facilitates continued Russian influence and Ukrainian dependency, thereby accelerating Ukraine's drift out of the Russian orbit. While Russian forces invaded Ukraine in a failed effort to prevent Kiev from signing its association agreement with the EU, Armenia, which was close to finalizing a similar agreement in the fall of 2013, was convinced to back out at the last minute, using subtler methods that reflected Yerevan's state of extensive dependence.

Similarly, former Georgian President Mikheil Saakashvili recognized the importance of his country's institutional linkages to Russia, which he sought energetically to break during his time in power following the 2003 Rose Revolution. Among Saakashvili's signature accomplishments was his overhaul of the police and intelligence apparatus, including the sacking of the intelligence chief he inherited from predecessor Eduard Shevardnadze and whom Putin had pressed him to keep. Underlying Saakashvili's reforms was a recognition that this corruption facilitated Russia's continued influence over the Georgian state, given the close links between the security services, big business, organized crime, and the state in both Russia and pre-revolutionary Georgia.[23] Overhauling the security apparatus helped break this nexus and deprive Moscow of one of its main transmission belts for influencing developments inside Georgia.

Ideology and Russian soft power

While the struggle between Russia and the West for influence in the post-Soviet region is not, as it was during the Cold War, primarily an ideological confrontation, Moscow uses ideology to shape the context within which its transmission belts operate. The concept of sovereign democracy has gone out of fashion in Moscow, but the underlying logic remains, supplemented in recent years by a renewed emphasis on efforts to show that Russia and its neighbors share a common but non-Western civilization which Russian leaders and thinkers term "Eurasia."[24]

Especially since Putin's 2012 return to the Kremlin, Moscow has deliberately developed this ideology to differentiate the post-Soviet world from the West. It owes much to the Eurasianist movement which originated among white Russian émigrés in the 1920s and was again taken up by anti-Soviet dissidents in the 1970s and 1980s, foremost among them the historian Lev Gumilev. Today, Eurasianism's most prominent mouthpiece is the Moscow State University Professor Aleksandr Dugin, who has become a prominent public intellectual under Putin, and especially since the start of the crisis in Ukraine—to the extent that he was placed on the US government's sanctions list.[25]

The essence of the Eurasianist ideology is that historical, cultural, and possibly biological factors separate the peoples of Eurasia (including Russians) from those of the Atlanticist West. While Gumilev and other Eurasianist ideologues point to deep-seated historical differences between Eurasia and the West, Putin adopts a more nuanced critique, and his embrace of Eurasianist ideas is heavily instrumental.[26] For much of his time at the apex of Russian politics, Putin identified Russia as a European, or a Western country.[27] As relations with the West have soured, Putin and his allies have increasingly advanced the argument that it is the West that has become unmoored from the common past that united it with Russia. In this telling, the West has become decadent by abandoning its Judeo-Christian roots in favor of a post-modern relativism that equates "large families with same-sex partnerships, belief in God with the belief in Satan."[28] Russia, in contrast, is portrayed as standing up for the "traditional" Western values that the West itself is in the process of abandoning.

Given the overlapping historical and cultural ties uniting societies across the post-Soviet region, this appeal resonates, including in places like Georgia where the bulk of the population has adopted a pro-Western political orientation largely in response to tensions with Russia dating back to the late Soviet period. LGBT rights have become a useful point of emphasis in Russia's ideological offensive, since populations in most of the post-Soviet region remain uncomfortable with homosexuality, which serves as an effective wedge issue for the Kremlin.[29] The Church, along with other Russian-backed institutions, has spread the narrative that "Western values" entail an acceptance of homosexuality which many post-Soviet citizens find distasteful. One of the most socially resonant (albeit inaccurate) arguments put forward by activist groups and Kremlin-backed media against Ukraine's efforts to sign an association agreement with the EU was the claim that the agreement would entail recognition of gay marriages performed in Europe.[30] In Georgia, the Saakashvili government sought to crack down on militant homophobia within the Church, which at times supported and even conducted mob violence against gay activists.[31] When Saakashvili was replaced in 2012 by the Georgian Dream coalition, pressure on the Church declined and clerics arrested for their part in anti-gay violence were released from prison.[32]

Russian money does not, then, create anti-gay sentiment in states like Georgia and Ukraine, but highlighting LGBT issues allows the Kremlin to mobilize large segments of the population in these countries behind the narrative that the West is a hostile, alien force. The political upshot is that Russia's neighbors would find a more congenial home in the Eurasian civilization that Moscow is creating. The use of LGBT rights as a wedge issue is not confined to the post-Soviet region either, as support for "traditional values" is an important tool of Russian soft power in Europe and even North America, where it is primarily expressed through support of quasi-NGOs and populist political parties of both Left and Right. QUANGOs and, to a lesser degree given the region's authoritarian political tendencies, parties are an important Russian soft power tool across the post-Soviet region as well.

Where foreign and domestic politics meet

Political parties and individual leaders in the post-Soviet states represent another point of leverage for the Kremlin. As oligarchs continue to dominate politics in much of the post-Soviet region, these figures and their business interests represent one important lever of Russian influence, even in countries like Georgia that have substantially liberalized their politics. Bidzina Ivanishvili, head of the Georgian Dream coalition that ousted Mikheil Saakashvili's government in 2013, was formerly a Russian citizen and made his fortune in Russia, where, among other business interests, he was the largest private investor in Russian gas giant Gazprom. Ivanishvili's opponents charge that his Russian connections made him a stalking horse for the Kremlin, though Ivanishvili has been at pains to deny working in Russian interests, and Georgian Dream was careful to appoint a government dominated—especially at first—by pragmatists.[33] That said, the domination of Georgian politics by a coalition of parties whose main loyalty is to an oligarch with a murky past remains a source of concern, even after Ivanishvili stepped down from his position as prime minister in November 2013 to become a kind of grey cardinal, operating what critics term a "parallel state."[34] While not openly pro-Russian, the lack of accountability, coupled with renewed economic ties to Russia, has become a source of concern for those worried about Moscow's ability to manipulate Georgian politics. Russian money is also suspected of contributing to the resurrection of Nino Burjanidze, a formerly pro-Western figure who, after a falling out with Saakashvili, set up her own party and adopted hard-line Eurasianist positions during Georgia's 2014 election campaign, and to the rise of the Alliance of Patriots, an anti-Western populist movement that took 5 percent of the vote.[35]

Given the extent of Russian influence in Armenia, Moscow's tie to Armenian party politics is more direct. The ruling Republican Party of Armenia (HKK) of President Serzh Sargsyan is openly aligned with Putin's United Russia Party. The two parties conduct consultations and organize reciprocal visits and events.[36] The opposition Prosperous Armenia Party (BHK), led by businessman Gagik Tsarukian, also maintains close ties to the Kremlin and to United Russia. Following Sargsyan's announcement of an effort to transform Armenia into a parliamentary republic (which critics charged would allow him to prolong his time in power), Tsarukian flew to Moscow for meetings with leaders of United Russia, a step that journalists interpreted as an effort to ensure Russian support—or at least neutrality—for his call to mobilize a popular anti-government campaign.[37] Though Tsarukian's efforts quickly collapsed, his visit to Moscow was telling. In Armenia's tenuous version of pluralism, Russia's hold on the economy and role as a security provider ensure it the role of kingmaker in Armenian domestic politics. Notably the BHK, like the HKK, supports Armenian membership in the Russian-sponsored Eurasian Economic Union.

Russian support for political parties and politicians is similarly evident in other parts of the post-Soviet region that maintain a degree of political openness, notably Moldova (not to mention the Baltic states and Ukraine). Russia openly supported Moldova's Party of Socialists, which won a plurality of 20.7 percent in the November 2014 parliamentary elections. During the election campaign, Socialist leader Igor Dodon (now President of Moldova) was received in Moscow by senior Russian leaders, including President Putin, while Russian Duma deputy Sergey Mironov was sent to Chişinău to participate in the Socialists' party congress. Russian state media, which are also widely followed in Moldova, gave the Socialists favorable coverage as well.[38] Another pro-Russian party in Moldova, Patria, or Homeland, was banned by the Moldovan Central Election Commission ahead of the election for receiving foreign (i.e. Russian) funds. Like Georgian Dream's Ivanishvili, the head of Patria is a local businessman, Renato Usatii, with close ties to the Russian establishment.[39]

As party politics are limited in the more authoritarian states of the former Soviet Union, including Azerbaijan, Russian soft power manifests itself more frequently through the often confusing web of QUANGOs supporting causes ranging from "family values" to environmentalism, as well as ethnic and religious organizations. The primary recipients of Kremlin support though are "pro-Russian youth groups, minority and separatist organizations and think tanks."[40] Among these groups are separatist youth movements active in Crimea, Transnistria, and Georgia's two break-away regions.[41] Overlapping with youth QUANGOs active in Russia, these groups organize in favor of separatism and ultimate unification with Russia. The main groups are the Eurasian Youth Movement (part of Dugin's network); *Nashi*, the pro-Kremlin movement notorious for its provocations against Kremlin opponents inside Russia; and *Proryv*, which focuses specifically on mobilizing pro-Russian sentiment in the separatist regions dotting the former Soviet Union.[42]

Moscow likewise plays on ethnic tensions in its multinational neighbors, whose ethnic patchwork is in no small part a deliberate legacy of Soviet nationality policy. In addition to the Abkhaz and Ossetians in Georgia, Russia is reported to back groups including the Gagauz in Moldova and the Lezgins and Avars in Azerbaijan (who also live on the Russian side of the border in the North Caucasus republic of Dagestan).

During the early 1990s, Russian intelligence supported the Lezgin terrorist group Sadval, which carried out bomb attacks in the Baku metro before a combination of Azerbaijani law enforcement and reduced Russian interest led to the group's decline in the 2000s. As relations between Baku and Moscow deteriorated around the time of the Georgian War, Russia began stepping up its support for Lezgin activists in Azerbaijan, including reportedly renewing its ties with Sadval (which by then no longer participated in violent actions), and sponsoring a conference in Moscow to provide a platform for various

Lezgin (and Avar) irredentists.[43] Azerbaijani officials today worry that renewed tensions with Russia, or a resumption of conflict with Armenia over Nagorno-Karabakh, could again lead Moscow to foment separatist violence among these minority groups.[44]

Similar concerns are expressed in Georgia, where various minority organizations have been accused of receiving Russian money.[45] These include the ethnic Armenians in the Samtskhe-Javaketi region along the Armenian–Georgian border, one of the poorest regions in Georgia. A Russian military base located in Samtskhe-Javaketi until 2007 allowed Moscow to recruit agents and collect information from the local population, which has chafed at Tbilisi's efforts to build new infrastructure through the region that connects to Turkey and Azerbaijan. The Saakashvili government carried out large-scale arrests of alleged Russian agents in Samtskhe-Javaketi, but an amnesty proclaimed by the new Georgian Dream government in 2013 saw most of these suspects released. The Georgian authorities are also reportedly concerned that Moscow is handing out passports to the area's ethnic Armenians, in line with Russian actions in South Ossetia and Abkhazia ahead of the 2008 war (not to mention Crimea).[46]

The Orthodox Church between religion and politics

One institution that plays an especially complex role in perpetuating Russian influence in the post-Soviet states is the Orthodox Church. Orthodoxy does not have a single supranational head analogous to the pope in Catholicism; rather, national churches typically maintain close ties to their state's government. Especially in the Orthodox world's more authoritarian states, the Church operates in close coordination with the secular authorities.

The Russian Orthodox Church remains the largest and most prominent member of the Orthodox community, and since Putin's return to the presidency in 2012, its relationship with the Kremlin has become increasingly close (though many Church hierarchs dating back to the Soviet period had close ties to the intelligence services, including, it is widely reported, current Patriarch Kirill I).[47] According to the Basics of the State Cultural Policy signed by President Putin in December 2014, Orthodoxy "played a special role in the formation of Russia's system of values."[48] The Church is frequently cited as the most respected institution in Russia, and it retains substantial influence abroad as well.

It also cooperates with the Kremlin's efforts to differentiate a Russian-led Eurasia from the West. Following the collapse of the USSR, the Church was an important player in efforts to elaborate a new "Russian Idea [*russkaya ideya*]" motivating Russia's society and politics. These efforts included an attempt to define an Orthodox variant of the United Nations' Declaration of Human Rights, as well as a "Russian Doctrine" asserting Russia's unique developmental path.[49] This rapprochement between the Kremlin and the Church was also influential in shaping Moscow's view of the whole post-Soviet region as a unique civilizational construct whose value system made it incompatible with Western institutions and ideologies, as the Church had remained a bastion of conservative thought even during Russia's experiment with Westernization in the 1990s.

At the same time, the presence of substantial Orthodox populations elsewhere in the former Soviet Union allowed the Church to play a unique diplomatic role on behalf of the Russian state's interests. In Ukraine, about a quarter of the population, and most of the ethnic Russians in the Donbas, adhere to the Patriarch of Moscow, and the Russian Orthodox hierarchy has been accused of providing moral and material support for the pro-Russian rebels.[50] Elsewhere in the former Soviet Union, most ethnic Russians continue looking to the Russian Orthodox Church, which has eparchies in Belarus, Estonia, Latvia, and Moldova, as well as episcopal sees in Kazakhstan and Uzbekistan (for all of Central Asia). To the extent that the Russian Orthodox Church reflects the interests of the Russian state, these branches across the former Soviet Union act as transmission belts.

In Georgia, which has its own autocephalous church dating back to antiquity, Russian influence is indirect, but no less significant. It affects appointment and promotion of clerics within the Georgian church hierarchy, and many Georgians point to a Russian campaign to raise the salience of LGBT rights and other social issues as means of undermining Georgia's anti-Western consensus.[51] Russian-backed NGOs, as well as the Georgian Orthodox Church, were prominent in mid-2014 protests against a bill in the Georgian parliament to ban discrimination on the basis of sexual orientation, while influential factions within the Georgian Church have called for rapprochement with Moscow as well.[52] Although the Georgian Orthodox Church maintains a complex relationship to Georgian nationalism (for instance, the Georgian Church is much more ambivalent about European integration than is the Kiev Patriarchate or the Ukrainian Autocephalous Orthodox Church), some Georgians worry that Moscow will also look to the Armenian Apostolic Church in Georgia, which serves the country's Armenian minority, as another potential transmission belt should the Georgian Church identify too closely with the political elites' European aspirations.[53]

A particularly sensitive issue has been the status of the Church in the occupied territories of South Ossetia and Abkhazia, which are, like the rest of Georgia, majority Orthodox, but whose canonical jurisdiction between Tbilisi and Moscow has been a point of contention since the Kremlin recognized South Ossetia and Abkhazia as independent states following the August 2008 war. Three months after the conclusion of fighting, a delegation from the Georgian Church obtained recognition from then-Russian Patriarch Aleksey II that the dioceses of South Ossetia and Abkhazia remained under the jurisdiction of the Georgian Patriarch. Nevertheless, prelates from the Russian Orthodox Church were soon operating in the occupied territories, notably Bishop Feofan of Stavropol and Vladikavkaz, a controversial figure with ties to the Kremlin establishment dating back to the 1980s. Besides his pastoral activities, Feofan acted as a go-between for South Ossetia's de facto president Eduard Kokoity and the hierarchy of the Russian Orthodox Church in Moscow. The Russian Patriarch also sent congratulations to the people of South Ossetia for achieving their independence—independence which only a handful of states besides Russia recognize.[54] In this way, the Church is acting to give substance to the notion of South Ossetian independence, even while remaining officially aligned with the position of the Georgian Church, and the wider Orthodox community.

The Armenian Apostolic Church is more insulated from Russian influence since it belongs to the Oriental Orthodox community and has historically not been in communion with the Russian and other Eastern Orthodox churches. Similarly, confessional politics play little role in Russian policy toward secular Shi'a Muslim Azerbaijan, where ethnicity more than religion serves as the principal lever for Russian soft power.

The South Caucasus in the "Russian World"

Throughout the South Caucasus (and the rest of the former Soviet Union), ethnic Russians, Russian speakers, and "compatriots" are a key constituency for Russia's influence operations. Putin asserted this protectorate most explicitly with regard to Ukraine. In his speech proclaiming the annexation of Crimea in February 2014, Putin noted that "Millions of Russians and Russian-speaking people live in Ukraine and will continue to do so. Russia will always defend their interests using political, diplomatic and legal means."[55]

Nor was this self-proclaimed responsibility limited to Ukraine. As Putin made clear in an address to representatives of Russian diplomacy in the summer of 2014, "our country will continue to actively defend the rights of Russians, our compatriots abroad, using the entire range of available means—from political and economic to operations under international humanitarian law and the right [of compatriots abroad] to self-defense"—presumably encompassing the kind of Russian military support provided to pro-Russian rebels in eastern Ukraine.[56]

Putin's invocation of the term "compatriots" [*sootechestvenniki*: literally those with a common Fatherland] is also significant, in that it extends Moscow's self-proclaimed right to intervene to those who do not even hold Russian passports. The term "compatriots" is codified in Russian law as essentially anyone who was a citizen of the USSR or who has "made a conscious choice in favor of a spiritual, cultural, or jurisdictional bond" with Russia.[57] Russia's first law on compatriots was adopted back in 1999, with the aim of facilitating the resettlement of ex-Soviet citizens in the Russian Federation, though the concept has evolved and received new prominence during the past several years.[58] Under Putin, the concept of compatriots has become an umbrella for Moscow's involvement across the former Soviet Union and beyond; even the United Kingdom has compatriot organizations that receive backing from the Russian state.[59]

Regardless of their citizenship, individuals identified as compatriots are entitled under this legislation to apply for a Russian passport. This provision of passports not only facilitates compatriots' resettlement in the Russian Federation; it allows Moscow to assert an internationally recognized right to intervene abroad in protection of its nationals. Ahead of the 2008 war in Georgia, Moscow was accused of handing out large numbers of passports to inhabitants of South Ossetia and Abkhazia; it did the same in Crimea in the years leading up to the 2014 annexation (despite Ukraine's prohibition on holding dual citizenship). Ukraine's foreign minister warned as early as 2008 that Russian efforts at "passportization" in Crimea were laying a foundation for future intervention.[60]

More recently, an amended Russian citizenship law created a fast-track procedure for Russian-speakers living on the borders of the former Soviet Union to claim Russian citizenship. The expedited ability to claim Russian citizenship appears to be particularly appealing to members of various ethnic minority groups across the former Soviet Union, where many states have pursued nation-building policies that privilege the dominant ethnicity. In Georgia, the Foreign Ministry was forced to deny media reports that the amended citizenship law was leading large numbers of Georgia's Armenian minority to queue up outside the Russian embassy to apply for Russian passports.[61]

All of these Russian speakers and compatriots fall under the rubric of what Moscow defines as the "Russian World" [*Russkii Mir*], a concept closely connected to the Eurasianist ideas of Dugin, Gumilev, and others.[62] Putin first mentioned the idea of a Russian World in late 2006 in a speech in St Petersburg, where he claimed "The Russian World can and must unite all those for whom the Russian language and culture are dear, regardless of where they live, in Russia or abroad."[63] Putin later asserted that inhabitants of the Russian world shared not only a common cultural framework, but also a "common genetic code," while Patriarch Kirill argued that the Russian World included not only ethnic Russians but all the Eastern Slavs of Belarus, Ukraine, and Russia, as well as non-Slavs who share their values.[64] More recently, Moscow has sought to confine its support of compatriots to those who actively participate in cultural or other organizations (many supported by the Kremlin), implying some level of adherence to Russianness.

This vagueness of definition nonetheless makes the Russian World concept at once useful as a foreign policy tool and potentially dangerous, given the challenge it poses to established Westphalian notions of sovereignty, which is tied to control of territory, allowing a government to restrict foreign states' activities on territory under its jurisdiction.[65] Above all, it lets Moscow itself determine just who is and is not a compatriot, thereby skirting around ambiguities of ethnicity, citizenship, religion, and other complicating factors.

A Russian World Foundation [*Fond Russkii Mir*] was established with Kremlin support in mid-2007 to facilitate the spread of Russian language and culture, and to protect the rights of Russian compatriots living abroad. The foundation, and the broader Russian World concept underpinning it, has become a central element in Moscow's efforts to assert influence over its post-Soviet neighbors. Headed by Vyacheslav Nikonov (best known for being the grandson of Stalin's Foreign Minister Vyacheslav Molotov), the Russian World Foundation oversees a network of Russia Centers in dozens of countries around the world, and manages relations with compatriot organizations, many of which also enjoy direct Kremlin support.[66]

While Moscow considers the South Caucasus as falling very much within the Russian sphere of influence which these concepts were devised to influence, the efficacy of the Russian World and compatriots concepts in the South Caucasus are limited compared to the situation in Ukraine or Moldova. For one, ethnic Russians make up a far smaller percentage of the population in the three South Caucasus countries than they do in Ukraine.[67] Moreover, Russia's history of military intervention against Azerbaijan (in Nagorno-Karabakh) and Georgia has caused elites and publics in both countries to turn against Russia, inclining them to favor closer ties with the West, even if pro-Western sentiment is fading, especially in Azerbaijan. Apart from the ethnic minorities in Nagorno-Karabakh, South Ossetia, and Abkhazia, all of whom are already beyond the de facto jurisdiction of Baku and Tbilisi, respectively, Russian World-type soft power lacks a natural constituency in either of these states. Meanwhile, Armenia's strategic and economic dependence on Russia make this sort of soft power less necessary as a tool of Russian influence.

Nonetheless, Russian officials are not above reminding inhabitants of the South Caucasus that the Russian World remains relevant for them as well. Invoking the potential threat from renewed conflict over Nagorno-Karabakh, chief Kremlin propagandist Dmitry Kiselev noted that "If Armenians want to feel safe, they have got to speak Russian," that is, they should continue identifying with the Russian World.[68] Similarly, Russian media suggested that if Georgia sought to integrate with the West through its association agreement with the EU, Moscow could look to the remaining non-Georgian population of the country as potential members of the Russian World.[69] Indeed, evidence of increased Russian engagement with the largely Muslim Georgian region of Ajaria, which Saakashvili forcibly brought back under Tbilisi's control in 2004—along with the Armenians of Samtskhe-Javaketi—suggests that the Kremlin continues to hedge its bets as Tbilisi remains focused on integration with Western institutions.

Conclusion

While Moscow's intervention in Ukraine raised the specter of a renewed Russian effort to upend the post-Cold War status quo militarily, Moscow retains an impressive variety of non-military tools to influence developments across its former hinterlands, above and beyond the capabilities that Moscow has demonstrated in Europe. Underpinning Russian soft power in the former Soviet Union are the continued cultural, economic, and political linkages between the Russian metropole and its one-time dependencies in Eastern Europe, the South Caucasus, and Central Asia. Various forms of Kremlin-backed "uncivil society" are perhaps the least understood and most pernicious type of non-military Russian power throughout the region. Such society groups are especially prominent in the South Caucasus, a region where many of Russia's more traditional tools of influence are less effective and Moscow faces a more complex and dynamic strategic environment. Nonetheless, hard power continues to lie behind Russian soft power in the South Caucasus, inasmuch as the Kremlin has military options here that are, at a minimum, likely to be more problematic elsewhere (as indeed Moscow has learned in Ukraine).

Russian soft power benefits from the continued status of the Russian language as a regional *lingua franca* despite efforts by local elites to promote national languages throughout the region. Especially among the older generation that still dominates the commanding heights of politics and business (albeit to a much lesser degree in Georgia), knowledge of Russian is practically universal, and Russian news sources are ubiquitous. Local elites recognize that the dominance of Russian media represents a vulnerability, and, to the extent possible, are seeking to ameliorate it, though the process will take time.[70]

Ethnic fragmentation is another asset from the perspective of Moscow's soft power efforts. Stalin, a Georgian, deliberately carved up the Soviet Union's constituent republics in such a way that most of them wound up with large, territorially concentrated minority groups. Deliberately or not, the presence of these minorities helped ensure that nationalist mobilization in the Soviet periphery tended to focus on local grievances rather than on Moscow's essentially colonial approach to ruling its non-Russian hinterlands. Today, these minorities provide Moscow with a useful lever for exerting influence throughout much of the former USSR. Georgia is most vulnerable on this score, with significant numbers of Ossetians, Abkhaz, Armenians, and Ajarians, among others, who do not necessarily line up with Tbilisi's political inclinations. A similar logic underpins Russian involvement in the Nagorno-Karabakh conflict, as well as the complexities of church politics throughout the post-Soviet region.

The operations of Russian soft power in the region testify to the continued existence of a post-Soviet political culture, one that Moscow has significant experience in manipulating and that the West often struggles to understand. The activists behind Georgia's Rose Revolution (and Ukraine's revolutions of 2004 and 2013) aimed to transform this political culture, creating a post-post-Soviet system of rule that would look more to the West and in the process undermine the traditional transmission belts that Moscow has relied on to maintain its sphere of "privileged interests." As such, Russia's hostility to "colored revolutions" owes much to this fear of losing control.

At the same time, Moscow never saw the colored revolutions as indigenous responses to corruption and misgovernment, so much as the products of Western political manipulation, orchestrated by Western governments and implemented by Western-funded NGOs.[71] The lesson which Moscow took from the colored revolutions was not that it should address the root causes of discontent before they boiled over into unrest, but that it should learn how to do the very things it was accusing the West of doing, creating its own (QUA) NGOs to promote not democracy, but a conservative ideology which coincided with the geopolitical push that Moscow was making to differentiate itself from the West. It also set out to take advantage of the implements it already had, including a dominant position in local media markets, financial resources, and ties to leading political and business figures to advance its geopolitical agenda.

One of the starkest differences between Russia's approach to soft power and that of the West is the deliberateness of the Russian variant. To be sure, the Kremlin seeks to portray itself in a positive light, in a Russian variant of the Puritan American preacher John Winthrop's "city upon a hill" metaphor, which has long resonated in American mythology. Yet Moscow also deploys this narrative in a highly strategic manner, especially within the former Soviet Union, where it continues to enjoy the most leverage and access. Uncivil society is a critical component of this larger soft power offensive, operating in tandem with hard power, diplomacy, and all the other tools of Russian power. To the extent that Russia has emerged as a revisionist power in the post-Soviet region, seeking to overturn the verdict of 1991 and reassemble some variant of a Russian sphere of influence, its soft power capabilities, especially its ability to create and mobilize uncivil society, will remain among its most effective tools, tools that the West is both morally and constitutionally incapable of matching.

7

TURKEY'S SOFT POWER IN A COMPARATIVE CONTEXT

THE SOUTH CAUCASUS AND THE MIDDLE EAST

Meliha Benli Altunışık

Joseph Nye first developed the concept of "soft power" in *Bound to Lead*,[1] in order to understand a new aspect of the US power dynamic. Nye defined soft power as the ability to achieve desired outcomes through attraction rather than coercion and payments.[2] It has been a topic of debate since its introduction, both in its conceptual clarity and its policy implications. In the meanwhile, the concept has also started to be widely applied to other states' policies, particularly to the middle powers. In this chapter, I will argue that the concept of soft power is also highly relevant to a parallel discussion that started in the post-Cold War era, namely the increasing room for maneuvering and thus relevance of regional powers. Several scholars have argued that the end of bipolarity created a space for regional powers to extend their influence in their regions.[3] This literature acknowledges that being a regional power is not only a factor of material power, but of acceptance in that particular region as well. Although soft power does not guarantee acceptance, it is intrinsically linked to it.

This chapter focuses on the soft power of a regional actor, Turkey, in a comparative context, comparing its engagements with the states of the South Caucasus (and Central Asia) to the countries of the Middle East. This is based on the argument that for Turkey the use of soft power was a tool to re-establish relations with and acquire acceptance in its neighborhood. In the case of the South Caucasus, Turkey attempted to reconnect with a region that it was cut off from for a long time due to the Soviet era and the Cold War. In the case of the Middle East, there was an effort to redefine its engagement after a decade of the securitization of its foreign policy in the 1990s. Although the use of soft power increased Turkey's visibility and presence, it is unclear if it changed the nature of Turkey's influence. Turkey's influence remained highly limited when faced with the realities of hard power politics, and was unable to develop a new set of policies that were accepted as legitimate and constructive by the regional actors that Turkey hoped to influence.

Focusing on Turkey's soft power in the South Caucasus and the Middle East allows for spatial and temporal comparisons. In developing its relations with the South Caucasus in the post-Soviet era in the 1990s, Turkey used several tools that could be considered soft power instruments without officially recognizing them as such. In contrast, in the 2000s, soft power was explicitly articulated in the speeches of government officials in explaining Turkey's foreign policy, particularly toward the Middle East. In both time periods, Turkey's larger policy objectives were to consolidate Turkey's regional power status, to intensify its political and economic ties, and to achieve comparative advantage vis-à-vis its rivals. To achieve these objectives, relatively similar instruments were used, although the ideological content has changed to some extent from the 1990s to the 2000s. Furthermore, Turkey's soft power has been received differently in different contexts, as its content has been interpreted differently by different actors. In this respect, the chapter argues that there are differences not only across these two regions, but also across different countries in the same region and even actors within them. Finally, in both cases Turkey's employment of soft power faced significant limitations and failed completely in some instances. More importantly, Turkey's soft power proved to be less sustainable in the face of a changing political and strategic context, particularly in the Middle East.

This chapter aims to compare Turkey's soft power in these two regions, its framing, narratives, and policies, as well as its evolution over time. The analysis draws on Nye's classification of soft power and discusses the sources of Turkey's soft power in the South Caucasus and the Middle East with regard to three aspects: foreign policy, domestic political ideas and ideology, and culture. One particular aspect that remains vague about Nye's concept of soft power relates to economic influence. Although economic power, including trade, investment, and even aid, is considered in his analysis as part of hard power, Nye also argued that when economic resources create a positive, attractive environment, they also produce soft power.[4] In the case of Turkey, this chapter will argue that both Turkey's aid as well as its trade and investment have played a positive role in creating a positive image of Turkey in the South Caucasus (and Central Asia) and Middle East. As such, these economic tools will also be considered as instruments of Turkey's soft power.

South Caucasus: soft power to reconnect with a region and beyond

After the disintegration of the Soviet Union in December 1991, Turkey became one of the first countries to recognize the newly established states in the post-Soviet space, including the three South Caucasus states of Armenia, Azerbaijan, and Georgia.[5] Turkey's interest in the Caucasus (and Central Asia) was not only in line with general regionalization of its foreign policy, but also with its expectation of an increased regional and thus global influence in the rapidly changing international system. A second general objective was to achieve greater roles in this region vis-à-vis its competitors, namely Iran and Russia. Third, Turkey was pursuing economic and energy interests in this region, which was presenting new opportunities. In addition to these material interests, as far as the so-called Turkic states are concerned there was a strong nationalist and ethnic narrative, especially initially, which emphasized Turkey's reconnection with a long-lost Turkish world. Soon these euphoric sentiments and expectations weakened and were replaced by more realistic objectives of intensifying Turkey's relations with these countries at all levels. Yet Turkey continued to work toward being an attractive country to the regional states and used soft power instruments to do so.

The collapse of the Soviet Union and the newly opened geopolitical landscape presented Turkey with new opportunities for building influence in the twenty-first century. This was particularly welcome at a time when Turkey was contending with the possibility of its declining strategic importance to the United States (US) and had already been rejected for membership into the European Union (EU), called the European Community at that time, in 1989.

The Minister of State at the time, Kamran İnan, argued that "once the international context has changed and the bloc system has ended," Turkey "whether it wanted or not, had to accept that it is a regional power."[6] The emergence of a new geopolitical space thus presented Turkey with an opportunity to play this role as a regional power. For the then Prime Minister, Süleyman Demirel (1991–3), this was to be expected as Turkey was "at the center of the newly emerging political and economic structure due to its unique cultural, geographical and historical position."[7] According to this view, all these changes conferred upon Turkey new responsibilities.

Approached from this perspective, Turkey was a source of attraction for mainly two reasons. First, a very important part of Turkey's soft power in the 1990s toward the South Caucasus and Central Asia was related to what Turkey represented, particularly in comparison to other regional competitors. The so-called "Turkish model" as a secular and democratic state based on a free market economy was seen as an alternative to Iranian and Russian models. Clearly, the Turkish model had its own limitations but was seen and promoted as being at a better place than its competitors. After all, these newly independent states were in the process of transition, and the question of what they were transitioning to was of utmost importance. According to Süleyman Demirel, "Turkey was an example to show that Islam, democracy, human rights, and market economy could co-exist in harmony."[8] Such a representation of Turkey was also supported and promoted by the US, as Washington was equally concerned about the rival models. For instance, in 1992 the US Secretary of State James Baker urged these countries to adopt the "Turkish model of secularism, liberal democracy and a market economy."[9] Finally, what came to be known as the Turkish model also had its supporters in the region. Particularly the second president of Azerbaijan, Abulfaz Elchibey, who was in power from June 1992 to June 1993, was a strong supporter of the "Turkish model" for Azerbaijan.[10] In addition to Elchibey's Azeri Popular Front (APF), the Musavat Party (Azerbaijan) and other parties in different countries such as the Azat Party (Kazakhstan) and Erk and Birlik (Uzbekistan) also supported the "Turkish model" and intensifying relations with Turkey.[11]

The second aspect of Turkey's attractiveness rested in its ability to help the newly independent states establish links with the rest of the world. Prime Minister Demirel in a press conference in March 1992 stated that Turkey was a "cultural center and historic magnet" for the newly independent states and claimed: "we simply believe that we can help these ... republics in their long overdue attempt to integrate with the world."[12] Again, in those early years of independence, regional states were keen to achieve Turkey's level of regional and global influence and power. In August 1992 Azerbaijani Foreign Minister Tofik Gasymov said, "we want Turkey's aid in establishing links with the world."[13] In fact, considering their neighbors, Turkey seemed to be the logical choice for their objective.

Using its institutional membership with several Western institutions, such as NATO and the Council of Europe, Turkey also presented itself as an attractive partner for the states in the South Caucasus and Central Asia and played an active role in establishing linkages between these states and the West. This was seen as necessary for these states to consolidate their independence from Russia. Yet Turkey was also influential in bringing these states into other regional groupings. For instance, they became members of the Economic Cooperation Organization (ECO) and were also invited to be the founding members of the Organization of the Black Sea Economic Cooperation (BSEC), a new multilateral organization established in 1992 on Turkey's initiative.

Especially in the 1990s, Turkey's engagement in the South Caucasus was limited to Azerbaijan and Georgia. Soon after Armenia's declaration of independence and Turkey's initial recognition of the new state, relations became strained. Armenia refused to recognize the border drawn and agreed upon in the 1920 Gümrü Treaty, between Turkey and the defunct Armenian Republic. The boundary was later confirmed by the 1921 Kars Treaty between the Soviet Union and Turkey. This development prevented the establishment of formal diplomatic relations. Soon, the Armenian diaspora and then Armenia's demand for Turkey to recognize the deportation and killing of Armenians during World War I under the Ottoman Empire as genocide created new tensions. Finally, the emergence of the Nagorno-Karabakh problem between Armenia and Azerbaijan introduced another constraint on the normalization of relations. Although at the beginning of March 1993 when the conflict first erupted "Turkey launched what it considered to be a serious bilateral attempt at mediation in the Armenian–Azerbaijani conflict," the Armenian invasion of Azeri territory led to Turkey's closure of the border with Armenia in 1993.[14] Azerbaijan, on the other hand, became the linchpin of Turkey's South Caucasus policy. Framing its approach in an ideational context of historical, cultural, and linguistic links, Turkey sought its economic and strategic interests with Azerbaijan. Georgia also became a country that Turkey engaged with intensely, and the two countries developed a close relationship that was quite unexpected. Tbilisi's interest in moving away from Russia and linking itself with Western institutions as well as common economic and energy interests brought the two countries together. Thus, Turkey's soft power was exercised mainly toward these two countries in the region.

As early as 1991 several high-level visits from Turkey took place to the newly established states of Central Asia and the South Caucasus. In one such visit in April–May 1992, then-Prime Minister Demirel gave a glimpse of the extent and the ambition of Turkey's vision in regards to this region. He announced US$ 1.1 billion in import credits and aid, encouraged these countries to get out of the ruble zone, promised to provide military training, and proposed the building of oil and gas pipelines to transport through Turkey. Demirel also encouraged these countries to switch to the Latin alphabet, and called for the establishment of direct transportation and communication links, including TV transmissions and the announcement of direct flights.[15] The agenda put forward by Demirel clearly pointed to the level of expectations that Turkey had. Although at the time it seemed far-fetched, almost all of these projects have since been realized.

Thus, soft power policies were just one aspect of Turkey's policy toward this region that aimed to strengthen bilateral relations strategically, politically, and economically. Ankara was determined to help these countries establish their independence and, subsequently, institutional links with Western organizations. Turkey's polices to increase its soft power in this region can be grouped under four headings: (1) Education, (2) Cultural links, (3) Religious activities, and (4) Aid, Training, and Economic Relations.

Education

Intensifying educational links with the countries of the South Caucasus and Central Asia has become the cornerstone of Turkey's policy toward these regions. As Lerna Yanık argues, education policy was based on two goals:

> Turkish elites, very optimistically, thought that educating today's students meant creation of the elites who later would be in charge of the transformation towards a market economy and democracy in their countries. More importantly, however, the goal was to create a stratum of people who would be well versed in Turkish culture and language, which then would act as a bridge between their countries and Turkey.[16]

Education policy had two elements. One was to grant scholarships to students at bachelor and postgraduate levels to study in Turkey; the other was the establishment of schools at different levels in these countries.

First, Turkey launched the "Great Student Exchange Project" in 1991, and the Ministry of National Education established the Department of Overseas

Education to manage the new scholarship program. The program started in the 1992–3 academic year and initially offered 7,000 higher education and 3,000 secondary education scholarships to students from the "Turkic countries," including Azerbaijan. As of 2010, the total number of university students in Turkey from the Turkic republics and Turkic communities was 6,294.[17] Figures specifically for Azerbaijan during the period 1992–8 show that 2,570 Azeri students were offered scholarships; among them 556 completed graduation; and 545 of them returned by 1998.[18]

Second, the Ministry of National Education established educational institutions in these countries. Turkey signed an education agreement with Azerbaijan in February 1992 for the reintroduction of the Latin script, educational reform, establishing Turkish schools, providing textbooks and teaching aids to Azerbaijani schools, and training courses for Azerbaijani students in Turkey. This was followed by a second agreement in May 1992 on cooperation "in teaching, expert services, technology and scientific research," and universities in Azerbaijan agreed to accept the scores from the Turkish university entrance exam.[19] Since 1994, the ministry has opened primary and secondary schools in Georgia, as well as a university and a vocational school. More significantly, various foundations in Turkey, especially the one linked to the Nurcu community of Fethullah Gülen, founded schools in the region.[20] By 1999 there were sixteen in Azerbaijan and four in Georgia. The total number of students educated in these schools amounted to 3,133.[21]

Cultural Contacts

Establishing cultural contacts with this region were seen as essential for the revitalization of ties and rebuilding bridges. Turkey's Ministry of Culture initiated a project which led to the establishment of the Turkish Culture and Arts Joint Administration (TÜRKSOY) in July 1993. The Ministry of National Education, together with its counterparts, launched a joint rewriting of history and literature books project in November 1992. Furthermore, on Turkey's initiative, the Summits of Turkic Speaking Countries' Heads of States began to be held in 1992 and were institutionalized with the establishment of the Cooperation Council of Turkic Speaking States (Turkic Council) in October 2009. The Secretariat of the Council was established in Istanbul. The state-owned Turkish Broadcast Organization (TRT) started its first transnational broadcasting and launched TRT *Avrasya* (Eurasia) in April 1992.

Religious activities

The Directorate of Religious Affairs (*Diyanet*) and its Foundation of Religious Affairs (TDV) were quite active from the beginning. Their activism in the South Caucasus is quite interesting considering that the majority of the population of Azerbaijan is Shia Muslim and Georgia is Orthodox Christian. Yet *Diyanet* was active in building and repairing mosques, supporting religious education by establishing schools, educating preachers, and sending religious material to these countries. In Azerbaijan a school of theology was established,[22] along with one secondary school and eight mosques (three in Baku, and one each in Gusar, Agdas, Nakhchivan, Yevlakh and Mekhtiabad) operated by *Diyanet*.[23] Several religious foundations also became active: the religious brotherhood of Osman Nuri Topbaş, linked to the Naqshbandiyya brotherhood, started a Koranic and a vocational school in Sheki, and a madrasa in Agdas. Another religious brotherhood, the Süleymancı movement founded by Süleyman Tunahan (who died in 1959), started missionary activity in the early 1990s.[24]

Aid, training, and economic relations

In response to transformations in the South Caucasus and Central Asia, the Turkish Cooperation and Coordination Agency (TIKA) was established in January 1992. The aim of the organization was initially to respond to the restructuring, adaptation, and development needs of the "Turkic" republics, but it also provided assistance to Georgia (see Table 1). Within this context, Turkey also offered training programs and seminars to government officials in these countries. One of these programs was aimed at training diplomats. Established in 1992 initially to train diplomats from the South Caucasus and Central Asia, the program still continues today with an expanded geographical reach, including the Middle East. Between 1992 and 1998 a total of 297 diplomats were trained by the program. In addition, there were seminars for bureaucrats, managers of banks, youth leaders, university rectors, news agencies, and teachers and other staff from ministries of education.[25] The total number of trainees who took part in these seminars between 1995 and 1999 was 910.[26]

Turkey welcomed the emergence of a "Turkic world" in the South Caucasus and Central Asia. It exploited the opportunities that emerged in the two regions to consolidate its international stature, present itself as a model, and act as a bridge to the outside world. In order to achieve these objectives, several policies were developed and institutions were established. To what extent were these policies influential? Has Turkey's soft power helped it achieve its objectives and increase its power and influence? By the end of the decade the glass was half full.

Table 1: Turkey's Official Development Assistance (ODA) to Azerbaijan and Georgia (2007–13) in million dollars

	Azerbaijan	*Georgia*
2013	28.68	11.13
2012	19.36	12.37
2011	26.48	7.38
2010	22.77	5.85
2009	27.20	13.77
2008	33.90	16.85
2007	36.22	7.84

Source: Compiled from TİKA, Turkish Development Assistance Reports, http://www.tika.gov.tr/en/publication/list/turkish_development_assistance_reports-24

It was soon clear that Turkey's initial euphoria was unfounded and its discourses were found patronizing by the recipient countries. On several occasions the leaders of these countries stated that they were freed from Soviet rule and were not looking for another "big brother." The limits of Turkey's optimism were exposed in the first Turkic summit held in Antalya in October 1992, when several regional countries expressed reluctance to go ahead with ambitious plans such as establishing a common market. Russia was quite clear about its distaste for such a gathering; and the countries in the South Caucasus and Central Asia were equally sensitive to Russia's concerns and did not want to antagonize them.[27] In fact, Turkey soon had to come to terms with the reality of Russia's return to these regions as a result of its "near abroad" policy.

The idea of being a model for governance was largely dropped and it soon became clear that these countries were not going to adopt an Islamic state nor follow the "Turkish model." Although the idea continued to surface from time to time (for instance, as late as 2000 then-Foreign Minister İsmail Cem said in an interview that "Turkey is a paradigm of modernization for Eurasian peoples who aspire for social change within a pluralist and secular democracy"),[28] it was largely set aside when Turkey itself began to pursue its own interests rather than involving itself in what was now considered the internal affairs of these countries. Furthermore, Turkey's own credentials as a pluralist democratic state were questionable. Even in the case of economic relations, Turkey's initial appeal began to crumble as some Turkish companies were accused of dumping poor-quality goods in the South Caucasus markets.

Turkey's significant role in these countries as a bridge to the outside world was prominent in the early 1990s, but began to diminish as these countries established their own links. In regard to the South Caucasus in particular, Turkey's foreign policy activism and attempts to play constructive roles were limited by its problems with Armenia. It was also limited by Azerbaijan's influence on Turkey's position in the Nagorno-Karabakh conflict. For instance, the proposal for a Stability Pact for the South Caucasus failed to materialize in 2000. However, Turkey was able to sustain close relations with Azerbaijan and Georgia. Contact with Georgia was deemed "exemplary" and proved that Turkey's appeal went beyond ethnic and/or religious ties. Moreover, Turkey has been largely instrumental in supporting these countries' quest for institutional links to several international organizations. Overall, Turkey was able to establish itself as an important political and economic actor in the region in the 1990s and formed close human contact with the populations through proliferating sets of policies and institutions.

When the Justice and Development Party (AKP) came to power, this marked both continuity and change for Turkey's engagement with the South Caucasus.[29] The trend toward more realistic policies continued. At the same time, the South Caucasus and Central Asia ceased to be a priority region for AKP as it turned its attention to the Middle East, with high expectations that were not so different from those that had existed for the South Caucasus and Central Asia in the 1990s. In the South Caucasus, Azerbaijan and Georgia generally remained important partners. A major change, however, was the relations with Armenia. As part of its "zero problems with neighbors" policy, the AKP government actively sought to normalize relations with Armenia. They even signed two protocols, the Protocol on Establishment of Diplomatic Relations and the Protocol on Development of Relations, under Swiss mediation for normalization of relations, in Zurich in October 2009. However, the process was stalled and the protocols remain unratified in their respective parliaments.[30] For Turkey the major cause of failure to execute the protocols was Azerbaijan. Alarmed by the possibility of normalization between Armenia and Turkey before the resolution of the Nagorno-Karabakh dispute, Baku launched a very powerful public diplomacy campaign in Turkey against the protocols, putting the government in a difficult position.

During AKP rule, previous policies to intensify educational, cultural, and religious ties as well as assistance continued. Especially with regard to education and assistance programs, there was a significant increase in terms of both resources and scope. This was in contrast with the 1990s, when the resources available were much more limited. In the 1990s Turkey had suffered from several economic crises. In fact, under such conditions some Turkish policymakers viewed Turkey's efforts in the South Caucasus and Central Asia as sacrifices.[31] From 1992 to 1997, Turkey spent about US$ 55 million on scholarships, which was apparently not enough to cover all costs. These problems were tackled more effectively in due course. During AKP rule the role of education as a soft power expanded significantly. A special program called Turkey Scholarships was initiated, and Turkey began to offer scholarships to students from all over the world, including the South Caucasus and Central Asia, on more attractive terms. Similarly, TİKA's role in this region continued, although the organization began to expand its operations in other regions, including the Middle East and Africa.

In the cultural sphere, a new institution was established: Yunus Emre Turkish Cultural Centers,[32] established in Baku (Azerbaijan) and Tbilisi (Georgia). However, cultural relations also started to develop, largely beyond the state level. Turkish mass culture, particularly TV shows and music, became quite popular in Azerbaijan. Generally, Turkey's image in Azerbaijan has been positive, but not as positive as expected, given the efforts. According to a survey conducted in 2003, 64 percent of respondents in Azerbaijan declared a positive attitude toward Turkey, highest among residents of Baku and western Azerbaijan.[33]

Economic relations with Azerbaijan and Georgia increased significantly in the 2000s. In 2013, the value of trade between the two countries was more than US$ 4 billion. Turkey's investment in that year was US$ 5.3 million, and more than 700 Turkish companies were doing business in Azerbaijan. Turkish construction companies so far have committed to US$ 9 billion worth of contracts.[34] Beginning in 2007, Turkey became Georgia's largest trading partner, and the Turkish company TAV built and operated the airports at Tbilisi and Batumi.[35] Similarly, Turkey's economic relations with Central Asia have also continued to grow, particularly focusing on trade, transportation, and communication. Turkey has also provided US$ 1 billion in foreign aid to Kazakhstan, Kyrgyzstan, Uzbekistan, and Turkmenistan over the last twenty years, one fourth of its total foreign aid for that period.[36]

Religious relations, on the other hand, have been the most problematic issue. The Azeri state became especially uncomfortable with the activities of religious foundations. Some groups, such as the Sufi Naqshbandiyya brotherhood and the

Association of Muslim Students in Azerbaijan, had to withdraw from official activity due to problems with registration.[37] President Erdoğan, as part of his fight against the Gülen movement, asked President Aliyev to close down the movement's schools during his visit to Azerbaijan in April 2014.[38] By then there were 11 high schools, 14 primary schools, and Qafqaz University.

Turkey's activism, particularly in Muslim areas of Georgia, also garnered some reaction. In Batumi and Ajara, where part of the population is Muslim, some Islamic movements from Turkey had been actively claiming to help the Muslim population there to rediscover their faith. However, these activities have sometimes attracted criticism, particularly from the Georgian Church, which is quite nationalist and generally hostile toward any kind of Islamic influence coming from abroad.[39] In summer 2013 angry protests broke out in Batumi over what was seen as "the influx of Turks" and government plans to rebuild an Ottoman-era mosque.[40]

Middle East: soft power as desecuritization

Unlike the South Caucasus, Turkey did not use soft power toward the Middle East in the 1990s. On the contrary, Turkey's response to perceived threats from the region was largely to apply its hard power, with the effect that it was considered mainly as a military power by the regional countries. Only in the 2000s, and especially after the coming to power of AKP, did Turkey begin to focus on soft power in its engagements with the Middle East. Then-Foreign Minister Ahmet Davutoğlu summed up this change when he said: Turkey "is trying to have a new style, in the sense of political rhetoric and tools; a new instrument. In summary I will call it soft power. Today, Turkey is using more soft power than hard power."[41] This shift can be explained by the twin goals of the AKP government. First, for ideological, economic, and strategic reasons, the new government aimed to improve relations with this region and decided that using soft power strategies would ease Turkey's acceptance in the region. Second, with the aim of transforming Turkey's domestic politics, including limiting the role of the military, AKP perceived desecuritization of Turkey's foreign policy in the Middle East as an aspect of its domestic goals.

Turkey's soft power in the Middle East focused on three elements. First, Turkey was framed as a "model" for the Arab world. Second, Turkey was presented as a link between the region and particularly Europe. Finally, Turkey's foreign policy became an important source of its soft power. Yet, Turkey began to face formidable difficulties in its role as a wielder of soft power, particularly after the Arab uprisings.

Up until the 2011 Arab uprisings, a significant part of Turkey's soft power was again about what Turkey represented. The meaning of the model, however, shifted slightly. Turkey under the AKP was framed as a successful combination of Islam with democracy and market economy. Turkey was no longer seen as a bastion of secularism, but rather as a country that had uniquely and successfully mixed religious conservatism, democracy, and integration with the global economy. Similar to the early 1990s, the US and the EU supported this narrative because it fit perfectly with the post-9/11 global context and the search for "moderate Islam" in the Islamic world. From this perspective, Turkey was representing a successful model of modernization, democratization, and globalization, and the electoral victory of a party with Islamist roots only strengthened this message. In the region as well, the advent of AKP to power increased interest in Turkey especially among the forces that were searching for political change, be it liberals, Islamists, or socialists. Additionally, Turkey's attractiveness was increased by its internal steps toward democratization, starting in the late 1990s and continuing especially during the early years of the AKP, as well as its economic successes.

The second element of Turkey's soft power was Turkey's claim to be a link between the region and the EU. Turkey became a candidate for EU membership at the Helsinki summit in December 1999. This decision led Turkey to adopt several constitutional and legal reforms. These led to the EU's 2002 decision to start accession negotiations with Turkey once it fulfilled the Copenhagen political criteria. This decision, together with the availability of financial assistance and AKP's desire to use the EU reforms to weaken the traditional state institutions, provided further incentive to reform. Among other changes, Turkey sought to decrease the role of the military in Turkish politics, and the reform process also encouraged the government to tackle other long-standing domestic problems, such as the Kurdish issue. The developments in Turkey–EU relations reinforced once again an image of Turkey that would link the Middle East with Europe. The Arab media were the most represented group at the European summit in Brussels in December 2004, when the decision to start the accession negotiations with Turkey was taken. It is claimed that approximately 200 Arab journalists covered the summit.[42]

Finally, Turkey's foreign policy became an increasingly important and paramount source of Turkey's soft power. The catchy phrase "zero problems with neighbors" emerged as one of AKP's chief foreign policy principles. This concept was implicitly critical of the country's previous foreign policy approach. The zero problems with neighbors discourse promised to minimize Turkey's threatening posture and to improve its relations with each of its neighbors. According to Davutoğlu, the zero problems with neighbors approach was going to contribute to Turkey's soft power:

> the adoption of a new discourse and diplomatic style, which has resulted in the spread of Turkish soft power in the region. Although Turkey maintains a powerful military due to its insecure neighborhood, we do not make threats. Instead, Turkish diplomats and politicians have adopted a new language in regional and international politics that prioritizes Turkey's civil economic power.[43]

In fact, during the early 2000s Turkey began promoting mutually beneficial regional economic ties. Visa requirements were lifted with Syria, Lebanon, Libya, and Yemen. Turkey's involvement in several mediation efforts in the region further consolidated its image as a constructive regional actor. Ankara sought to reconcile Lebanon's squabbling factions, to attempt mediation between Israel and Syria, to achieve Palestinian reconciliation, to help facilitate the participation of Iraqi Sunni groups in the 2005 parliamentary elections, and to pursue a diplomatic solution to the Iranian nuclear issue. Last but not least, the AKP government's, and especially Erdoğan's, harsh criticism of Israel after the Gaza War of 2008/9 increased Turkey's popularity in the Middle East. This was most evident in the opinion polls conducted by a Turkish think tank TESEV after 2010.[44] However, the picture has changed dramatically since the Arab uprisings. This is in part due to the damage to Turkey's image as a soft power, the deterioration of its relations with most regional countries, and the emergence of the idea that Turkey is part of the problem instead of the solution in several countries.

Up until the Arab uprisings, Turkey's policies to increase its soft power in the Middle East can be examined under three headings: (1) Education, (2) Cultural links, (3) Aid, training, and economic relations.

Education

Turkey sought to expand educational cooperation with the Arab world during this period. Initially these efforts remained partial. For instance, before the deterioration of relations with Syria, several projects were developed to intensify educational exchanges. The Turkey–Syria Universities Forum was established, consisting of five universities from Turkey and three from Syria. The two countries also signed protocols on research cooperation and on the exchange of faculty, staff, and students. However, the real jump in the number of students from the Arab world occurred with the initiation of the Turkey Scholarship program. Unlike the South Caucasus and Central Asia, however, the activity of religious foundations in the field of education in the Middle East remained almost non-existent. The Kurdistan Regional Government (KRG) in Iraq proved to be the exception. The 2003 Iraq War and the establishment of the KRG provided an opportunity for the Gülen movement to establish a foothold in the region. Currently, the movement is believed to operate nineteen schools in the KRG region, educating 5,500 students, including Arabs, Turkmens, and Kurds.[45] More significantly, however, the movement opened its first school in Cairo in 2009, the Turkish Salahaldin International School.

Culture

Cultural relations between Turkey and the Middle East have traditionally been quite limited. As an indication of improving ties between Turkey and the Arab world in the mid-2000s, Turkey joined Jordan and Syria in projects to rewrite history textbooks to rid them of mutual prejudices. In Algiers, Rabat, Beirut, Alexandria, Cairo, and Amman, Yunus Emre Turkish Cultural Centers were established with the aim of providing language courses and promoting Turkish culture, history, literature, and art.

Turkey also launched a 24-hour state television channel, TRT 7 *al-Turkiyya*, to broadcast in Arabic to the Arab world. Prime Minister Erdoğan stated at the opening ceremony: "Turks and Arabs are like the fingers of a hand. We belong to the same history, the same culture and above all the same civilization ... TRT 7 *al-Turkiyya* was launched to become our common language, or common screen, our common passion."[46] The discourse reflected the new image that Turkey was trying to build in the Arab world, but also covered the fact that TRT 7 was the voice of Turkey, not necessarily a "common screen."

Yet, most significantly, Turkey has also emerged as a source of attraction owing to its cultural output. Since 2004 Turkish TV dramas have become popular throughout the Arab world. The first of these, *Nour*, became a media phenomenon. When the final episode was broadcast on MBC, a Saudi-owned, Dubai-based, pan-Arab network, a record 85 million Arab viewers watched it.[47] One consequence of the popularity of Turkish TV dramas has been a general upsurge in the number of Arab tourists visiting Turkey in recent years. Tours of TV series locations have become a major attraction for Arab visitors to Turkey.[48] The attraction of these TV dramas is generally considered to arise from cultural proximity and their presenting "an accessible modernity that is not wholly taken from the West, and political drama enacts a counter-hegemonic narrative that puts Turks in particular and Middle Easterners in general in the role of heroes."[49]

Although *al-Turkiyya* has been branding the image of Turkey in line with government policy, Turkish drama series have been produced by the private sector. However, as Kraidy and al-Ghazzi argue, the government "still recruited the culture industry with its productions and glitzy stars in its nation-branding efforts."[50] The now very famous Turkish actors and actresses, frequently interviewed by the Arab media, have become faces for Turkish products and found support from Turkey's diplomats in the Arab world. In fact, the government announced that they would support media producers who create products that boost Turkey's image.[51] As Kando argues, even for the non-state actors to wield soft power the state acts at least "as a facilitator, creating an environment conducive for others to generate 'soft' power."[52]

Aid, training, and economic relations

During AKP rule, TIKA began to expand its activities in the Arab world. The amount of aid to this region particularly increased after the Arab uprisings (see Table 2).[53]

Some of the more prominent elements of the AKP's foreign policy during these years were the growing contacts and dialogue among state officials as well as civil society. Young diplomats, journalists, and academics from the region were invited to Turkey not only for meetings but also training programs, hosted over long periods of time, so that the delegates could observe the workings of their Turkish counterparts, conduct interviews, and attend lectures. The economic bureaucracy, Turkish businesses, and business associations played an important role in engaging the Arab world economically and transmitting their experiences. The Undersecretariat for Foreign Trade was engaged with its counterparts in the Arab countries, particularly Egypt, Syria, and Iraq, in the implementation of bilateral economic agreements. Through these engagements, Turkey's experience in transitioning to a free market economy was shared. Similarly Turkish business associations, such as the Turkish Foreign Economic Relations Board (DEIK) and the Turkish Union of Chambers (TOBB), became active in the Arab countries. Parallel to these relations was an increase in Turkey's economic relations with the Arab world.[54]

It is evident that AKP has deployed soft power instruments in the Middle East. However, how attractive to the region has Turkey become as a consequence? One method of assessing Turkey's attractiveness is to look at relevant polling data. TESEV conducted two sets of public opinion polls in the region before the Arab uprisings, both of which demonstrated Turkey's high and increasing popularity.[55] In a 2010 survey Turkey emerged as the most positively regarded foreign country in Jordan, the Palestinian Territories, Lebanon, Iran, Syria, and Saudi Arabia.[56] The surveys also indicated that Turkey was perceived as an influential regional actor. There was clear support for its mediation in the Israeli–Palestinian conflict (overall 78 percent) and a belief that Turkey's impact on peace in the Middle East was positive (overall 76 per cent). In the region 66 percent saw Turkey as a possible "model" for the Middle East. In the Palestinian territories (77 percent), Jordan (76 percent), Syria (75 percent) and Lebanon (71 percent) support for this proposition was higher still. Turkey was also seen as a successful illustration of the compatibility of Islam and democracy, and again higher percentages than the regional average were recorded in the above listed countries. Finally, Turkey was identified as the strongest economy in the Middle East by the respondents in all countries except Iran, where Turkey came behind Iran and Saudi Arabia. This contrasts dramatically with a survey conducted by Zogby International in March–April 2002.[57] In that survey, the respondents' attitudes toward Turkey were found to be very negative, above only the UK, the US, and Israel in the list. The change in this data suggests that there was a substantial shift in how Turkey was perceived by the public in the Middle East.

Table 2: Turkey's bilateral development assistance to the Arab world, 2007–12 (million dollars)

	2007	*2008*	*2009*	*2010*	*2011*	*2012*	*Total*
Algeria	0.18	0.19	0.22	0.51	0.49	–	1.59
Egypt	0.72	0.95	0.91	1.30	3.51	503.2	510.59
Iraq	46.68	47.68	51.33	39.31	27.83	19,39	184.54
Jordan	1.1	1.4	0.93	1.75	1.58	–	6.76
Lebanon	1.08	25.69	11.53	26.82	7.06	–	72.18
Libya		1.71	0.91	1.01	53.11	3.10	59.84
Morocco	0.38	0.49	0.49	0.45	0.75	–	2.56
Oman	0.02	0.02	0.17	0.06		–	0.27
Palestine	14.22	20.18	48.20	27.83	25.92	51.23	187.58
Syria	5.69	4.11	4.62	9.52	162.03	1019.93	1205.9
Tunisia	0.56	1.29	0.70	0.34	0.49	60.39	63.77
Yemen	0.08	0.44	1.24	6.01	0.45	4.52	12.74
Total	70.71	104.15	121.25	105.91	283.22	1662.48	–

Source: Compiled from Turkish Cooperation and Coordination Agency, *Türkiye Kalkınma Yardımları Raporları* (Turkey Development Assistance Reports), http://www.tika.gov.tr/en/publication/list/turkish_development_assistance_reports-24

Turkey's attractiveness also increased among opinion-makers in the region.[58] More importantly, the Arab debate about Turkey has become more nuanced. In particular, Turkey began to appear in the debate about the region's politics and international relations.[59]

Up until the Arab uprisings, Turkey's diplomacy and use of soft power succeeded in enhancing Turkey's political and economic interests. Turkey was accepted as an important regional player, became part of regional politics, and was generally seen as a constructive player. According to Kirisci, between 2002 and 2010 Turkish trade increased threefold with Syria, nearly fourfold with Maghreb countries, fivefold with the Gulf countries and Yemen, and sevenfold with Egypt. The number of Arab tourists to Turkey increased considerably, from 332,000 in 1991 to nearly 1.9 million in 2010.[60]

Yet, even before the uprisings there was criticism of Turkey's soft power. First, the increasing popularity of Turkey in general, and AKP in particular, started to create anxiety especially among the political elites. Thus, "Arab public discourse began to interpret all things Turkish as an integrated part of the AKP government's policy that seeks economic and geopolitical gain in the region."[61] In the cultural realm Turkey's soft power also generated negative responses of its own. Conservatives in the region condemned Turkey's TV dramas for their "moral laxity." Saudi Arabia's Grand Mufti issued a fatwa against the series *Nour* and called it "subversive" and "un-Islamic."[62] Thus, alongside the attraction there has also been resistance to Turkey's soft power.

These criticisms withstanding, Turkey was able to transform its earlier negative image in the Arab world in a major way and has benefited politically and economically from that transformation. In a paper on the general picture at the beginning of the Arab uprisings, al-Ghazzi and Kraidy observe that:

> Noting the limits of and challenges to Turkey's dependence on soft power, particularly in light of the Arab uprisings, the article argues that the Turkish government has succeeded in constructing a positive image of Turkey as a politically and economically rising power. We contend that this success depends on the AKP government's multiple strategies of using popular culture, broadcasting, rhetoric, and economic branding techniques in a soft power push that aims to enhance Turkey's regional geopolitical and economic clout.[63]

Yet the trajectory of the Arab uprisings, and particularly the Syrian crisis and Turkey's responses, eventually challenged and to a large extent undermined Turkey's soft power in the region. Ironically, the political contestation that spread from Tunisia to almost all Arab countries could have been Turkey's moment. After all, the AKP government has cultivated a positive image with the Arab public and was looked upon positively by various opposition groups.

In fact, soon after the start of the uprisings the issue of the "Turkish model" came to the fore. Yet, the meaning of the Turkish model differed depending on the context in which it was raised. For instance, right after the ousting of Hosni Mubarak, the Turkish model was discussed in the context of civil–military relations in Egypt. Particularly those who were concerned about the mounting Islamist power viewed the Turkish historical experience in civil–military relations as a useful model. However, this understanding of the Turkish model was not promoted by the AKP government as it tried to curb the role of the Turkish army in politics. Among other aspects, it is precisely this side of the AKP that raised interest amongst Islamists in the Arab world, some of which came to view the AKP, rather than Turkey, as a model. Overall, the meaning of the Turkish model narrowed after the Arab uprisings, being largely reduced to the AKP model, and at most the model of Turkey as a country combining Islam and democracy. Muslim Brotherhood groups in Egypt, Tunisia, Libya, and Syria also began to use the AKP model to give messages of moderation to domestic and international audiences.

However, the Arab transitions also exposed the limits of the appeal of Turkey's model. The Turkish model used to mean different things to different people prior to the uprisings, but has subsequently been subsumed exclusively into the AKP experience and the transformation of political Islam. Such a shift in the understanding of the Turkish model alienated Islamists and non-Islamists alike. Secular forces have been critical of the AKP's support for Islamists. On the other hand, at times even Islamists raised eyebrows at Turkish interventions. During his "Arab Spring" tour to Egypt, Tunisia, and Libya, Prime Minister Erdoğan openly declared that while he was a devout Muslim, the state should be secular, triggering acute criticism in Egypt. The deputy leader of the Brotherhood's Freedom and Justice Party, Essam al-Arian, said: "We welcome Turkey and we welcome Erdoğan as a prominent leader but we do not think that he or his country alone should be leading the region or drawing up its future."[64]

More significantly, Turkey's foreign policy toward the region in general ceased to be an important element of Turkey's soft power. Turkey's policies since the Arab uprisings, particularly its involvement in the Syrian crisis and the AKP government's support for Muslim Brotherhood groups, have tarnished its image as a constructive power and adversely affected its branding itself as a benign regional power working for the good of the whole region.

A second problem is Turkey's own domestic challenges. Nye argues that political values can be best converted into soft power when a country lives up to them at home and abroad. However, in both spheres Turkey's soft power has had limitations. At home the AKP government has been increasingly accused of "electoral authoritarianism",[65] or majoritarianism, becoming intolerant of criticism and dissent. The government's crackdown on the Gezi protests, its pressures on the media, and its overall slippage into authoritarianism are followed in the region and have undermined Turkey's soft power.

Conclusion

Turkey has used soft power toward the South Caucasus (and Central Asia) starting in the 1990s, and the Middle East in the 2000s. In order to create a positive image Turkey tried to develop an attractive narrative and branding, also developing several policies and establishing institutions to facilitate closer relations with the countries in these regions. Both the sources and the instruments of Turkey's soft power showed some remarkable similarities but also significant differences between these two periods. In general, the narrative in the 1990s was based on an ethnic/nationalist "Turkic" ideology, whereas the 2000s saw a neo-Ottoman and an Islamic ideology, although there is some mixture of the two for both periods as well.

In the 1990s, Turkey used soft power toward the newly independent states of the South Caucasus and Central Asia. The dominant narrative there was based mainly on the "Turkic" ties, and yet the staunchly secular governments of the time did not refrain from using the Religious Directorate as well as private religious communities to expand Turkey's influence. When the AKP came to power, its policies toward these regions continued to be a mixture of nationalist and religious perspective. Toward the Middle East, however, the AKP relied heavily on historical ties and responsibility, which is neo-Ottomanism in disguise, as well as Islamic solidarity. Yet, the Religious Directorate and private religious communities were largely absent. Instead, conservatism and "moralpolitik" were used to brand Turkey. Erdoğan particularly was presented as the defender of Muslims everywhere.

The sources of soft power were similar during both periods, which is particularly interesting in light of the claim by AKP about the "newness" of its foreign policy. It is clear that many of the same arguments and instruments were used in the pre-AKP periods as well. "Turkey as a model" branding was used, albeit with slightly different definitions, and Turkey's role in linking these regions with the "West" was emphasized. Foreign policy was more actively used in the 2000s on a regional scale, whereas in the 1990s it was more on a bilateral basis. For the South Caucasus, problems in Turkey's relations with Armenia prevented a regional foreign policy approach.

Soft power was utilized to achieve political, economic, and strategic objectives. Overall, soft power was used to reconnect with these regions, and in the Middle East additionally for desecuritization. Thus, evaluating Turkey's soft power in these regions wielding an influence requires an analysis of the achievement of its foreign policy objectives. In the case of the South Caucasus (and Central Asia), particularly after scaling down its expectations, Turkey achieved its aim of becoming a significant actor in the region and realizing most of its economic and energy interests. As explained above, over the years, Turkey has developed beneficial economic relations and become a significant transit country for the hydrocarbon resources of this region after the inauguration of the Baku–Tbilisi–Ceyhan oil pipeline and the Baku–Tbilisi–Erzurum natural gas pipeline. Turkey has stopped seeing its relations with this region and with Russia as a zero-sum game and thus developed quite close relations with Russia as well. Yet, regional developments such as the Russia–Georgia conflict over Abkhazia and South Ossetia in 2008, as well as Azerbaijan's opposition to normalization of Armenian–Turkish relations, continue to impose limitations for Turkey's regional aspirations.

Regarding the Middle East before the Arab uprisings, Turkey was able to transform its negative image in the region and benefited politically, strategically, and economically from it. Yet the major transformations that were unleashed by the Arab uprisings and the AKP government's subsequent responses to them eventually undermined Turkey's influence in the region. Turkey lost its political clout and economic benefits, and saw its popularity become more fragmented. The AKP government's anti-Assad regime stance continues to be popular with some, but drags Turkey to sectarian fault lines that deepened after the Syrian crisis. That being said, Turkey's welcoming of millions of Syrian refugees has created a positive image. Hosting about 2 million refugees, Turkey was the third largest government donor of humanitarian assistance in the world in 2013.[66] Yet even among its supporters, Turkey's image as a regional power has been tarnished by looking unable to implement effectively what it preached.

Thus, the case of Turkey as a soft power contributes to our understanding of its use as a means to achieve foreign policy objectives. An analysis of Turkey's soft power faces the challenge of "intangibility."[67] This is, in fact, a general problem in the analysis of the concept of soft power:

> While very few would dismiss Nye's intuitively plausible arguments about the importance of and necessity to cultivate soft power out of hand, it is extremely dif-

> ficult (methodological difficulties notwithstanding) to determine how and to what extent soft power would enable a state to achieve its political goals.[68]

Nye's response to the issue of intangibility is that whether soft power resources can be converted into behavioral power will depend "upon the context" and that country's "skills in power conversion."[69] In the case of Turkey's soft power, changes in the context in the Middle East due to the Arab uprisings have been important in that respect. The intensification of hard power struggles and increasing fragmentation imposed limitations on soft power. Yet the agency, that is to say the AKP government, and its choices were equally important. The choices that were made did not lead to power conversion but rather diminished Turkey's influence in the region.

8

THE GÜLEN MOVEMENT AND TURKISH SOFT POWER IN THE SOUTH CAUCASUS AND THE MIDDLE EAST

Bayram Balci

Literature on the concept of "soft power" is rich and abundant with many case studies from different countries around the world. Joseph Nye initially forged the term "soft power" in his book *Bound to Lead* and expanded upon the concept in a number of other major works.[1] According to Nye, "hard power" resources, such as military and economic assets, are now less effective in interdependent international policies than they were in the past. In the modern era, the ability of a nation to generate charisma and attraction is the crucial and ultimate form of soft power. A country may serve its interests better by inspiring respect, admiration, and emulation than by using coercion.[2]

So what constitutes a country's soft power? Nye identified three fundamental sources: the country's culture (whether attractive to others or not); its political values (as a source of inspiration for others); and its foreign policies (perceived by others as legitimate and as having moral authority). But there are other sources of soft power: for example, economic resources can serve as a means of both soft and hard power.[3] As Nye underscores, soft power is more of a descriptive concept than a normative concept, and like any other form of power, can be wielded for good or bad purposes. The success of soft power depends on a country's ability to create credibility, trust, and attraction. Joseph Nye's works were initially conceived to explain the United States' foreign policy. Once applied to other powers, such as the European Union, Japan, India, or Turkey, his theories are also helpful in helping to explain their particular stand on the regional or international scene.[4]

While Meliha Altunışık discusses the theoretical and practical aspects of Turkish soft power more broadly in another chapter, this chapter will focus on a concrete case study in Turkey's close neighborhood. Broadly, this chapter examines the exceptional role played by a social and religious organization that is unique in the Muslim world, namely the movement of Fethullah Gülen. This chapter will address the following questions: To what extent did the Gülen movement contribute to the development of Turkey's soft power in both the South Caucasus and the Middle East? Reciprocally, how did the Gülen movement benefit from the government's support and prestige to develop its own influence? Finally, yet equally as important, we shall question the durability of the bond between Gülen and Turkey's soft power through the lens of the clash between Gülen, the charismatic leader of the *hizmet* movement, and Recep Tayyip Erdoğan, the even more charismatic leader of the Turkish executive power since 2002.

The Gülen movement in the Turkish context

Today's *hizmet* ("service") and yesterday's *cemaat* ("community" or "congregation") movements are rooted in movements dating back to the late 1960s. Born in 1938, Fethullah Gülen grew up in the eastern part of Turkey, where traditionally conservative and religious ideas are dominant.[5] Like many of his contemporaries in the region living close to the Soviet border, Fethullah Gülen also grew up with anti-communist sentiments. Significantly, he acquainted himself with the ideas of *naqshibendiyya*, a prestigious Sufi brotherhood of Central Asian origin that had become very influential in Turkey. Additionally, the ideas of Sait Nursi, a leading religious thinker and activist whose ideas and legacy are still very widespread in contemporary Turkey, deeply influenced Gülen's own beliefs.[6] Fethullah Gülen's career is strongly associated with the *Diyanet*, the official state body that manages religious issues in Turkey. As an official imam employed by this state institution, he worked in different cities, notably in Izmir where he gradually formed his own organization in the 1970s and 1980s, an unprecedented success in Turkish religious history. Even the most dedicated scholars, who have scrutinized the "movement," the "*cemaat*," or the "*hizmet*" for years, have some difficulty defining it beyond its most basic religious, social and economic features.

Religiously speaking, the movement subscribes to a moderate Turkish Sunni Islam with a significant Sufi dimension, a quality shared by most Turkish Islamic movements.[7] The young Fethullah Gülen was an anti-communist nationalist, who displayed a clear admiration for a strong state, and was an early and authentic admirer of the Ottoman legacy. Different from other Turkish movements, the Gülen *cemaat* is very active in the social sphere, especially in education and the media. Its members manage strong media groups as well as an impressive network of private schools, prep schools, private dormitories, and other educational institutions across the country.

Moreover, since Turkey established a state-controlled economy in the 1980s for a more liberal system, members of the *cemaat* have also invested in the trade and business sectors. In his sermons, Fethullah Gülen himself praises the good Muslim for being a successful businessman.[8] His repeated exhortations for balancing Islamic faith and ethics with economic success and the spirit of capitalism have convinced analysts that his approach could be compared to Calvinism.[9] The comparison is particularly relevant if you consider how the *cemaat* prioritizes education, trade, business, and social activities, and how in doing so it bears resemblance to the Christian missionary schools of the late nineteenth and early twentieth centuries that were involved in the modernization of many Eastern societies, especially in the declining Ottoman Empire. Indeed, institutions like Robert College or Lycée Notre Dame de Scion in Istanbul, among others, provided strong and modern education to a whole new generation of Turkish elites. In addition to its prioritization of an elitist education, the Gülen movement's relatively secretive operational system, which some of its detractors have called infiltration, allowed us to compare it to the Jesuit phenomenon in a previous work.[10]

For decades until the end of the Cold War, the movement's activities were limited to Turkey. In 1991, the collapse of the Eastern Bloc played a significant role in facilitating the internationalization of the *cemaat*. The new global geopolitical context created new opportunities for the movement, especially in neighboring countries also marked by the Ottoman legacy. Turkey welcomed the emergence of new independent countries in the Balkans, Central Asia, and the Caucasus, countries with which it shares several historical, cultural, linguistic, and religious affinities.[11] Coupled with the West's worries about the possible development of Saudi or Iranian dark influences, the West pushed forward the so-called "Turkish model" for a Muslim and secular liberal democracy, and encouraged these countries to cooperate with Turkey.[12] Although the Western political and diplomatic circles judged Turkey's democracy imperfect, with its liberal economy and secular institutions, it was the best transitional alternative to the old Soviet system. The West's backing gave wings to the new Turkish foreign policy. The Gülen *cemaat* benefited from the opening of the Balkans, Central Asia, and the Caucasus, because they were then able to test their methods outside national borders. They developed businesses, started media, implemented hundreds of schools, and altogether their actions made a difference. Their achievements in Central Asia were treated in a previous work.[13] This chapter will focus on the *hizmet*'s involvement in two other regions of high interest for Turkey: the South Caucasus and the Middle East. Because interests have varied from one region to another, the *hizmet*'s approach has varied accordingly. As such, we shall treat each region separately.

However, before analyzing and measuring the Gülen movement's impact, we shall identify and define these actions. What does it take to receive a "Gülen" label which does not exist otherwise? In Turkey as well as in other countries, a "Gülen" school, business, or newspaper is generally unofficially labeled as such, or as "Fethullahçi," not because Fethullah Gülen himself or his organization is the owner, but simply because the actual owners and managers consider Fethullah Gülen as a spiritual leader or source of inspiration. Because there is no direct and open link of ownership or allegiance, it is difficult to know for sure if an establishment is or is not affiliated with the movement, and to what extent. Indeed, Gülen sympathizers subscribe to his ideas and prescriptions at different degrees and apply his principles and philosophy in their day-to-day management at different levels. Furthermore, even though the core of the management is strongly influenced by the ideas of Gülen, some team members, driven only by self-interest and pure career pragmatism, might ignore Gülen's ideas and remain unaware of his influence. Similarly, in some non-Muslim countries, it happens that some *cemaat* sympathizers operate a Gülen school or establishment with a large majority of non-Muslim students and beneficiaries.

The Gülen movement in the South Caucasus

The absence of diplomatic relations between Turkey and Armenia limits Turkish presence and/or influence in the South Caucasus to Georgia and

Azerbaijan. Although there are various informal businesses developing economic ties between Turkey and Armenia[14] and several Turkish NGOs working for the Turkish–Armenian reconciliation, like the Hrant Dink foundation, the Gülen movement did not take any kind of initiative toward Armenia. Instead, it carefully avoids the tough and controversial issues, like the Armenian genocide, about which Gülen remained extraordinarily and surprisingly silent. Although entirely absent from Armenia, the *hizmet* is extremely dynamic in the other southern republics of Azerbaijan and Georgia.

Azerbaijan

Azerbaijan is crucial to Turkey for many reasons. Both countries share a common Turkish identity; they speak almost the same language and oppose the same historical adversary: Armenia. They differ only with respect to their religious beliefs. While both are attached to secularism, Turkey is mainly Sunni whereas Azerbaijan is 65 percent Shia. During the early twentieth century, both Azerbaijan and Turkey were similarly influenced by the European revolutionary and modernization trends from which Turkism and pan Turkism emerged. Moreover, Azerbaijan benefits from Turkey's extensive sympathy, because currently a large part of Turkey's population is of Azeri and other Turkic Caucasian extraction. These descendants of Azeris, who fled their country after the Russian conquest of the Caucasus and the later takeover by the Soviets, still have strong affinities with the homeland. In 1991, when Azerbaijan became independent from the Soviet Union, Turkey and Azerbaijan established excellent bilateral relations.[15] As such, the political and social context was favorable for the Gülen movement to develop and implement its activities in Azerbaijan. The first Gülen schools in Azerbaijan opened in 1992 in Nakhichevan, an Azerbaijani enclave between Armenia, Iran, and Turkey. Gradually, many other establishments were opened in the rest of the country. In alignment with the movement's attention to the social sphere, education remains the number one priority of the *hizmet*'s strategy. In Azerbaijan, this network of at least twenty high schools, more than thirty prep schools, numerous dormitories, and the prestigious Kafkaz Univesity were implemented and managed by several business associations under the supervision of the *Çağ Öyretim* education company, before President Erdoğan eventually urged his homologue Aliyev to close the education institutions down in January 2014.[16] To this day, many Turkish students are hosted in Gülen establishments in Azerbaijan, and reciprocally many Azeri students who graduated from Gülen schools in Azerbaijan are hosted in Turkey in various *hizmet*-affiliated dormitories and schools.

In addition to education, the *hizmet* was also active in the media sector. The *Zaman* daily news still has an Azerbaijani newspaper edition, *Zaman Azerbaijan*; a radio station, *Burç FM*; and the *S TV* channel which is counted among the very popular channels in Turkey and has developed a branch in Baku in the Azeri language.

Georgia

Georgia ranks second on the Turkish priority list for the South Caucasus. As in the case of Turkish Azeris, there are many Turkish citizens of Georgian extraction. Most of them belong to Muslim minorities of Georgia, primarily Abkhazians, Ajarians, and Azeris. Indeed, when the Russian army conquered the South Caucasus, many Muslim communities, threatened in their identity and faith by a non-Muslim rule, fled and immigrated to the neighboring Ottoman Empire. Later, when the Soviet Union collapsed, many Turks of Caucasian origin then played a significant role in the establishment of relations between Turkey and their historical homeland, Georgia. The Gülen movement once again benefited from favorable conditions for the renewal of good relations and from Turkish official support for any kind of Turkish presence in this region. Turkish policy-makers perceived Georgia as a gate to the Turkic world, to Azerbaijan and even further, to the Caspian basin. At the same time, Turkey is a window to Europe for Georgia.[17] Both countries are partners in the BTC pipeline for the transportation of Caspian oil and gas to European markets.[18]

The Gülen movement made the most of this opportunity for developing and implementing its activities. Just before the dissolution of the Soviet Union in 1991, several Gülen disciples crossed the Sarpi border, explored the Ajaria area, and initiated an educational program, beginning with the construction of a small school in Batumi. Later on, the movement funded other schools in other Georgian cities, Kutaisi and Tbilisi. In addition to its usual network of high schools, a Gülen-affiliated university was also founded in the capital city of Tbilisi: the Black Sea University,[19] managed by the private company Caglar Educational Institutions. Moreover, there are several Turkish language centers across the country to meet the demand by business people or students who want to develop business with Turkey or study in Turkey. As anywhere else, the Gülen-affiliated schools reject the practice of active proselytism, but they do contribute to the diffusion of a Turkish influence.

Now, do they proceed differently in Western Asia, the Middle East, and especially in Iraq and Egypt where the *hizmet* is the most active? Or do they apply the same methods there as anywhere else?

The Gülen movement in the Middle East

The Middle East, and specifically the Arab countries, are not a top priority for the *hizmet* for a simple reason. At the beginning of his career, the nationalist and relatively chauvinist Fethullah Gülen viewed the Arabs negatively, accusing them of perverting the good nature of Islam, which he believed was better defended and encouraged under Ottoman protection. Originally, the Gülen movement was similarly hostile to many other ethnic and religious groups in addition to the Arabs, such as Iranians, Christians, and Shias. Only in its gradual transnationalization did the movement shift to a more open vision of other Muslim and non-Muslim communities. A good illustration of the radical transformation of his ideas is his vision of Jews, who transformed from enemies to friends.[20]

Gülen's interest in Arab countries developed quite late. As in the South Caucasus, he did not try to initiate a strong dialogue with the Shia and Iran, a stance that persists to this day. However, after he left Turkey in 2009 for self-imposed exile in Pennsylvania, his world's vision evolved drastically. He began to diversify his movement and began developing initiatives everywhere in the world, targeting countries where Turkey had not had strong relations before, like Africa where Turkish policy has since benefited from Gülen's networks.[21] The opening to the Arab countries also occurred with this shift in vision. The *cemaat*'s interest in this region really began with the translation of Sait Nursi's abundant writing into Arabic.[22] The publisher of the translation of the *Risale i Nur*, the Sözler editions, is close to the *cemaat*.

Gülen's emerging interest in the Arab countries was even more explicitly demonstrated by the development of another initiative. In 2010, the movement of *Hira*, a symbolic name referring to the cavern where the Prophet Muhammad received the revelation from Allah, launched a journal in Arabic. The journal purports to be a scientific journal seeking to reconcile Islam with science and modernity. Fethullah Gülen himself signs all the editorials and Turkish authors write the majority of the articles in *Hira*, although an increasing number of Arab thinkers do contribute. Thematically, *Hira* focuses on the Turkish legacy to Islamic civilization and insists upon the golden age of Ottoman history, which it depicts as an age of peace and tolerance, leaving the violent episodes of its domination and repression in some provinces of the empire untold. Curiously enough, the journal also ignores the mutually negative perception that Arabs and Turks have of one another, preferring to build anew a more positive image based on the best of their common cultural and religious grounds.

Hira has cooperated with other Gülen-affiliated foundations and Arab partners to organize numerous prestigious international conferences in Cairo, with the objective of increasing the cultural and scientific ties between Turkey and the Arab world. One of the most successful of these conferences was held in 2010 in cooperation with the Arab League and the University of Cairo. For three days participants debated "the future of reforms in the Arab World [and] comparative experiences with the Gülen movement."[23] Since its inception, this conference has attracted many prestigious intellectuals, including the rector of Al Azhar University.

In the education sector, at least three "colleges" operating as high schools were inaugurated in Egypt in 2010, in the cities of Cairo, Beni Suef, and Alexandria. More impressively, a large international school was founded the same year in New Cairo; it was named after Salahuddin Ayubi, better known as Saladin, the Sultan of Egypt and Syria who recaptured Jerusalem from the Crusaders in 1187. It is provided with state-of-the-art equipment, and classes are taught in three languages: English, Arabic, and Turkish. During my visit to the school in 2010, the annual ceremony of graduation was attended by both Turkish and Egyptian officials, as well as by the Secretary General of the Organization of Islamic Cooperation, Ekmeleddin Ihsanoğlu, an international diplomat who holds both Turkish and Egyptian citizenship and was head of the second largest inter-governmental organization after the UN from 2005 to 2014.

Iraq, and more specifically the Kurdish region under the control of the Kurdish Regional Government (KRG), is where the Gülen movement's presence is the most massive, despite two major and recurrent obstacles. Within the movement's ideology, Turkish nationalism plays the role of both a catalyst and an inhibitor. Additionally, the Kurdish province of Iraq has been a constant threat to Turkey's security, and Turkish presence and actions there have been the preserve of the Turkish military.

As mentioned earlier, Turkish nationalism is a founding pillar of the *cemaat*. Although Sait Nursi was an ethnic Kurd, and the movement counts many Kurds in its ranks, Turkish patriotism has always been a fundamental dimension of the movement's ideology. Consequently, the *hizmet* in Turkey faced difficulties in establishing activities in the Kurdish regions of Turkey, where the movement faces challenges from the PKK, a nationalist and irredentist Kurdish movement that dominates the Kurdish political and social sphere in Turkey. Perceived accurately as an agent of Turkish nationalism and an "instrument for the turkification" of these Kurdish regions, the *cemaat* is under close watch by the PKK and struggles to implement activities in this highly resistant Kurdish environment.[24] Similarly, the implementation of the *cemaat* in the Kurdish region of Iraq was not an easy achievement.

The second obstacle for a strong Turkish presence in Iraq and in the Iraqi Kurdish region was the role that the Turkish military played in regional politics until the mid-2000s.[25] Since the beginning of Kurdish PKK guerrilla warfare against Turkey in 1984, the northern mountains of Iraq served as a safe haven for the Kurdish separatists. Security and military issues concerning the PKK thus dictated the course of Turkish–Iraqi relations. As a security state,[26] Turkey did not allow other Turkish non-military actors, not to mention religious movements like the *cemaat*, to interfere in politics and national security issues. Consequently, the *cemaat*'s presence in Iraq remained limited between 1994 and 2005.[27] They were able to establish six to eight schools, primarily in the KRG region, but the local Kurdish population remained wary and suspicious of the Turks. However, these schools benefited from the massive support of the Turkmen minority because of the cultural and linguistic affinities which the minority shares with Turkey.

When the AKP (*Adalet ve Kalkınma Partisi*) came to power in 2002, things changed in Turkey. The AKP shifted the focus of its foreign policy from securitization to desecuritization of the state. The demands for democratization in the context of Turkish candidacy to the European Union justified the AKP reforms to limit the role of the army in Turkish politics. More specifically, the Turkish army lost most of its prerogatives in foreign policy, especially in the management of Iraqi policy. The AKP government and the Turkish foreign ministry then became the prevailing decision-makers in the Turkish establishment. Because of the ideological proximity between the AKP, the Turkish business companies known as the "Anatolian Tigers," and the Gülen movement, it thus became easier for the *cemaat* to implement its activities in Iraq. The Kurdish region of Iraq became an important market for Turkish business companies, especially for those based in eastern Turkey where the population is also predominantly Kurdish.

2007 was a crucial year for the development of *cemaat* schools in Iraq for at least two reasons. In addition to marginalizing the Turkish military, the AKP adopted a more pragmatic approach to the Kurdish issue, to which the *cemaat* contributed by helping to develop more pacified and positive relations. The first improvement came from the *Abant Plalateformu*, a powerful think tank affiliated with the *cemaat*, which specialized in the organization of debates and conferences on various political and social issues. Two major events organized by this leading think tank had a positive impact on Turkey–KRG relations. The first conference, titled "The Kurdish Problem: The Way to Find Together the Path to Peace," was organized in Bolu in 2009.[28] Its final declaration insisted on the fraternity between Kurds and Turks and recommended the Turkish government to befriend the KRG. The following year, the *Abant Plalateformu* organized a similar conference in Arbil, which concluded with the same recommendations for the rapprochement between Turkey and the KRG, and also firmly condemned ethno-nationalism.[29]

These positive steps and initiatives improved Turkey's image among Kurds and encouraged the *cemaat* to develop activities further, leading to the number of Gülen schools in Iraq increasing considerably. Between 1994 and 2002 the number of Gülen schools grew from eight to almost thirty. A university opened its doors in Arbil and rapidly became very attractive for young Kurdish elites. In this most favorable context,[30] *Fezalar*, the business company that runs the schools, became a key player in the Kurdish educational system, as well as in the bilateral political relations between the Turks and the Kurds of Iraq.

The Gülen movement: cause or consequence of Turkish soft power in West Asia?

The *cemaat's* actions are so intertwined with AKP official policies that it is not simple to determine whether Gülen is the cause or effect of Turkey's increasing soft power in Western Asia. The movement both considerably contributed and at the same time benefited from Turkey's emergence as a regional power. Moreover, Turkish diplomacy has supported the *hizmet* as much as Turkish diplomacy has also made the most of the *hizmet's* successes and achievements in the educational sector.[31]

So how do we get to the bottom of their complementary actions, so as to measure the impact, influence, and soft power of the Gülen movement alone in Western Asia? For starters, the Gülen movement undeniably increased Turkish influence in these countries in Western Asia. Beginning with language instruction and bilingual Turkish and English education, the Gülen schools expanded the Turkish language beyond the Turkic-speaking countries, and raised the Turkish language to an international ranking behind English, French, or Arabic. Thanks to the Gülen schools, many students among the younger generations across the Middle East, the Caucasus, and Central Asia, where the schools are very active, now speak Turkish.

The Gülen movement has also promoted a positive image of Turkey and of the Turkish Islamic synthesis that made the country a leader among Muslim nations. In the Arab countries, where the memories of Ottoman imperialism and domination shed a dark light on modern Turkey's image, the Gülen schools have helped to transform previously negative perceptions.[32] The schools have also helped improve perceptions of Turkey in the Kurdish region of Iraq, where Kurds once viewed Turkey through the lens of the Turkish army's war against the PKK guerrilla in the south-east of the country.[33] Interviews with Turks and Kurds who worked together in Iraq show that at the beginning it was hard for the *hizmet* to work there because of suspicion against Turks; but with time, there have been positive results.

We have observed the same phenomenon in Georgia. Because of the separatist conflicts in Abkhazia and Ossetia, Georgians are suspicious and wary of foreign influences, especially those originating from Turkey.[34] The Georgians have not forgotten the Ottoman domination that lasted several centuries in Ajaria. Although bilateral relations are good between Turkey and Georgia, Turkey is still perceived negatively among the Georgian population, partly because of the old fear of domination, and partly because of the Georgian church's resistance against Turkish influence. In 1991 when Georgia became independent, the Muslims of Georgia, mainly in Ajaria and less extensively the Azeri minorities of the Kvemo Kvartly region, received special support from various Islamic movements in Turkey. This assistance was viewed by some Georgians as Turkish proselytism. In the case of the Gülen movement's activity in Georgia, however, open proselytism has been absent, and this low-profile approach of avoiding criticism has worked for the improvement of Turkey's image among Georgians.

In Azerbaijan, Turkey receives good press, which has enabled the *hizmet* to root itself deeply in Azerbaijani society and reinforce the already good relations between Turkey and Azerbaijan. Azerbaijan is the country where the *hizmet* has "converted" most of the nationals to its cause, and this indigenization made the *hizmet* and Fethullah Gülen very influential.

In terms of business and trade, the Gülen business associations are also very active. As already mentioned, business and exports paved the way for the movement's transnationalization. Business networking has constantly involved the movement in bilateral relations. In every country there is a Turkish and local business association whose objective is to reinforce economic cooperation with Turkey. To promote economic cooperation, these business associations organize business trips to Turkey on a regular basis for entrepreneurs, as well as influential personalities like journalists, intellectuals, and decision-makers, to meet with potential Turkish partners.[35] They might be judged lightly, but these trips are extremely important in terms of soft power, because they are a good opportunity to enlarge the Gülen network with people and partners who may not adhere to the movement's ideology, but support its actions and development. In other words, economic and business-driven pragmatism outbalances proselytism, but at the same time this new "invisible hand" reinforces the *cemaat*'s influence on bilateral relations in the respective countries where they operate, and back home in Turkey.

Likewise, the Gülen movement has benefited from the Turkish government's support for its activities abroad. The first example of this positive and reciprocally beneficial relationship between Turkish diplomacy and the Gülen movement was in Central Asia. Just after the dissolution of the Soviet Union, when the Gülen movement arrived in Uzbekistan, a country of considerable importance to the *cemaat*, Turkish diplomacy was also facing a dilemma. The Gülen schools and business activities were the main, if not unique, Turkish non-governmental initiative in the country. Because the conservative AKP was not yet in power, the then Kemalist and secular establishment had serious reservations openly supporting a religious movement like the Gülen *cemaat*. But there was no time for hesitation, so the Turkish diplomats in Central Asia chose to support and promote the Gülen schools for what they were: a wonderful promotional tool for Turkish culture, excellence, and prosperity. Therefore, the Turkish diplomats went to the local Uzbek or Kazakh authorities to reassure them that the Gülen schools were to be trusted. In the case of Central Asia, the diplomats' support was essential because the suspicious and authoritative regimes would not have let a private foreign organization operate without state guarantee. Similarly, in Azerbaijan, Georgia, Iraq, and Egypt, Turkish diplomacy did not spare its support for the *hizmet* movement's educational and commercial initiatives. When the first schools opened in Azerbaijani Nakhichevan in 1992, Süleyman Demirel (who was Turkey's president at the time) had personally met with the Azerbaijani leader Heydar Aliyev, requesting that he help the Turkish schools. The same official and governmental support was provided to the Gülen schools in Iraq, where the prevalence of insecurity and instability made the state guarantees even more vital.

Successive Turkish governments supported the Gülen movement in these strategically critical countries on other matters too. Even before the AKP came to power, and increasingly after it did in 2002, every official Turkish visit to these countries included a visit to the Turkish schools to promote them, make them visible, and reassure them with state protection. Even the most secularist Turkish diplomats and analysts were supportive of the Gülen movement for its successes and achievements, more because of pragmatism than because of their allegiance to the ideas of Fethullah Gülen. But this official Turkish support has demonstrated itself to be confusing to the recipient countries. In Central Asia, the Caucasus, and the Middle East these schools are usually known as "Turkish schools" and are incorrectly thought to be state-controlled public schools. People and officials often ignore the very existence of the Gülen movement behind them.

Both Turkish diplomacy and the Gülen movement took advantage of this cooperation. In all these countries, the different Turkish governments granted their support for the promotion of a positive image of Turkey among the populations and elites of Western Asia. This alliance, which had begun with the Soviet collapse and opening of the Turkish economy, enabling the Gülen movement to grow abroad, ended in 2013 after several years of crisis between Gülen and the presiding AKP. The reasons for and consequences of the break between Recep Tayyip Erdoğan and Fethullah Gülen, and its impact on Turkey's policy in Western Asia and beyond, are dependent upon an analysis of the *raison d'être* of this alliance.

Back in the early 2000s, both the AKP and Gülen movement had converging interests. Both share the same social grass roots, that is, the conservative Anatolian elites that had been excluded and marginalized by the more Westernized Kemalist elites for many years.[36] Their interpretation of Islam shared commonalities, although the AKP was historically and relatively more influenced by the Muslim Brotherhood ideology, and Gülen by the more mystical Sufi Islam of Central Asian origin. Despite minor differences, the political Islam of the AKP and the more social Islam of the *cemaat* shared enough of a common ground to build an alliance. This common ground also shared a common rival in the powerful military and the Kemalist elites who were both very suspicious of these two religious forces, believing the AKP and Gülen movement to be nurturing a hidden agenda to impair the secular character of the country. The alliance helped to shake the omnipotence and the omnipresence of the military.[37]

Together, Erdoğan and Gülen put an end to the supremacy of the army in both domestic and foreign affairs. Under their alliance, a lot of high-ranked generals were sent to jail for real or alleged attempts to organize a coup against the democratically elected government. But once the common enemy of the army and Kemalist establishment were drawn aside, personal and ideological discrepancies rose to the surface. Gradually, their alliance and friendship eroded into a more suspicious and competitive relationship. Eventually the former allies became rivals, their dispute an open fight on Turkish ground and beyond.[38] Within Turkey, the AKP now considers Gülen to be an obstacle to its supremacy over state institutions, while the *hizmet* condemns the AKP harshly for its increasingly anti-democratic authoritarianism. On the international scene, the first divergence occurred in 2010 with the Gaza crisis. The AKP government, judging that it had been tricked and humiliated in its relations with Israel, began a more assertive policy of support for Palestinians. When the Turkish *Mavi Marmara* humanitarian convoy, under the unofficial hospices of the AKP government, tried to break the embargo against Gaza in May 2010, provoking an Israeli raid and the resultant death of nine Turkish citizens, the condemnation of the Turkish initiative by Fethullah Gülen was an unexpected surprise for Erdoğan.[39] Fethullah Gülen criticized Erdoğan's anti-Israel policy for many reasons, among which his desire to maintain good relations with the pro-Israeli circles in the US should not be underestimated. Additionally, Gülen, aligned again with the US stance, has also distanced himself from Erdoğan's stand on the Iranian nuclear issue. Finally, with regard to the Syrian crisis, Erdoğan and Gülen once again disagreed. At the beginning of the Syrian crisis, both Turkey and the US opposed Bashar al Assad. With time Erdoğan and Obama grew apart on their response to the Syrian crisis, and the Gülen movement, partly ideologically and partly strategically in its personal competition against the AKP, adopted a more pro-Obama position.

The ultimate break occurred in December 2013. The Gülen movement knew that the AKP was determined to eradicate the *hizmet* in Turkey, especially when in October 2013 the government announced its decision to close its prep schools, leaving the *cemaat* no choice but to strike back. Thanks to sympathizers working in the police and the judiciary, the *hizmet* revealed via social media several cases of corruption among high-ranking officials, some of whom had close ties to the Erdoğan government, and some who were members of Erdoğan's own family. Vindictive and paranoid, the Turkish prime minister is now waging a war against the *hizmet*. Numerous members or alleged members of the Gülen movement were sacked or removed from the police and judiciary sector, and some were arrested. The repression expands outside national borders, as the *hizmet* draws much of its strength from its transnational network. Given Erdoğan's stance against the *hizmet*, what are his chances of eradicating the *hizmet*? And how will his actions impact Turkish foreign policy?

Turkish diplomacy has radically changed its position toward the *hizmet* since the break and has become its first adversary on the ground. Unsurprisingly, right after the local elections of March 2014, which resulted in a national plebiscite for the AKP and Erdoğan in power, the Turkish prime minister paid a visit to Azerbaijan. Because Azerbaijan is a staunch ally of Erdoğan's government and at the same time the most massive and diverse field of investment for the *hizmet*, with dozens of schools, a university, and hundreds of affiliated companies, the Turkish prime minister's visit was an intentional choice. As previously mentioned, the activism of the *hizmet* in Azerbaijan more than anywhere else relies on a strong "indigenized" group of sympathizers to the Gülen cause, more than on the presence of Turkish expatriates. Many of these sympathizers have reached high-ranking positions in schools and business management, and rumor has it that some of them have already infiltrated the highest Azerbaijani administrative bodies. Concerned by their invisible, yet potentially harmful influence on positive Azerbaijani–Turkish relations, Erdoğan publicly urged the Aliyev administration to close all Gülen schools and adopt a more cautious attitude toward the Gülen movement.[40] His request has been partly satisfied.[41] Indeed, the Azerbaijani government has changed the status of the *hizmet*-affiliated schools, putting them under much more severe scrutiny, and most significantly has expelled a special adviser, Elnur Aslanov,[42] from the presidential administration, due to his links with the Gülen movement.

It also appears that Turkish embassies abroad received specific recommendations from Ankara to end their cooperation with the Gülen schools, and instead now preach against their "pernicious" activities. The case studies of two African countries just after the crisis are very informative about the extent of the break between Turkish diplomacy and the Gülen movement. In Senegal, where the Turkish ambassador was more of a Kemalist and, as a diplomat, did not show concern about the personal dispute between Erdoğan and Gülen, he remained neutral by trying not to take part in the fratricide duel. As such, the *hizmet* schools in Senegal were not directly targeted by any attack or pressure from the Turkish embassy.

The situation was rather different in the neighboring Mauritania, where the Turkish ambassador had a special profile. As a loyal servant to Erdoğan and the AKP ideology, he joined the diplomacy after Erdoğan made him ambassador.

The interview we conducted with him showed the extent of his passion for the dispute between Erdoğan and the *hizmet*. Consequently, it would be no surprise if Ankara's recommendations to have all schools closed and the *hizmet* local interests frozen were applied in Mauritania under his term.

In Georgia, Iraq, and Egypt, the Turkish government's "crusade" against the *hizmet* has been more subtle. In Georgia, the movement is not powerful enough to threaten Erdoğan's image; and, more importantly, the Gülen movement's presence in Georgia is the preferred Turkish presence in their country for the Georgian authorities who know that, compared to other Turkish Islamic movements, the *hizmet* is less focused on proselytism. Indeed, Islamic activism operated by Turkish movements among Muslims in Ajaria is mainly the work of Süleymancilar, a powerful Islamic organization in Turkey. In Egypt, the *hizmet* interests are safe. Whereas the relations between Abelfattah al Sissi and Erdoğan, because of the latter's link to the Muslim Brotherhood and former president Mohammad Morsi, are extremely bad. Surprisingly enough, in Iraq where the *hizmet* is very active in an extremely delicate political environment, the Turkish government has not sought to harm the *hizmet* educational initiatives, at the risk of jeopardizing a very fragile balance.

Both in Turkey and abroad, the war between Erdoğan and the *hizmet* movement has weakened the Gülen movement. However, as the general elections on 7 June reflected a clear defeat for Erdoğan and his AKP party, who did not achieve the necessary numbers to change the Turkish Constitution, there is good reason to think that this defeat foreshadows a new course of weakness for Erdoğan despite his combat against the Gülen movement. Because his authoritarianism has become more and more apparent, Erdoğan has tarnished his image abroad, which will weaken his ability to convince foreign countries to limit the presence and influence of Gülen-affiliated institutions.

On 15 July 2016, a major political cataclysm occurred in Turkey, when elements within the Turkish military took part in an attempted *coup d'état*. The coup, intended to overthrow President Erdoğan, was quickly thwarted, and the president was able to reassert his authority within twenty-four hours. The details and circumstances of the failed *coup d'état* remain largely unclear, but the Turkish government immediately attributed it to Fethullah Gülen, whose followers had allegedly infiltrated many state institutions, including the armed forces. Whether true or not, whatever the degree of Gülen's implication in the *coup d'état*, the movement is more than ever considered to be a "terrorist organization" by the Erdoğan government, and the president has launched an aggressive purge within the state bureaucracy, the military, and academia of alleged Gülen followers.

Significantly, Erdoğan has not limited his all-out war against Gülen to Turkey. Following the coup attempt, Erdoğan directed Turkish embassies abroad to do what they could to undermine the Gülen movement and its global reach. Specifically, Turkish embassies began demanding that host countries halt the operations of Gülen-affiliated schools. The responses of the host states have been varied, with some, like Pakistan, closing Gülenist schools, while others refusing to do so. In Azerbaijan, the government closed Gafgaz University because of its Gülen affiliation. Since December 2013, Gülen schools have been placed under the Azerbaijani state's firm control, and some Turkish citizens have been barred from managing the schools. The governments of Georgia and Iraqi Kurdistan did not change their attitude toward the Gülen schools. For them, control over their educational system was a question of sovereignty and they were not susceptible to pressures from a foreign government.

Perhaps an even more important reason for balking at Turkish demands, however, has to do with the type and level of education services that the Gülen movement guarantees. The Gülen schools are generally known for providing high-quality education in English, and have produced many wealthy and powerful alumni. Moreover, for more than twenty years, they have operated legally and have catered to elite and well-to-do families. Suddenly closing them, ostensibly because of an internal Turkish power struggle, would be both disruptive and politically costly for host governments.

Insofar as Turkish soft power in West Asia and the South Caucasus is concerned, the *coup d'état* is likely to have disastrous consequences in certain respects. The end of the alliance between Turkish diplomacy and the Gülen movement will limit the impact of Turkish schools, and will also impede the continued diffusion of Turkish language, culture, and influence. Nevertheless, the perseverance of Gülenist schools in other countries, especially in places where they have become financially autonomous from Turkish business circles, is likely to continue the mantle of the Gülen movement, or at least Gülen's spirit. This will most likely sustain and perhaps even spread Turkish soft power.

Conclusion: the place of Turkey in Western Asia with or without Gülen by AKP's side

While they were allies, the Turkish government and the Gülen movement helped to develop a powerful Turkish presence and influence in their immediate regional environment and beyond. Placing Turkey on the worldwide map was beneficial to both sides; but now the break will likely harm both sides, an outcome for which both share responsibility. The *hizmet* could not and would not approve the AKP's authoritarian turn, and the *hizmet's* politicization away from its initial mystic and apolitical identity challenged and threatened the government. The break leaves no winner, but one loser: Turkish soft power, not only in Western Asia but everywhere that it made a difference and made a promising opening for Turkish influence.

It will not be easy now for Ankara to clean its tarnished international image after the *hizmet* launched a media conspiracy campaign exposing its authoritarian excesses and corruption scandals. As a result, the AKP lost all credibility as a so-called "Turkish model." In terms of soft power, Turkey lost much of its ability to attract and persuade as a model of moderate Islam, combining harmoniously with democracy and a liberal market economy. The *hizmet* is no longer by the AKP's side to balance its decisions with a sense of measure, and this might weigh negatively on Turkey's isolation in the international scene.

But Turkey and the AKP government are not the only losers in this major political crisis. The *hizmet* will also make a bad harvest in Turkey and abroad. For many years, Gülen and his followers pretended that the *hizmet* was only a social movement advocating the conciliation of Islam with modernity and science, insisting on the concept to serve humanity (*hizmet etmek*) and denying any kind of political or leadership ambition. However, what happened in December 2013 showed that they are not so immune to political influence and power. The *hizmet* may have lost a round against the AKP government, but the confrontation continues. The impressive political power it has demonstrated by infiltrating the police and judiciary will also probably tarnish its international image as a social and humanitarian organization. It might jeopardize the future of their own assets, schools, media outlets, and businesses in countries where the regimes have come to realize that they were not as innocent as they claim to be.

As for the direct consequences on Turkey's place and influence in Western Asia, the break between Erdoğan and Gülen that spread to the government against the international interests of the *hizmet* will compromise Ankara's ambitions to become a regional power of influence. In the South Caucasus, Turkey is already losing ground to the advantage of Russia, which is operating a strong comeback in its historical areas of influence. In the Middle East, Turkey is engulfed in the Syrian crisis and finds itself more isolated than ever in the fight against the Islamic State organization and in the disintegration process that undermines Iraq and Syria. Marginalized in the South Caucasus to the benefit of Russia, Turkey is losing ground in the Middle East to the benefit of Iran, which is the winner of this grand transformation of the Middle East.

PART III

THE TRAVAILS OF STATE-BUILDING

9

THE ARMENIAN IMPERATIVE

CONFRONTING AND CONTAINING OLIGARCHS

Richard Giragosian

In the wake of the collapse of the Soviet Union, the three states of the South Caucasus region, Armenia, Azerbaijan, and Georgia, were ill-prepared and generally ill-equipped for the challenges of independence. For much of the past decade and a half, each of these three states has pursued a difficult course of economic and political reform, marked by a transition that varied in both consistency and commitment. And as a region with a shared history, all three countries have also struggled to overcome a common legacy of seven decades of Soviet rule.

Historically, the region of the South Caucasus has long served as an arena for competition of interests among rival powers, including the Russian, Turkish, and Iranian empires. This historical legacy of external pressure has been further exacerbated by domestic institutional weakness and vulnerability. This internal fragility has only continued, with each of these three countries still hindered by the burden of several unresolved, low-intensity conflicts that have further contributed to a serious degree of regional instability and national insecurity.

More specifically, the region is also plagued by a set of fundamental internal challenges, ranging from incomplete democracy, and the related predominance of "strongmen over statesmen," to economic mismanagement and widespread corruption. Each of these factors has significantly impeded the course of economic and political reforms in each country. But in terms of a steady erosion of political legitimacy, the most daunting challenge, however, has been the emergence of a new commercial–political elite, commonly referred to as "oligarchs," which has distorted and deformed both the reform effort and the process of state-building in recent years.

As an informative case study, the oligarchic elite in Armenia pose an especially challenging test to institutional capacity and political will, given their inherent position as an entrenched obstacle to developing viable democratic institutions and building a sound market-based, rule-governed economy. Moreover, the emergence of so-called "oligarchs" in Armenia, or more accurately, through the formation of several commodity-based cartels, stands as a significant and pressing problem, as the power and influence of this oligarchic elite have become so entrenched that they now threaten the next stage of economic reform, and may seriously undermine the sustainable development of the country. And for Armenia, the country was hobbled by an especially unique post-Soviet experience, marked by the onset of independence during a state of war with neighboring Azerbaijan and having to recover from a serious earthquake. Yet there are several common traits and legacies among the former Soviet states in the South Caucasus that help to explain the emergence of oligarchs, or a business–political elite region-wide.

The post-Soviet experience

Given the shared challenge of overcoming the legacy of decades of Soviet economic mismanagement and central planning, one of the more fundamental challenges to economic reform in these post-Soviet transition states has been to adopt market-based economic structures and to adapt to the demands of the free market. This shift to capitalism has been no easy task, however, and has been characterized by a long and painful transition. For many of the populations of these three countries, the economic stability and order of the old Soviet system was abruptly replaced by the insecurity and chaos of entrepreneurship and unfamiliar market-driven economic demands in the post-Soviet era. For a small elite, however, the period ushered in a new opportunity, unfettered by rules or laws and endowed with as much reward as risk.

During this period of initial transition, the region quickly forged its own unique system for commerce and trade. What made commerce in these countries unique was the combination of distinct factors facing each country. While each country sought free trade, with an added recognition of the need for competitiveness, for the emerging business class this also necessitated an open business environment. For the South Caucasus, however, this was no easy task in light of pressure from unresolved conflicts and the restraints from closed borders and limited trade routes.

For Armenia's new business elite, these structural challenges posed greater problems than for her neighbors. One of the most obvious and immediate of these challenges was the blockade of Armenia imposed by Azerbaijan and Turkey. This blockade, which still continues, was especially significant as it went well beyond a simple closure of borders to encompass a near-full disruption of trade, transport, and energy links. Its effects were further magnified by Armenia's landlocked status, and never fully offset.

The initial impact of the blockade when it was imposed in the 1990s was, of course, an immediate and devastating shortage of foodstuffs and basic commodities, an abrupt and severe energy crisis, and a period of economic isolation. The immediate effects forced Armenia to adapt quickly to the sanctions by concentrating on its sole remaining external trade link, northward through Georgia. Although this led to a degree of dual dependence—on Georgia for trade access and on Russia as a major trading partner—the fact that Armenia was forced to adapt developed as a key competitive advantage. This adaptability was more than a mere weathering of adversity; it was sheer survival. And it was that adaptation in which Armenian business was able to excel, and in relative terms far outpaced its neighbors.

It was this very set of restraints and obstacles that provided the opportunity for the rise of the "oligarchic" commercial elite, however. More specifically, a new business elite, many with either strong ties to political officials or endowed with criminal links, rose to power and wealth by exploiting and maximizing the lack of open borders which thereby impeded competition; by maximizing "conflict economics"; and by building monopolies over scarce consumer commodities. Within the war period of the 1990s, each of these three countries witnessed the rise of the so-called oligarchs. And through this first decade of reform, this new oligarchic elite was able to enhance their wealth and power in each country: Armenia, Azerbaijan, and Georgia, mimicking in many ways the much larger problem of oligarchs in Russia.

Moreover, from a broader regional perspective, later assessments consistently rated the business environment in Armenia much higher than its neighbors. For example, compared to Azerbaijan and Georgia, Armenia's business environment has been hailed as the most open and least restrictive in the region. Despite its energy wealth, Azerbaijani businesses also face substantial challenges, such as problems of investment freedom, inadequate property rights, and corruption. But there has been more progress in recent years in Georgia, which is now highly rated for its "business freedom," and for posting gains in curbing corruption. Yet this was also a problem, as the oligarchic elite was by then firmly entrenched within the rising commercial class in the Caucasus.

Defining the Armenian oligarch

The term "oligarch" is an old reference, often used in the context of the "robber barons" of the mid- to late-nineteenth-century United States or semi-criminal businessmen exercising an inordinate degree of power and influence in many developing countries such as Mexico, Indonesia, and the Philippines. More recently, the term oligarch assumed an updated meaning, referring to the emergence of a post-Soviet commercial elite, most notably in Russia and Ukraine, who used close ties to both the new states and links to the criminal underworld to garner significant wealth and power during the early privatization in these countries of transition.[1]

Moreover, the popular meaning of an "oligarch" has come to mean "a very wealthy and politically well-connected businessman ... who is the main owner of a large business and has close ties with the ruling political elite."[2] Some analysts have gone further, revealing the case of "state capture" to characterize the relationship between big businessmen, or oligarchs, and the state, demonstrating how the oligarchs influence the state through different means.[3] Over time, within the context of such "state capture," the growing power and wealth of the oligarchs assumed an elevated status of "corporate oligarchy," whereby their power, both governmental and operational, was effectively but informally divided among a small elite group of inside individuals, most often with some common origin or shared power base, and generally conducting business well beyond the confines of the rule of law or state regulation. Such corporate oligarchy is also usually endowed with state-granted monopolies or semi-monopolies, backed by their privileged position both within the broader market and within the political system.[4]

From a broader strategic perspective, the emergence of the oligarchs was also a result of isolation and insignificance. For a landlocked country limited by its small size in terms of both demography and territory, the threat of isolation stems from the constraints of closed borders, the collapse of regional trade and transport, and an exclusion of all regional development projects. With Armenia's borders with Azerbaijan and Turkey both sealed since the early 1990s by the blockade, the imperative for Armenia is to overcome the limits of geography. This threat of isolation involves the danger of becoming disconnected from the globalized marketplace and from the technological and economic changes inherent in the process of globalization. In addition to the relative isolation of the country, Armenia also faces a second, related threat of insignificance, defined by the limits of a small landlocked country with two of its four borders closed.

Armenia as a case study

In the case of Armenia, even more than other post-Soviet states, the oligarchs represent several factors, demonstrated by their role in the following five core areas:

(1) undermining the authority and credibility of state ministries, regulatory bodies, and agencies, backed by privileged access and collusion with customs and tax bodies;
(2) curbing competition by enforcing a closed and rigid market, bolstered by dominant market share and control over the import of key commodities and semi- or near-monopolies on the import and sale of consumer goods;
(3) distorting and deforming the efficacy of the reform program, while impeding the development of an emerging middle class and hindering private sector growth;
(4) exercising an inordinately close linkage between business and politics;
(5) threatening the longer-term sustainable development of the country by damaging the overall investment climate and diminishing prospects for economic growth.

In terms of the first factor, the undermining of the very authority of the Armenian state, the oligarchs' routine practice of under-paying or evading taxes has consistently deprived the state of much needed tax revenue, which, in turn has unfairly shifted much of the tax burden onto the country's weaker small- and medium-sized enterprises (SMEs). The credibility of the state is also weakened by the oligarchs' disregard for the law, often demonstrated by their virtual impunity from the law. This has tended to exacerbate the state's already limited degree of legitimacy, as the oligarchs also personify the deeper disparities in wealth and income, thereby only magnifying popular discontent.

Second, as commodity-based cartels, oligarchs tend to thwart competition in two ways: by enforcing a closed and rigid market through their dominant hold over the import (and to a lesser degree, export) of key commodities; and, by acting as "barriers to entry" for new firms, often leveraging their dominant market share to undercut or force out new market entrants. Third, as powerful political actors, often able to intervene and interfere in state policy enforcement, the oligarchs, both individually and as a group, are able to distort the efficacy of the government's reform program. Fourth, on a structural level, the political power of oligarchs, most notably as members of parliament, demonstrates the more difficult challenge of separating business from politics. A fifth element of the challenge posed by the oligarchs stems from their longer-term threat to the country's goal of sustainable development by damaging Armenia's overall investment climate by impeding the rule of law, undermining the integrity of contracts, ignoring property rights, and disregarding labor laws, thereby greatly weakening investor confidence.

The rise of the "oligarchs"

The absence of such economic institutions in the region, and the resulting weak regulatory framework in each state, has allowed a pattern of flagrant abuse and excess to emerge relatively unchallenged by the authorities. This lack of an adequate institutionalization of economic regulation and enforcement has permitted the emergence of a new class of economic elite. This new elite, the so-called "oligarchs," have acquired economic power at the expense of state power, depriving the state of both tax revenue and defoliating the country of national assets. In the case of the Russian and other former Soviet economies, this new class of oligarchs has tended to exploit the privatization process: firstly to gain economic power, but with an additional appetite for political power that also inherently threatens the success of democratization and political reform.

A second problem associated with the rise of a powerful oligarchic elite is seen in economies endowed with natural resources, like Azerbaijan. Ironically, natural resource wealth has tended to hinder political modernization and economic development in significant and far-reaching ways. As "unearned riches" hinder the development of political institutions and weaken the rule of law, such resource-rich states have come to be called "trust-fund" states, relying on the attractively easy revenue derived from energy or other resources rather than facing the challenging task of forging institutions and economic structures capable of garnering national wealth of their own.[5] Examples of such "trust-fund states" abound, and are geographically diverse, ranging from Saudi Arabia to Nigeria to Venezuela.

For Armenia, these structural shortcomings were only compounded by an equally daunting set of challenges, ranging from the inherent limits of its small size and landlocked geography to a virtual "state of war" with Azerbaijan over the unresolved Nagorno-Karabakh conflict. And within this context, Armenia embarked on a difficult path of state-building, bolstered by ambitious economic and political reforms. Against that backdrop, the abrupt and unexpected collapse of the Soviet Union left Armenia largely unprepared for the urgency of independence.

Therefore, in the case of the Armenian oligarchs, there are both similarities with the theoretical model outlined above and important differences, reflecting the unique conditions in the early period of post-Soviet Armenian independence that gave rise to their emergence. An important distinction in the case of the emergence of the Armenian oligarchic model from other post-Soviet states was the unique circumstances in Armenia at the very onset of independence, consisting of several factors.

First, even during the Soviet period, there was a relatively thriving "black market" or informal economy in Armenia, notable for its innovative strategies to circumvent Soviet laws and regulations, and its capacity to overcome the limits of centralized planning and the closed distribution of goods and services. While this informal "grey economy" later helped ease Armenia's difficult early period of transition to a market economy by offering a degree of experience and familiarity with an open market, the semi-legal or even outright criminal underworld in Armenia also posed early challenges to state rule and enforcement in the early years of independence.[6]

A second factor contributing to the unique conditions in Armenia allowing for the emergence of the oligarchic system was the specific conditions in the country in the immediate aftermath of the collapse of the Soviet Union. Moreover, several developments even during the period prior to independence tended to foster the emergence of oligarchs. For example, Armenia was beset by two seminal events: the eruption of the Nagorno-Karabakh conflict triggering a subsequent war with Azerbaijan in February 1988, and a devastating earthquake in December 1988. The latter event, the earthquake, encouraged private groups to assume control of the distribution of critical supplies, such as medicine and food stocks, and to channel humanitarian aid to the earthquake area in the absence of any coordination or capacity by the weak central authorities of the last Soviet Armenian government.

But it was the Nagorno-Karabakh war that was most significant for creating the conditions for the birth of an entrenched oligarchic system in Armenia. During this time, the combination of the sudden and unexpected collapse of the Soviet Union and the outbreak of war led to a severe disruption of trade and transport routes, cut key energy links, and triggered a near blockade of the country by neighboring Azerbaijan and Turkey. Given these conditions, this early phase of independence, marred by war, blockade, and economic collapse, culminated in severe shortages of food, electricity, fuel, and other critical products and consumer goods.

These conditions also predetermined the development of a subsequent closed, oligarchic economic system, and seriously distorted reform, as the state was unable to overcome the scarcity of goods. The weakness of the state further led to the recruitment and retention of oligarchs, both on an individual basis and through small groups or cartels, who then assumed responsibility for the production and distribution of goods and services. This role was only bolstered by their additional role in supplying the emerging Armenian military, serving the state as logistical agents, often justified by military necessity.

Within this closed economic system and facing little state oversight or regulation, several commodity-based cartels emerged, bolstered by a powerful combination of criminal links and political influence. Their power also stemmed from the opportunities for power and profit inherent in exploiting "conflict economics" through monopolistic positions controlling scarce consumer commodities. These cartels and semi-monopolies quickly solidified their power as "agents of the state," preventing any competition and securing dominant positions over the import and export of key consumer goods, raw materials, and foodstuffs.

More broadly, a third, related factor that led to the emergence of oligarchic cartels was the consequence of the "conflict economics" of the Karabakh war, which also helped them to garner political influence, as their support for a feeble and war-weary state increased demonstrably. This was also due to the fact that the Armenian government at the time was largely preoccupied with economic measures in other areas, including land reform, privatization, and the introduction of a stable national currency. The power of these cartels quickly expanded beyond commodities, however, and similar to other post-Soviet states, they leveraged their links with the state and political power to acquire inordinate wealth and assets during the privatization process. At the same time, they further consolidated their power by positioning themselves at the top of the rapidly developing networks of patronage and corruption within the state system.

Over time, the cartels adopted more sophisticated means of expanding their power, including using collusion to fix and enforce commodity prices, barring competitors from emerging, and securing exclusive state procurement contracts. Furthermore, the early absence of economic institutions and the weak regulatory framework tended to support a pattern of flagrant abuse and excess by the cartels that went relatively unchallenged by the authorities. This lack of an adequate institutionalization of economic regulation and state enforcement provided the foundation for the emergence of this new class of economic elite. Over time, Armenia's oligarchs were able to extend their informal networks of political power through informal cartels and commodity-based semi-monopolies and now wield significant economic and political power. Moreover, this oligarchic elite has further acquired both substantial wealth and significant economic–commercial power, most often at the expense of state authority, depriving the state of both tax revenue and defoliating the country of national assets through the privatization process. Transforming into a new business elite, the oligarchs, many with either strong ties to political officials or endowed with criminal links, now exercise their power, position, and privilege by exploiting and maximizing the isolation caused by the country's (still) closed borders, impeding competition, and maximizing their near-monopoly and dominant market hold over the import (and export, in some cases) of core commodities, such as gasoline, aviation fuel and heating oil, and basic staple goods, ranging from flour to sugar.

Against this backdrop, the real danger stems more from complacency and inaction, while for Armenian business, given the small size of the national economy, there is a serious need for the state to tackle monopolies and to open the economy further through transparency and competition. Although the emergence of near-monopolies in the Armenian business sector has not been as profound or as powerful as in other former Soviet states, they have created two especially serious problems for the overall Armenian economy. First, the rather unique form of Armenia's oligarchic business tends to stifle economic growth by restricting the export–import trade sector. The second, net result is an overall weakening of economic growth, barriers to competition, and serious disincentives for foreign investment. In Armenia's case, these results reinforce the structural limits of being economically isolated and geographically landlocked.

Barriers to entry and impediments to market competition

In terms of the direct impact on market competition, the oligarchs, as a business elite with close ties to political officials, are a primary obstacle by virtue of their monopoly positions in controlling scarce consumer commodities. Thus the real danger for Armenia stems from complacency; and for Armenian business, especially given the small size of the national economy, there is a serious need for the state to tackle monopolies and to open the economy further through transparency and competition.

Although the emergence of monopolies in the Armenian business sector has not been as profound or as powerful as that of other of the former Soviet states, it has created two especially serious problems for the overall Armenian economy. First, the rather unique form of Armenia's business monopolies, unlike their counterparts in the case of Russia, for example, comprise informal cartels based on a dominant control over the import and export of specific key commodities. Such a stranglehold has serious economic consequences, as it tends to stifle economic growth by restricting the export–import trade sector. The net result is an overall weakening of economic growth, barriers to competition, and a serious disincentive for foreign investment.

The second economic impact of these commodity-based cartels or monopolies is their role in obstructing the rise and expansion of new firms and businesses. This too harms overall job creation and maintains the closed and limited nature of the national economy.

In larger economies, such "cronyism" has resulted in high "transaction costs," whereby corruption becomes entrenched, even to the point of actually weakening the state by depriving it of much needed tax revenue. It also limits economic growth in the short run, and constrains competition in the long run, which in turn leads to higher prices and slower innovation. Thus, the cumulative effects are devastating for the national economy overall and for society in particular. But as seen in the model of Armenian business in particular, such a failure to tackle the closed, monopolized economy also threatens to destabilize and further isolate the country.

Obstacles to SME development

The influence, presence, and power of the Armenian oligarchs has weighed heavily against competition and the emergence of small- and medium-sized enterprises (SMEs). Commodity-based cartels and monopolies continue to pose a serious problem for the country's economic development, especially as the government has failed to introduce more effective application of anti-monopoly mechanisms, or reduce administrative costs for small and medium-sized enterprises. Despite having one of the most advanced regulatory systems among the former Soviet states, Armenia still needs to improve transparency. As things stand now, Armenia lacks the necessary combination of critical laws and effective enforcement, particularly in the area of anti-monopoly and anti-trust laws. This weakness is exacerbated by excessive state control over some key sectors of the economy.

Given the prevalence of generally weak state regulatory institutions and a pronounced lack of political will to confront corruption and break up cartels and semi-monopolies, the now entrenched power and position of the oligarchs stands as a direct threat to reform and, at least, an indirect threat to the state itself, especially in terms of tax evasion or under-reporting of profit and income. The oligarchic system has had a devastating impact on Armenia, eroding the power and authority of the state, which can neither tax the oligarchs nor police their business interests. In this context, the state now faces an uphill battle if it is to regain control of the economic system.

Against this backdrop, the real danger for Armenia stems from complacency and for Armenian business. Especially given the small size of the national economy, there is a serious need for the state to tackle monopolies and to open the economy further through transparency and competition. Although the emergence of monopolies in the Armenian business sector has not been as profound or as powerful as in other former Soviet states, the net result is an overall weakening of economic growth, barriers to competition, and a serious disincentive for foreign investment. The second economic impact of these commodity-based cartels or monopolies is their role in obstructing the rise and expansion of new firms and businesses.

This too harms overall job creation and maintains the closed and limited nature of the national economy. In Armenia's case, this not only reinforces the landlocked limits on the Armenian economy, but creates a reinforcing cycle: where the monopolies benefit from closed borders and reinforce their control over key sectors of the economy. As with lessons from similar cases, the only effective way to tackle this problem has been to introduce "anti-trust" legislation strong enough to counter and contain the oligarchic cartels. Ultimately, it is the implementation and enforcement of the laws and legislation that matters most. In addition, there are also negative effects from the oligarchic system on the country's tax assessment and revenue collection system, as well as a deeper structural problem in the Armenian taxation system. Because the state cannot generate revenue from these oligarchs, state revenue has instead traditionally relied on proceeds from value added tax (VAT), most of which emanates from imported goods. Accounting for a little more than half of all state revenue, VAT has now become the leading source of state revenue, far beyond the meagre collection of corporate profit tax.

Yet after past years of double-digit economic growth, such a discrepancy between dangerously high reliance on VAT and a meagre rate of corporation tax is worrisome for two reasons. First, such an overreliance on VAT for overall tax collection is not sustainable over the long term and, as the low level of corporate tax revenue demonstrates, has only deferred more serious budget shortfalls while tax evasion and under-reporting has gone unpunished. In addition to this structural problem, the high dependence on VAT-related tax revenue rather than more significant corporation and import taxes tends to impose an unfair tax burden on the country's lower and still-emerging middle classes, as individual consumers are increasingly forced to endure even higher sales and value added taxes that beset the medium- and large-scale business enterprises.

The influence of the oligarchs

Just as the rise of the oligarchs has been based on their personal, political, and military ties and connections, assessing the influence of the oligarchs, both individually and collectively, depends on their personal standing and reputation, as well as the usually opaque allegiances and alliances with each other. As is the case with most countries, economic clout and wealth are usually closely linked with political power and influence, often with a nation's wealthy elite holding a disproportionate amount of power and influence. Recognizing the threat posed by the combination of wealth and political power, democratic reformers have sought to construct "checks and balances" designed to counter such power. And although there were many times when a small wealthy elite was able to acquire and exercise too much power, the institutional system of checks and balances always tended to restore a natural balance over the longer term.

But, for countries lacking strong democratic institutions like Armenia, there is a tendency for personal politics over policy politics.[7] This dominance of politics of personalities has only encouraged Armenia's individual oligarchs to acquire and exercise inordinate personal influence. While this personal influence stems from a network of close connections, including personal friendship, with a varied number of officials and political figures, the informal nature of their influence is inherently insecure. In other words, the degree of their influence is dependent on their personal standing and relationship with political officials, a limitation that makes their power dependent on official favor, as they must remain in good standing or else risk losing some or all of their influence. Given this inherent insecurity in the longer-term influence of the oligarchs, there is a related danger that they exceed any informal limits on their influence.

Over the past several years, the expanding influence of the oligarchs has been matched by significantly greater pubic visibility, at times even embarrassing their political patrons. More recently, as this higher visibility has fostered an "arrogance of power" among many of the most prominent oligarchs, there has been a pronounced public backlash, with many oligarchs having become the objects of public derision and popular disdain. This negative backlash has also been magnified by the public flaunting of wealth and flouting of the law by the oligarchs, which for a small country like Armenia is especially threatening to the widening disparities of wealth and growing poverty.[8]

Business and politics

As the early source of the oligarchs' economic power was rooted in the Karabakh war and the period's conflict economics, their political power also emanates from their military role during the early period of the war. The ceasefire in 1994 halted hostilities but merely "froze" the underlying conflict, so the resultant uneasy period of "neither peace nor war" allowed this newly emerging oligarchic elite to accumulate and consolidate yet greater power. Steadily securing power from even within the government of the first president, Levon Ter-Petrosyan, the oligarchs provided key support for a virtual *coup d'etat* initiated by then-Defense Minister Serge Sarkisian, Prime Minister Robert Kocharian, and former Defense Minister Vazgen Sarkisian, which culminated in the forced resignation of Ter-Petrosyan in February 1998. The first two were natives of Nagorno-Karabakh, Sarkisian having led the small but impressive Karabakh armed forces, and Kocharian having previously served as the Karabakh head of state. As their power and ambition grew, both men came to be seen as a new "Karabakh" political elite, eventually assuming near-complete control of Armenia proper, with the oligarchs providing key backing and conveniently "switching sides" for a new political master.

The most revealing aspect of the end of the Ter-Petrosyan government was not the resignation itself, but the context. The ousting of Ter-Petrosyan was prompted allegedly by his moderate approach to the Karabakh issue and justified by a pretext of Armenian national security. Assuming the presidency in subsequent elections, the rise of Robert Kocharian demonstrated the ascendancy of this Karabakh elite, which then consolidated control and mastery of most of the oligarchs, as well as much of the country's networks of crime and corruption.[9] The end result was a new government dominated by political figures who not only shared common roots with Karabakh natives, but who had also gained power and legitimacy because of the Karabakh conflict.

After a period of commercial consolidation, the entrenched position of the oligarchs in Armenia has been matched by the close relationship between business and politics. In recent years, the convergence of economic and political power has become even further consolidated, as the members of the new "oligarchic elite" were formally elected to the Armenian parliament in 2003 (and have returned in each subsequent parliamentary election), raising obvious concerns over the integrity of governance and public policy in Armenia. More specifically, the longer-term worry is demonstrated by the clear conflict of interests and dubious ethics inherent in allowing powerful "businessmen" to become parliamentarians and, at least theoretically, being able to influence and even legislate economic and political reforms.

The emergence of a number of powerful oligarchs in the political arena poses more problems. It is most apparent from the pressure they can bring to bear as parliamentarians, and from their new-found structural ability to influence and impede reforms from the inside. Their direct role within national politics also highlights the risks posed by cozy relationships between business and politics, and by the power of a commercial–political elite as an impediment to the development of viable democratic institutions, by hindering market-based, rule-governed economic reforms.

More specifically, after securing (and retaining) a number of seats in the Armenian parliament, the oligarchs' political role as deputies demonstrates a convergence of corporate, state, and in some cases even criminal interests.[10] In addition to influencing the formulation of public policy and garnering substantial leverage over the course of governmental policies, this oligarchic elite has come to embody the difference between the power to rule and the responsibility to govern. In the case of other former Soviet economies, this new class of oligarchs has tended to exploit the privatization process to gain economic power first, but has exhibited a subsequent appetite for political power. It is that new-found political role that inherently threatens the course of democratization and political reform.

The most significant element of the relationship between business and politics is the utility of the oligarchs as key pillars of support for the authorities in terms of vote-buying and election-related activities, as well as campaign and party financing. This political utility has served to strengthen the ruling party machine in Armenia, at both local and national levels. Even more distressing, although Armenia's recent election cycle has passed,[11] the oligarchs are likely to continue to play an important role in terms of conflict within the ruling elite. More specifically, the oligarchs may become more actively engaged in a looming struggle for power as an important new period of political transition opens, perhaps driven by a perception of weakness in President Sarkisian's position as a "lame duck," having been elected to a second, final term with no clear successor. For this reason, they may seek to engage more deeply in the political process now, and become more politically active (and even less loyal), in order to exert more influence or even control the fight for succession as the broader transition to a post-Sarkisian elite begins.[12]

Oligarchs in parliament

Despite the steady accumulation of political power and influence through the 1990s, the oligarchs did not formally enter the Armenian parliament until 2003. Driven largely by a motivation to acquire status, as well as parliamentary immunity, a considerable number of oligarchs ran in the May 2003 parliamentary election. In terms of political allegiance, most of them were closely affiliated with the ruling Republican Party of Armenia, although a few were individually aligned with smaller parties. Since then, however, nearly all of the oligarchs became "independents," standing for re-election as candidates for the majoritarian seats, rather than running on party lists for the proportional seats.[13]

Most interestingly, there was also a case of party formation, as seen by the United Labor Party, which was very much the creation of the oligarch Arsenian, and was formed a mere three months prior to the election. As one of the more serious oligarchs, Arsenian's business interests are concentrated on the oil and cigarette trade, as well as owning a number of other businesses, including the Kentron TV station which he acquired in 2003, just prior to the election.[14]

The success of the oligarchs in their first election was largely due to their ability to outspend their rival candidates, often by a 10:1 proportion. Despite a general lack of political experience or campaigning skill, by choosing to stand in single-candidate constituencies, the oligarchs were able to maximize their inherent advantages by focusing their efforts and money on overwhelming any opponent in the district; although in some cases in prior elections, they either forced or bribed some candidates to stand aside in favor of their own candidacies, further undermining the democratic process.

Another significant aspect of their political stature in past parliamentary elections was the more sophisticated demonstration of political strategy by some of the more serious oligarchs. For example, Hrant Vartanian, an oligarch with extensive business interests through Grand Holding, was able to secure the election of several of his employees and friends, as well as his son. Closely aligned with the Armenian Revolutionary Federation (ARF)-Dashnaktsutiun party, Vartanian was able to pressure that party to add several of his chosen candidates to their party list, and after providing financial assistance and campaigning volunteers, ensured the election of Samvel Sahakian and Armenuhi Hovhanissian (two senior executives of the Masis Tobacco Company, owned by Vartanian), Araik Grigorian (the director of Vartanian's Avshar Winery), and Vartanian's son, Mikayel Vartanian.

The move was significant beyond the display of political acumen, as it also revealed the possibility that other oligarchs might recruit and secure the election of loyal employees and relatives as new, younger and more acceptable candidates in the future. Such an option would ensure that the interests and influence of the oligarchs would be continuously protected, while avoiding the scrutiny of openly holding seats in parliament.

Since then, however, there has been a concerted effort to pare down and limit the number of oligarchs in parliament. For example, since the parliamentary elections of 2008 and 2012, almost half of the initial group of oligarchs were not returned to parliament, although that reduction also includes several oligarchs who assumed other state positions or official responsibilities. Nevertheless, many of the more "publicly unacceptable" oligarchs were encouraged to stand aside after serving their one term in parliament. But in many ways, the May 2012 parliamentary election represented a clash between the government and the oligarchs.

For several months prior to the May 2012 election, Prime Minister Tigran Sarkisian and President Serzh Sarkisian himself both publicly vowed that the new parliament would no longer have oligarchs as deputies. After an initial public promise by many of the leading oligarchs not to return as deputies, the oligarchs then decided to challenge the government more directly, refuting their earlier promise and forcing the government to back down. In the end, many of the oligarchs ran for re-election and easily kept their seats in parliament. It was, in many ways, a public humiliation for the Sarkisian government, in which the oligarchs challenged the state, and won, with little state response or retaliation.

Overall, the presence of oligarchs in parliament has had little real effect on Armenian politics, however. For the overwhelming majority of the oligarch deputies, the appeal of parliament is nothing more than simple status and basic immunity, confirmed by both their voting record and attendance at parliamentary sessions. And given their lack of interest in ether voting or attending sessions, there has been little real danger of oligarchs understanding the potential power in using the legislative process to distort or deform public policy. Yet that danger is real, and at some point the oligarchs may realize the effectiveness of using their mandates to enact laws to benefit their corporate interests directly.

Privileged position and political will

Since the acquisition of a dominant market share and control over the import and export of a wide range of core commodities, the oligarchs have also benefited from an informal system of special privileges, in terms of de facto exemptions and special treatment regarding tax and customs enforcement. This special arrangement is driven by the close working relationship between the leading oligarchs and senior officials of the Armenian State Revenue Committee (SRC), which comprises both the state tax and customs bodies.

Now in his second and final term, Armenian President Sarkisian has generally overcome the dangerous legacy of distrust, discontent, and crisis of confidence that he first inherited upon taking office. In a broader sense, there is also a fresh opportunity for President Sarkisian for political will and leadership, based on his desire to leave a legacy that may last well beyond his second term. And with no successor, there is ample room for bold political courage, and most notably to confront the entrenched power of the oligarchs.

Moreover, there is a further opportunity for change because of the fact that politics in Armenia is now entering a new period of dynamic change, driven by a fundamentally different nature of political conflict and the onset of a new period of political transition. In terms of new political conflict, a serious division has emerged within the ruling political elite, emanating from a deep rivalry between current President Serzh Sarkisian and his predecessor, former President Robert Kocharian, and matched by an open "battle by proxy" between Sarkisian's dominant Republican Party and the country's number two party, Prosperous Armenia, widely seen as the political creation of

Kocharian. At the same time, on a deeper level, the Armenian president's term reflects a closing chapter in the country's political history. Although Sarkisian's February 2013 re-election was most clearly defined by a serious lack of competition, he is viewed as the "last of the Mohicans," as the last of a specific Armenian political elite. With no clear successor, Sarkisian represents the last representative of the political elite that came to power in Armenia from Nagorno-Karabakh and because of the Karabakh conflict, exploiting a political vacuum and embracing a nationalist political discourse at that time.

Moreover, the present Armenian political landscape also marks the opening of a new political transition, with the rise of a new, younger generation of political figures. This newly emerging political elite has no direct connection to Karabakh or reliance on the nationalist politics of that conflict, and gained political, and financial, power as they rose up through the Armenian political system. But being younger and different does not necessarily make this new elite more democratic. Rather, the more significant factor is the political transition and the emergence of a new elite which will force open a closed and rigid political system, offering more space and greater hope for more mature politics in Armenia.

Oligarchs and the economics of power

In most countries, economics and politics far too often intertwine, with a nation's wealthy elite holding too much power and influence. The dangers from such a close relationship between economic and political power have long been understood, and have even been reflected in the historical maxim that "power corrupts, and absolute power corrupts absolutely." Recognizing the threat posed by the combination of wealth and political power, democratic reformers have sought to construct "checks and balances" designed to counter such power. And although there were many times when a small wealthy elite was able to acquire and exercise too much power, the institutional system of checks and balances always tended to restore a natural balance over the longer term.

But for countries without resilient democratic institutions, there is little recourse, as the state lacks the capability to check or balance the power of the rich. This problem is evident in the case of the post-Soviet states, whose transition to market economics and pluralistic democracy has been beset with profound obstacles. These post-Soviet countries also face a deeper paradox, whereby essential political and economic reforms are susceptible to being thwarted by the very same wealthy elite that they seek to curb and control. Moreover, the weakness of the rule of law in such transition states further impedes the early stages of reform, exacerbating the inherent vulnerability to the influence of such elites, well before the establishment of a durable democracy.

For a small country like Armenia, the disparities of wealth and power become only more apparent, and much harder to correct. And in the case of Armenia, the economic system has been distorted, with commodity-based cartels and monopolies garnering a dangerous degree of power and position within the economy. In recent years, the convergence of economic and political power became even further consolidated, as a new "oligarchic elite" was formally elected to the Armenian parliament. The emergence of such a dominant and exclusive body raises obvious concerns over the integrity of governance and public policy in Armenia. More specifically, the longer-term worry is demonstrated by the clear conflict of interests and dubious ethics inherent in allowing powerful "businessmen" to be responsible for formulating and legislating economic and political reform. Once the wealthy elite acquired a new, formal role in Armenian politics, a virtual culture of impunity became even more firmly entrenched. At the same time, governance in Armenia was increasingly expressed through a new "arrogance of power," where the state abdicated its responsibility to serve and protect the public. Naturally, this only fostered a greater sense of apathy and disengagement among ordinary Armenian citizens.

Taking on the oligarchs

In order to confront and curb the powerful oligarchs, there are several measures that may be adopted in Armenia, Azerbaijan, and Georgia. Of course, the twin challenges of corruption and the oligarchs are interrelated, and are also mutually reinforcing, as the shadow economy promotes corruption within the tax system, while corruption tends to foster a permissive view of the oligarchs. But on their own, both problems are direct challenges to the country. And ironically, unlike the commonly held perception of the state benefiting from corruption and the shadow economy, both also threaten the state, by depriving it of sizeable tax and customs revenues. One obvious conclusion is that, like much of what is wrong in the region today, there is a lack of political will. It is political will that is needed to reform and bolster the tax and customs services by ending the permissive and passive approach to tax evasion and avoidance. This permissiveness serves as the "hothouse" for a culture of impunity that has allowed both corruption and the shadow economy to flourish.

Although these new economic problems pose new threats to social and economic stability, this new crisis is made only worse by the already serious disparities in wealth and income. These disparities, evident in a mounting social divide between the small wealthy elite and the much bigger proportion of ordinary citizens, have magnified the rise of the so-called "oligarchs" in Armenia. In fact, there is an interesting lesson from the case of the Russian oligarchs: for Russia's oligarchs, the recent economic crisis weakened them considerably, with most now begging the Russian state for loans and assistance. The underlying weakness of oligarchs—any oligarchs, not just the Russian or the Armenian variety—is that their "business empires" are based on state patronage and debt, and are not built on true business models or activities.

For many of the Russian oligarchs, the crisis exposed the fragile "house of cards" that underpinned their businesses, and revealed their vulnerability. It is this vulnerability that is now spurring the Russian state to retake control over several key sectors of the Russian economy, as the oligarchs are being stripped of much of their economic clout and even political power during this crisis. In the case of Armenia, however, unlike Georgia, for example, the state seems to lack the will to adopt such tactics. Sadly, Armenia's oligarchs have only consolidated their power through the control of several commodity-based cartels, controlling the imports of nearly all important commodities and exercising powerful influence over exports.

But like the Russian case, Armenia's oligarchs are also vulnerable, with a sharp fall in commodity prices, a slump in demand, and an end to easy credit combining to pose new threats to their personal wealth and power. Although, unlike Russia, the Armenian state lacks the resources to rescue these failing businesses, it has also failed to seize the opportunity to take on the oligarchs. Whether in terms of failing to pay their fair share of taxes, or due to their illegal cartels and semi-monopolies, the oligarchs represent one of the most serious threats to the state, flaunting their power and diminishing the authority of the government. Equally troubling, the oligarchic structures are also obstacles to development, robbing the state as much as the population of economic opportunities and competition. What is needed is a serious campaign to regulate these oligarchic business interests, enforce and break up the illegal commodity-based cartels, and hold the oligarchs to account, forcing them to meet their tax obligations and respect existing laws and regulations. Only then can the countries of the region overcome a general lack of legitimacy and crisis of confidence.

Conclusion

For Armenia, the outlook for successfully tackling and restraining the oligarchs seems rather bleak. The absence of effective institutions and the resulting weak regulatory framework have allowed a pattern of flagrant abuse and excess to emerge relatively unchallenged by the authorities. This lack of institutionalization is especially evident in terms of economic regulation and enforcement, and has permitted the emergence of a new class of economic elite in Armenia. This oligarchic elite has steadily acquired economic power at the expense of both society and state power, depriving the state of tax revenue and defoliating the country of national assets.

The emergence of "oligarchs" as a new elite wielding excessive power is neither a new phenomenon nor limited geographically. The challenge of containing such oligarchs has been prevalent in many countries, including 1900s America. In the American case, the oligarchs, or "robber barons," of early industrial capitalism included such well-known patriarchs as Carnegie, Rockefeller, and Vanderbilt. As these oligarchs extended their informal networks of control throughout the booming American economy, they also created informal cartel-based semi-monopolies. But the mounting domestic outrage over such monopolistic abuses led to the creation of a most effective weapon: anti-trust legislation. Success against these American oligarchs was achieved by more than just the weapon of anti-trust laws: it was the political will to use this legislative tool and the hardy rule of law to enforce it that were the keys to victory. Moreover, it took an American leader, President Theodore Roosevelt, courageous enough to confront the power of the oligarchs, to restore the natural equilibrium of the US economy.

In the case of the Russian and other former Soviet economies, this new class of oligarchs has tended to exploit the privatization process to gain economic power initially, but then also to pursue political power that inherently threatens the course of democratization and political reform. In the Russian case, the threat is also to the regime itself. Such a perception is at the heart of the ongoing drama between Russian President Vladimir Putin and the small group of super-oligarchs. Having enjoyed years of political power in a trade-off for their financial support for the former Russian President Boris Yeltsin, they have faced a very different fate in Putin's pursuit of a strong Russian state. In many ways, the clash between the state and the oligarchs was inevitable. Some Russian oligarchs chose exile while others opted for acquiescence. Fewer still were bold enough or arrogant enough to cross the line and confront Putin's political will.

And in the case of Latin America, much of the economic growth over the past century was spurred by a form of state-sponsored capitalism, with local oligarchs in alliance with the military and the state bureaucracy, exercising inordinate control over key sectors and industries of the economy. This system led to policies of distorted trade, with high tariffs and arbitrary regulations that only exacerbated widening divides of economic inequality and social disparity. This further impeded Latin America's overall political development in favor of authoritarian regimes, only interrupted by an occasional military intervention. This Latin American pattern was finally broken by the one country in the region that was able to replace the oligarchic economic structure with free markets. As Chile was the first to end the economic domination of the oligarchs, it also became the first to achieve lasting stability and a prosperous economy in the region.

The key to defeating the power of the oligarchs is to attack their main vulnerability: the source of their money. This is related to the broader campaign against corruption, with the rule of law (and political will) again playing a crucial role, and it involves tackling the economic monopolies and cartels that fuel and finance the oligarchs. Generally, such cartels and monopolies flourish within "closed" economies, averting the transparency and competition that dominate the more open marketplace. These cartels and monopolies also become entrenched by bargaining with elements of the state. In Armenia, given the small size of the national economy, transparency and competition are rather easy to avoid. And despite efforts to limit or break up monopolies, without the rule of law and political will very little can be reasonably expected. In larger economies, such as in the East Asian region, this "cronyism" has resulted in state policies aimed at restricting foreign and domestic competition, in return for providing an avenue for lucrative shares to the state elite.

In both cases, however, there is a high "transaction cost" to such arrangements. It fosters and promotes widespread corruption, even to the point of actually weakening the state by depriving it of much-needed tax revenue. It also limits economic growth in the short run, and constrains competition in the long run, which in turn leads to higher prices and slower innovation. Thus, the cumulative effects are devastating for the national economy overall and for society in particular. And for Armenia, with its small, infant economy and still engaged in a difficult transition, such a situation only threatens to destabilize and isolate the country further.

In order to confront and curb the powerful oligarchs, there are several measures that need be adopted. While obviously the twin challenges of corruption and the threat posed by the oligarchs are interrelated and also mutually reinforcing, both problems are direct challenges to the state's power. And ironically, unlike the commonly held perception of the Armenian state benefiting from corruption and the shadow economy, they harm the state, by depriving it of sizeable tax and customs revenues and by undermining state authority.

Whether in terms of failing to pay their fair share of taxes, or due to their illegal cartels and semi-monopolies, the oligarchs represent one of the most serious threats to the state, flaunting their power and diminishing the authority of the government. Equally troubling, the oligarchic structures are also obstacles to development, robbing the state as much as the population of economic opportunities and competition.

Subsequently, what is needed is a serious campaign to regulate these oligarchic business interests, enforce and break up the illegal commodity-based cartels, and hold the oligarchs to account, forcing them to meet their tax obligations and respect existing laws and regulations. The imperative now is the need for a renewed commitment to defeating the power of the oligarchs by attacking the economic monopolies and cartels that fuel and finance the oligarchic system.

It is the relationship between power and economics that holds the key to weathering the crisis now facing Armenia. More specifically, the inverse of the "economics of power" linkage—the "power of economics"—is the most effective avenue toward correcting the Armenian crisis. The "power of economics" offers a new sense of "creative destruction" capable of overcoming the economic power and influence of the oligarchic system. And the power of economics is multifaceted, including the "shocks" to the closed system from, first, an internal budget crisis driven by low tax collection and the need to rein in corruption and fight monopolies. A second shock to the system would come from an open border with Turkey and the subsequent competition that an open border would bring to the Armenian marketplace.

Third, and most significant, is the need to realize that the Armenian state can no longer maintain the current economic system. Weathering the economic crisis necessitates an end to the state's reliance on the twin evils of corruption and oligarchic cartels and monopolies. Faced with an already apparent shortage of political legitimacy, the Armenian state can no longer sustain the closed economic system that has deformed and distorted the country in recent years. Although these economic problems pose new threats to social and economic stability, this new crisis is only made worse by the already serious disparities in wealth and income. These disparities, evident in a mounting social divide between the small wealthy elite and the much bigger proportion of ordinary Armenians, have magnified the rise of the so-called "oligarchs."

This is especially crucial in light of the recent assessments of the Armenian economy by the International Monetary Fund (IMF), which show that Armenia is now facing deeper long-term problems. This means that the Armenian state will only continue to face declining revenue, dwindling investment, and an end to even the mirage of economic growth that the previous government used to hide its political shortcomings behind.

What is needed is a serious campaign to regulate these oligarchic business interests, enforce and break up the illegal commodity-based cartels, and hold the oligarchs to account, forcing them to meet their tax obligations and respect existing laws and regulations. Only then can the Armenian government begin to address its already serious lack of legitimacy and crisis of confidence.

Such a state effort to target the oligarchs' stranglehold on business is the first step to meeting the government's plans to develop small- and medium-sized business. And such a move would also send a serious message in support of the state's effort to fight corruption, which has long been seen as too little, too late. Although the Armenian government is increasingly coming to the realization that it is the economic crisis, even more than the current political stalemate in the country, that poses the most serious threat to stability, the imperative now is to take on the oligarchic cartels. And as the lessons from Russia reveal, the time to tackle the oligarchs is now, while they are weakened by the economic and financial crisis, otherwise it will be too late—too late for the state, and much too late for the country.

10

UNDERSTANDING VARIATION IN CORRUPTION AND WHITE-COLLAR CRIME

GEORGIA AND ARMENIA

Alexander Kupatadze

This chapter examines the internal and external causes of variations in corruption and white-collar crime through a comparative case study of Georgia and Armenia. This chapter argues that, from the domestic perspective, different outcomes in relation to ethnic conflicts as well as differences in terms of the political elite's stability (a radical changeover of political elites in Georgia versus a continuation of existing elite networks in Armenia) explain the varying degrees of corruption and white-collar crime rates between the two states. From the external dimension, this chapter states that the varying attitudes toward Russia and amenability to Western influence have provided different incentives to reform in Georgia and Armenia, and resulted in different outcomes in reference to corruption.

Given that Georgia and Armenia share similar histories, the variation in the levels of white-collar crime and corruption between these two countries has remained a puzzle. Both are small Caucasian countries that share the history of invasions, as well as the experience of having been part of the Tsarist Empire and subsequently the Soviet Union. Both states have served as a battleground for expansionist empires from even earlier eras, including the Romans, the Persians, and the Ottomans. While their spoken and written languages are different, as are their alphabets, both cultures share an allegiance to Christianity, which has fueled some sense of an overarching religious identity. Both Armenia and Georgia are also small states that have learned to survive and adapt to difficult geopolitical and economic conditions. Additionally, in both countries, ethnic identity persisted throughout the Soviet era despite Russian assimilation policies.

The case selection allows us to control the number of variables that affect the levels of corruption. This includes political systems or the degree of democracy/authoritarianism,[1] political and economic competition,[2] colonial heritage and age of democracy,[3] as well as economic capacity, prospects for European Union accession, international trade openness,[4] and foreign direct investment levels.[5] The following table sums up some of the similarities.

Table 1: Armenia and Georgia

	Armenia	*Georgia*
Political system	Presidential	Presidential (until Oct. 2013)
Electoral system	Mixed	Mixed
Media freedom	Medium	Medium
Democracy (Freedom House 2013)	Partly free	Partly free
GDP (official exchange rate) (US$)	$10.61 billion (2015 est.)	$13.75 billion (2015 est.)
Ethnic homogeneity	98% Armenian	84% Georgian
Large reserves of natural resources (oil, gas, etc.)	No	No

Source: data on democracy and political system is derived from Freedom House Reports, available at https://freedomhouse.org/reports; data on demographics, economy, media and natural resources is derived from *CIA World Factbook*, https://www.cia.gov/library/publications/the-world-factbook/.

Although Armenia has not engaged in an active process of reform, its corruption rates were much less than those of Georgia in the 1990s. A key shift occurred when Georgia became the "anti-corruption achiever" after its Rose Revolution in 2003, which provided a window of opportunity for the incoming political elite.[6] A group of young reformers, led by US-educated lawyer Mikheil Saakashvili, launched a radical break with the formerly corrupt past and was soon credited by the World Bank's "Doing Business" report as being among the world's top reformers.[7] In contrast, Armenia experienced only superficial reforms and limited success in fighting corruption during this time period. However, as in countries such as Ukraine and Kyrgyzstan, where similar reform processes succeeded only partially, in Georgia there has also been limited success against corruption, despite the efforts of the young reformers.[8] Hence it is important to look at why and how the window of opportunity was used in Georgia, rather than taking it for granted.

Two sets of factors, internal and external, define diverging levels of corruption and white-collar crime. Internally, the Rose Revolution of 2003 provided a window of opportunity that was used by a young, structurally and ideologically cohesive group of reformers, willing and able to implement wide sweeping reforms in Georgia. These reforms eliminated corruption in areas where state officials and the public interact. In Armenia, conversely, the political elite have had a vested interest in keeping the status quo, which has undermined radical reforms and perpetuated corruption. The elite continuity in Armenia is partially an outcome of the Nagorno-Karabakh conflict that solidified the dominance of corrupt interest groups in the state. Externally, the antagonism between Russia and the Georgian political elites for their deviation from "post-Sovietness" provided incentives for anti-corruption reforms. These incentives were further strengthened by the unanimity of Georgian political elites to develop closer ties with the EU and NATO. In the case of Armenia,

Chart 1: Control of corruption, worldwide governance indicator, World Bank[9]

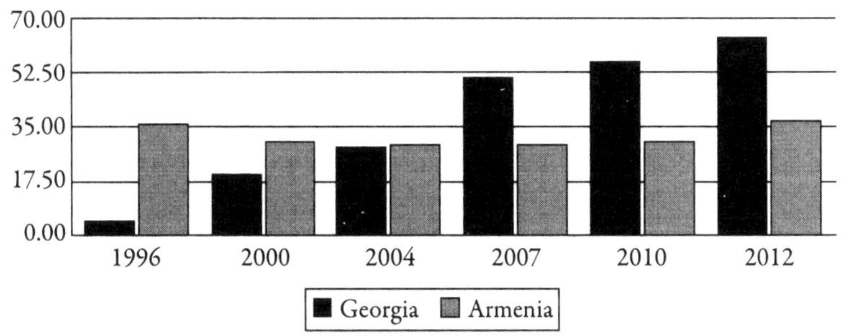

their "strategic partnership" with Russia did not provide any of these incentives. Moreover, political elites have been divided in their willingness to integrate with Euro-Atlantic blocs.

Hence, I first discuss the issues of elite continuity/discontinuity in the two countries and provide evidence pertaining to how it led to diverging outcomes in corruption levels. Then I focus on the ethnic conflicts that the two countries experienced in the 1990s, and elaborate on how the outcomes of these two conflicts have influenced corruption. Lastly, I discuss different trajectories in the foreign policies of the two countries, and explain how this divergence has also impacted the variation in corruption rates between the two countries. This chapter focuses on the period from 2004 to 2012, the time of reform in Georgia when the radical divergence between the two countries occurred.

Elite-level variables and corruption

In Georgia, corruption was largely tolerated during Shevardnadze's era in exchange for loyalty to the regime.[10] In 2001, bribes to state officials were estimated at between $75 and $105 million,[11] while state revenues for the same year were $499 million.[12] Subsequently, the state could not pay wages to the vast majority of its employees, and salaries were delayed for months. Hence, corruption and bribery engulfed every level of the state apparatus.[13] For instance, a number of the Ministry of Fuel and Energy's officials are accused of embezzling $380 million, an amount equal to half of the foreign aid awarded for the reconstruction of Georgia before the Rose Revolution.[14] Ministers were often engaged in business activities, which resulted in conflicts of interest and sometimes outright corruption.[15] For instance, Fridon Injia, the Minister of Communications in the 1990s, emerged as a major entrepreneur in the communication sector while holding the government portfolio. Corrupt interest groups permanently derailed all anti-corruption initiatives.[16] This widespread and unpunished abuse of office was among the reasons for public protests that emerged following the rigged elections in November 2003. These protests culminated with the removal of Eduard Shevardnadze from power, following which a group of young reformers took office, led by Mikheil Saakashvili. From the very beginning of his presidency, Saakashvili prioritized building efficient state institutions, and introduced sweeping public sector reforms. Fighting corruption and organized crime were key elements of Saakashvili's state-building project. In general, his administration concentrated on state-building rather than state-democratization.[17] The economic model of Singapore, as well as historic strongmen and state-builders such as Mustafa Kemal Atatürk and Charles de Gaulle, inspired Saakashvili's decisions.

In pursuing state-building, Saakashvili's team demonstrated an impressive level of dedication and commitment. At the forefront of their agenda were new anti-corruption legislations, a zero-tolerance policy toward crime and corruption, neo-liberal economic policies, and reforms of key institutions central to combating corruption, such as the police and prosecution apparatuses.

These radical reforms have been implemented under very specific conditions. There was a generational change in the Georgian ruling elite. Many members of Saakashvili's team had a civil society background, like the Interior Minister Ivane Merabishvili, Secretary of the Security Council Giga Bokeria, and Tbilisi Mayor Gigi Ugulava. The core of the team had graduated from Western educational institutions. They demonstrated a high degree of structural and ideological coherence rooted in neo-liberal ideology with strong right-wing and market-friendly orientations.[18] Saakashvili was thirty-seven years old when he took office, and many of his cabinet members were in their late twenties or early thirties. Furthermore, the government succeeded in attracting young educated personnel at middle and lower levels of bureaucracy with competitive salaries. Many of these young bureaucrats were highly motivated, full of new ideas and, most importantly, zealously committed to institutional integrity.[19]

Significantly, there was also a temporary breakdown in the state–business nexus. Initially the Saakashvili team was only peripherally involved in large businesses, and had only one or two financiers, such as the natural gas trader David Bezhuashvili. Members of the Shevardnadze family had monopolized most of the licit and illicit economic resources.[20] Hence the incoming political elite were less beholden to economic interest groups in the period of most radical reform that took place between 2004 and 2007. The 2004 elected parliament mostly consisted of young activists and a few businessmen from the ruling United National Movement (UNM) faction.[21] The radical changeover from the old political elite, the cohesiveness of the new political elite, and the breakdown of collusive networks between businessmen and politicians were crucial for the implementation of radical and wide-sweeping reforms.

The new government adopted a zero-tolerance policy to white-collar crime. In late 2003, Prime Minister Zurab Zhvania said in a press conference that there "will be a real fight against corruption. All those who are responsible for misappropriation of people's property will be held accountable."[22] Many previous government officials were imprisoned, some of whom were released soon after paying substantial fines under the framework of a newly adopted plea-bargain system.[23] The zero-tolerance policy and the use of near-universal incarceration led to a dramatic increase in the prison population: it quadrupled from 6,119 prisoners in 2003 to 24,114 prisoners in 2011.[24]

The criminal justice approach was supplemented by neo-liberal economic policies focusing on reducing red tape, simplifying state regulations, and optimizing bureaucracy. These measures led to a dramatic decrease in corruption, especially in sectors where citizens' interactions with state officials were most frequent, such as in registering property, licensing businesses, and declaring taxes.[25] However, Saakashvili's government faced continuous criticism of the persistence of "elite level" corruption. During the period between 2003 and 2010, about 1,000 public officials faced charges of corruption, including six members of parliament and 15 deputy ministers, according to Georgia's Justice Ministry.[26]

Unlike the "big bang approach" in Georgia, the Armenian elite promoted the idea of "evolution." The entrenched interest groups have largely maintained their influence throughout the past decades. Armenian presidents Levon Ter-Petrosyan (held office 1991–8) and Robert Kocharian (held office 1998–2008) both managed to manipulate interest groups to their own political and material advantage. In contrast to Georgia, Armenia has been continuously ruled by a group of young communists (Komsomol) and members of the "Karabakh clan." After President Ter-Petrosyan lost power in 1998, due to the revolt orchestrated by his inner circle, two subsequent presidents, Kocharian and Serzh Sargsyan, have also been keen to co-opt powerful interest groups to secure their power.[27] This constrained the anticipated reforms, as these groups were interested in maintaining the status quo. In 2009, Prime Minister Tigran Sarkisian complained that the existing system would not allow for exposing and punishing officials who maintained extensive and illegal business interests.[28]

Thus in Armenia elite continuity contributed to the perpetuation of corruption and white-collar crimes, as entrenched networks and their personal interests prevented the reformation of state institutions. The Tax Enforcement and Customs agencies have generated illicit income for the oligarchs through their own complicity. This financed the ruling bargain between the state and its constituencies. Businessmen who oppose the state risk losing their businesses and becoming targets of selective anti-corruption investigations, as was the case for Khachatur Sukiassian.[29] At the same time, those who are allied to the oligarchs receive preferential treatment.[30] The case of MP Ruben

Hayrapetyan[31] indicates how police investigations and court judgments can be undermined in favor of the oligarchs.[32]

In ostensible efforts to counter corruption, the Armenian government has pursued highly selective police investigations and carried out court judgments against certain political targets, in what President Sargsyan called going "after bigger fish."[33] Between 2010 and 2012, several cases were filed against high-ranking embezzlers and white-collar criminals on a limited scale.[34] The political opposition and political analysts have been skeptical about these arrests, with some claiming that they have been a result of intergovernmental conflicts, rather than a genuine good-faith effort to fight corruption.[35] Some other cases filed against high-profile officials have lacked government attention. For example, in 2012 a foreign court fined MP Vardan Ayvazyan for demanding a bribe from the Global Gold Mining Company while he served as minister of environment. However, the Armenian prosecutor did not investigate the alleged corruption.[36] Moreover, in 2012 a member of parliament was arrested in Tbilisi for running a Cyprus-based company, along with Prime Minister Sarkisian and an archbishop, which was involved in illegal trading of diamonds with Sierra Leone.[37]

In contrast to Georgia, the domination of the old corrupt oligarchy went unabated in Armenia. The post-Soviet practice of securing and developing businesses through informal, and sometimes illicit, deals produced networks of politicians, entrepreneurs, and criminals that have blurred the public–private line since the early 1990s.[38] The early privatization policies in Armenia resulted in the convergence of corporate, state, and in some cases illicit or criminal interests.[39] This was exacerbated by corrupt government officials, at both national and local levels, who maintained direct, partial, or indirect control over emerging private firms.[40] Some of the wealthy elite were appointed regional governors. Often protected by the political leaders in Yerevan, these "regional feudals" run the regions as their personal fiefdoms, enjoy immunity, and avoid punishment for recurring crimes such as violence and embezzlement.[41]

Importantly, some of the earlier achievements of the anti-corruption efforts in Georgia have also been reversed since 2008. While legal deregulation was implemented swiftly, Georgia did not turn into the "the Switzerland of the Caucasus."[42] Near the completion of the re-privatization process in 2007 and 2008, new oligarchs appeared, including a former minister and a close friend of Saakashvili. They were joined by older oligarchs who were carry-overs from the previous regime and shifted loyalty overnight. Together they funded the UNM after the Rose Revolution.[43] Centralized mechanisms for bribe collection have disappeared, but clientelism has emerged where the state distributes resources among its allies. The government is believed to have awarded public contracts to "friendly" companies in exchange for political support. In return, the owners of these companies contribute financially to the ruling UNM.[44] However, broadly, corruption schemes have disappeared, bribery in lower- and medium-level bureaucracy has decreased dramatically, and what was formerly private profiteering of elites has been replaced by clientelist policies aimed at maintaining and consolidating political power. None of this occurred in Armenia. A radical temporary breakdown of the state–business nexus, and a new cohesive and united political elite, resulted in Georgia's divergence from Armenia's continued trajectory of corruption. This is inherently linked with the way that ethnic conflict has unfolded in the two countries.

Ethnic conflicts and their impact

Both Georgia and Armenia experienced prolonged ethnic wars in the 1990s. Georgia fought separatist movements in Abkhazia and South Ossetia from 1992 to 1994, and Armenia was at war with Azerbaijan in the region of Nagorno-Karabakh from 1991 to 1994. Georgia lost against the separatist movements, and Abkhazia and South Ossetia became de facto independent and partially recognized states. Armenia won the war in Karabakh, and claimed control over Azerbaijani territories. Nagorno-Karabakh became de facto autonomous, but still officially recognized as part of Azerbaijan.

The struggle for Nagorno-Karabakh became central to Armenia's political identity, and a key part of its post-Soviet state construction.[45] It contributed to the formation of political elites in Armenia with two presidents, Kocharian and Sargsian, hailing from the region and both representing the so-called "Karabakh clan." The conflict has established a very special role for the power ministries (Ministry of Defense and Ministry of Interior) of Armenia. This new political elite controlled the key financial streams that financed the war, and most importantly emerged as key players in Armenia's post-war business sector.

The outcome of the Nagorno-Karabakh war explains the relatively low corruption levels in Armenia compared to Georgia in the early years of transition. Armenia never went through the sort of chaos and criminalization of the state that was rampant in Georgia during the 1990s. Instead, the victorious veterans of the Nagorno-Karabakh war quickly restored order, controlled crime, and established a stable regime.[46] Due to the high cohesiveness of the regime, the Armenian state was able to maintain a monopoly over power, and effectively deploy forces to maintain order and prevent non-state actors' insurgencies. For example, Vano Siradegyan, Minister of Interior, was successful in keeping mafia bosses out of Armenian politics.[47] However, the dominance of the Karabakh clan over all aspects of Armenian politics led to the development of widespread corruption.

In contrast to Armenia, Georgian military forces were defeated twice in the early 1990s. Ethnic conflicts thus directly contributed to the weakening of the state and the strengthening of semi-criminalized armed groups, one of the most notorious of which was the Mkhedrioni. These criminal networks successfully hijacked the weak central authority, which at some point had lost control over more than 20 percent of the country. Until President Eduard Shevardnadze outlawed the group in 1995, the leader of the Mkhedrioni band, Jaba Ioseliani, was virtually ruling Georgia by controlling most levers of the state.

Unlike Georgia, the Armenian state had to reward the national heroes who gained reputation and prestige during the war with Azerbaijan. Many former leaders of armed movements were granted government positions in law enforcement agencies and other government institutions, as well as lucrative shares in various business sectors.[48] The origins of some of the contemporary oligarchic structures can be traced back to the "power ministries" during the war, especially in the Ministries of Defense and Interior.[49] Most importantly, these ministries, especially the Ministry of Defense dominated by older officers, have remained most resistant to internal reforms that undermine the power of the old guard.[50] Thus, the war has crystallized the dominance of political and military leaders of the Karabakh movement in Armenia.[51]

Many Armenian leaders still manipulate the Nagorno-Karabakh issue for their own political gain.[52] This reflects the crucial differences in the political elites' agendas. Armenian elites are reluctant to reform, fearing that this would weaken the central government and lead to losing on the Karabakh issue; by contrast, Georgian political elites are trying to reform in order to attract Abkhazians and Ossetians into a single common state.[53]

The decrease of corruption and white-collar crime rates in Georgia was a result of the radical elite changeover that brought to power a new generation of young leaders committed to building a strong state. This group of leaders transformed the political and economic environments, and eliminated corruption in lower and medium rings of bureaucracy. In Armenia, the continuity of the political elites reinforced the dominance of interest groups that aim to maintain the corrupt equilibrium. This was exacerbated by the war in

Nagorno-Karabakh that cemented the political and economic powers of the Karabakh movement's leaders, and diminished incentives to reform.

Russia versus the West: incentive structure for reform

There are fundamental differences in terms of incentives for anti-corruption reform as Georgia has drifted closer to the EU while Armenia remains in the Russian orbit. For obvious reasons, it is rather difficult to argue that the close alliance with Russia causes corruption, but it is evident that this kind of alliance does not provide incentives for reform.

Georgia has long been oriented toward the West, and it was widely understood among the Georgian political elite that the rule of law is a prerequisite for conforming to Western and European social and legal standards. The adoption of a democratic model of governance, practiced in different European countries, unified different factions of the political elite, current authorities, and political opposition. The absolute majority of political parties' leaders, interviewed in 2010,[54] supported integration into the EU.[55] As an influential member of Saakashvili's team, Giga Bokeria, once said: "there is no other environment. There is no other family we can move to."[56] This attitude has promoted strong ties between the Georgian political elite and their counterparts in Europe. As the experience of central and south-eastern Europe suggests, these ties provided means and motivations for the political systems to become more transparent.[57] There is no such unanimity for EU integration in Armenia. The study of Armenian elites[58] reveals only a slight difference among those who prefer EU integration (26 percent) and those who prefer integration with Russia and CIS countries (22.5 percent).[59]

The existence of countervailing powers that provide alternative sources of support enhances the bargaining power of the countries to ward off external demands for reform.[60] The foreign policy vectors of Georgia and Armenia went on two different trajectories. On the one hand, the war with Azerbaijan and the historical animosity with Turkey (a result of the Armenian genocide in 1915) left Armenia with few alternatives other than Moscow. On the other hand, Georgia, due to Moscow's backing of its break-away regions, had few alternatives but to ally with the West (US and European Union). Since the mid-1990s, Georgia has sought integration with NATO and drifted away from the Russian orbit. Georgia and Russia were engaged in a short war in August 2008, and there have not been diplomatic relations between the two countries since then. The aggression with Russia did not leave Georgia with many foreign policy choices. Moreover, concerns about the co-option of Georgian security forces and antagonism with Russia gave strong incentives to crack down on corruption in law enforcement agencies.[61]

Furthermore, Saakashvili has reiterated several times that Georgian leadership is building "alternative governance model in post-Soviet Eurasia," meaning a government marked by low levels of corruption, in contrast to how Russia functions.[62] The reforms are also believed to be bringing Georgia closer to Europe. In 2011, Thornike Gordadze, a Georgian minister, said at the Croatia Summit of Senior European and North American Leaders, stemming from its efforts to get closer to the EU, "Georgia is fighting geography with successful reforms," and the first example of these successful reforms is "the elimination of corruption and organized crime."[63] Hence, the Georgian political elite has explicitly chosen to divert the country from the Russian path of development. The impact of their antagonism toward Russia is visible in the fight against corruption, and is exacerbated by the drive to get closer to the EU and NATO. There were no such incentives in the case of Armenia.

On the contrary, Armenia never wanted to join NATO, and has drifted closer to Russia over the past two decades. Military cooperation with Russia often translates into subsidized arms sale. The common security umbrella provided by the Collective Security Treaty Organization (CSTO) is an effective counterbalance to the armament of Azerbaijan financed by petrodollars. Russia also has a crucial stake in this relationship, especially after the war with Georgia and the need for military presence in the South Caucasus.[64] The nature of Armenian–Russian relations did not necessitate any changes in the Armenian government's *modus operandi*.[65] Armenian political elites describe their foreign policy as "multi-vector"; however, Armenia's dependency on Russia for economic and political support is striking. The Armenian political system follows the Russian model.[66] Armenia has a strong centralized executive branch, corrupt courts that lack independence, and controlled media.[67] The Armenian elite still value the former Soviet model of rule, as demonstrated by the 2014 AREG survey which showed that 35 percent of the interviewed political parties' leaders thought that the Soviet Union's political regime was more effective than the current system.

Russian control over the Armenian economy has rapidly increased over the last decade, mainly through suspicious deals. Russian firms own all of Armenia's telecommunications network, virtually the whole energy sector (including the nuclear power plant at Medzamor), its railway network, and the local remnants of the Soviet-era defense industry, most of them acquired during the presidency of Robert Kocharyan (1998–2008) in exchange for debt relief or subsidized energy supplies. Since the 2008 war, Georgia has no longer been dependent on Russia as far as its energy imports are concerned. That being said, Russian companies are still active in Georgia's oil sector, telecommunications, mining, fertilizer industry, in addition to running two hydropower stations, the Tbilisi electricity distribution plant, and a major bank.[68]

Armenia, like Georgia, had the opportunity to sign the Association and Free Trade agreements with the EU in 2013. In an unexpected move in September 2013, Serzh Sargsyan announced "a dramatic U-turn in Armenian policy."[69] While meeting with Vladimir Putin in Moscow, Sargsyan confirmed that Armenia would join the Russian-led Customs Union, and would support Moscow's efforts to "integrate" the former Soviet space. That decision effectively put an end to Armenia's hope to partner with the EU.[70]

The impetus for reforms in Armenia is most likely to come from the Armenian diaspora in the West. They have been voicing their concerns after several cases of losing businesses and money due to government decisions influenced by bribery and lobbying.[71] The diaspora community also commissioned a comprehensive analysis of Armenia's corrupt networks.[72] Yet the impact has been limited, as powerful local interest groups undermine the calls for change.

In summary, unlike Armenia, the Georgian political elite has been more amenable to Western pressures, and keener to drift away from political interest groups. These two crucial distinctions resulted in different outcomes. Because Armenia is politically and economically more dependent on Russia, and its elite divided on the integration with the West, there are fewer incentives for anti-corruption reforms in Armenia, as compared with Georgia.

Conclusion

This chapter has discussed two Caucasian states and accounts for the diverging outcomes in corruption levels of Georgia and Armenia. It analyzed a number of variables, including issues related to the political elites, outcomes of ethnic conflicts, and international pressures. It has argued that, domestically, the radical political elite changeover, the ideological and structural cohesiveness of the new political elite, and the temporary breakdown of the state–business nexus pushed Georgia and Armenia into two divergent paths. Externally, two crucial conditions, namely the amenability to Western influence and the drive to divert from the "Russian way" of governance, contributed to the two divergent trajectories of the countries.

Similar to the Caucasian cases studied in this chapter, two Baltic countries followed the same path. In the early 1990s, Estonia succeeded in its anti-corruption reforms, whereas Latvia has lagged behind since then.[73] In Estonia, it was the team of young liberal intellectuals led by Mart Laar that implemented radical reforms.[74] Whereas in Latvia, efficiency was undermined by the heterogeneous elites with Soviet nomenclature hangovers and lack of ideological unity and intra-elite trust.[75] Moreover, the impact of Western countries such as Finland and Sweden was greater on government policies in Estonia, while the influence of Russia was much more significant in Latvia, to the extent that it delineated the overall efficiency of government performance.[76] Given these parallels, the findings from this chapter may have the potential to be generalized.

11

BAKU

CREATING A PERSIAN GULF PARADISE ON THE CASPIAN SEA

Anar Valiyev

Baku is the capital of Azerbaijan and the largest city in the Caucasus region, located on the Absheron peninsula with a territory covering over 2,130 square kilometers, which is then divided into twelve administrative districts. From a historical perspective, Baku has been an industrial city, oil having been the major commodity that turned the small fortress into a city. The birth of a new Baku as an industrial city can be dated to 1847, following the drilling of the first industrial oil well.[1] The period from the 1870s until World War I has been called the "first oil boom," or the golden age of the development of Baku. From this period till 1917, Baku witnessed the rise of magnificent buildings in a Baroque style that was completely alien to the architecture of a Muslim city at that time. By 1913, Baku was producing almost 95 percent of all Russian oil and 55 percent of total global oil production.[2] Geographic location, as well as the presence of natural resource wealth, predetermined the course of urban planning in Baku. Located on a peninsula surrounded by the biggest lake in the world, the profile of Baku is defined by several natural factors: including the sea, the landscape, the climate, and limestone, a material that was used for construction of many of its historical buildings. The Soviet period of Baku was marked by further expansion of the oil industry and a growing population, which needed more accommodation. Between the late 1950s and mid-1980s, the government therefore prioritized housing; in order to solve the problem created by increased immigration of rural people into the city, the Soviet administration invested heavily in the construction of cheap five-storey buildings. During this time, many micro-rayons (micro-districts) were also constructed in Baku, reflecting the central socialist urban planning concept of "Ideal Communist City Planning."

Since the disintegration of the Soviet Union, Baku has undergone a tremendous transformation. In this context, demographic trends for the last decade have been quite favorable toward the development of Baku, with a constant increase in population due to the high net in-migration from the rural areas of Azerbaijan. The official population of the capital reached 2.2 million in 2014, whereas Ganja, the second largest city of Azerbaijan, had only 322,000 inhabitants.[3] Unofficial estimates are even higher, however, as it is estimated that up to 3.5–4 million people live in or commute to the city every day. Consequently, it is not surprising that Baku exerts a disproportionally significant influence on the national economy. The total GDP of Azerbaijan in 2014 was $63 billion, almost 71 percent of which was generated in Baku.[4]

The city continues to be the leading recipient of investment, most of which is funneled into the construction industry. Demographic pressure and the demand for new apartments forced the city to invest heavily in construction, with new high-rise towers constantly erected across the downtown area. In addition, government investment also favors Baku, directing major funds toward infrastructure projects, city gentrification (beautification), and renovation. The post-Soviet transition toward a market economy has enabled Baku to make tremendous progress in urban development and to become one of the fastest growing cities in the region of the Caucasus and Central Asia. As in many other Central and Eastern European countries, the rate of post-socialist urban change in Baku has been striking, with privatization being "the leitmotif of post-socialist urban change."[5] Meanwhile, the city was constantly looking for a model of development, and many experts, architects, and tourists could not resist comparing Baku with Dubai. In this chapter we shall aim to look at the development pattern of Baku and its attempts to emulate the model of Dubai, or other Gulf cities like Doha. We shall try to answer the question of whether Baku will be able to copy the pattern of the "Pearl of the UAE" successfully, or if it will fail because of both indigenous and exogenous factors.

In the steps of Dubai and Doha

Post-Soviet urban transformation in Baku was characterized by many positive developments. Within two decades the city's landscape had changed completely: most notably, new high-rise buildings, plazas, and business centers were built. The logic of this development in Baku highlights how the government and urban elites were trying to turn the city into a main tourist destination of the region as well as an economic powerhouse similar to Dubai. Baku's development after 2004–5 resembled Dubai's rapid expansion. The first common characteristic between Baku and Dubai was the desire of the authorities to turn their respective cities into transportation hubs. For Baku, the desire to become the transportation hub for Central Eurasia stemmed from the success experienced by two other rising cities: Singapore and Dubai.

Today, the main projects undertaken by Baku resemble the path and plans implemented by these two cities. Rashid Port, the Jabal Ali Port and Free Economic Zone, Dubai International Airport, and many other state-of-the-art projects stand as vivid examples for Baku's development. Although the figure of Lee Kuan Yew, prime minister of Singapore, is referred to less, nevertheless Singapore's strategies for becoming a transportation hub are actively copied by Baku. It is not surprising, then, that the figure of Sheikh Rashid bin Said Al-Maktum, the former vice president of the UAE, who is seen as responsible for Dubai's rapid development and is a frequent visitor to Baku, is similarly much revered.

Baku's development after 2004–5 resembles Dubai's rapid expansion; but Baku is trying within a decade to accomplish what Dubai accomplished over an almost 45-year period. Additionally, just as the Dubai rulers tried to turn the city into a transportation hub by constructing Port Rashid and Jebel Ali, the government of Azerbaijan made a strategic decision to construct a new modern port 60 km south of Baku. This remarkable project on the Caspian Sea, dubbed the "jewel of the Caspian," includes the construction of Alyat port, the Alyat International Logistics Center, and Alyat Free Economic Zone. It is estimated that completion of the new port will cost around $870 million, and will enable the transportation and processing of around 10 million tons of cargo and 40,000 containers a year. In later stages this number will reach twenty-five million tons of cargo and one million containers. However, in order to be able to connect the region with the rest of Eurasia, it has also become necessary to reconnect several links.

The South Caucasus formerly lacked railroad connection with Europe. In 2007, the presidents of Azerbaijan, Turkey, and Georgia signed an agreement for the construction of the Baku–Akhalkalaki–Kars railroad, which would unite these three countries. Until that decision, Turkey only had railroad connections up to Kars and then to Gyumri in Armenia. Meanwhile, Azerbaijan had railroad connections to Tbilisi. The Karabakh conflict and complications related to it did not allow Armenian participation in the project. Thus, the absence of railroad connections directly between Georgia and Turkey was a major element missing from an uninterrupted transportation corridor from Central Asia to Turkey and Europe. The Azerbaijani government provided Georgia with a $700 million loan to construct the missing link between Akhalkalaki and Kars, as well as to modernize the existing route. Once the revitalized railroad is launched, it will be able to carry 20 million tons of cargo and about three million passengers. The launch date is currently delayed until sometime in 2017.

The second strategy that Baku borrowed from Dubai is one called "supply driven demand." Dubai's success in attracting an increased number of tourists by building luxurious hotels led Baku to believe in the strategy of "build it and they will come," which is the perception that the supply of hotels will attract the demand for them. Therefore, following what was done in Dubai, brand new hotels such as the Marriot, Hilton, Jumeirah, Kempinski, and Four Seasons have been opened in Baku.

The third strategy that Baku has employed is to construct iconic image-making buildings. Like Dubai with its iconic Burj Khalifa, Jumeirah, and Palm Islands, Baku has also attempted to lure the attention of the world to this kind of attraction. One such example of a grand project from the post-Soviet period is the construction of the Baku Flame Towers, which are gradually becoming a visual symbol of the city (for example, they are frequently depicted on postcards bought by visitors). The towers symbolize the long history of fire worshippers who considered Azerbaijan as the birthplace of the prophet Zoroaster. The Baku Flame Towers include a residential tower that offers 130 residential apartments over thirty-three floors; a hotel tower with 250 rooms and sixty-one serviced apartments; and an office tower that provides 33,114 square meters of office space.

In addition to the iconic Flame Towers, the Heydar Aliyev Center is another pearl of the construction boom in Baku. Occupying 57,519 square meters and opened in May 2012, it hosts a conference hall, library, and museum. Designed by the late architect Zaha Hadid, it is one of the many buildings built in Baku over the last four years that represent a move away from the Soviet-dominated past and toward a cohesive Azerbaijani national identity. The center is part of a larger redevelopment area and is expected to be the hub of the city's intellectual and cultural life. Last but not least of these construction achievements is the residential Khazar Islands project. This project, spearheaded by the local company Avesta, covers 3,000 hectares. It will consist of 41 different-sized islands and 19 districts in the Caspian Sea. The archipelago will cover an area of twenty-four sq km: eight km in length and three km in width. The total length of the boulevard islands will be fifty km. The project was first envisaged in 2010, and construction is now well underway. It is expected that, when completed in 2022–3, it will host one million residents.

The overall cost of construction of these artificial islands is estimated at $100 billion, $30 billion coming from foreign investors and another $30 billion from apartment sales. According to the project, completely renovated apartments will cost around $4000–$5000 per square meter.[6] What is immediately clear is the striking similarity between the Khazar Islands and Palm Islands in Dubai, which were constructed for similar reasons. But what is surprising is the enthusiasm of business people and government officials: none of the parties involved seems willing to imagine the huge problems and dangers that may plague this ambitious project.

The attraction of tourists is not the only objective of the business elites: the successful example of Dubai has also encouraged them to consider turning Baku into a business center for the region. Similar to Dubai's policy to create cluster-type satellite cities, such as Dubai Internet City or Dubai Media City, the business elites, with the support of the government, proposed the construction of Baku-city, which is a twenty-nine sq km coastal area designated for business facilities.[7] In terms of its target audience, Baku-city is intended for business people, diplomats, bankers, and students seeking to enjoy their leisure time. Consequently, it will not include housing for employees, although Baku-city will also include an allocation of certain lots of land destined for the construction of university campuses. Currently, most of the universities are located in the downtown area, or close to the city center, which results in periodic overcrowding of central facilities. By transferring the universities from the downtown area to the outskirts of the city, the business class hopes to be able to divert the flow of people and subsequently ease the pressure on transportation and other facilities of the city. This would then give business people access to the original university property downtown, which could be converted for business use, thus providing an additional return on their original investment. This plan mimics Dubai's similar policy for university clusters located in one area of the city.[8]

All these projects take time to get implemented and bring benefits. While the elites of Azerbaijan are hungry for attention, the strategy of getting noticed predominated over other strategies. Urban theory often suggested that urban spectacles or one-off events like the Olympic Games constituted large-scale, spectacular productions, where advertising, entertainment, TV and mass media would combine to stimulate consumer demand and tourism-oriented development.[9] Spectacular urban development agendas were frequently justified on the basis of developmentalist thinking, which equated national progress and "modernity" with economic development, "defined for policy purposes in terms of growth, productivity, and competitiveness rather than in terms of welfare."[10] But these types of events, the key example of which is the Olympic Games, are only short-term and demand massive investment. The classical example of failure was the 1976 Montreal Olympics, which left that city with "white elephant facilities" and a financial burden that has haunted policy-makers for the last couple of decades.[11]

Nevertheless, these types of events do attract a large number of tourists and the interest of international media, providing opportunities for the host nation, especially a small one, to showcase its achievements. Moreover, this kind of event has a boosting effect on national pride and strengthens its identity. Just as Doha has tried to become a hub for international media with Al Jazeera, the World Cup, and other events, Baku has also tried to bring international events to the city.

In 2012, Azerbaijan received the chance to test the ability of Baku to host high-profile international events when an Azerbaijani team of singers won the Eurovision song competition in 2011. In accordance with the rules of the competition, Baku then had to host the 2012 Eurovision event. Initially, Baku was not equipped to hold such a large-scale event, because it lacked both a major venue and also the infrastructure facilities; but immediately, Baku invested huge sums in the event, most of which were infrastructure projects. During the short period of nine months, the government built and launched the Crystal Hall, a new convention hall for holding the song contest; and then spent up to $600 million on additional projects associated with enhancements and city development, although the direct cost for the coordination of the event totaled only $34.3 million.

Eurovision was the first event to put Baku and Azerbaijan at the center of entertainment for Europe. This was the first time that Azerbaijan was able to associate itself with the rest of Europe. According to an independent NGO Internet Forum in Azerbaijan, the searches on Azerbaijan through Google increased eight times during the month following the victory in 2011, while searches for Baku as a destination doubled. Meanwhile on TripAdvisor, interest in Azerbaijan grew by over forty times. Finally, Baku hosting the Eurovision contest in May 2012 put queries about Azerbaijan into the ten most popular searches for May.[12]

As well as helping Azerbaijan to gain visibility on a wider scale, Eurovision enhanced the identity of Azerbaijanis. These events dramatically strengthened the sense of European or Western identity among large segments of the population, and especially those in the political and cultural elite. The Azerbaijani population was able to obtain a first-time opportunity to actually "live" in a European cultural milieu. For many people it was fundamental to their reappraising the roots of belonging to Europe while keeping national traditions and values.[13] The opening and closing ceremonies of the song contest featured motifs from Azerbaijani culture and traditions, while the rest of the show represented European traditions.

For the last two decades, Baku has typically earned huge resources from the sale of oil;[14] but from 2010, Baku began to move away from oil as the sole source upon which to build its state legitimacy at home and abroad, and began to invest in national culture, sport, cuisine, and other elements to promote a cohesive state identity. From this perspective, the European Games became the second grandiose project after Eurovision, in both of which Baku tried to brand itself alongside Europe and the world. In this context, Baku tried to use the model of Doha, Qatar, to try to attract as many athletic events as possible. After its success with Eurovision and some other events of regional significance, the Azerbaijani authorities felt that the country could host a larger event on an international scale, so they made a bid for the 2020 Olympic Games. Based on initial studies that put the hosting cost at $20 billion, the authorities suggested that oil revenues and private investment could finance it. By the time of the bid to the Olympic Committee, Azerbaijan had already built thirteen new sporting complexes to bolster Baku's candidacy, with twenty-three additional buildings underway and scheduled to be completed by 2012–14. However, Baku lost the Olympic bid to Tokyo in 2012. So the planners then shifted their strategy to attracting smaller-scale or second-tier events, ostensibly with the aim of improving the city's portfolio for another Olympic bid in 2024. On 8 December 2012, the 41st General Assembly of the European Olympic Committee decided to hold the first ever European Games, and the committee awarded Baku the right to host the inaugural European Games in 2015. The decision was the result of a secret ballot, in which the forty-eight votes produced thirty-eight in favor, eight votes against, and two abstentions. As Azad Rahimov, Minister of Youth, put it:

> It will be a major chance to show Baku to the world as a European country, as a Muslim, but secular state, as a good bridge between East and West, between the Muslim Orient and the Christian Europe, and to show the beauty of the country, [its] very ancient history, our music, art, food and hospitality. It is very important for a country that gained independence only 23 years ago to position itself on the map of Europe as a European country. Very often the question [is asked] "Where is Azerbaijan?" After the Eurovision song contest [which the country hosted in 2012, after winning in 2011] and after the European Games, most people will know the answer.[15]

Planners were highly focused on preparing for the 2015 European Games, which were expected to bring to Baku 6,000 athletes from forty-nine countries. The European Games featured up to twenty sports, including fifteen summer Olympic and two non-Olympic sports. The Baku European Games Operations Committee (BEGOC) was established to facilitate the organization of the Games; as BEGOC's Chief Operating Officer Simon Clegg announced, "This is going to be the most fantastic show ever staged in Azerbaijan, one that will make the Eurovision song contest seem like a small, local event."[16] Attracting high-quality athletes was an important first step, Clegg contended, and it was accomplished by ensuring that sixteen of the twenty participating sports could use the Baku Games as a qualifying or ranking event for the Rio 2016 Olympics. Baku also wanted to ensure that the Games were broadcast all over the world, from Australia to South America.

To ensure maximum attendance, the government altered its immigration policy to waive visa requirements for all participating athletes and officials in possession of an accreditation card. Additionally, all foreign spectators received visas upon arrival based on proof of purchase of tickets. Some 6,000 athletes and 3,000 officials from the National Olympic Committees of Europe participated in the Games, which, as Clegg believed, became the "second most important event in the history of Azerbaijan after the signing of the contract of the century in 1994," referring to the deal with an international consortium to develop the giant Azeri, Chirag, and deep-water Gunashli (ACG) oilfields.[17]

It was estimated that the 1,600 staff and 12,000 volunteers that BEGOC hired would walk away with new skills and an appetite for volunteering in sporting and other types of events. In addition to the European Games, Azerbaijan hosted an international Formula 1 event in 2016, the Chess Olympiad, the Islamic Games, and, having already bid twice for the Olympic Games, it may ultimately host the event in 2024 or 2028.

Initial estimates placed the costs of the 2015 European Games at around $1 billion, including the construction of a $720 million Olympic stadium that was inaugurated in June 2011 by Azerbaijan's President Aliyev, alongside presidents Sepp Blatter of FIFA and Michel Platini of UEFA.[18] The construction was finished by May 2015 and seated 65,000 viewers.[19] Within the stadium precinct there were also warm-up and training facilities for athletes that included seating for up to 2,000 spectators, parklands, and parking facilities, as well as a new Athletes' Village. Meanwhile, numerous other facilities were constructed to host the event, including thirteen newly constructed luxurious buildings for 5,000 athletes. Although the preparations concentrated on new construction, planners also intended to repurpose some older Soviet-era structures, as well as the recently built Crystal Hall. For Baku, the major concern was to ensure international recognition and a good image; therefore the appointment of Dimitris Papaioannou, the former artistic director of the Athens 2004 Olympic Games ceremonies, to a similar position at the European Games 2015 opening ceremony spoke volumes about Baku's intention to stage a show to remember.

The opening ceremony of the European Games at the new Olympic stadium exceeded all expectations, according to the local media commentators. Baku spent around $100 million on this ceremony, and was even able to bring in Lady Gaga to sing the John Lennon song "Imagine." Traditional music and about 2,000 female dancers and artists set the stage for the flame-lighting ceremony, which officially opened the games, followed by a presentation of the literary writing of the famous twelfth-century Azerbaijani poet, Nizami Ganjavi. Another $140 million was spent on the closing ceremony, to conclude the seventeen-day event.

To impress international visitors, it is essential to have all the attributes of a major city: an international airport, signature buildings by big architects, impressive infrastructure, and cultural complexes.[20] By the end of 2014, Baku had achieved most of these attributes. In particular, the newly inaugurated terminal at Baku airport is an architectural masterpiece. Constructed in a triangular shape with rounded off angles, it is designed to manage about three million passengers. The terminal also offers luxury shopping and leisure areas. Several new magnificent buildings have also been constructed in Baku. The SOCAR Tower, the tallest building in Baku and the entire Caucasus, became home to the State Oil Company at the beginning of 2015. Similar to the Lakhta Center (formerly known as Gazprom City) in St Petersburg, Russia, it is supposed to symbolize the might and power of the largest taxpayer of Azerbaijan and Georgia, which is SOCAR. Built in the style of structural expressionism and designed by Heerim Architects from South Korea, the twin-towered project rises from an elongated, canopy-like podium and snakes its way skywards. The towers have thirty-two floors at a height of 173 meters. Covering a ground area of 12,000 sq m and providing 100,000 sq m of usable space, the headquarters mainly houses office space, but also has conference and sports facilities, guest house and retail spaces, and food outlets for the 2,000 employees.

Despite some criticism, Azerbaijan has generally been able to fulfill its goal of image-making and branding. The country has attracted the attention of Europe and brought parts of Europe to Baku. The European Games were successful for Baku, since they highlighted Azerbaijan's modernity and its rise to international prominence. Officials claimed that the Games were a promotional opportunity for Azerbaijan because not many people knew very much about the city previously. Through international media efforts, however, more people worldwide were exposed to Baku through the European Games. The rights for showing the Games were sold to European, US, and Canadian companies. They also secured translation of the Games to the Middle East and North Africa. In China 447 million households were able to watch through CCTV, in addition to fifty-six million households in Japan, and thirty million households in India.

Even before the European Games, Azerbaijan confirmed bringing Formula 1 European Grand Prix to Baku in July 2016. For this event, Hermann Tilke's architectural firm produced an urban highway project to stretch into the center of Baku. Baku as host for Formula 1 puts them on a par with Monaco, Singapore, and other major cities. The organizers planned that during the race through Baku, the cars would move in parallel with the boulevard and make a circle around the Old City—a national historical and architectural reserve, which is considered to be the most ancient part of Baku and is listed as a UNESCO World Heritage Site. Azad Rahimov, Minister of Youth and Sport, spoke of the country's location at the crossroads of eastern Europe and western

Asia as a new "frontier": "Azerbaijan is a modern European country that has established a reputation as a center of sporting excellence. The deal to bring Formula 1 racing to Baku is a very significant new chapter in our ongoing success to attract the world's largest sporting events to our country."[21] In addition to the Formula 1 event, in April 2015 Baku signed an agreement with the Islamic Solidarity Sport Federation to hold the IV Islamic Solidarity Games (ISG) in 2017. The procedure for voting on the location of the IV Islamic Solidarity Games was held in Jeddah on 23–24 July 2013. The banner of the Federation was already transferred to Azerbaijan during the opening ceremony of the III Islamic Solidarity Games in the Indonesian city of Palambang on 22 September 2013. The Islamic Solidarity Games will be held in May 2017 and include competitions in twenty sports. Participants will lodge in the Athletes' Village initially built for the European Games of 2015. "We are delighted to have secured this highly important and prestigious event for our nation," said Konul Nurullayeva, head of the international relations department of the NOCA. "We strongly believe that the Islamic Solidarity Games is one of the most significant and exciting initiatives for Muslim communities around the world and we are proud to contribute to the development of the event."[22] Similarly, speaking at the ISG selection ceremony, the vice president of the National Olympic Committee, Dr Chingiz Huseynzada, affirmed Azerbaijan's leading role in the regional advancement of sport: "After our success in securing the 2015 European Games, the hosting of the fourth ISG in 2017 will make another important contribution to our standing both in the Muslim and international communities. We are a strong Islamic nation and are committed to helping and inspiring our friends around the world."[23]

Finally, the success of the European Games encouraged the Azerbaijani government to think about bidding for the 2024 Olympic Games. As Sports Minister Rahimov stated, Azerbaijan could host the event if IOC requirements for the host nation were reduced. Baku's bid for the 2016 and 2020 Olympics failed due to a lack of infrastructure and other requirements, receiving poor ratings on infrastructure during IOC inspections for the 2016 and 2020 bids. However, both inspections were conducted before the major building program for the European Games.[24] The good news for Baku is that the IOC adopted a reform package in 2014 entitled "Olympic Agenda 2020," which aims in part to cut the costs for hosting the Olympics and encourages maximizing the use of existing venues. The IOC also instituted a new "invitation phase" for potential bid cities to discuss their plans and vision with IOC officials.

Emulating Dubai and Doha: success or failure?

Overall, recent investments indicate that urban elites are more concerned with making Baku appealing to foreigners and turning it into a tourist destination, rather than a city for its citizens. With high prices for almost everything and an influx of oil money not supported by production, Baku is becoming an extremely expensive city for both visiting and inhabiting. And here the most important question that politicians, policy-makers, and elites should answer is whether all these projects and initiatives are sustainable. It seems that Baku is following Dubai's model on certain parameters. The first similarity is government-led development. As in Dubai, Azerbaijan's government, and not the private sector, has taken the lead. What private sector involvement there has been is divided among the business groups closely associated with the government. It allows the government to obtain financial support, if needed, for any type of project. Moreover, government-led development with no public involvement makes decision-making in Baku as rapid as it has been in Dubai. Decisions on strategic issues, such as building a new facility, sports center, industry or port, are taken very quickly by the government. Last but not least is the similarity in supply-generated demand. Like Dubai, Baku is trying to build everything to over-capacity, against the advice of experts. Whether it is a hotel, housing, or grandiose projects such as the Khazar Islands, the logic of the business elites can be explained by the phrase "supply goods or service and let it generate its own demand."[25] Thus, generally, it appears that Baku is applying Dubai's model within certain parameters.

However, the two cities do have significant differences that could undermine Baku's chances of emulating Dubai. First, geographical constraints prevent Azerbaijan from becoming a truly significant regional player. Countries or cities that become successful are usually ports with access to an ocean. Singapore, Hong Kong, Doha, and Dubai are all hubs of sea trade with easy access to neutral waters. Baku, with certain exceptions, could be considered a landlocked city, since the Caspian Sea does not have access to the ocean.

Second, unlike Dubai or Doha, Azerbaijan does not have enough resources for implementing larger projects. Unlike Dubai, Baku is the capital of a state where almost 80 percent of the budget and GDP is generated. Thus, a big share of its income is distributed across the country. Third, Azerbaijan's economy is not diversified. Due to the high income generated by oil, the non-oil sector of the country's economy is marginal. Moreover, Azerbaijan could be characterized as rentier state. Unlike Dubai or Singapore, whose economies are characterized as knowledge-based with high growth, high value-added products, and global mobility, Azerbaijan's economy is not diverse at all and the major source of income depends on a highly volatile commodity—oil.

Finally, Dubai's success was highly dependent on historical circumstances of international surplus capital looking for profitable investment possibilities in the 1990s and early 2000s. Dubai was lucky to be able to take advantage of the opportunity to create a significant build-up of physical and human assets within a relatively short time. On the other hand, Azerbaijan's rapid development began during a period of world financial and economic crisis, when excess capital rushed to save the economies of Europe and other states. The only investment that spurred development in Azerbaijan was government money received from oil sales, making it even more difficult for Azerbaijan to become a real regional player.

Moreover, the sustainability of a number of projects in Baku is under question. Although government officials and the business people involved are largely enthusiastic, none of the involved parties seems willing to imagine the huge problems and dangers that may plague their ambitious projects. For example, there are several issues that could make the Khazar Islands project unfeasible in Baku. First, the price of apartments will not allow the average Azerbaijani to buy them (even with a mortgage). The number of people capable of buying such apartments will hardly reach 5 percent of the intended number of residents. Second, unlike Palm Jumeirah, it is hard to imagine that foreign investors or celebrities would buy apartments in a volatile region with uneasy neighbors. Despite the waning success of the Nakheel company (constructor of the Palm Islands project) to sell their apartments, however, Baku has not reconsidered the nature of the project. By the end of 2016, the company heading the Khazar Islands project declared bankruptcy and the project has been postponed indefinitely.

Last but not least is the problem of the absence of tourists despite the mega-infrastructure built for them. The influx of oil money allowed Baku to create many businesses whose interests are closely vested in the development of the city. Most of the capital investments that poured into Baku went mainly into construction and tourism. Growth is the major component of both. Despite the positive effect of international events upon Azerbaijan's tourism, the recurring issue of the absence of tourism persists. The Eurovision song contest, the World Cup Soccer for girls under seventeen, and other international events held in Baku in 2012–13 had a positive impact on the number of tourists visiting the city. For example, in 2012 the number of people staying in hotels and hotel-type complexes in Azerbaijan increased by 22.5 percent compared to

2011, amounting to 624,900 guests.[26] The great majority of visitors entered the country through Baku. Meanwhile, the number of overnight stays also increased compared to previous years: at least 57.3 percent of the total number of overnight stays were registered in Baku, with the remainder in other regions of the country. However, low occupancy rates remained the main problem for hotels and hotel-type facilities in Azerbaijan. In 2012 the average occupancy rate was around 13.7 percent, while in Baku it was only slightly higher.[27] It is worth mentioning that without international events, the occupancy rate would be much lower.

Despite disappointing tourist numbers, the number of luxury hotels in Baku is increasing every year. In 2012, top brand hotels such as Jumeirah, Marriott, and Four Seasons opened in Baku, which now boasts seventeen five-star hotels. In 2013 was added the Fairmont Hotel located in the Flame Towers, as well as the Kempinski. According to Marina Usenko, the Moscow-based executive VP of Jones Lang LaSalle Hotels, in 2009 Baku had only 4,400 hotel rooms; in 2010 the number increased by 1,200 rooms (a 29 per cent increase); in 2011 were added 800 more rooms; and in 2012–13 a further 1,200.[28] The growth in the number of five-star hotels is understandable: most clients are corporate business people either working in the Azerbaijani government or having close ties with it; and hotel business is an easy investment and a lucrative enterprise. However, despite the fact that the government claims an increasing number of tourists in Azerbaijan, all these numbers are somewhat artificial and constitute mostly ethnic Azerbaijanis living in Russia or Georgia who frequently cross the border. The Ministry of Tourism labels them as tourists, making the statistics very attractive. In reality, it is difficult to calculate the real tourist numbers, but apparently the number is not high. Expensive hotel prices, unreasonable costs for entertainment downtown, as well as the visa regime introduced in 2010, have all made Baku less attractive. Marina Usenko reckoned that by the end of 2015 the number of hotel rooms would increase by 260 percent, raising the question of whether the city is in danger of becoming "overhoteled," at least in the luxury category:

> Baku is a nice and attractive city, but for a city of just two million people current number of rooms is redundant. Concerning business travelers, most of the impact from the construction and installation boom related to the petroleum business is now over. So unless the Azerbaijani authorities reposition the country to attract more business and leisure travelers (business meetings, conferences and other events), I don't see the high-end hotel market as sustainable.[29]

Kemal Bayik, director of marketing for the Four Seasons Baku, echoes her, stating that demand is now primarily from the UK and US, where major oil companies are located.[30]

Meanwhile, despite many positive changes, Baku has not been able to avoid problems that often plague developing cities, and which are mostly absent or not visible in Dubai and Doha. As in many other cities, these problems included a retreat from planning, a lack of institutional coordination, poor implementation of laws, chaotic development patterns, suburban sprawl, and a surge in informal construction. Moreover, the impact of transformation was felt in the loss of open spaces in urban areas, the privatization of the public realm, and social stratification. However, while in Central and Eastern European cities the process of transformation has been accompanied by a decentralization of power and the increased role of public participation and NGOs, in Baku governmental policies have led to further centralization, as well as an absence of democratic participation. Indeed, a Byzantine system of governance inherited from Soviet times, as well as ineffective resource management and corruption, have hampered the city's sustainability and precluded reforms in public administration. At the same time, the absence of a clear vision creates endemic problems, such as environmental pollution, urban sprawl, informal construction of dwellings, as well as political and administrative fragmentation. One major issue facing Baku's development is the absence of a Master Plan that would guide the development of the city. The last Master Plan was designed and introduced in 1984 and expired in 2005. As Christine Kessides has argued, the usual socialist city "was structured with little regard to the logic of market forces and the spatial transformation of the post-socialist urban areas in accord with the principles of market efficiency has required significant adjustments in the spatial arrangement of urban activities."[31] Baku's original Master Plan did not envision the collapse of the central economy and its transformation into a market economy. The city's new economy required new types of buildings for the banking sector, hotels, business and commercials projects among others. Moreover, the original plan did not anticipate the explosion of Baku's population. Thus, without a Master Plan, Baku is developing in an unorganized fashion, and the absence of zoning is leading to chaotic construction.[32] In fact, such a situation favors the business elites. Without proper plans and zoning ordinance requirements, business corporations can construct any type of building at random in Baku, regardless of the consequences. Indeed, development and construction have proceeded so fast that the situation with planning and zoning in Baku is exacerbated by the fact that no single agency has been given a unifying and coordinating responsibility over it. Several agencies and committees oversee such work without coordinating with each other. The absence of a regulating body also adds to the problem of quality housing and construction. By contrast, during the Soviet period some restrictions existed in terms of building height, due to Baku's location in an earthquake-prone zone. These restrictions were lifted in the post-Soviet period, and the justification for lifting these restrictions is now being debated. It is true that since independence there has been only one significant earthquake, in 2000, and that the few newly built high-rises that existed at that time did not suffer significant damage. However, over the last fifteen years the number of high-rise buildings has increased significantly, and concerns for safety continue to grow. The rapid growth of Baku's population has also affected the housing market considerably: the collapse of the Soviet Union and the inability of a Master Plan to reflect such dramatic changes has led to complete chaos in the housing market. Thus, the absence of vision for the city's development also differentiates Baku from Gulf cities.

Finally, the absence of democratic decision-making processes is another problem for Baku (although this does not differentiate Baku from the Gulf countries). Bakuvians are losing the feeling of ownership of their city. They have now started to believe that their city no longer belongs to them, feeling uncomfortable in their environment, which has led to a passive attitude towards the decision-making process. People also believe that protests will not lead to any change. In this context, one remarkable feature of the redevelopment of Baku is the absence of grass-roots organizations. In many cities, such as Prague, Moscow, or Kiev, there are citizen groups trying to influence the process by seeking information, writing petitions, and providing alternative expert opinions, although they are not always successful. However, in Baku, civil society is not engaging with urban development in this way, and the rather large and active NGO community of Baku is remarkably uninterested in the process of urban transformation.

Many people interviewed by the author also complained about the fact that government and urban authorities do not inform them about proposed projects. At the policy-making level, there is a clear lack of information. The public is usually informed about redevelopment projects after decisions have already been made, the projects approved, and the construction or renovation about to begin. So the general public does not participate in the process of making decisions about development, even though such issues have a profound effect on their lives. The process is now even less participatory than in the pre-Soviet period, when urban projects had to be at least approved by the City Council; and thus the Soviet legacy of centralization and inaccessibility continues.[33]

Conclusion

Having explored some of the major issues relating to the urban development of Baku, it is still very difficult to define a possible future model for the city. Indeed, it appears that none of the current global models is a particular fit for the city. In fact, Baku already displays some of the features characteristic of all models, in that it has the vitality of the Western European inner city neighborhoods; the suburbanization of the North American style, with eroding downtowns and the creation of edge cities; eroded levels of public services, as well as a rapid growth of informal houses in poverty-ridden areas; and finally the booming economy and huge investments of Dubai, Abu Dhabi, Doha, and Singapore. Nevertheless, after examining the construction and infrastructure projects, the gentrification of the city center, as well as massive investments in landmark buildings, it is becoming clear that the Baku administration and government are trying to increase the city's attractiveness.

The current strategy of Baku could be considered as one of the elements of post-political urban propagation, or active promotion of a city. In Baku, the strategy has evolved into large-scale urban development schemes, including constructing iconic new buildings, revamping local infrastructure, and creating a new urban imagery. In this context, Dubai continues to be the most suitable model for the overall needs of Baku, even though the two cities do not have much more in common. However, the urban planners in Baku are increasingly seeking to create new images for their cities and states through grandiose urban development and hosting major international spectacles. The expansionist agenda in Baku, unlike in Dubai, therefore serves three purposes: (1) distributing financial and political patronage; (2) promoting a positive image of the state for both international and domestic consumption; and (3) creating a sense of unity in society.

Moreover, elites have also been able to use these projects for their state-making efforts: using resource wealth, officially and otherwise, to cultivate credit for transforming the country and setting it on track for a new era of modernity, while painting these three developmental goals as a "gift" to the people from the state. Moreover, the perception of urban development among the city elites is skewed toward an understanding that the "Dubai-zation" of

Baku is the fastest shortcut toward becoming a world, or global, city. However, it seems that these elites fail to understand the unique geographical situation, financial resources, as well as historical moment that enabled Dubai to emerge as a world city.

By contrast, Baku lacks these latter three major components. Consequently, random construction combined with environmental degradation continues to have a negative effect on the image of Baku. Therefore, since it is not currently possible to adopt the Dubai model, the city could follow the model of European cities such as Prague, Paris, or Amsterdam and preserve its historical heritage, which could have the benefit of attracting more tourists than with its current strategy of building skyscrapers. Sadly, in the current situation in which Baku appears to follow Dubai's lead, the city administration fails to pay attention to the other attractive factors that would make the city more cosmopolitan, tolerant, and vibrant, while enabling the city to become more competitive in comparison with other cities of the region.

12

CONCLUSION

Mehran Kamrava

Since the early 1990s, Iran and Turkey have been engaged in a—mostly friendly—chess match in the South Caucasus. As the ideological foundations of Russian and US hegemony in the South Caucasus have eroded, space has opened up for new entrants in the region. This has enabled Iran and Turkey, two middle powers with rising regional and global aspirations, to exert power and influence in the South Caucasus. What has emerged in the process has been a new great game, with Iran and Turkey as the main protagonists. And the South Caucasus has become the main arena where the game is played.

In addition to soft power, the two countries have resorted to trade, and more specifically to energy politics, especially to pipeline politics, as the means of expanding their influence in the South Caucasus region. Among other things, both have sought to turn the region into energy consumers, or, more accurately, a critical component in an east–west corridor of both energy and essential goods.

For its part, Turkey, itself energy-dependent, has sought to catapult itself into being a regional geopolitical force by first ensuring its own energy supplies, principally from Azerbaijan and also from Iran and Russia, and by efforts aimed at becoming an important energy transit state and a leading energy hub. Winrow's analysis demonstrates that these two objectives are both intertwined and also inherently political. One of the central goals of Turkish policy-makers is to turn the country into a major re-exporter of natural gas from Russia and Iran, and possibly also from Turkmenistan and the Kurdish Regional Government, into Europe. There are multiple complicating factors at work here. Turkey's plan hinges on uninterrupted supplies of gas from Russia and Iran, despite the fact that these two countries have at times had their gas supplies intentionally or unintentionally interrupted. Similarly, Turkey's relations with Europe have been fraught in recent years, at times complicated by the seemingly maverick diplomacy of President Erdoğan, the unfolding civil war in Syria, and the refugee crisis in Europe.

Meanwhile, an important factor in Iran's relationship with its northern neighbor Azerbaijan has been ethnicity, as the latter has sought to strengthen its ethnic identity in the region. Over the course of the last century or so, Iran and Azerbaijan have pursued decidedly different processes of state- and nation-building. For the Republic of Azerbaijan, a sovereign and independent country since the collapse of the Soviet Union in 1991, Azeri ethnicity plays a central defining element in the construction of Azeri nationalism. For Iran, Persian ethnicity has played a similarly important role in Iranian national identity. The Islamic Republic has also been careful to promote a narrative of national harmony and ethnic diversity—of Iranian Azeris as well as other non-Persian populations across the country—under its own official rubric. But, as Ahmadi shows in this volume, equally central, especially as a counter-strategy to the ethnic nationalism promoted by Baku, has been the Iranian state's promotion of Islamic and Shiite elements in Iranian national identity. In the ensuing competition between the two nationalisms, ethnicity has emerged as a central force, but not one that has the potential to derail the national project in either of the countries, or, for that matter, good-neighborly relations between them.

Turkey and Iran are not the only countries seeking to expand their soft power in the South Caucasus. Given its enduring historic, political, economic, and cultural linkages with the region, Russia already has a first-starter's advantage as compared to others insofar as its soft power is concerned. This soft power is less in the form of ideology or national identity, but is rooted instead in the form of professional associations and civil society organizations, or, as Mankoff labels them, "uncivil society." Fragile and still-unfolding processes of state-building continue to provide space across the South Caucasus for non-governmental organizations of all kinds. Some of these NGOs have spread with direct encouragement, support, and funding from Western governments and entities such as the US-based National Endowment for Democracy. Others—in the form of media organizations, cultural groups, or (Eastern Orthodox) religious associations—have mushroomed through Russian support precisely to counter the ensuing localization of a Western-oriented narrative. Their efforts have been aided by the perseverance of a post-Soviet political culture that remains dominant among local elites, for most of whom the Russian language continues to be the *lingua franca*. Russia's hegemonic aspirations in the South Caucasus may have receded, but, as Mankoff reminds us, its shadow and influence remain highly consequential to the region, not just as a military superpower but as a historic and cultural entity with considerable clout and leverage.

Beginning in the 1990s, Turkey also made a concerted effort to expand its soft power in the South Caucasus. This effort has occurred at two levels, the distinguishability of which is more apparent at some points as compared to others. At the state level, as Altunışık outlines, the Turkish government engaged in a branding campaign that was part of a new, diplomatically proactive foreign policy meant to emphasize Turkey's historic and ideational ties to the region. This emphasis on regionalism was aided by the expansion of Turkish construction companies across the South Caucasus on the one hand, and the growing popularity of Turkish cultural products, especially music and television soap operas, on the other.

There was a second level at which Turkish soft power began manifesting itself in the South Caucasus, this time with what may be described as semi-official support. This soft power was in the form of the spread of the Gülenist (or *hizmet*) movement, which enjoyed a close, symbiotic relationship with Turkey's ruling AKP (*Adalet ve Kalkınma Partisi*) in the 1990s. Initially, the spread of the Gülen movement in the South Caucasus, and elsewhere, was seen by the Turkish state as another facet of its expanding soft power. But by the late 2000s, the relationship between the AKP and the Gülen movement had deteriorated to the point that President Erdoğan directed the blame for the July 2016 attempted coup against him at none other than Fethullah Gülen himself. Balci maintains that the break between the two may lessen the appeal of Turkey's soft power in the South Caucasus. There are no doubt other variables at work, including the expansion or contraction of Russian and Iranian soft power in the region, the evolution of the Gülen movement itself, and the fortunes of the AKP and especially President Erdoğan in Turkey's post-coup environment.

One of these variables includes the direction in which local processes of state-building in Georgia, Armenia, and Azerbaijan evolve. As Giragosian and Kupatadze amply demonstrate in relation to Armenia and Georgia, fragile and at best semi-democratic processes of state-building, as well as unregulated liberalization of local markets, have opened up space for the rise of powerful oligarchs, many of whom are closely linked with the political elite. These oligarchs are both beneficiaries of, and participants in, systems of corruption that permeate the political economies of the South Caucasus. Compromised in the process have been consolidation of democracy on the one hand and economic development on the other. Azerbaijan's oil and gas resources may have given it a façade of growth and riches—with Baku hailed as "the Dubai of the Caspian"—but structural and political underdevelopment, as well as pervasive poverty, still characterize the country. In all three countries, political development, and the consolidation of the state, have yet to be realized.

For now, chronic political and economic underdevelopment are only likely to increase the appeal of, and space for, competition by external actors in the South Caucasus. Russia, the United States, the European Union, Turkey, and Iran all have and will continue to vie for power and influence in the region. The competition between the US and EU on the one side and Russia on the other is not new and is part of a larger contest for spheres of influence not just in the South Caucasus but also in Central Asia, in the Baltic, in Ukraine, and elsewhere. Iran and Turkey are relatively new entrants, and while careful not to actively antagonize each other, they do seek to expand their own influence and power across the region. Not surprisingly, Iranian–Turkish competition in the South Caucasus is also influenced by developments elsewhere, including the relationship each country has with the US and Russia, domestic political developments in their own capitals, and the direction of the Syrian civil war, in which both countries are deeply involved.

Even more consequential to Iranian–Turkish competition in the South Caucasus are political developments within the three countries of the region. Reflecting Georgia's deeply divided political culture, the country's political elites remain fractured between those for whom Russia poses a serious national threat and those for whom Russia is a power not to be ignored. The political ascension of one group of elites over another determines the extent to which actors other than Russia—the US, the EU, Turkey, and Iran—are seen as viable, and valuable, partners in diplomacy, trade, commerce, and protection. In Armenia, it is generally not Russia that is perceived as a threat but rather Turkey, and therefore the country maintains relatively close relations with Iran. For its part, the Islamic Republic does not mind that Baku looks askance at its relations with Yerevan, given the role that ethnic nationalism plays in the state-building process in Azerbaijan and its possible consequences for Iran's own ethnic politics.

As middle powers with regional aspirations, Iran and Turkey see the South Caucasus region as an ideal arena for expanding their reach and influence. As post-sanctions Iran finds greater space for diplomacy and trade, the ensuing competition between the two neighboring countries is likely to intensify in the coming years. For both states, trade and soft power are the most viable tools for expanding their influence. In the long run, the competition in trade is only likely to benefit the three states of the South Caucasus. But it is also likely to keep the multiple conflicts that have ravaged the region over the last several decades—especially between Armenia and Azerbaijan, Russia and Georgia, and even the historic animosity between Turkey and Armenia—frozen and without a solution in sight.

Frozen conflicts, cross-border tensions and mistrust, ethnic politics and competing national identities, middle power rivalries and clashing aspirations, economic and political underdevelopment, malleable non-governmental and civil society organizations, politically-motivated external cultural influences, and rule by elites with suspect democratic credentials at best and by corrupt oligarchies at worst are all likely to be the enduring features of the great game currently unfolding in West Asia in general and in the South Caucasus in particular. For the foreseeable future, there is no reason to believe that any of these developments will be reversed, much less resolved.

NOTES

1. THE GREAT GAME IN WEST ASIA

1. My own aversion to jargon notwithstanding, resort to specialized terminology is often unavoidable. For elaborate discussions on and definitions on geopolitics and geostrategy, see Saul Bernard Cohen, *Geopolitics of International Relations*, 3rd edn (Lanham, MD: Rowman and Littlefield, 2014); Dodds and David Atkinson, eds, *Geopolitical Traditions: Critical Histories of a Century of Geopolitical Thought* (London: Routledge, 2000); Colin Flint, *Introduction to Geopolitics*, 2nd edn (London: Routledge, 2012); and Gearóid Ó Tuathail, Simon Dalby, and Paul Routledge, eds, *The Geopolitics Reader*, 2nd edn (London: Routledge, 2006).
2. For a valuable study of the subject that focuses on the cases of Venice, the Ottoman Empire, and Ming China, see Jakub J. Grygiel, *Great Powers and Geopolitical Change* (Baltimore, MD: Johns Hopkins University Press, 2006).
3. David Fromkin, "The Great Game in Asia," *Foreign Affairs*, Vol. 54, No. 4 (Spring 1980), p. 936.
4. Ralf Dahrendorf, "A New World Order: Old Forces, New Riddles, No Answers," in Roger Morgan et al., eds, *New Diplomacy in the Post-Cold War World* (London: Palgrave Macmillan, 1993), pp. 293–300.
5. Philip Robins, "The Foreign Policy of Turkey," in Raymond Hinnebusch and Anoushiravan Ehteshami, eds, *The Foreign Policies of Middle East States*, 2nd edn (Boulder, CO: Lynne Rienner, 2014), pp. 328–30.
6. Anoushiravan Ehteshami, "The Foreign Policy of Iran," in Hinnebusch and Ehteshami, *The Foreign Policies of Middle East States*, pp. 271–84.
7. Uwe Halbach, "The European Union in the South Caucasus: Story of a hesitant approximation," in Friedrich-Ebert-Stiftung, ed., *South Caucasus—20 Years of Independence* (Berlin: Friedrich-Ebert-Stiftung, 2011), p. 304.
8. See Michael E. Bonine, Abbas Amanat, and Michael Ezekiel Gasper, eds, *Is There a Middle East? The Evolution of a Geopolitical Concept* (Stanford, CA: Stanford University Press, 2012).

9. Halbach, "The European Union in the South Caucasus: Story of a hesitant approximation," p. 300.
10. Thomas de Waal, "The Conflict of Sisyphus—The elusive search for resolution of the Nagorno-Karabakh dispute," in Friedrich-Ebert-Stiftung, ed., *South Caucasus—20 Years of Independence*, pp. 146–7.
11. Of the various conceptualizations of state-building, one of the more theoretically sophisticated analyses is offered by David Waldner in his *State Building in Late Development* (Ithaca, NY: Cornell University Press, 1999), ch. 2.
12. Jeronim Perovic, "From Disengagement to Active Economic Competition: Russia's Return to the South Caucasus and Central Asia," *Demokratizatsiya*, Vol. 13, No. 1 (Winter 2005), pp. 61–85.
13. Andrey Ryabov, Russian interests and strategies in the South Caucasus," in Friedrich-Ebert-Stiftung, ed., *South Caucasus—20 Years of Independence*, p. 267.
14. Ibid., p. 271.
15. Andrey Makarychev, "Russia's policies in the South Caucasus after the crisis in Ukraine: the vulnerabilities of realism," in Fuad Chiragov et al., *The South Caucasus: Between integration and fragmentation* (Baku: SAM, 2015), p. 25.
16. Ryabov, "Russian interests and strategies in the South Caucasus," p. 267.
17. Keith Johnson, "Turkey's Reckless Gas Game," *Foreign Policy*, 11 May 2015, http://foreignpolicy.com/2015/05/11/turkeys-reckless-gas-game-russia-putin-turkish-stream/
18. Ryabov, "Russian interests and strategies in the South Caucasus," p. 268.
19. Ibid., p. 276.
20. Makarychev, "Russia's policies in the South Caucasus after the crisis in Ukraine: the vulnerabilities of realism," p. 19.
21. Ibid., p. 26.
22. Ryabov, "Russian interests and strategies in the South Caucasus," p. 278.
23. Nicu Popescu, "ENP and EaP: Relevant for the South Caucasus," in Friedrich-Ebert-Stiftung, ed., *South Caucasus—20 Years of Independence*, p. 317.
24. Halbach, "The European Union in the South Caucasus: Story of a hesitant approximation," p. 301.
25. Gulshan Pashayeva, "Security challenges and conflict resolution efforts in the South Caucasus," in Chiragov et al., *The South Caucasus*, p. 39.
26. Popescu, "ENP and EaP: relevant for the South Caucasus," p. 319.
27. Halbach, "The European Union in the South Caucasus: Story of a hesitant approximation," p. 303.
28. Pashayeva, "Security challenges and conflict resolution efforts in the South Caucasus," p. 43.
29. Richard Giragosian, "US National Interests and Engagement Strategies in the South Caucasus," in Friedrich-Ebert-Stiftung, ed., *South Caucasus—20 Years of Independence*, p. 251.

30. Ibid., p. 241.
31. Rajan Menon, "The New Great Game in Central Asia," *Survival*, Vol. 45, No. 2 (Summer 2003), p. 187.
32. Giragosian, "US National Interests and Engagement Strategies in the South Caucasus," pp. 242–3.
33. Ibid., p. 249.
34. Matthias Jobelius, "Introduction," in Friedrich-Ebert-Stiftung, ed., *South Caucasus—20 Years of Independence*, p. 16.
35. Dieter Boden, "Conflict Settlement for Abkhazia and South Ossetia: Lessons and prospects," in Friedrich-Ebert-Stiftung, ed., *South Caucasus—20 Years of Independence*, p. 124.
36. de Waal, "The Conflict of Sisyphus," p. 140.
37. Gernot Erler, "Europe's Interest in a Peaceful and Stable South Caucasus," in Friedrich-Ebert-Stiftung, ed., *South Caucasus—20 Years of Independence*, p. 17.
38. de Waal, "The Conflict of Sisyphus," p. 137.
39. Ibid., p. 145.
40. Ibid., p. 144.
41. Ibid., p. 143.
42. Jobelius, "Introduction," p. 18.
43. Michael B. Bishku, "The South Caucasus Republics: Relations with the U.S. and the EU," *Middle East Policy*, Vol. 22, No. 2 (Summer 2015), p. 41. The Armenian diaspora, of course, started being formed prior to the collapse of the Soviet Union, as not all Armenians outside the country left since its independence.
44. Boris Navasardian, "Politics and Governance in Armenia: The Prospects for Democracy," in Friedrich-Ebert-Stiftung, ed., *South Caucasus—20 Years of Independence*, p. 100.
45. Mikayel Zolyan, "Armenia's 'Velvet Revolution': Successes and Failures," in Friedrich-Ebert-Stiftung, ed., *South Caucasus—20 Years of Independence*, p. 58.
46. Navasardian, "Politics and Governance in Armenia," p. 96.
47. Ibid., p. 97.
48. Zolyan, "Armenia's 'Velvet Revolution,'" p. 56.
49. Navasardian, "Politics and Governance in Armenia," p. 92.
50. Ara Nranyan, "Armenia: 20 years of integration into capitalism—consequences and challenges," in Friedrich-Ebert-Stiftung, ed., *South Caucasus—20 Years of Independence*, pp. 194–5.
51. Jobelius, "Introduction," p. 19.
52. Navasardian, "Politics and Governance in Armenia," pp. 100–101.
53. Nranyan, "Armenia: 20 years of integration into capitalism," p. 200.
54. Zolyan, "Armenia's 'Velvet Revolution,'" p. 56.
55. Navasardian, "Politics and Governance in Armenia," p. 93.
56. Zolyan, "Armenia's 'Velvet Revolution,'" p. 43.

57. Dennis Sammut, "Armenia—stuck between a rock and a hard place," in Chiragov et al., *The South Caucasus*, p. 48.
58. Navasardian, "Politics and Governance in Armenia," p. 96.
59. Stepan Grigoryan, "Armenian–Turkish relations under the new geopolitics," in Friedrich-Ebert-Stiftung, ed., *South Caucasus—20 Years of Independence*, p. 159.
60. Ibid., p. 164.
61. Navasardian, "Politics and Governance in Armenia," p. 95.
62. Bishku, "The South Caucasus Republics," pp. 46–7.
63. Giragosian, "US National Interests and Engagement Strategies in the South Caucasus," p. 247.
64. Nika Chitadze, "Geopolitical Interests of Iran in South Caucasus and Georgian-Iranian Relations," *Journal of Social Sciences*, Vol. 1, No. 2 (2012), p. 7.
65. Data collected from World Integrated Trade Solution, World Bank, www.worldbank.org
66. Kakha Gogolashvili, "In search of Georgia's economic model," in Friedrich-Ebert-Stiftung, ed., *South Caucasus—20 Years of Independence*, p. 174.
67. Archil Gegeshidze, "Georgia's Political Transformation: Democracy in Zigzag," in Friedrich-Ebert-Stiftung, ed., *South Caucasus—20 Years of Independence*, pp. 30–31.
68. Matthias Jobelius, "Georgia's authoritarian liberalism," in Friedrich-Ebert-Stiftung, ed., *South Caucasus—20 Years of Independence*, p. 79.
69. Ibid., p. 83.
70. Gegeshidze, "Georgia's Political Transformation," p. 34.
71. Boden, "Conflict Settlement for Abkhazia and South Ossetia," p. 124.
72. Gegeshidze, "Georgia's Political Transformation," pp. 26–7.
73. Boden, "Conflict Settlement for Abkhazia and South Ossetia," p. 125.
74. Gegeshidze, "Georgia's Political Transformation," p. 29.
75. Giragosian, "US National Interests and Engagement Strategies in the South Caucasus," p. 245.
76. Kornley Kakachia, "Europeanisation and Georgian foreign policy," in Chiragov et al., *The South Caucasus*, p. 17.
77. Gegeshidze, "Georgia's Political Transformation," p. 38
78. Jobelius, "Georgia's authoritarian liberalism," p. 81.
79. Ibid., p. 84.
80. Ibid., p. 85.
81. Gogolashvili, "In search of Georgia's economic model," p. 181.
82. Ibid., p. 189.
83. Bishku, "The South Caucasus Republics," p. 41.
84. Gegeshidze, "Georgia's Political Transformation," p. 25.
85. Erler, Europe's Interest in a Peaceful and Stable South Caucasus," p. 8.
86. Boden, "Conflict Settlement for Abkhazia and South Ossetia," p. 129.

87. Ibid., p. 132.
88. Quoted in Bishku, "The South Caucasus Republics," pp. 42–3.
89. Kakachia, "Europeanisation and Georgian foreign policy," p. 11.
90. Bishku, "The South Caucasus Republics: Relations with the U.S. and the EU," p. 40.
91. Kakachia, "Europeanisation and Georgian foreign policy," p. 12.
92. Anar M. Valiyev, "Parliamentary Elections in Azerbaijan: A Failed Revolution," *Problems of Post-Communism*, Vol. 53, No. 3 (May–June 2006), pp. 27–8; Shahin Abbasov, "Azerbaijan: Achievements and missed opportunities," in Friedrich-Ebert-Stiftung, ed., *South Caucasus—20 Years of Independence*, p. 108.
93. Arif Yunusov, "Twenty years of independence in Azerbaijan," in Friedrich-Ebert-Stiftung, ed., *South Caucasus—20 Years of Independence*, pp. 73–4.
94. Abbasov, "Azerbaijan," p. 108.
95. Ibid., p. 109.
96. Yunusov, "Twenty years of independence in Azerbaijan," pp. 64–6.
97. Ibid., p. 62.
98. Abbasov, "Azerbaijan: Achievements and missed opportunities," pp. 111–12.
99. Ibid., p. 112.
100. Ibid., 116.
101. Ibid., p. 121.
102. Anar Valiyev, "Victim of 'War of Ideologies': Azerbaijan after the Russia-Georgia War," *Demokratizatsiya*, Vol. 17, No. 3 (Summer 2009), p. 280.
103. Max Fisher, "Oops: Azerbaijan released election results before voting had even started," *Washington Post* (9 October 2013).
104. Abbasov, "Azerbaijan: Achievements and missed opportunities," p. 115.
105. Valiyev, "Parliamentary Elections in Azerbaijan," p. 17.
106. Anar Valiyev, "Azerbaijan: Islam in a Post-Soviet Republic," *Middle East Review of International Affairs*, Vol. 9, No. 4 (December 2005), p. 1.
107. Yunusov, "Twenty years of independence in Azerbaijan," p. 72.
108. Abbasov, "Azerbaijan: Achievements and missed opportunities," p. 119.
109. From 1997 to 2009, for example, Azerbaijan's economy grew by 14 percent per year, thanks almost entirely to oil and gas revenues. Anar Vliyev, "Azerbaijan's Economic Model and its Development since Independence," in Friedrich-Ebert-Stiftung, ed., *South Caucasus—20 Years of Independence*, p. 222.
110. Amanda Paul, "Iran's foreign policy in the South Caucasus: Between pragmatism and realpolitik," in Chiragov et al., *The South Caucasus*, p. 56.
111. Erler, "Europe's Interest in a Peaceful and Stable South Caucasus," p. 7.
112. Vliyev, "Azerbaijan's Economic Model and its Development since Independence," p. 234.
113. Ibid., p. 229.
114. Ibid., p. 230.

115. Ibid., p. 231.
116. Farhad Mammadov, "Azerbaijan's Foreign Policy—A New Paradigm of Careful Pragmatism," in Chiragov et al., *The South Caucasus*, pp. 30–31.
117. Giragosian, "US National Interests and Engagement Strategies in the South Caucasus," p. 245.
118. Abbasov, "Azerbaijan: Achievements and Missed Opportunities," p. 122.
119. Mammadov, "Azerbaijan's Foreign Policy," p. 29.
120. Valiyev, "Victim of 'War of Ideologies'", pp. 284–5.
121. Giragosian, "US National Interests and Engagement Strategies in the South Caucasus," p. 244.
122. Bishku, "The South Caucasus Republics," p. 40.
123. Emil Souleimanov, Maya Ehrmann, and Huseyn Aliyev, "Focused on Iran? Exploring the Rationale Behind the Strategic Relationship Between Azerbaijan and Israel," *Southeast European and Black Sea Studies*, Vol. 14, No. 4 (2014), p. 471.
124. Souleimanov, Ehrmann, and Aliyev, "Focused on Iran?", p. 473.
125. Ibid., p. 478.
126. Ibid.
127. Ibid., p. 473.
128. Ibid., p. 476.
129. Chitadze, "Geopolitical Interests of Iran in South Caucasus and Georgian-Iranian Relations," p. 6.
130. Robert Olson, *Turkey–Iran Relations, 1979–2004: Revolution, Ideology, War, Coups and Geopolitics* (Costa Mesa, CA: Mazda, 2005), p. 42.
131. Ibid., pp. xxvii–xxviii.
132. Hongying Wang and Erik French, "Middle Range Powers in Global Governance," *Third World Politics*, Vol. 34, No. 6 (2013), p. 985.
133. See, for example, Miles Kahler, "Rising powers and Global Governance: Negotiating Change in a Resilient Status Quo," *International Affairs*, Vol. 89, No. 3 (2013), pp. 711–29; and Kevin Gray and Craig N. Murphy, "Introduction: Rising Powers and the Future of Global Governance," *Third World Politics*, Vol. 34, No. 6 (2013), pp. 183–93.
134. Andrew Cooper and Daniel Flemes, "Foreign Policy Strategies of Emerging Powers in a Multipolar World: an introductory review," *Third World Politics*, Vol. 34, No. 6 (2013), p. 948.
135. Chitadze, "Geopolitical Interests of Iran in South Caucasus and Georgian-Iranian Relations," p. 6.
136. Most notably, tensions between Iran and Saudi Arabia, especially after the lifting of EU sanctions against Iran following the resolution of questions around the country's nuclear program, can be explained through the prism of two regional middle-power rivalries. For more on this issue see Mehran Kamrava, "Iranian

Foreign and Security Policies in the Persian Gulf," in Mehran Kamrava, ed., *International Politics of the Persian Gulf* (Syracuse, NY: Syracuse University Press, 2011), pp. 184–206.

137. Mohammed Ayoob, "Beyond the Democratic Wave in the Arab World: The Middle East's Turko-Persian Future," *Insight Turkey*, Vol. 13, No. 2 (2011), p. 57.
138. Olson, *Turkey–Iran Relations*, p. 11.
139. See also Gawdat Bahgat, "Iran–Turkey Energy Cooperation: Strategic Implications," *Middle East Policy*, Vol. 21, No. 4 (Winter 2014), p. 2.
140. Ibid.
141. Ibid., p. 1.
142. Chitadze, "Geopolitical Interests of Iran in South Caucasus and Georgian–Iranian Relations," p. 7.
143. Grigoryan, "Armenian–Turkish Relations under the New Geopolitics," p. 168.
144. Paul, "Iran's Foreign Policy in the South Caucasus," p. 53.
145. Chitadze, "Geopolitical Interests of Iran in South Caucasus and Georgian–Iranian Relations," p. 5.
146. Paul, "Iran's Foreign Policy in the South Caucasus," p. 54.
147. Chitadze, "Geopolitical Interests of Iran in South Caucasus and Georgian–Iranian Relations," p. 8.
148. Paul, "Iran's Foreign Policy in the South Caucasus," p. 55.
149. Chitadze, "Geopolitical Interests of Iran in South Caucasus and Georgian–Iranian Relations," p. 10.
150. Ibid., 9.
151. Bishku, "The South Caucasus Republics," p. 51.
152. Johnson. "Turkey's Reckless Gas Game."
153. Burcu Gultekin Punsmann, "Turkey's Interest and Strategies in the South Caucasus," in Friedrich-Ebert-Stiftung, ed., *South Caucasus—20 Years of Independence*, p. 280.
154. Ibid., p. 284.
155. Ibid., p. 287.

2. WEST ASIA SINCE 1900: LIVING THROUGH THE WRECK OF EMPIRES

1. For the rise and ideology of the Islamic State, see Patrick Cockburn, *The Rise of Islamic State: ISIS and the New Sunni Revolution* (London: Verso Books, 2015); Graeme Wood, "What ISIS Really Wants," *New Yorker* (March 2015), and the subsequent exchange of letters on this theme.
2. Writing on one aspect of modernization, Tom Nairn says that "Urbanisation is the smooth-sounding, impersonal term for what was often an agonising process: the fearful undertow of modernity. During it, rural emigrants look backwards as much as forwards, and pass from the remembrance to the often elaborate reinvention of the worlds that they have lost." Tom Nairn, "The Curse of Rurality," in John A. Hall,

ed., *The State of the Nation: Ernest Gellner and the Theory of Nationalism* (Cambridge: Cambridge University Press, 1998), p. 108.

3. Leon Carl Brown, *International Politics and the Middle East: Old Rules, Dangerous Game* (Princeton, NJ: Princeton University Press, 1984), p. 5. For the original academic concept of "informal empire" over client states (as opposed to direct imperial rule), see J. Gallagher and R. Robinson, "The Imperialism of Free Trade," *Economic History Review*, Vol. 6, No. 1 (1955).
4. Ibid., p. 17.
5. See Hugh Poulton, *Top Hat, Grey Wolf and Crescent: Turkish Nationalism and the Turkish Republic* (London: Hurst, 1997), pp. 50–62.
6. See Selim Deringil, *The Well-Protected Domain: Ideology and the Legitimation of Power in the Ottoman Empire, 1876–1909* (London: I. B. Tauris, 2011).
7. See Handan Nezir Akmese, *The Birth of Modern Turkey: The Ottoman Military and World War I* (London: I. B. Tauris, 2005); Alan Palmer, *The Decline and Fall of the Ottoman Empire* (London: John Murray, 1992), pp. 189–221; Poulton, *Top Hat, Grey Wolf and Crescent*, pp. 50–86.
8. For Kemalist moves against religion, see Umut Azak, *Islam and Secularism in Turkey: Kemalism, Religion and the Nation State* (London: I. B. Tauris, 2010), pp. 9–13, 21–60.
9. Poulton, *Top Hat, Grey Wolf and Crescent*, p. 90.
10. Anatol Lieven, *The Baltic Revolution: Estonia, Latvia, Lithuania and the Path to Independence* (New Haven, CT: Yale University Press, 1993), p. 293.
11. David Fromkin, *A Peace to End All Peace: The Fall of the Ottoman Empire and the Creation of the Modern Middle East* (London: St Martin's Press, 1991), p. 562.
12. Michael C. Hudson, *Arab Politics: The Search for Legitimacy* (New Haven, CT: Yale University Press, 1977), p. 99. See also William Montgomery Watt, *Islam and the Integration of Society* (London: Routledge, 2010).
13. Fromkin, *A Peace to End All Peace*, p. 17.
14. Hudson, *Arab Politics*, p. 257: "By the end of World War II, the Hashemites in both Iraq and Transjordan had forfeited their claim to lead the national movement as a result of their collaboration with the British to crush radical nationalists like Gailani."
15. See, for example, Nelson Moe, *The View from Vesuvius: Italian Culture and the Southern Question* (Berkeley, CA: California University Press, 2002), pp. 179–83 ("The Supreme Argument of Force"), on the subjugation of southern Italy by northern Italian liberalism. See also Denis Mack Smith, *The Making of Italy, 1796–1866* (London: Macmillan, 1988), pp. 364–78.
16. Francesco Trinchero, quoted in Moe, *The View from Vesuvius*, p. 145.
17. For the authoritarian and military character of Italian liberalism after unification, see Moe, *The View from Vesuvius*, pp. 126–83; Smith, *The Making of Italy 1796–1870*, pp. 371–94. For the Bronte revolt and its suppression, see Lucy Riall, *Under the Volcano: Revolution in a Sicilian Town* (Oxford: Oxford University Press, 2013).

18. See Erica Benner, "Nationalism: Intellectual Origins," in John Breuilly, ed., *The History of Nationalism* (New York: Oxford University Press, 2013), pp. 36–51; James J Sheehan, *German Liberalism in the Nineteenth Century* (London: Methuen, 1982), pp. 274–83.
19. Delmer M. Brown, *Nationalism in Japan: An Introductory Historical Analysis* (Berkeley, CA: University of California Press, 1955), pp. 91, 104.
20. Barrington Moore, *Social Origins of Dictatorship and Democracy: Lord and Peasant in the Making of the Modern World* (London: Penguin, 1966), pp. 246 ff.
21. Moore, *Social Origins of Dictatorship and Democracy*, p. 493. Eugen Weber, *Peasants into Frenchmen: The Modernization of Rural France 1871–1914* (London: Chatto and Windus, 1977).
22. Heinz Ziegler, *Die Moderne Nation* (Tuebingen, 1931), quoted in Bassam Tibi, *Arab Nationalism: Between Islam and the Nation State* (London: Macmillan, 1997), p. 33.
23. In a very belated recognition of the importance of nationalism as a check to Islamism, David Brooks of the *New York Times* wrote in February 2015 that "Young Arab men are not going to walk away from extremism because they can suddenly afford a Slurpee. They will walk away when they can devote themselves to a revived Egyptian nationalism, Lebanese nationalism, Syrian nationalism, some call to serve a cause that connects nationalism to dignity and democracy and transcends a lifetime." "The Nationalist Solution", *New York Times* (20 February 2015). He did not however acknowledge that it has been above all US and Israeli actions that have shattered the nationalist legitimacy of Arab states.
24. Tibi, *Arab Nationalism*, pp. 88–9.
25. See Steve Coll, *Ghost Wars: The Secret History of the CIA, Afghanistan and Bin Laden, from the Soviet Invasion to September 10, 2001* (London: Penguin, 2004), pp. 65–6, 67, 72, 261, 277, 398; for Saudi relations with the Taliban, see pp. 294–7. For further writing on Saudi Arabia's role in supporting Islamist radicalism in Pakistan and Afghanistan, see Hassan Abbas, *The Taliban Revival: Violence and Extremism on the Pakistan–Afghanistan Frontier* (New Haven, CT: Yale University Press, 2014), pp. 57, 64–8, 185, 213–15; Riaz Mohammad Khan, *Afghanistan and Pakistan: Conflict, Extremism and Resistance to Modernity* (Washington, DC: Woodrow Wilson Center Press, 2011), pp. 184–7, 67–70, 186–7. For Saudi Arabia's funding of Sunni sectarian extremists in Pakistan, see Khaled Ahmed, *Sectarian War: Pakistan's Sunni–Shia Violence and its Links to the Middle East* (Karachi: Oxford University Press, 2011).
26. Interviews with the author in Kabul and Camp Leatherneck, Helmand, November 2013.
27. For Reza Shah's achievement in laying the basis for modern Iranian nationalism, see Richard W Cottam, *Nationalism in Iran* (Pittsburgh, PA: University of Pittsburgh Press, 1979), pp. 99ff.

28. Albert Hourani, *A History of the Arab Peoples* (New York: Warner Books, 1991), pp. 411ff. For the centrality of hostility to Israel and anti-imperialism to Arab state legitimacy in the 1960s and 70s, see Hudson, *Arab Politics*, pp. 107–18; Tibi, *Arab Nationalism*, p. 24; Nazih N. Ayubi, *Over-stating the Arab State: Politics and Society in the Middle East* (London: I. B. Tauris, 2006), p. 265.
29. Ibid., 216.
30. For the collapse of the Libyan state, see Peter Cole and Brian McQuinn, eds, *The Libyan Revolution and its Aftermath* (London: Hurst, 2015). For the civil war in Syria, see Emile Hokayem, *Syria's Uprising and the Fracturing of the Levant* (London: Routledge, 2013). For the historical background, see John McHugo, *Syria: A Recent History* (London: Saqi Books, 2015).
31. Quoted in Hudson, *Arab Politics*, p. 368. For the centrality of nationalist pan-Arab rhetoric to this legitimacy from the 1950s on, see Hudson pp. 27ff.
32. Ibid., p. 2.
33. Ibid., pp. 87, 99ff. For the continuity of rural traditions of kinship authority, see for example Richard T. Antoun, *Arab Village: A Social Structural Study of a Transjordan Peasant Community* (Bloomington, IN: Indiana University Press, 1972); Michael Gilsenan, *Lords of the Lebanese Marches: Violence and Narrative in an Arab Society* (London: I. B. Tauris, 1996). For the origins of patrimonialism in the Ottoman Empire, see Hourani, *A History of the Arab Peoples*, pp. 285ff; Perry Anderson, *Lineages of the Absolutist State* (London: NLB, 1974), pp. 376ff.
34. See Steffen Hertog, *Business Politics in the Middle East* (London: Hurst, 2013); John Waterbury, "Endemic and Planned Corruption in a Monarchical Regime," *World Politics*, Vol. 25, No. 4 (1973), pp. 533–55; Robert Springborg, *Family, Power and Politics in Egypt: Syed Bey Marei—His Clan, Clients and Cohorts* (Philadelphia, PA: University of Pennsylvania Press, 1982); Ellen Lust, "Competitive Clientelism in the Middle East," *Journal of Democracy*, Vol. 20, No. 3 (2009), pp. 122–35.
35. For the historical centrality of the struggle of states against kinship, see Ernst Gellner, *Muslim Society* (Cambridge: Cambridge University Press, 1983), pp. 326 ff; Francis Fukuyama, *The Origins of Political Order From Prehuman Times to the French Revolution* (London: Profile Books, 2011), pp. 49–110, 189–244, 437–84; idem, *Political Order and Political Decay from the Industrial Revolution to the Globalisation of Democracy* (London: Profile Books, 2014), pp. 3–22, 285–385, 524–48. For kinship and the state in the Middle East, see Ayubi, *Over-stating the Arab State*, pp. 125ff, 326ff.
36. See Ali M. Ansari, *The Politics of Nationalism in Modern Iran* (Cambridge: Cambridge University Press, 2012): "Nationalism is the determining ideology of modern Iran ... in all its manifestations [it] has been the ideological reference point to which all competing ideologies have ultimately had to adhere, and within which most have been subsumed. Nothing exemplifies this process better than the ideo-

logical transformation of an Islamic Revolution which aspired to universality but which within a decade had defined itself as an Iranian Islamic revolution to distinguish itself from other movements emerging around the world, and to emphasise a pre-eminence and exclusivity most commonly associated with nationalist ideologies."

37. As observed first, of course, by Ibn Khaldun in the *Muqadimah*.
38. For the importance of the struggle against kinship and tribalism in modern Iranian state development, see Cottam, *Nationalism in Iran*, p. 59.
39. Hisham Sharabi, *Neopatriarchy: A Theory of Distorted Change in Arab Society* (Oxford: Oxford University Press, 1992), p. 14.
40. Ayubi, *Over-stating the Arab State*, pp. 263ff; Robert Springborg, *Family, Power and Politics in Egypt* (Philadelphia, PA: University of Pennsylvania Press, 1982).
41. Tibi, *Arab Nationalism*, p. 232; see also pp. 65, 209. See also Charles Glass, *Tribes With Flags: Adventure and Kidnap in Greater Syria* (London: Avalon, 2000), Introduction.
42. Ayubi, *Over-stating the Arab State*, pp. 3ff.
43. Ibid., pp. 311ff.
44. For the history of the Nagorno-Karabakh dispute, see Thomas de Waal, *Black Garden: Armenia and Azerbaijan Through Peace and War* (New York: New York University Press, 2004); Charles King, *The Ghost of Freedom: A History of the Caucasus* (New York: Oxford University Press, 2008), pp. 210–21.
45. For the establishment of Aliyev's rule in Azerbaijan, see Shireen Hunter, "Azerbaijan: Searching for New Neighbours," in Ian Bremmer and Ray Taras, eds, *New States, New Politics: Building the Post-Soviet Nations* (Cambridge: Cambridge University Press, 1997), pp. 437–70; Thomas Goltz, *Azerbaijan Diary* (London: Routledge, 1999).
46. For the origins and course of the Abkhaz conflict, see Gueorgui Otyrba, "War in Abkhazia: The Regional Significance of the Georgian-Abkhaz Conflict," in Roman Szporluk, ed., *National Identity and Ethnicity in Russia and the New States of Eurasia* (New York: M. E. Sharpe, 1994).
47. See Richard Sakwa, "Great Powers and Small Wars in the Caucasus," in Matthew Sussex, ed., *Conflict in the Former USSR* (New York: Cambridge University Press, 2012).
48. For the history of Georgia since independence, see Stephen Jones, *Georgia: A Political History Since Independence* (London: I. B. Tauris, 2015); Donald Rayfield, *Edge of Empires: A History of Georgia* (London: Reaktion Books, 2012), pp. 381–401.
49. For the failure of state development policies which helped lead to the Arab Spring revolutions, see Adeel Malik and Bassem Awadallah, "The Economics of the Arab Spring," *World Development*, Vol. 45, No. 5 (2013), pp. 296–313.

3. PIPELINE POLITICS IN IRAN, TURKEY, AND THE SOUTH CAUCASUS

1. Stephen J. Flanagan, "The Turkey–Russia–Iran Nexus: Eurasian Power Dynamics," *Washington Quarterly*, Vol. 36, No. 1 (Winter 2013), pp. 163–78; see pp. 165, 175.
2. Ibid., p. 169.
3. Ibid., pp. 173–4.
4. Richard Giragosian, "Armenia's Search for Independence," *Current History*, Vol. 113, No. 765 (October 2014), pp. 284–9; see p. 284.
5. Elkhan Nuriyev, *The South Caucasus at the Crossroads: Conflicts, Caspian Oil and Great Power Politics* (Berlin: Lit Verlag, 2007), p. 273.
6. Ariel Cohen and Kevin Decorla-Souza, "Security Issues and US Interests in the South Caucasus," in Fariz Ismailzade and Glen E. Howard, eds, *The South Caucasus 2012: Oil, Democracy and Geopolitics* (Washington, DC: Jamestown Foundation, 2012), pp. 187–217; see p. 206.
7. Albert Bressand, "Natural Resources Investment Relations and Regional Energy Strategies," in Fariz Ismailzade and Glen E. Howard, eds, *The South Caucasus 2012: Oil, Democracy and Geopolitics* (Washington, DC: Jamestown Foundation, 2012), pp. 131–49; see p. 148.
8. Ibid.
9. Ibid.
10. Bahram Amir Ahmadian, "Iran's Opportunities and Challenges in Caucasus," *Iran Review* (6 July 2011), available at www.iranreview.org/content/Documents/Iran%E2%80%99s_Opportunities_and_Challenges_in_Caucasus.htm
11. Mandana Tishehyar, "Iran–Russia Energy Relations," *Iran Review* (8 July 2011), available at www.iranreview.org/content/Documents/Iran_Russia_Energy_Relations.htm
12. Jim Nichol, "Armenia, Azerbaijan, and Georgia: Political Developments and Implications for US Interests," *Congressional Research Service* (2 April 2014), available at fas.org/sgp/crs/row/RL33453.pdf
13. Nika Chitadze, "Geopolitical Interests of Iran in South Caucasus and Georgian-Iranian Relations," *Journal of Social Sciences*, Vol. 1, No. 2 (2012), pp. 5–12; see pp. 6–7.
14. Marcel de Hass, Andrej Tibold, and Vincent Cillessen, eds, *Geo-strategy in South Caucasus: Power Play and Energy Security States and Organizations* (The Hague: Clingendael Institute, Netherlands Institute of International Relations, November 2006), available at http://www.clingendael.nl/sites/default/files/20061100_cscp_haas.pdf
15. Nuriyev, *South Caucasus at the Crossroads*, p. 277.
16. Simone Tagliapietra, "Turkey as a Regional Natural Gas Hub: Myth or Reality?", *Review of Environment Energy and Economics*, 16 January 2014.
17. Ibid.

18. Suleyman Elik, *Iran–Turkey Relations, 1979–2011: Conceptualizing the Dynamics of Politics, Religion and Security in Middle-Power States* (London: Routledge, 2011), p. 146.
19. Tagliapietra, "Turkey as a Regional Natural Gas Hub".
20. Elik, *Iran–Turkey Relations*, pp. 147–8.
21. Nuriyev, *South Caucasus at the Crossroads*, p. 275.
22. Alex Vatanka, "Tangle in the Caucasus: Iran and Israel Fight for Influence in Azerbaijan," *Foreign Affairs* (15 January 2013), available at www.foreignaffairs.com/articles/138753/alevatanka/tangle-in-the-caucasus
23. Nuriyev, *South Caucasus at the Crossroads*, p. 276.
24. Ibid.
25. P. L. Dash, *Caspian Pipeline Politics, Energy Reserves and Regional Implications* (New Delhi: Pentagon Press, 2008), p. 69.
26. Flanagan, "The Turkey–Russia–Iran Nexus: Eurasian Power Dynamics," pp. 175–6.
27. Chitadze, "Geopolitical Interests of Iran in South Caucasus and Georgian–Iranian Relations," pp. 5–12; see p. 5.
28. Nuriyev, *South Caucasus at the Crossroads*, p. 287.
29. Kaweh Sadegh-Zadeh, "Iran's Strategy in the South Caucasus," *Caucasian Review of International Affairs*, Vol. 2, No. 1 (Winter 2008), pp. 1–7; see p. 7.
30. Anthony H. Cordesman, Bryan Gold, Robert Shelala, and Michael Gibbs, *US and Iranian Strategic Competition: Turkey and the South Caucasus*, Center for Strategic and International Center (CSIC), 6 June 2013, p. 52, available at http://csis.org/files/publication/130612_turk_casp_chap9.pdf
31. Chitadze, "Geopolitical Interests of Iran in South Caucasus and Georgian–Iranian Relations," p. 7; and Sadegh-Zadeh, "Iran's Strategy in the South Caucasus," pp. 4–5.
32. Brenda Shaffer, "Iran's Role in the South Caucasus and Caspian Region: Diverging Views on the US and Europe," in Eugene Whitlock, ed., *Iran and its Neighbors: Diverging Views on a Strategic Region* (Berlin: Stiftung Wissenschaft und Politik (German Institute for International and Security Affairs, 2003), pp. 17–22; see p. 21; available at http://belfercenter.ksg.harvard.edu/files/shaffer.pdf
33. Nigar Oruova, "Caspian Summit in Astrakhan finalizes with Breakthrough," *Azernews*, 30 September 2014, available at www.azernews.az/region/71361.html
34. Evanthia Balla, "Turkish and Iranian Interests and Policies in the South Caucasus," Norwegian Peacebuilding Resource Center (NOREF), Policy Brief, April 2013, available at http://peacebuilding.no/var/ezflow_site/storage/original/application/4b0857e9346d1c11fcfe98dc3a42c49a.pdf
35. "Iran Seeks to Trade Electricity with Russia, Azerbaijan," *Caspian Barrel*, 11 October 2014, available at http://caspianbarrel.org/?p=20539, accessed on 28 February 2015.

36. Balla, "Turkish and Iranian Interests and Policies in the South Caucasus."
37. Iran's population is divided along ethnic and linguistic lines. The CIA estimates that Iran's ethnic population is divided by roughly the following percentages: Persian 61%, Azeri 16%, Kurd 10%, Lur 6%, Baloch 2%, Arab 2%, Turkmen and Turkic tribes 2%, and other 1%. Its linguistic differences are: Persian 535, Azeri Turkic and Turkic dialects 18%, Kurdish 10%, Gilaki and Mazandarani 7%, Luri 6%, Balochi 2%, Arabic 2%, and other 2%. The country is far more unified in religious terms with 89% Shi'ite, 9% Sunni, and 3% other. See Cordesman, Gold, Shelala, and Gibbs, *US and Iranian Strategic Competition: Turkey and the South Caucasus.*
38. Cordesman, Gold, Shelala, and Gibbs, *US and Iranian Strategic Competition: Turkey and the South Caucasus*, p. 53.
39. Balla, "Turkish and Iranian Interests and Policies in the South Caucasus."
40. Since a 1994 ceasefire suspended hostilities between Armenian and Azerbaijani forces, the conflict has been subject to an international mediation effort aimed at negotiating a resolution of the contrasting principles of self-determination (supported by Armenia) and territorial integrity (upheld by Azerbaijan). The mediation effort has been managed by the Organization for Security and Cooperation in Europe (OSCE) through the so-called "Minsk Group," a tripartite body chaired by France, Russia, and the United States.
41. Cordesman, Gold, Shelala, and Gibbs, *US and Iranian Strategic Competition: Turkey and the South Caucasus*, p. 142.
42. Ibid., p. 142.
43. Charles Kennedy, "Caspian Sea Set to Become a Major Hub for Natural Gas Production," 3 September 2013, available at www.oilprice.com/Latest-Energy-News/World-News/Caspian-Sea-Set-to-Become-a-Major-Hub-for-Natural-Gas-Production.html
44. Shaffer, "Iran's Role in the South Caucasus and Caspian Region: Diverging Views on the US and Europe," p. 19.
45. Clement Therme, "Iranian Foreign Policy Towards the South Caucasus: Between Revolutionary Ideals and Realpolitik," Academia.edu, available at https://www.academia.edu/3224368/Iranian_Foreign_Policy_towards_the_South_Caucasus_Between_Revolutionary_Ideals_and_Realpolitik
46. Manochehr Dorraj and Nader Entessar, "Iran's Northern Exposure: Foreign Policy Challenges in Eurasia," *Occasional Paper*, No. 13, Center for International and Regional Studies, 2013, pp. 1–27; see p. 20.
47. Giragosian, "Armenia's Search for Independence," p. 285.
48. Ibid.
49. Sadegh-Zadeh, "Iran's Strategy in the South Caucasus," p. 7.
50. Cordesman, Gold, Shelala, and Gibbs, *US and Iranian Strategic Competition: Turkey and the South Caucasus*, p. 65.

51. Tornike Sharashenidze, "The Role of Iran in South Caucasus," International Relations and Security Network, 27 February 2013, available at http://www.isn.ethz.ch/Digital-Library/Articles/Special-Feature/Detail/?lng=en&id=158505&contextid774=158505&contextid775=158498&tabid
52. Cordesman, Gold, Shelala, and Gibbs, *US and Iranian Strategic Competition: Turkey and the South Caucasus*, p. 65.
53. Ibid.
54. Ibid., p. 66.
55. Abdollah Baei Lashaki, Masoumeh Rad Goudarzi, and Davood Amraei, "The Roots of Tension in South Caucasus: The Case of Iran–Azerbaijan Relationship," *Journal of Politics and Law*, Vol. 6, No. 4 (2013), pp. 141–8; see p. 142.
56. Nuriyev, *South Caucasus at the Crossroads*, p. 271.
57. Ibid.
58. Chitadze, "Geopolitical Interests of Iran in South Caucasus and Georgian-Iranian Relations," p. 8.
59. Nuriyev, *South Caucasus at the Crossroads*, pp. 81–2.
60. Chitadze, "Geopolitical Interests of Iran in South Caucasus and Georgian–Iranian Relations," p. 9.
61. Sadegh-Zadeh, "Iran's Strategy in the South Caucasus," p. 7.
62. Chitadze, "Geopolitical Interests of Iran in South Caucasus and Georgian–Iranian Relations," p. 10.
63. Cordesman, Gold, Shelala, and Gibbs, *US and Iranian Strategic Competition: Turkey and the South Caucasus*, p. 95–6.
64. Alex Vatanka, "Iran: Peacemaker in the Caucasus," *National Interest*, 13 November 2014, available at http://nationalinterest.org/feature/iran-peacemaker-the-caucasus-11672
65. Tornike Sharashenidze, "The Role of Iran in South Caucasus," International Relations and Security Network, 27 February 2013, available at http://www.isn.ethz.ch/Digital-Library/Articles/Special-Feature/Detail/?lng=en&id=158505&contextid774=158505&contextid775=158498&tabid=
66. Bayram Sinkaya, "Turkey–Iran Relations in the 1990s and the Role of Ideology," *Perceptions: Journal of International Affairs*, Vol. X, No. 1 (Spring 2005), pp. 1–16; see p. 12.
67. Ibid.
68. For further information on this issue, see "Turkey–Azerbaijan strategic alliance treaty and Russia–Armenia military agreement: Status-quo in the South Caucasus remains unchanged," *ANALYTICS*, available at http://en.apa.az/news/128191
69. Balla, "Turkish and Iranian Interests and Policies in the South Caucasus."
70. Ibid.
71. Ekpen James Omonbude, *Cross-Border Oil and Gas Pipeline and the Role of the Transit Country: Economics, Challenges, and Solutions* (New York: Palgrave/Macmillan, 2013), p. 89.

72. Nuriyev, *South Caucasus at the Crossroads*, p. 250.
73. Ibid., p. 281.
74. Ibid.
75. Balla, "Turkish and Iranian Interests and Policies in the South Caucasus."
76. Ibid.
77. Nuriyev, *South Caucasus at the Crossroads*, p. 285.
78. Ibid., p. 284.
79. Walter Laqueur, *Putinism: Russia and its Future with the West* (New York: St Martin's Press, 2015), p. 8.
80. Ibid., p. 97.
81. Marlene Laruelle, *Russian Eurasianism: An Ideology of Empire* (Baltimore, MD: Johns Hopkins University Press, 2008), p. 197.
82. Ibid., pp. 197–8.
83. Graham E. Fuller, *The New Turkish Republic: Turkey as a Pivotal State in the Muslim World* (Washington, DC: United States Institute of Peace Press, 2008), pp. 173–4.
84. Sinkaya, "Turkey–Iran Relations in the 1990s and the Role of Ideology," p. 14.
85. US Energy Information Administration, EIA, "Iran," 22 July 2014, available at http://www.eia.gov/countries/cab.cfm?fips=ir
86. Ibid.
87. Michael A. Reynolds, "Why Turkey Has Been Quiet About Crimea," *Current History*, Vol. 113, No. 765 (October 2014), pp. 290–92; see p. 292.
88. Ibid., p. 292.
89. Sara Miller Llana, "Europe's New Realism Toward Russia," *Christian Science Monitor Weekly Magazine*, 7 April 2014, p. 32.
90. Maryam Pashang, "Ukraine's Crisis and Role of Iran in Europe's Energy Security," *Iran Review*, 23 March 2014, available at www.iranreview.org/content/Documents/Ukraine-s-Crisis-and-Role-of-Iran-in-Europe-s-Energy-Security.htm
91. Paul R. Pillar, "The Need for Iranian Oil and Gas," *National Interest*, 22 April 2014, available at http://server1.nationalinterest.org/blog/paul-pillar/the-need-iranian-oil-gas-10325
92. Pashang, "Ukraine's Crisis and Role of Iran in Europe's Energy Security."
93. Jeremie Kasongo, "Russia vs. Turkey: Consequences of a New Eurasia Clash," Linkedin.com, 27 December 2015, available at https://www.linkedin.com/pulse/russia-vs-turkey-consequences-new-eurasian-clash-j%C3%A9r%C3%A9mie-kasongo, last accessed on 9 August 2016.
94. Kadri Kaan Renda, "Turkey's Neighborhood Policy: An Emerging Complex Interdependence," *Insight Turkey*, Vol. 13, No. 1 (2011), pp. 89–108.
95. Matthew Sussex and Roger E. Kanet, *Russia, Eurasia, and the New Geopolitics of Energy: Confrontation and Consolidation* (New York: Palgrave Macmillan, 2015), p. 80.

96. Neil MacFarquhar and Tim Arango, "Erdogan and Putin Seek to Put Syria Rift in Past," *New York Times*, (9 August 2016), pp. A4 and A8.
97. Ibid., p. A4.
98. Neil MacFarquhar, "Russia and Turkey Vow to Repair Ties as West Watches Nervously," *New York Times*, 10 August 2016, p. A6.
99. Ibid.
100. Elik, *Iran–Turkey Relations*, p. 174.
101. Alidad Mafinezam and Aria Mehrabi, *Iran and its Place Among Nations* (Westport, CT: Praeger, 2008), pp. 54–5.
102. Ibid., p. 59.
103. Mohammed Ayoob, "Turkey and Iran in the Era of the Arab Uprisings," in Fawaz A. Gerges, ed., *The New Middle East: Protest and Revolution in the Arab World* (New York: Cambridge University Press, 2014), pp. 402–17; see p. 410.
104. Bill Park, "Turkey, the US and the KRG: Moving Parts and the Geopolitical Realities," *Insight Turkey*, Vol. 14, No. 2 (Summer 2012), pp. 109–24; see p. 120–21.
105. Ibid., pp. 122–3.
106. Michael Eppel, "Kurdish Nationalism's Moment of Truth," *Current History*, Vol. 113, No. 767 (December 2014), pp. 362–8; see p. 364.
107. Ibid., p. 346.
108. Ayoob, "Turkey and Iran in the Era of the Arab Uprisings," pp. 415–16.
109. Mafinezam and Mehrabi, *Iran and its Place Among Nations*, p. 58.
110. Ayoob, "Turkey and Iran in the Era of the Arab Uprisings," p. 416.
111. Ibid., p. 416.
112. Elik, *Iran–Turkey Relations*, p. 166.
113. Ibid., p. 167.
114. Ibid.
115. Siamak Adibi and Fereidun Fesharaki, "The Iranian Gas Industry," in Bassam Fattouh and Jonathan Stern, eds, *Natural Gas Markets in the Middle East and North Africa* (Oxford: Oxford Institute for Energy Studies, 2011), p. 289.
116. Ibid.
117. Ibid., pp. 158–60.
118. "Turkey Seeks to Build Iran Pipeline Amid Uncertain Environment, *Today's Zaman*, 9 February 2014, available at http://www.todayszaman.com/news-338859-turkey-seeks-to-build-iran-pipeline-amid-uncertain-environment.html
119. Cordesman, Gold, Shelala, and Gibbs, *US and Iranian Strategic Competition: Turkey and the South Caucasus*, p. 15.
120. Elik, *Iran–Turkey Relations*, p. 160.
121. Scott Peterson, "Iran and Turkey: Rivals in Syrian War, but Friends in Trade," *Christian Science Monitor*, 9 June 2014, available at www.csmonitor.com/World/Middle-East/2014/0609/Iran-and-Turkey-rivals-in-Syrian-war-but-friends-in-trade-video

122. Roland Elliott Brown, "Siamese Rivals: Iran and Turkey," Iranwire.com, 9 June 2014, available at http://en.iranwire.com/features/5813/
123. William Armstrong, "Turkish–Iranian Relations Since 1979: Asymmetry of Interest?", *Hurriyet Daily News*, available at www.hurriyetdailynews.com/turkish-iranian-relations-since-1979-assymetry-of-interest—.aspx?pageID=238&nID=40546&NewsCatID=474
124. Ibid.
125. Atilla Yezilada, "Turkey and the rise of ISIS: The consequences of benign neglect," *The Mark News*, 14 July 2014, available at www.themarknews.com/2014/07/14/turkey-and-the-rise-of-isis-the-consequences-of-benign-neglect/
126. Taylor Goel, "Vital role of Turkey's Ruling AKP in the Rise of ISIS," *Liberation*, 19 August 2014, available at www.liberationnews.org/akps-vital-role-in-the-rise-of-isis/
127. Nuriyev, *South Caucasus at the Crossroads*, p. 259.
128. Cordesman, Gold, Shelala, and Gibbs, *US and Iranian Strategic Competition: Turkey and the South Caucasus*, pp. 48, 59.
129. Bülent Aras, "Turkey and Iran Discussing the Future Under the Impact of the Arab Spring," Al Jazeera Center for Studies, 5 May 2013, available at http://studies.aljazeera.net/en/reports/2013/05/20135572011282586.htm
130. George Friedman, *The Next Decade: Where We've Been ... and Where We're Going* (New York: Doubleday, 2012), pp. 117–18.
131. Elik, *Iran, Turkey Relations*, p. 197.

4. TURKEY'S ENERGY POLICY IN THE MIDDLE EAST AND SOUTH CAUCASUS

1. Ahmet K. Han, "Turkey's Energy Strategy and the Middle East: Between a Rock and a Hard Place," *Turkish Studies*, Vol. 12, No. 4 (December 2011), p. 607.
2. Tuncay Babalı, "Regional Energy Equations and Turkish Foreign Policy: The Middle East and the CIS," *Insight Turkey*, Vol. 12, No. 3 (2010), p. 150.
3. Aad Correlje and Coby Van der Linde, "Energy Supply Security and Geopolitics: A European Perspective," *Energy Policy*, Vol. 34, No. 5 (March 2006), pp. 532–43.
4. For an extensive discussion of the terms "securitization" and "politicization" with regard to threats and political procedures, see Barry Buzan, Ole Waever, and Jaap de Wilde, *Security: A New Framework for Analysis* (Boulder, CO and London: Lynne Rienner, 1998).
5. Ahmet Davutoğlu, "Turkey's Foreign Policy Vision: An Assessment of 2007," *Insight Turkey*, Vol. 10, No. 1 (2008), p. 78.
6. Hakan Fidan, "A Work in Progress: The New Turkish Foreign Policy," *Middle East Policy*, Vol. 20, No. 1 (Spring 2013), pp. 91–6. For more discussion on soft power

and Turkey's foreign policy, see the chapters by Altunışık and Balcı in this volume.

7. Kemal Kirişci, "The Transformation of Turkish Foreign Policy: The Rise of the Trading State," *New Perspectives on Turkey*, Vol. 40 (2009), pp. 29–57.
8. Turkish Ministry of Energy and Natural Resources, "International Projects and Pipelines," accessed 8 April 2015, http://www.enerji.gov.tr/en-US/Pages/International-Projects-and-Pipelines
9. Altay Atlı, "Businessmen as Diplomats: The Role of Business Associations in Turkey's Foreign Economic Policy," *Insight Turkey*, Vol. 13, No. 1 (2011), pp. 121–2.
10. Malik Mufti, "A Little America: The Emergence of Turkish Hegemony," *Middle East Brief*, Vol. 51 (May 2011), pp. 1–4, accessed 17 April 2015, http://www.brandeis.edu/crown/publications/meb/MEB51.pdf
11. Miriam Prys, "Hegemony, Domination, Detachment: Differences in Regional Powerhood," *International Studies Review*, Vol. 12, No. 4 (December 2010), p. 494.
12. Sandra Destradi, "Empire, Hegemony and Leadership: Developing a Research Framework for the Study of Regional Powers," *GIGA Working Paper* 79 (June 2008), pp. 11–12, accessed 7 July 2015, http://www.giga-hamburg.de/en/empire-hegemony-and-leadership-developing-a-research-framework-for-the-study-of-regional
13. "Turkey's 2.9 pct Growth in 2014 Fails to Meet Target," *Hürriyet Daily News*, 31 March 2015, accessed 9 April 2015, http://www.hurriyetdailynews.com/turkeys-29-pct-growth-in-2014-fails-to-meet-target.aspx?pageID=238&nID=80398&NewsCatID=344
14. T. C. Enerji ve Tabii Kaynaklar Bakanlığı, *2015 Yılı Bütçe Sunumu* (13 November 2014), p. 10, accessed 9 April 2015, http://www.enerji.gov.tr/file/?path+ROOT%2f1%2fDocuments%2fBütçe+Konuşması%2f2015+Yılı+Plan+Bütçe+Komisyonu+Konuşması.pdf
15. T. C. Enerji Piyasası Düzenleme Kurumu, *Petrol Piyasası 2014 Yılı Sektör Raporu* (2015), p. 2, accessed 2 July 2015, http://www.epdk.org.tr//documents/petrol/rapor_yayin/PPD_RaporYayin20141.pdf
16. Orhan Coşkun and Hümeyra Pamuk, "Turkey's First Nuclear Power Delayed, 'Not Ready Before 2022,'" *Reuters*, 23 March 2015, accessed 9 April 2015, http://www.reuters.com/article/2015/03/23/us-turkey-nuclear-delay-idUSKBNOMJ1DJ20150323
17. "Turkish Energy Min. Slams 'Biased' EU Parliament Report," *Anadolu Agency*, 15 June 2015, accessed 7 July 2015, http://www.aa.com.tr/en/economy/537848-turkish-energy-min-slams-biased-eu-parliament-report
18. T. C. Enerji Piyasası Düzenleme Kurumu, *Doğal Gaz Piyasası 2014 Yılı Sektör Raporu* (2015), pp. 1, 7, accessed 7 July 2015, http://www.epdk.org.tr/documents/dogalgaz/rapor_yayin/DPD_RaporYayin2014.pdf

19. T. C. Enerji ve Tabii Kaynaklar Bakanlığı, *2015 Yılı Bütçe Sunumu*, p. 75.
20. "BOTAŞ: 2020 Yılında Gaz İhtiyacı 70 Milyar Metreküp Olacak," *Enerji Enstitüsü*, 16 November 2012, accessed 9 March 2014, http://enerjienstitusu.com/2012/11/16/botas-2020-yilinda-gaz-ihtiyaci-70-milyar-metrekup-olacak
21. "Political Concerns Mar Turkish Stream Project," Euractiv.com, 11 March 2015, accessed 9 April 2015, http://euractiv.com/sections/energy/political-concerns-mar-turkish-stream-project-312815
22. Paul Stevens, *Transit Troubles: Pipelines as a Source of Conflict* (London: Royal Institute of International Affairs, 2009).
23. Adam N. Stulberg, "Strategic Bargaining and Pipeline Politics: Confronting the Credible Commitment Problem in Eurasian Energy Transit," *Review of International Political Economy*, Vol. 19, No. 5 (2012), p. 809.
24. T. C. Enerji Piyasasi Düzenleme Kurumu, *Doğal Gaz Piyasası 2014*, p. 15.
25. Erkan Erdoğdu, "Turkey's Energy Strategy and its Role in the EU's Southern Gas Corridor," *Istituto Affari Internazionali* Working Paper 14, No. 1 (February 2014), p. 8, accessed 10 April 2015, http://www.iai.it/sites/default/files/iaiwp1401.pdf
26. Einar Wigen, "Pipe Dreams or Dream Pipe? Turkey's Hopes of Becoming an Energy Hub," *Middle East Journal*, Vol. 66, No. 4 (Autumn 2012), p. 601.
27. Patrick Heather, "Continental European Gas Hubs: Are They Fit for Purpose?", *Oxford Institute for Energy Studies* NG 63 (June 2012), p. 5, accessed 10 April 2015, http://www.oxfordenergy.org/wpcms/wp-content/uploads/2012/06/NG-63.pdf. The discussion on different types of energy hubs is largely taken from this paper.
28. Gulmira Rzayeva, "Natural Gas in the Turkish Domestic Energy Market: Policies and Challenges," *Oxford Institute for Energy Studies*, NG 82 (February 2014), p. 52, accessed 10 April 2015, http://www.oxfordenergy.org/wpcms/wp-content/uploads/2014/02/NG-82.pdf
29. T. C. Enerji ve Tabii Kaynaklar Bakanlığı, *2015–2019 Stratejik Planı* (2014), p. 31, accessed 10 April 2015, http://www.enerji.gov.tr/File/?path=ROOT%2f1%2fDocuments%2fStratejik+Plan%2fETKB+2015–2019+Stratejik+Plani.pdf
30. John Roberts, "Turkey as a Regional Energy Hub," *Insight Turkey*, Vol. 12, No. 3 (2010), p. 44.
31. "Kurdish Oil Revenue Exceeds $1B, Turkey's Halkbank Holds $400M Share," *Daily Sabah*, 26 September 2014, accessed 12 April 2015, http://www.dailysabah.com/energy/2014/09/26/kurdish-oil-revenue-exceeds-1b-turkeys-halkbank-holds-400m-share
32. "Genel Energy's Production and Revenues Rise in 2013," *Digital Look*, 15 January 2014, accessed 15 March 2014, http://www.digitallook.com/newsaim_bulletin/genel_energys_production_and_revenues_rise_in_2013_d121417814.html
33. Amiram Barkat, "10 Bids for Leviathan Export Tender to Turkey," *Globes*, 23 March 2014, accessed 4 April 2014, http://www.globes.co.il/en/article-10-bids-for-leviathan-export-tender-to-turkey-1000926526

34. "Turkey's Turcas Says Starts Talks to Buy Natural Gas from Leviathan Field," Reuters, 22 April 2014, accessed 12 April 2015, http://uk.reuters.com/article/2014/04/22/turcas-petrol-israel-gas-idUKL6N0NE3O720140422
35. Sharon Udasin, "Report: Turkey Forbids Completion of Gas Deal with Israel until Peace Deal with Gaza Achieved," *Jerusalem Post*, 6 August 2014, accessed 12 April 2015, http://www.jpost.com/Enviro-Tech/Report-Turkey-forbids-completion-of-gas-deal-with-Israel-until-peace-with-Gaza-achieved-370192
36. "Turkish Government Decides Against TPAO Investment in Iranian Energy Sector," *Platts*, 12 February 2014, accessed 13 April 2015, http://www.platts.com/latest-news/natural-gas/istanbul/turkish-government-decides-against-tpao-investment-26708443
37. David Ramin Jalilvand, "Iran's Gas Exports: Can Past Failure Become Future Success?" *Oxford Institute for Energy Studies*, NG 78 (June 2013), p. 23, accessed 13 April 2015, http://www.oxfordenergy.org/wpcms/wp-content/uploads/2013/06/NG-78.pdf. For an alternative view of Iran's gas export options, see the chapter by Monshipouri in this volume.
38. Merve Erdil, "Turkey Rejects Iran's Gas Export Proposal," *Hürriyet Daily News*, 17 April 2015, accessed 19 April 2015, http://www.hurriyetdailynews.com/turkey-rejects-irans-gas-export-proposal.aspx?pageID=238&nID=81214&NewsCatID=348
39. "Turkey Cannot Afford Disruption in Ties with Russia, Says Erdoğan," *Turkish Daily News*, 1 September 2008, accessed 16 March 2014, http://www.hurriyetdailynews.com/default.aspx?pageid=438&n=turkey-cannot-afford-disruption-in-ties-with-russia-sayserdogan-2008–09–01
40. Aura Sabadus, "Turkey: Dispelling Unhelpful Myths," naturalgaseurope.com, 18 May 2015, accessed 18 June 2015, http://www.naturalgaseurope.com/turkey-dispelling-unhelpful-myths-23750
41. Vladimir Socor, "Aliyev, Erdoğan Sign Intergovernmental Agreement on Trans-Anatolian Gas Pipeline to Europe," *Eurasia Daily Monitor*, Vol. 9, No. 122 (27 June 2012), accessed 27 June 2012, http://www.jamestown.org/programs/edm/single/?tx_ttnews%5Btt_news%5D=39545&tx_ttnews%5Bback-Pid%5D=587&no_cache=1#.UzWGN01FCP8
42. "Intergovernmental Agreement between the Government of the Republic of Turkey and the Government of the Republic of Azerbaijan Concerning the Trans Anatolian Natural Gas Pipeline System," 26 June 2012, accessed 3 July 2015, http://www.tanap.com/content/file/TANAPIGA.pdf
43. Mushvig Mehdiyev, "Turkey Seeks to Strengthen Ties with Azerbaijan," azernews.az, 26 February 2015, accessed 13 April 2015, http://www.azernews.az/azerbaijan/78276.html
44. "Uluslararası Projeler," BOTAŞ, accessed 15 March 2014, http://www.botas.gov.tr/index.asp

45. Marat Gurt,"Turkmenistan Inks Deal with Turkey to Supply Gas to TANAP Pipeline," Reuters, 7 November 2014, accessed 14 April 2015, http://www.reuters.com/article/2014/11/07/turkmenistan-turkey-tanap-idUSL6N0SX2QK20141107
46. "Turkey, Turkmenistan Seal New Energy Deals," *Today's Zaman*, 3 March 2015, accessed 14 April 2015, http://www.todayszaman.com/diplomacy_turkey-turkmenistan-seal-new-energy-deals_374197.html
47. Saleha Mohsin and Mikael Holter, "Statoil Sells Shah Deniz Stake to Petronas for $2.25 Billion," Bloomberg, 13 October 2014, accessed 14 April 2015, http://www.bloomberg.com/news/articles/2014–10–13/statoil-sells-shah-deniz-stake-to-petronas-for-2-25-billion
48. Ashgabat Declaration, European Commission, Brussels, 1 May 2015, accessed 3 July 2015, http://ec.europa.eu/commission/2014–2019/sefcovic/announcements/ashgabat-declaration_en
49. Gareth Winrow, "Turkey, Russia and the Caucasus: Common and Diverging Interests," Chatham House Briefing Paper (12 November 2009), pp. 6–7, accessed 7 July 2015, http://www.chathamhouse.org/publications/papers/view/109168
50. "Gazprom, Turkey's BOTAŞ Could Build 63 bcm Undersea Gas Pipeline—Gazprom CEO," Reuters, 1 December 2014, accessed 17 April 2015, http://www.reuters.com/article/2014/12/01/us-russia-gas-turkey-pipeline-idUSKCN0JF33D20141201
51. Rufiz Hafizoğlu, "Turkish Stream to Compete with TANAP—Turkish Minister," en.trend.az, 28 January 2015, accessed 17 April 2015, http://en.trend.az/business/economy/2357914.html
52. "Gazprom Cuts Gas Price to Turkey to no Benefit of Customers," *Today's Zaman*, 27 February 2015, accessed 17 April 2015, http://mobile.todayszaman.com/business_gazprom-cuts-gas-price-to-turkey-to-no-benefit-of-customers_373795.html
53. A. Makris, "Russia, Greece Sign Deal on TurkStream Gas Pipeline," *Greece.Greek Reporter*, 19 June 2015, accessed 7 July 2015, http://greece.greekreporter.com/2015/06/19/russia-greece-sign-deal-on-turkstream-gas-pipeline.
54. "Turk Stream: The Realm of if, if, if...," naturalgaseurope.com, 12 February 2015, accessed 17 April 2015, http://www.naturalgaseurope.com/european-gas-conference-2015-turkish-stream-8855
55. Jonathan Stern, Simon Pirani, and Katja Yafimava, "Does the Cancellation of South Stream Signal a Fundamental Reorientation of Russian Gas Export Policy?", *Oxford Energy Comment* (Oxford Institute of Energy Studies, January 2015), p. 6, accessed 17 April 2015, http://www.oxfordenergy.org/wpcms/wp-content/uploads/2015/01/Does-cancellation-of-South-Stream-signal-a-fundamental-reorientation-of-Russian-gas-export-policy
56. "Turk Stream: The Realm of if, if, if..."
57. "European Gas Demand Fell 11% One Year in 2014 to 409 bcm: Eurogas," *Platts*,

26 March 2015, accessed 17 April 2015, http://www.platts.com/latest-news/natural-gas/london/european-gas-demand-fell-11-on-year-in-2014-to-26049067

58. European Energy Security Strategy, COM (2014) 330 Final, European Commission, Brussels, 28 May 2014, pp. 2, 15, accessed 17 April 2015, http://eur-lex.europa.eu/legal-content/EN/TXT/PDF/?uri=CELEX:52014DC0330&from=EN
59. "Mysterious '08 Turkey Pipeline Blast Opened New Cyberwar," Bloomberg, 10 December 2014, accessed 17 April 2015, http://www.bloomberg.com/news/articles/2014–12–10/mysterious-08-turkey-pipeline-blast-opened-new-cyberwar
60. "Azerbaijan Resumes Gas Flows to Turkey from Shah Deniz—BP," Reuters, 11 June 2012, accessed 17 April 2015, http://af.reuters.com/article/energyOilNews/idAFL5E8HBB2J20120611; A. Taghiyeva, "Turkish Ministry: Explosion on Baku-Tbilisi-Erzurum Gas Pipeline a Terror Act," en.trend.az, 4 October 2012, accessed 17 April 2015, http://en.trend.az/business/energy/2072926.html
61. Barak Ravid, "In Secret Meeting, Israel and Turkey Renew Reconciliation Talks," *Haaretz*, 22 June 2015, accessed 7 July 2015, http://www.haaretz.com/news/diplomacy-defense/premium-1.662476

5. THE CLASH OF NATIONALISMS: IRANIAN RESPONSE TO BAKU'S IRREDENTISM

1. See, for example, Theda Skocpol, ed., *Visions and Methods in Historical Sociology* (Cambridge: Cambridge University Press, 1984).
2. See Alireza Asgharzadeh, *Iran and the Challenge of Diversity: Islamic Fundamentalism, Aryanist Racism, and Democratic Struggles* (New York: Palgrave Macmillan, 2007); Abbas Vali, *Kurds and the State in Iran: The Making of Kurdish Identity* (London: I. B. Tauris, 2010); and Alam Saleh, *Ethnic Identity and the State in Iran* (New York: Palgrave Macmillan, 2013); Mostafa Vaziri, *Iran as Imagined Nation: The Construction of National Identity* (Washington, DC: Paragon House, 1993); and Rasmus Christian Elling, *Minorities in Iran: Nationalism and Ethnicity after Khomeini* (New York: Palgrave Macmillan, 2013).
3. See Anthony D. Smith, *The Antiquity of Nations* (London: Polity Press, 2004).
4. Hamid Ahmadi, "Unity within Diversity: Foundations and Dynamics of National Identity in Iran," *Critique: Critical Middle Eastern Studies*, Vol. 14, No. 1 (Spring 2005), pp. 123–40; "Iran and the Arab Spring: why Iranians did not follow the Arabs?" *Asian Politics and Policy*, Vol. 5, No. 3 (July 2013); "International Politics, Political Elites and the Question of Ethnicity in Iran," *Iran and the Caucasus*, Vol. 17, No. 1 (March 2013); "Islam and Nationalism in Iranian Contemporary Society and Politics," *Iranian Review of Foreign Affairs*, Vol. 1, No. 1 (Spring 2010), pp. 193–223; *Bonyaad Haaye Hoviyyat-I Melli Irani* [The foundations of Iranian national identity] (Tehran: Pajuheshkadey-i Motaaleaat-i Ijtemaai, 2010); *Ghowmiyyat va*

Ghowmgeraai dar Iran [Ethnicity and ethnic politics in Iran] (Tehran: Nashre Ney, 2009).

5. The best example of such works is Brenda Shaffer, *Borders and Brethren: Iran and the Challenge of Azerbaijani Identity* (Cambridge, MA: MIT Press, 2002).
6. Kaveh Bayat, *Azerbaijan Dar Mowj Khize Tarikh: Negahi be Mabahese Mellion Iran va Jarayede Baku Dar Taghire name Aran be Azerbaijan 1296–98* [Azerbaijan confronting the devastative waves of history: a glance at the discussions between Iranian nationalists and Baku media on changing the name Aran into Azerbaijan, 1918–20] (Tehran: Shiraze, 1379/1990).
7. On pan-Turkism, see Jacob Landau, *Pan-Turkism, from Irredentism to Cooperation* (London: Hurst & Co., 1995).
8. Touraj Atabaki, "Ethnic Diversity and the Territorial Integrity of Iran: Domestic Harmony and Regional Challenges," *Iranian Studies*, Vol. 38 (2005).
9. Ahmad Kasravi, *Tarikhe Hejdah Sale Azerbaijan* [Eighteen years history of Azerbaijan] (Tehran: Amir Kabir, 1378/1998), p. 873.
10. Kaveh Bayat, *Tufan Bar Farazr Ghafghaz: Negahi be Monasebate Iran va Jomhurihaye Azarbaijan, Armanestan va Gorjestan dar Dowreye Nakhoste Esteghlal 1917–1921* [Storm over the Caucasus: regional relations of Iran with Republics of Azerbaijan, Armenia and Georgia in the first period of independence, 1917–1921] (Tehran: Entesharate Vezarate Kharejeh, 1380/2001), pp. 149–51.
11. Reza Azari Shahrezai, *Hay'ate Fogholadeh Ghafghaziyeh* [Extraordinary mission for the Caucasus] (Tehran: Vezarate Kharejeh, 1379/2000).
12. On the Iran–Azerbaijan confederation, see *Azerbaijan Democratic Republic Documents: Great Britain Archives*, compiled by N. A. Maxwell (Baku: Azerbaijan National Academy of Science, 2008); Mansure Etehadiyeh and Syruse Sa'dvandian, *Majmueh Mokatebat, Asnad, Khaterate va Asare Firuz Mirza Firuz (Nosrat al Dowleh)* [A collection of communications, documents, memories and the works of Firuz Mirza Firuz] (Tehran: Nashre Tarikhe Iran, 1369/1990); Bayat, *Tufan Bar Faraze Ghafghaz*, pp. 188–96.
13. Jamil Hasanli searched the Soviet Archives on Baku and found these three documents. For the full text of the documents, see "New Evidence on the Iranian crisis of 1945–46: From the Baku Archives," Woodrow Wilson Center for Scholars, http://www.wilsoncenter.org/publication/new-evidence-the-iran-crisis-1945–46
14. Jamil Hasanli, *Faraz o Forude Firgheye Democrate Azarbaijan* [The ups and downs of Azerbaijan Firghe Democrat], trans. Mansur Homami (Tehran: Nashre Ney, 1387).
15. Hamid Mollazadeh, *Raazhaye Sar Be Mohr: Nagofte Haye Vaghaye'e Azerbaijan* [Unrevealed secrets: untold stories about Azerbaijan events] (Tabriz: Mahde Azadi, 1997).
16. Cameron S. Brown, "Observations from Azerbaijan," *Middle East Review of International Affairs*, Vol. 6, No. 4 (December 2002), p. 68.

17. Shaffer, *Borders and Brethren*, pp. 73–4.
18. Eric Hobsbawm and T. Ranger, eds., *The Invention of Tradition* (Cambridge: Cambridge University Press, 1983).
19. Benedict Anderson, *Imagined Communities: Reflections on the Origin and Spread of Nationalism* (London: Verso, 1983).
20. David Nissman "The Origins and the Development of the Literature of 'Longing' in Azerbaijan," *Journal of Turkish Studies* (1984), pp. 199–207.
21. David Nissman, "Baku Looks South," *Prism*, Vol. 1, No. 2 (12 May 1995), http://www. amestown. org/single/ tx_ttnews%5Btt_news%5D=6197&tx_ttnews%5BbackPid%5D=217#.VUEB8_lViko
22. Nacaf Nacafov, Samad Mirzayev, et al., *Azerbaijan–Iranian Relations* (Baku: FAR Center for Economic and Political Research, 1996).
23. Shaffer, *Borders and Brethren*, pp. 132–3.
24. Svante Cornell, "Small Nations and Great Powers: A Study of Ethno-political Conflict in the Caucasus," (Richmond: Curzon Press, 2001), p. 318.
25. *Turan*, 21 April 1999, quoted in Cameron S. Brown, "Wanting to have their Cake and their Neighbor's too: Azerbaijani Attitudes toward Karabakh and Iranian Azerbaijan," *Middle East Journal*, Vol. 58, No. 4 (Autumn 2004), p. 588.
26. Ibid.
27. *Turan*, 23 April 1999, quoted in ibid., p. 589.
28. Author interview with Iranian Azeri students, Tehran.
29. Nasib Nasibli, "Azerbaijan–Iran Relations: Challenges and Prospects" (Event Summary. Event Report, Kennedy School of Government, Harvard University, 1999), http://belfercenter.ksg.harvard.edu/publication/12750/azerbaijan_iran_relations.html
30. Nasib Nasibli, "The Azerbaijan Question in Iran: A Critical Issue for Iran's Future," *Caspian Crossroads* (Winter 1998), www.zerbaijan.com/azeri/nasibzade2.html
31. Brown, "Wanting to have their Cake," p. 589.
32. Ghayratli Azari, 'GunAz TV Koja Istade Ast? Tahlile Mohtavaye Televisione GunAz TV," [Where does GunAz TV stand? A content analysis of GunAz TV], (9 Shahrivar 1393/31 August 2014), Http:www.pantorkism.blogfa.com/
33. Nasib Nasibli, "Most of Our Compatriots, Residing in Iran, Consider themselves to be Iranians, not Azerbaijani," http://www.today.az/news/politics/49617.html
34. Brown, "Wanting to have their Cake," p. 592.
35. Emil Souleimanov, Kamil Pikal, and Josef Kraus, "The Rise of Nationalism among Iranian Azerbaijanis: A Step toward Iran's Disintegration?" *Middle East Review of International Affairs*, Vol. 17, No. 1 (Spring 2013), p. 38.
36. Brad Knickerbocker, "Attacking Iran: Did US just torpedo Israeli deal for a base in Azerbaijan?" *Christian Science Monitor* (29 March 2012).
37. Cornell, *Small Nations and Great Powers*, p. 318.
38. Khadija Ismayilova, "Azerbaijani Tempers Flare over Iranian TV's Criticism of

Peres Visit," *Asbarez*, 2 July 2009, http://asbarez.com/blog/archives/65952; "Azerbaijani Foreign Minister Urges Iran to end Broadcasting into Southern Azerbaijan," *CACI Analyst*, 25 October 2003, http://old.cacianalyst.org/?q=node/1623; "Baku appeals to Iran's state broadcaster over libelous reports," *Azernews*, 23 June 2011, http://www.azernews.az/ Azerbaijan/33348. html

39. Hema Kotecha, *Islamic and Ethnic Identities in Azerbaijan: Emerging Trends and Tensions* (Baku: OSCE, 2006), p. 28.
40. Ibid.
41. For a letter from Ayatollah Lankarani to the people of Azerbaijan, see "Statement of Ayatollah Shaikh Muhammad Jawad Fazel Lankarani regarding the Implementation of the Apostasy Ruling on Rafiq Taqi," http://www.fazellankarani.com/english/news/4931/. A group named "Majmae Defa az Hoghughe Azarihye Musalmane Jahan" [League for the defense of Muslim Azeris of the World] wrote a letter to Grand Ayatollah Sistani and the UN Human Right Council on the situation of those it called Muslims in Azerbaijani Jails. See http://qafqaz.ir/fa/?p=5612
42. Altay Goyushov, "Islamic Revival in Azerbaijan," *Current Trends in Islamic Ideology*, Vol. 7 (Hudson Institute: Center on Islam, Democracy, and the Future of the Modern World, 2008), p. 78.
43. Ibid., p. 29.
44. Javid Azizi, "Dowlate Baku va Tadavome Mobareze ba Azadi Hejab" [Baku government and the continuation of the struggle against the freedom of the hijab], *Irane Shomali*, 2008, http://irshomali. persianblog. ir/tag/; "Protests in Iran against ban on wearing hijab in Azerbaijan," *Panorama*, 7 February 2011, http://www.panorama.am/en/society/2011/02/07/hejab/
45. Elmira Kianpour, "Eurovision Bahane-ee baraye E'teraz" [Eurovision: A pretext for protest], in Hossein Ahmadi, ed., *Jomhuri-e Azarbaijan: 23 sal Takapoo baraye Dowlat va Mellat Sazi* [The Republic of Azerbaijan: 23 years of bustle for state and nation-building] (Tehran: Moasseseye Motaaleaate Tarikhe Moaser, 1393/2014), pp. 257–78; see also Giorgi Lomsadze, "Azerbaijan: Pop Music vs. Islam," *Eurosatnet*, 21 May 2012, http://www.eurasianet.org/print/65433
46. Antidze Margarita, "Iran's 'gay' Eurovision jibes strain Azerbaijan ties," Reuters, 22 May 2012, accessed 15 July 2012, http://in.reuters.com/article/2012/05/22/azerbaijan-iran-idINL5E8GM61H20120522
47. "Iran recalls envoy to Azerbaijan ahead of Eurovision," *AFP*, 22 May 2012, http: www.english.alarabiya.net/ articles/ 2012/ 05/22/215722.html
48. Felix Corley, "Azerbaijan: Imam and Driver in Pre-trial Detention, Conscientious Objector Imprisoned," Forum 18 News Service, 14 May 2013.
49. Mina Muradova, "Azerbaijan: Mosques Close in Baku, 'Capital of Islamic Culture,'" Euroasianet, 26 May 2009, http://www.eurasianet.org/departments/insightb/articles/eav052709b.shtml

50. Shahla Sultanova, "Azerbaijan Tightens Grip on Islamic Literature," *IWPR* [Institute of War and Peace Research] (2013), http://islamicommentary.org/2013/03/shahla-sultanova-azerbaijan-tightens-grip-on-islamic-literature/
51. Fariz Ismailzade, "The Rise of Islam in Azerbaijan," *IAGS* [Institute for the Analysis of Global Security] (2005), http://www.iags.org/n0328053. htm
52. Goyushov, "Islamic Revival in Azerbaijan," p. 73.
53. Ibid., p. 77.
54. Reza Nassaji, "Revayati az Naradan: Paytakhte tashayyo va Musighi Azerbaijan" [A narrative from Naradan: the capital of Shi'ism and the music of Azerbaijan), *Jahannews*, 3 April 2013, http://jahannews.com/vdchk wnik23nqkd.tft2.html
55. Idrak Abbasov, "Azeri Muslims Protest Theologian's Arrest," *Global Voices*, 9 April 2013, https:// iwpr.net/global-voices/azeri-muslims-protest-theologians-arrest; "Protest action in Nardaran," *ContactAz*, 10 December 2014, ttp://www.contact.az/docs/2014/Social/121000099435en.htm#; Etibar Mammadov, "Protest Staged in Nardaran", *APA*, 21 January 2015, http://en.apa.az/ xeber protest_ staged _in_ nardaran_221988.html
56. "Shooting in Nardaran kills 4," *Today Az*, 26 January 2006, http://www.today. az/print/news/society/ 22539.html
57. See, for example, Baytollah Ja'fari, "Sedaye Mazlumiyyate Nardaran" [The voice of innocence of Nardaran], Vijeh Namey-e Aran (Tabriz: Moasseseye Farhangi-ye Aran, 1381/2002), pp. 142–9; "Baztabe Koshtare Mardome Mazlume Nardaran dar Matbuat" [The reflection of the killings of the innocent people of Nardaran in the press], *Misaagh*, No. 112 (Tir 1381/ July 2002), p. 6; "Koshtar-e Nardaran Dar Jomhuri-ye Azarbaijan" [Killings of Nardaran in the Azerbaijan Republic], *Misaagh*, No. 113 (Khordad 1381/June 2002), p. 3.
58. For a more extensive analysis of the Shiite and pro-Iranian religious groups in the Azerbaijan Republic, see Arif Yunusov, *The Islamic Factor in Azerbaijan* (Baku: Institute for Peace and Democracy, 2013).
59. See http://bizimyol.info/news/10512.html
60. Natiq Cavadli, "Eicin Manafov: Xamneyi ağa bizim Dini liderimizdir..." [Elcin Mnafov: Khamenei is my religious leader], *Bizim Yol*, 31 August 2012, http://bizimyol.info/news/2231.html
61. By nationalists, I do not mean merely those who are active members of nationalist political parties, but those who generally lean to Iran's national interests, and its cultural and political legacy. Though some may even have affiliation with political parties, most are intellectuals, researchers, academicians, and journalists; for them Iran is more important than other references of identity. The more proper term is perhaps *Iran Dust* (one who likes Iran).
62. Hamid Ahmadi, *Bonyadhay-e Hoviyyate Melli-e Irani*, pp. 179–82.
63. Morteza Saghebfar, "Nasionalisme Irani va Masaleye Melliat ha" [Iranian nationalism and the question of nationalities], *Negahe Now*, No. 4 (Day 1370/January 1991), pp. 17–48.

64. Kaveh Bayat, "Nasionalism e Turk" [Turkish nationalism], *Negahe Now*, No. 4 (December 1991), pp. 54–75.
65. Mostafa Rahimi, "Nasionalism, Mellat Gerai va Democracy" [Nationalism, nationality, and democracy], pp. 121–30.
66. For Varjavand's letter, see "Matne kamele name-ye Dr. Parviz Varjavand be Mohammad Khatami" [The full text of Parviz Varjavand's letter to Mohammad Khatami], http://iranchehr.com/?p=4315
67. Hamid Ahmadi, *The Politics of Ethnic Nationalism in Iran* (PhD dissertation, Carleton University, Ottawa, 1995).
68. Such Iranian pan-Turkists include Mohammad Taghi Zehtabi, former member of *Firghe Democrat* who was teaching in Baku and returned to Iran after the Iranian Revolution of 1979; Javad Hay'at, a physician who graduated in Turkey and died in Baku in 2014; and Hussein Seddigh, who was in permanent contact with pan-Turkist circles in Turkey and the republic of Azerbaijan. The latter's ideas and activities were disclosed in a long journal article by a pro-Iranian nationalist Azeri researcher. See Masoud Mojdehi, "Doshmani ashekar va bi pardeh ba Iran o Irani, Farsha va zabane Farsi" [Open and unveiled animosity with Iran and Iranian, Persians and the Persian language], *Faslnameh-e Tarikhe Moasere Iran*, Vol. 15, No. 60 (Zemestan 1390/Winter 2012), pp. 87–133.
69. Mohammad Reza Khubruye Pak, *Federalism dar Jahan e Sevvom* [Federalism in the third world] (Tehran: Nashre Hazar, 2010); *Naghdi Bar Federalism* [A critique of federalism] (Tehran: Shirazeh, 1998).
70. Kaveh Farrokh, *Pan-Turanism Takes Aim at Azerbaijan: A Geopolitical Agenda*, http://iranpoliticsclub.net/ library/ english-library/pan-turanism1/index.htm. Another book by Farrokh on the early history of the de-Iranization policy of Russia on the Iranian conquered land will be published as *History of De-Iranianization in the Southeast Caucasus and the Promotion of Separatism in Azerbaijan* (Yerevan: Yerevan State Universit, forthcoming). For other related works by Farrokh, see Kaveh Farrokh and Rouben Galichian, "The Clash of Histories in the Southern Caucasus," *Iran Nameh*, Vol. 28, No. 4 (Winter 2013), pp. 160–67; Kaveh Farrokh, "The role of Imperial Russia in severing Iran–Caucasus cultural links," *Amordad-Nameh*, No. 31 (2011), pp. 2–9.
71. See Tirdad Bonakdar, "Zamine haye paydayeshe Bohrane Ghowmi Dar Iran," *Iranshahr* (18 shahrivar 1386/9 September 2007), http://iranshahr.org/?p=285; Tirdad Bonakdar, "Zabane Madari va Hoghughe Baynolmelal," [Mother language and international law], *Ruznameh Ghanun* (7 Bahman 1392/27 January 2014, p. 5).
72. As an Iranian Baluch, she has been active in the main dailies of Tehran, writing articles and interviews with academics on subjects related to Iranian national identity and ethnicity. See Narjeskhatoon Barahui, "Negahi be sarzamin va mardome Baluchestan" [Take a look at the land and people of Baluchistan], *Faslame-ye Motaleate Melli* No. 1 (1378/1998).

73. Habibollah Fazeli, "Be bahaneye Naghsh Afarini haye Dowlate Baku Alayhe Iran," [The Baku government's role against Iran], *Zendeginews* (Bahman 1390/27 January 2012); "Varzesh va Siasate Hoviyyat" [Sport and the politics of identity], *Pajuheshnam-ye Olume Siasi*, Vol. 7, No. 2 (Bahar1391/Spring 2012).
74. Mohammad Ali Bahmani Ghajar, *Tamamiyyate Arzi Iran, Sayri dar Tarikhe Marzhaye Iran* [Iran's territorial integrity: a review of the history of Iran's frontiers] (Tehran: Moassese-ye Motaleat va Pajuheshhaye Siasi, 1390/2011).
75. Loghman organized one of the first internet sites, *Ruznamak*, devoted to Iranian identity and deconstructing anti-Iranian ethnic discourses. After its closure by the authorities, he founded *Iranshahr*, another internet website still active. See Mas'ud Loghman, "Dastane Babak Khorramdin Ya Tahrife Tarikhe Azarbaijan" [The story of Babak Khorramdin, or deviating from the history of Azerbaijan], http://rouznamak.blogfa.ir/post-113.aspx; Mas'ud Loghman, "Adabiyyat-e Pan Turkisti dar Ruznameye Jam-e jam" [Pan-Turkist literature in Jame Jam newspaper], *Iranshahr* (9 Day 1386/30 December 2007), http://iranshahr.org/?p=406
76. Oghab Ali has a publishing house for subjects mainly related to Iranian identity in the realm of ethnicity, such as Firuz Mansuri and Khubrooye Pak books.
77. Musawi Ghuhe wrote his MA dissertation on Self-Determination in International Law at Payam Norr University in the late 2000s.
78. See for example Mohammad Ali Bahmani Ghajar, *Tamamiyyate Arzi Iran, Sayri dar Tarikhe Marzhaye Iran* [Iran's territorial integrity: a review of the history of Iran's frontiers] (Tehran: Moassese-ye Motaleat va Pajuheshhaye Siasi, 1390/2011).
79. The founders of *Pasaargad* included a Kurd (Habibollah Fazeli), an Azeri (Hojjat Kazemi), and a student from Fars province (Sadegh Jowkar).
80. It changed its name to *Dide bane Aghvame Irani* [Iranian ethnicities monitor] and moved to Telegram in early July 2015.
81. This association has published an occasional magazine called *Irane Bozorge Farhangi* [The culture of Greater Iran]. In its No. 3 (Winter 2014) it had three articles dealing with the Iranian Azerbaijan crisis of 1945–6, the Dadaqorqud story and its irrelevancy to Azerbaijani culture, and the presidential election in the Azerbaijan Republic in 2013. See *Irane Bozorge Farhangi*, No. 3 (Zemestan 1392/Winter 2013), pp. 31–4, 97–8, 130–31.
82. Though it concentrated on the challenge of pan-Arabism against Iran, its journal, *Mehraain*, used to cover Iranian Azerbaijan and the challenge of pan-Turkism too.
83. This information was collected through my personal interview with Alireza Afshari, May 2015.
84. On the coordinative council, see Alireza Afshari, *Defa'e az Tarikh* [In defense of history] (Tehran: Nashre Shoorafarin, 1394/2015), pp. 47–51.
85. See *Mehraain*, No. 6 (Bahar 1384/Spring 2005), p. 2. The 4th gathering was held in Hamadan in 1383/2004.
86. Enayatollah Reza, *Aran: az Dowrane Bastan ta Aghaze Ahde Moghul* [Aran: From

ancient times to the beginnings of the Mongol era] (Tehran: Markaze Asnad va Tarikhe diplomacy, 2001); *Azarbaijan va Aran: Albaniyaye Ghafghaz* [Azerbaijan and Aran: The Caucasus Albania] (Tehran: Bonyade Mowghoofat Afshar, 1993).

87. Iraj Afshar, *Zabane Farsi dar Azerbaijan* [Farsi language in Azerbaijan] (Tehran: Bonyade Mowghoofat Afshar, 1999); Hossingholi Katebi, *Zabanhaye Bastani Azaerbaijan* [The ancient languages of Azerbaijan] (Tehran: Pazhang, 2000).
88. Ahmadi, *The Politics of Ethnic Nationalism in Iran;* Hamid Ahmadi, *Ghowmiat va Ghowm Gerai dar Iran.*
89. Ahmad Kazemi, *Pan-Turkism va Pan-Azerism: Mabani, Ahdaf va Natayej* [Pan-Turkism and pan-Azerism: foundations, results, and goals] (Tehran: Abrare Moaser, 2006).
90. Gholamreza Ensafpour, Tarikh, *Tabar va Zabane Mardome Azarbaijan* [The history and language of Azerbaijani people] (Tehran: Entesharate Fekre Ruz, 1377/1998).
91. Ali Morshedizad, *Roshanfekrane Azari va Hoviate Melli va Ghowmi* [Azeri intellectuals and national and ethnic identity] (Tehran: Nashre Markaz, 2001).
92. Ali Azari, *Ghiyame Shaykh Mohammadi Khiabani dar Tabriz* [The revolt of Sheikh Mohammad Khiabani in Tabriz] (Tehran: Safiali Shah, 1362/1983); Ahmad Kasravi, *Ghiyame Shaykh Mohammadi Khiabani* [The revolt of Sheikh Mohammad Khiabani] (Tehran: Nashre Markaz, 1376/1997).
93. Salar Seifoddini, "Melli Gerai-e Bedune Mellat: Negahi be Farayande Mellatsazi dar Jomhuri-e Azarbaijan" [Nationalism without nation: a look at the nation-building process in the Republic of Azerbaijan], in Hossein Ahmadi, ed., *Jomhuri-e Azarbaijan: Bist o se sal takapu baraye dowlat va Mellatsazi*, pp. 183–217.
94. Hossein Ahmadi, an Iranian researcher from Talish, has provided a relatively comprehensive analysis of such formal historical texts in the Azerbaijan Republic's educational system; see Hossein Ahmadi, "Baresi-e ketabhay-e Darsi Jomhuri-e Azarbaijan" [A review of the educational books in the Republic of Azerbaijan], in Hossein Ahmadi, ed., *Jomhuri-e Azarbaijan: Bist o se sal takapu baraye dowlat va Mellatsazi*, pp. 11–47. In a more recent systemic study, Salar Seifoddini, the Iranian Azeri researcher, has given a comprehensive analysis of pan-Turkist historiography in the Azerbaijan educational system; see Salar Seifoddini, "Chaleshhaye Tarikhnegari-e Varroneh: Naghdi bar Maktabe Tarikhnegari-e Ghafghaz" [The challenges of reverse historiography: a critique of the Historiography School of the Caucasus], *Faslnameye Tahghighi Motaaleaati Azar-Araan*, Vol. 13, Nos. 40–41 (Zemestan 1393-Bahar 1394/Winter 2014-Spring 2015), pp. 57–93.
95. Hamid Ahmadi, "Dowlate Modern va Aghwame Irani: Shalude Shekani Paradaym haye Rayej" [Modern state and Iranian ethnic groups: deconstructing the prevalent paradigms], in Rasul Afzali, ed., *Dowlate Modern Dar Iran* [The modern state in Iran] (Qom: Daneshgahe Mofid, 1386/2007), pp. 361–413.
96. Hooshang Taale, *Tarikhe Tajziyeh Iran: Talashe Nafarjam Baraye Tajziyehe*

Azarbaijan [The history of Iran's disintegration: failed efforts at the separation of Azerbaijan] (Rasht: Entesharate Samarqand, 1388/1999); Hooshang Taale, "Khaste Mardome Nkhjavan Baraye Payvaste dobare be Iran" [The Nakhjavan people's demand to join Iran again] *Aran*, Vol. 8, No. 23 (Bahar 1389/Spring 2010); Hamid Ahmadi, "dar Azerbaijan Che Gozasht?" [What happened in Azerbaijan?], *Ettelaate Siasi Va Eghtesadi*, Nos. 181–2 (1381/2002), pp. 44–61.

97. Though Akhunzadeh, born of Iranian parents, was raised in Russia, or the later Azerbaijan Republic, he was one of the first admirers of Iranian romantic nationalism, the heritage of ancient Iran, and played an active role in Iranian intellectual circles of the late nineteenth and the early twentieth centuries. See Reza Beigdalu, *Bastangeraai dar Tarikhe Moasere Iran* [Archaic nationalism in contemporary Iranian History] (Tehran: Nashre Markaz), pp. 40–52; Hafez Farman Farmayan, "The Forces of Modernization in the Nineteenth Century Iran," in William R. Polk and Richard l. Chambers, eds, *The Beginning of Modernization in the Middle East* (Chicago: Chicago University Press, 1968), p. 141.
98. See Ervand Abrahamian, "Kasravi: The Integrated Nationalist of Iran," *Middle Eastern Studies, Vol.* 9, No. 3 (1973), pp. 271–95.
99. See Hossein Kazem Zadeh Iranshahr, *Tajalliate Ruhe Irani dar Advare Tarikhi* [Manifestations of Iranian spirit in historical periods] (Berlin: Entesharate Iranshahr, 1342/1963).
100. One of the leading intellectuals of the constitutional revolution and the Pahlavi era, whose magazine *Kaaveh*, published in Berlin 1916–19, represented the organ of Iranian nationalists before the rise of the Pahlavi state. Taqizadeh was one of the first Muslim intellectuals writing on pan-Turkism. See his French article: Hasan Taqizadeh, "Les Courants Politiques dans la Turquie Contetemporaine," *La Revue du Mond Musulman* (1912). For a Farsi translation of the article, see Iraj Afshar, ed., *Maghalate Taghizadeh*, Vol. 4 (Tehran: Toos, 1386), pp. 11–59. In one of his reports written when Taqizadeh was governor of Khorasan, revealed after the revolution of 1979, he warned about what he called "khatare Nejade Zard" [the danger of the yellow race). For this report, see Bastani Parizi, *Hasirestan* (Tehran: Elm, 1382), p. 382; Sepehr H. Joussefi, *Seyyed Hasan Taqizadeh: A Political Biography in the Context of Iranian Modernization* (Masters thesis, University of Utrecht, 1998).
101. Afshar was the first Iranian intellectual to suggest the idea of pan-Iranism as a counter-argument against pan-Turkism. See Mahmoud Afshar Yazdi, *Ganjineye Maghalat: Jelde Aval, Maghalate Siasi ya Siasatnameh Jadid* [A treasury of articles, Vol. 1, Political articles or The new book of politics] (Tehran: Bonyade Mowghufat Afshar, 1368/1999), p. 528.
102. Though Arani is considered one of the founders of the Iranian Marxist left, he had strong Iranian nationalistic tendencies and wrote on the Iranianness of Azerbaijan in reaction to the pan-Turkist circles in Turkey of the 1920s. See Taqi

Arani, "Azarbaijan ya yek Masaleye Hayati va Mamati Iran" [Azerbaijan, or A question of life and death for Iran], *Farangestan*, No. 5 (1304/1925).

103. Zoka was a prolific researcher on ancient Iran and its national heritage. See Yahya Zoka, "Nowruz dar Tarikh va Taghvim" [Nowruz in history and calendars], *Abrar Eghtesadi* (Farvardin 1383/April 2004); Yahya Zoka, "Aya Hakhamaneshian Zartoshti Budand?" [Were the Achaemenid Zoroastrians?], *Bokhara*, No. 3 (1998), pp. 22–50; Yahya Zoka, *Guyeshe Kringan: Taati* [Kringan accent: Taati] (Tehran: Ketabkhaneh Danesh, 1322/1943).
104. He used to write on Iranian history, Persian language, Shahnameh of Ferdowsi, and translated books on ancient Iran, Cyrus the Great, the Great Darrius, and the history of Persian literature. See Sadegh Rezazadeh Shafagh, "Sattar Khan Sardare Melli" [Sattar Khan the national hero], *Ettelaate Siasi va Eghtesadi*, Nos. 227–30 (Mordad-Aban 1385/July–October 2006), pp. 234–45. "Negahi Gozara be Zendegi Yek Ensane Mandegar: Dr Rezazadeh Shafagh, Yeki az Monadiane Vahdate Melli Iran," *Hafteh*, http://www.hafteh.ca/articles/culture/4111-fa-812.html
105. See his nationalistic poetry for Iranian Azerbaijan during the Soviet occupation: Mohammad Amin Riahi, *Dar Rahe Nejate Azarbaijan: Ash'aare Melli va Vatani* [For the liberation of Azerbaijan: national and patriotic poems] (Tabriz, 1325/1946).
106. Salim Naysari was born in Tabriz and his main interest has been Farsi literature and language. He founded the Faculty of Literature at Shiraz University, and is considered amongst the vanguard of the modern method for teaching Farsi language in Iran.
107. Born in Takab, Anvari is one of the pioneers of Persian language and literature, and a prolific author on the subject in Iran. As one the main editors of *Farhange Sokhan* [Sokhan Encyclopedia], he had an important role in returning Ferdowsi's status to Salmas, after its removal by municipal authorities in western Azerbaijan province in early 2015. Recently, he has said that "I testify that most Azeris love the Farsi language and sixty percent of Farsi language teachers and professors are Azeris." See http://anjom.ir/bozorgdashtha/2428-bozorgdashtd rhasananvari.html
108. Professor of Persian literature at Tabriz University. He conducted original research on "Azari," the native Iranian language of Azerbaijan, before its Turkification. See Manuchehr Mortazavi, "Asar va Asnade Marbut Is Zabane Dirin e Azerbaijan" [Works and documents related to the old language of Azerbaijan], *Nashriyeh Daneshkade Adabiyat va Olume Ensani Daneshgah Tabriz*, No. 115 (1354/1975), pp. 445–79; Manuchehr Mortazavi, *Zabane Dirine Azerbaijan* [The old language of Azerbaijan] (Tehran: Bonyad Mowghufate Afshar, 1384/1995). He also wrote on *Shahnameh*, the national Iranian epic. See Manuchehr Mortazavi, *Ferdowsi va Shahnameh* [Ferdowsi and Shahnameh] (Tehran: Toos, 1385/1996).

109. One of the prestigious teachers in Tabriz before the revolution of 1979, Nasehi has written on the activities and policies of *Firghe* and his leader Ja'far Pishevari during the crisis of 1945–6. See Ebrahim Nasehi, *Gha'ele-ye Azarbaijan dar Rahgozare Tarikh va Chehre-ye Pishevari dar Ayeene-ye Firghe Democrat* [Azerbaijan dedition in the passage of history and Pishevari's image in the mirror of Firghe-ye Democrat] (Tehran: Entesharate Setudeh, 1393/2014).
110. He was one of the first Azerbaijani to write on the Iranian identity of Azerbaijan in the aftermath of the 1945–6 crisis, the role of the Soviets, and Firghe's policies. See Ali Dehghan, *Sarzamine Zardosht* [The land of Zaratostra] (Tehran: Ibne Sina, 1347/1968).
111. Ahmad Kasravi, *Azari ya Zabane Bastane Azarbaijan* [Azeri, or the ancient language of Azerbaijan] (Tehran: 1304/1925). This book has been repeatedly republished in Iran. Kasravi is widely hated by pan-Turkist circles in the Azerbaijan Republic and Iran, where they consider him a traitor to Azeris.
112. See, for example, Shireen Hunter, "Azerbaijan: Search for Identity and New Partners," in I. Bremmer and R. Taras, eds, *Nations and Politics in the Soviet Successor States* (Cambridge: Cambridge University Press, 1993), p. 235; for instance Bakhtiar Vahabzadeh, a famous poet in the Azerbaijan Republic, accused Iranian Azeri professor Yahya Zoka of being a "traitor to his ancestors and sons" because of his Iranian nationalist tendencies and writings. See S. Enders Wimbush, "Divided Azerbaijan: Nation Building, Assimilation and Mobilization between Three States," in William O. McCagg and Brian Silver, eds, *Soviet Asian Ethnic Frontiers* (New York: Praeger, 1979), p. 62.
113. Bayat, "Nasionalism e Turk" [Turkish nationalism].
114. Kaveh Bayat, *Pan-Turkism va Iran* [Pan-Turkism and Iran] (Tehran: Shirazeh, 1387/1998).
115. See Kaveh Bayat, *Azerbaijan Dar Mowj Khize Tarikh: Negahi be Mabahese Mellion Iran va Jarayede Baku Dar Taghire name Aran be Azerbaijan 1296–98* [Azerbaijan confronting the devastating waves of history: a look at the discussions between Iranian nationalists and Baku media on changing the name Aran to Azerbaijan, 1918–20] (Tehran: Shiraze, 1379/1990).
116. Ibid.
117. Firuz Mansuri, *Motaleati dar Bareye Tarikh, Zaban va Frahang Azerbaijan* [Studies in the history, language and the culture of Azerbaijan] (Tehran: Moassesye Motaleate Trikhe Moasere Iran, 1379/2000).
118. Ibid., pp. 628–46.
119. Ibid., pp. 79–114.
120. Firuz Mansuri, *Farhange Vajegane Azari: ya Gozareshe Hamanadi ha ba Digar Guyesh Haye Iran* [A dictionary of Azeri words and terms: or A report about their similarities to other accents in Iran] (Tehran: Nashre Hazare Kerman, 1393/2015).

121. Ibid., p. 16.
122. Ibid., pp. 16–17; Mansuri, *Motaleati Dar Bareye*, pp. 730–40.
123. Hunter, "Azerbaijan: Search for Identity and New Partners."
124. Ibid.
125. Ibid.
126. Touraj Atabaki, "Recasting Oneself and Rejecting the Other: Pan-Turkism and Iranian Nationalism," in Eric Jan Zucher and W. Van Schendel, eds. *Identity Politics in Central Asia and Muslim World* (London: I. B. Tauris, 2001).
127. Touraj Atabaki, *Azerbaijan: Ethnicity and Autonomy in Iran after the Second World War* (New York: St Martin's Press, 1993).
128. See for instance Touraj Atabaki, "Ethnic Diversity in Iran and Iranian National Identity," *Iran Nameh* (journal of Foundation for Iranian Studies), Vol. 25, Nos. 2–23 (2009); Touraj Atabaki, "Ethnic Diversity and the Territorial Integrity of Iran: Domestic Harmony and Regional Challenges," *Iranian Studies*, No. 38 (2005).
129. He has presented the idea of the decline in Iranian political thought. See Javad Tabatabai, *Zavale Andisheye Siasi dar Iran* [The decline of political thought in Iran] (Tehran: Kavir, 1373/1994).
130. Javad Tabatabai, "Pan Turkism Malghamci az Bisavadi va BiSho'uri Ast" [Pan-Turkism is an amalgam of ignorance and stupidity], *Mehrnameh*, No. 29, http://www.azariha.org/?lang=fa&muid = 53&item=748
131. Sayyed Javad Tabatabai, "Tarikhe Jomhuri Azarbaijan dar dele Tarikhe Iran Jay Darad" [The history of the Azerbaijan Republic is located at the heart of Iran's history] *Tarhe Now* 6, no. 218 (4 Khordad 1392/25 May 2013), http://www.azariha.org/?lang=fa&muid=53&item=685
132. My personal discussion with Izadi.
133. He translated Shireen Hunter's article "Azerbaijan: Search for Identity and New Partners" and published it in his journal in Ardabil. See Shireen Hunter, "Azerbaijan Dar Jostejuye Hoviyyat va Shorakaye Jadid," trans. Rajab Izadi, *Hafte Nameh Ardabil*, Nos. 14–15 (1Ordibehesht and 29 Khordad 1378).
134. Rajab Izadi, "Negahi be Yek Dame Chalet Barware Hoviyyate Azerbaijan," [Looking to a decade of challenge over Azerbaijan's identity], in Hamid Ahmadi, ed., *Iran, Hoviyyat, Melliat va Ghowmiyyat* [Iran: identity, nationality and ethnicity] (Tehran: Moseseye Towseye Olume ensani, 1383/ 2004). This book has been translated into Turkish as Hamid Ahmedi, *Iran: Ulusal Kimlik Insasi*, tercume Hakki Uygur (Istanbul: KURE Yaninlari, 2009).
135. In his forthcoming book on the Islamic Revolution in Ardabil (Tehran: Markaze Asande Enghelabe Islami), Izadi has analyzed the performance of *Firghe Democrat* and the reaction of Ardabil's people to it in 1945–6.
136. Jamshidi Raad has given several lectures at the universities of Tabriz, Orumiyeh, and other cities of Iranian Azerbaijan on the Iranian identity of Azaris; and orga-

nized annual seminars, including in 2007 and 2008, commemorating the Salvation day of Azerbaijan on 12 December, for which he used to invite both Azeri and non-Azeri professors and intellectuals. Among his books was one about Babak Khorrramdin, whom pan-Turkist literature introduce as a Turk but Jamshidi Raad argued for his Iranian identity. See Ja'far Jamshidi Rad, *Babak Khorramdin* (Tehran: Mozakereh, 1390/2011).

137. See Fariba Sadeghi, "Hoviyyate Irani, Farhange Irani: Mosahebe ba Bahram Amir Ahmadian" [Iranian identity, Iranian culture: an interview with Bahram Amir Ahmadian], *Sepideh Jame Jam*, No. 15 (Khordad 1386/June 2007), pp. 8–10.
138. Amir Ahmadian, *Ravabete Iran va Jomhuriye Azarbaijan*.
139. In a critical review of the book, one Iranian Azeri researcher wrote that *Ata Yordu* is in fact an anti-Iranian manifesto than an accurate history. See Karim Mojtahedzadeh, "Naghde ketabe Ata Yordu" [A critique of Ata Yordu's book], *Misaagh*, No. 124 (Aban 1381), p. 3.
140. Ibid. For a critical content analysis of *Ata Yordu* written by Iranian Azeris, see Karim Mohammad Zadeh, "Naghde Ketabe Ata Yordu" [A critique of *Ata Yordu*], *Misaagh*, No. 124 (Aban 1381/November 2002), p. 3.
141. Ataollah Abdi and Maram Lotfi, "Pzhvake Zaman dar Jaynamhaye Azerbaijan Dar Manabe-e Kohan [The reflection of time in the place names of Azerbaijan in old documents], *Faslnameye Motaleate Melli*, Vol. 15, No. 58 (1393/2014), pp. 49–71.
142. Ataollah Abdi, Reza Rahimi, and Mohammad Ayvazi, "Tab'in-e Ruykardhaye Ghowmiyyati dar Shoarhaye Entekhbati-e Namzadhaye Rriasat Jomhuri" [Explaining the ethnic approaches of the candidates in presidential elections], *Faslnamey-e Geopolitics*, Vol. 10, No. 3 (Autumn 1393/2014), pp. 95–121.
143. Ataollah Abdi and Mojtaba Maghsudi, "Hamgerai Dar Azerbaijan" [Integration in Azerbaijan], *Faslnameye Motaleate Melli*, Vol. 14, No. 53 (1392/2013), pp. 51–72.
144. See for example Hezbe Tudeh Iran, *Azadligh Yolunda Mubariza* [The struggle on the road of liberty] (Baku: no place, no date, 2 vols.).
145. Rahim Nikbakht and Asghar Haidari, *Firghe Democrat dar Sarab be Ravayate Asnade Montasher Nashode* [*Firghe Democrat* in the city of Sarab according to unpublished documents] (Tehran: Markaze Asnade Mjlese Showraye Islami, 1388/ 2009); Rahim Nikbakht and Manijeh Sadri, *Paydayeshe Firghe Democrat Azerbaijan be Ravayate Asnad va Khaterate Montasher Nashode* [The emergence of *Firghe Democrat* Azerbaijan as narrated by unpublished documents and memories] (Tehran: Mosesseye Motaleate Tarikhe Moaser, 1386/2007). Other Iranian Azeris have also described *Firghe's* atrocities during 1945–6; see an interview with Behzad Mohammad Khani, whose grandfather was killed by *Firghe* forces: "Negahi be Nehzate Mihan Parastane Arasbaran" [Take a look at the Arasbaran patriotism movement] in *Tabrize Bidar* (11 Esfand 1391/1 March 2013), http://tabrizebidar.ir/mosahebe/45531

146. Rahim Nikbakht, *Naghshe Azerbaijan dar Tahkime Hoviyyate Irani* [The role of Azerbaijan in Iranian identity consolidation] (Tehran: Vezarate Olum, Tahghighat va Fannavari, 1387/2008); Rahim Nikbakht, *Azerbaijan va Hoviyyate Melli* [Azerbaijan and national identity] (Tabriz: Iran Shenakht, 1393/2014).
147. Bahram Amir Ahmadian, *Rabete Iran va Jomhuriye Azarbaijan* [Iran–Azerbaijan Republic relations] (Tehran: Vezarate Kharjeh, 1387/2008).
148. One such conference, organized by *Vatan Yoli* and Dashtebani, was held in January 2013 in Tehran as "Chalesh Haye Tamamiate Arzi Iran" [The challenges of Iran's territorial integrity].
149. *Vatan Yoli, Nashriyeh Daneshjuyane Azerbaijani Daneshgah Tehran* [Journal of Azerbaijani students of Tehran University], No. 19 (August 2012).
150. Abu'l Majd Muhammad ibn Masu'd Tabrizi, *Safine-ye Tabriz: A Treasury of Persian Literature* (Tehran: Tehran University Press, 2001).
151. For more information on the book and its content, see http://dictionary.sensagent.com/safina-yi%20tabriz/en-en/
152. Nasrollah Pourjavadi, "Safine-ye Tabriz, Kashfi Bozorg dar Tarikh va Farhange Azarbaijan" [Safine Tabriz: A great discovery in the history and culture of Azerbaijan], http://www.cloob.com/c/_parlaq_/115560
153. On this, see Ahmad Kasravi, *Tarikhe Hejdah Sale Azerbaijan* [Eighteen years history of Azerbaijan] (Tehran: Amir Kabir, 1378/1998).
154. *Iran Zamin, Nashriye Siasi, Farhangi, Eghtesadi va Ejtemai Daneshjui* [A political, cultural, economic, and social student journal], No. 2 (January 2009).
155. See, for example, "Setam Melli: Afsaneh ya Vagheiyyat; an interview with Ghorban Abbasi," [National oppression: myth or reality, an interview with Ghorban Abbasi], *Navay-e Azarbaijan*, No. 105 (2 Mehr 1392/24 September 2013). In this interview, Abbasi, an active pro-Iranian nationalist Azeri student of political science in Marand, presents historical evidence of Iranian identity of Azerbaijan.
156. "Poems in Farsi in Nizami Ganjavi's mausoleum to be replaced by analogues in Azerbaijani language," *Trends*, 22 August 2013, http://en.trend.az/azerbaijan/society/2181361.html
157. "Najafi be Dabire Kolle Unesco E'teraz Kard" [Najafi submitted his protest to UNESCO's secretary general], *Diplomacy Irani*, 12 October 2013, http://www.irdiplomacy.ir/fa/page/1922772/%.html. Besides Najafi, Mohsen Paakain, the Iranian ambassador in Baku at the time, protested against the action and said: "calling Nizami a non-Persian poet is as surprising as saying that Victor Hugo, the French poet, was an Arabic-speaking poet."
158. This refers to Nizami's poems on Iran in his works, including a frequently cited verse in Iranian from Nizami's *Haft Paykar* as follows:

    the world is the body, Iran is the heart
    such comparison should not bring shame

since Iran is the heart of the earth
the heart is certain to be better than the body

See Kazem Abedini Motlagh, ed., *Kolliate Hakin Nizami Ganjavi* [Nizami Ganjavi collected poems] (Tehran: Entesharate Adineye Sabz, 1391), pp. 565–6.

159. See "Campaigne Hakim Nizami Ganjavi Dar Shabakeye Ejtemai Facebook E'elame Mojudiat Kard" [Campaign for Nizami Ganjavi announced on social media's Facebook], *Aran News*, 7 September 2013, http://fa.arannews.com/?MID=21&type=news&BasesID=2&TypeID=15&id=40121#sthash.bAFIOgrt.dpbs
160. A seminar was held in Tehran, in Seraye Ahle Ghalam, on Azar 1392 (December 2013) about "Tahavvolate Azarbaijan Pas az Jange Jahani Dovvom" [Post-World War II developments in Iranian Azerbaijan]. The following year (December 2013), it was held in the University of Tehran's Faculty of Letters, dealing with *Firghe Democrat* in 1945–6.
161. See Salar Seifoddini, "Irane Shomali Kojast?" [Where is northern Iran?], *Misaagh*, No. 222 (Mehr 1385/October 2006).
162. Hushmand is the most active Iranian Kurd in ethnic and national issues of Iran, and is a particularly prolific writer on Kurdish issues in Iran, Turkey, and Iraq.
163. Fazeli is an Iranian Kurd, whose writing on Iranian nationalism and identity have been published in Iranian print media.
164. Salar Seifoddini, "Asl 15 Ghanoone Asasi: Zarayef, Bayadha va Nabayadha" [Article 15 of the Constitution: delicacies, should and should nots], *Ruznameh Ebtekar*, 13 April 2014. See also his interview with the daily newspaper *Ghanoon* on the issue: "Salar Seifoddini: "Dowlat Baraye Amuzeshe Zaban Madari Taklife Ghanooni Nadarad" [The government has no legal obligation to teach mother tongue], *Ghanoon*, 14 April 2015, p. 11.
165. *Express* attacked the seminar as a chauvinistic gathering in which the famous Iranian nationalist chauvinists had presented a negative image of *Firghe Democrat* and its leader, J'afar Pishevari. See "Dorugh Pardazi Ruznameh Express Baku va Gunaz TV Alayhe Seminare Tahavolate Siasi Iran Pas az Jange Jahani Dovvom (Firghe Democrat) [Baku newspaper *Express* and GunAz TV spread lies about Iran's development after World War II seminar (*Firghe Democrat*)], http://www.azariha.org/?muid=53&item=1429. See also GunAz TV's reaction at http://www.gunaz.tv/?id=2&sID=76830&lang=2
166. Salar Seifoddini, "Enghelabe Mashruteh va Zayeshe Goftemane Melli" [The constitutional revolution and the emergence of the national discourse], *Shargh Newspaper*, No. 1594 (14 Mordad 1391/5 August 2012), p. 29; Salar Seifoddini, "Ta'sire Jonbeshhaye Siasi Manteghei bar Revayathaye Farhangi-Tarikhie Kurdha" [The impact of regional political movements on the Kurds' cultural–historical

narratives], *Ketabe Mah: Tarikh va Joghrafia*, No. 189 (Day 1392/January 2014), pp. 24–35.

167. See for instance Salar Seifoddini, "Stalin va Masaleye Melli" [Stalin and the national question], *Sahrgh Newspaper*, No. 1685 (12 Esfand 1391/2 March 2013), http://sharghdaily.ir/Vijeh/496/%D8%A. Salar Seifoddini, "Nationalism Ghowmi dar Ghafghaze Jonubi va ta'sire an Bar Amniate Mantaghe" [Ethnic nationalism in South Caucasus and its regional impact], *Faslname Diplomacy Solhe Adelaneh*, No. 10 (Zemestan 1393/Winter 2015), available at http://peace-ipsc.org/fa/%D9%86. Salar Seifoddini, "Haghe Ta'ine Sarnevesht va Sue Estefadeye Bonyad Geraai Ghowmi az An" [Self-determination and its misuse by ethnic fundamentalism], http://www.azariha.org/?lang=fa&muid=36&item=683
168. Roshanak Astaraki, "Hojjat Kalashi: Tanesh ba Iran, Noi Hoviyyat Jui Baraye Dowlate Baku" [Tension with Iran: a kind of identity-seeking by the Baku government], *Rahe Digar*, Vol. 1, No. 219 (24 Farvardin 1392/13 April 2013), rahe-digar.net/1392/01/24/10680
169. Ibid.
170. See Reza Chehreghani Barcheloui, "Shahnamey-e Ferdowsi, Nakhostin Manzumey-e Paydari," [Shahnameh of Ferdowsi, the first epic of steadfastness], *Misaagh*, Nos. 191–2 (Mordad 1384/July–August 2005).
171. See for instance Mohammad Jalali, "Zabane Farsi, Zabane Melli va Taarikhie Mellat Iran ya Mellate Fars?" [Farsi language, national and historical language of the Iranian nation, or the Fars nation?], *Misaagh*, No. 213 (Khordad 1385/June 2006), p. 7.
172. See for instance Asghar Sherdust, "Gostareshe Sher va Adabe Farsi dar Jomhuri Azarbaijan" [The spread of Persian poetry and literature through the republic of Azerbaijan], *Misaagh*, no. 169 (Shahrivar 1383/August 2004), p. 5; Bahram Masumi, "Shahnameh dar Ghafghaz" [Shahnameh in the Caucasus], *Misaagh*, Nos. 178–83 (Day-Esfand 1383/January–March 2004); Mohammad their Khosroshahi, "Zanane Parsi Pajuhe Ghafghaz" [Women in the Caucasus who have researched the Persian language], *Misaagh*, Nos. 195–200 (Shahrivar-Azar 1384/August–December 2005).
173. Shahriar, "Ferdowsi va Shahnameh Javedane and" [Ferdowsi and *Shahnameh* remain eternal], *Misaagh*, No. 122 (October 2002), p. 5; Amin Pasha Jalali, "Azarabadegan dar Shahkare Javidane Ostade Toos" [Azerbaijan in the eternal masterpiece of Toos Mentor], *Misaagh*, No. 189 (Tir 1384/ July 2005), p. 5; Manuchehr Mortazavi, "Mozu' va Ruhe Shahnameh" [The subject and spirit of *Shahnameh*], *Misaagh*, No. 230 (Bahman 1385/February 2006), p. 5.
174. Such as the detention of Haji Nuriov, the deputy of the party. See *Misaagh*, No. 104 (19 Azar 1380/January 2002), p. 6.
175. Zartosht Alizadeh, "Doshmani ba Iran be Zarar Jomhuri Azerbaijan Ast"

(Hostility with Iran is against the benefits to the Azerbaijan Republic," *Misaagh*, No. 104, p. 3.

176. See Mohammad Reza Gholizadeh, "Firghe Democrat va Tajrobeye Azarbaijan" [*Firghe Democrat* and Azerbaijan's experience], *Misaagh*, Nos. 205–6 (Bahman 1384/February 2006); "Firghe Democrate Shoravi dar Azarbaijan e Iran" [The *Soviet Firghe Democrat* in Iranian Azerbaijan], *Misaagh*, Nos. 207–9 (Esfand 1384/March 2006]; "Gushe I Az Jenayate Firghe Democrat Dar Azarbaijan be Ravayate Farmandeye Lashkare Tabriz dar 1324" [Part of *Firghe Democrat*'s crimes in Iranian Azerbaijan, as told by General Derakhshani, commander of the Tabriz garrison in 1945], *Misaagh*, No. 212 (Khordad 1385/June 2006), p. 6.
177. See the report of the meeting between *Misaagh* chief editor and staff with Isa Gambar, leader of the Musavat Party, in *Misaagh*, No. 126 (Day 1381/January 2003), p. 3.
178. See for instance Ahmad Kazemi, "Az Safare Baku" [Trip to Baku], *Misaagh*, Nos. 164–70 (Tir-Shaharivar 1383/July–August 2004); "Esteghbal Gostardeye Matbooat va Ruznameh Negarane Jomhuriye Azerbaijan az Ruzname Neagrane Irani" [Azerbaijan Republic's media and journalists welcome Iranian journalists], *Misaagh*, No. 136 (Khordad 1381/June 2002), p. 3. See also "Baku dar Negahe Dovvom" [Baku, a second view], a series of reports by a *Misaagh* journalist in Azerbaijan Republic, published during 1381–2 (2002–3).
179. Nasser Hamrang, *Az Badkubeh va Chizhaye Digar: Yaddasht haye Safar be Jomhuri-e Azarbaijan* [From Baku about many things: travel notes from the Republic of Azerbaijan] (Tabriz: Jamiyyate Vatan, 1384/2005).
180. Jalal Mohammadi, "Iran Kanoone Ma'navi Azari hayed Jahan" [Iran, the spiritual center of world Azerbaijanis], *Vatan*, No. 1 (Shahrivar 1383/August 2004).
181. *Vatan: Gahnameye Dakheli Jamiate Vatan*, No. 2 (Khordad 1385/July 2006), p. 15.
182. Jalal Mohammadi, "Farsi Zabane Tarikhi va Melli-e Hameye Aghwame Irani ast" [Farsi is the historical and national language of all Iranian ethnicities], *Mehr News*, March 2014. Mohammadi arranged this interview on the day of mother language when pan-Turkist circles stress the formalization of the Turkish language for Azerbaijan.
183. Alireza Hosseinpour, "Aran ya Azarbaijan?" [Aran or Azerbaijan?], in *Vije Nameh Aran* (Tabriz: Moasseseye farhangi-ye Aran, 2002), pp. 10–21.
184. On this conference held in 2013, see the special issue of *Aran* on the Karabakh crisis: "Gozareshe Conference Baybalmelalie Gharabagh" [A report on the internal conference on Karabakh], *Azar-Aran: Faslname Tahghighi Motaleati Moaseseye Farhangi Aran*, Nos. 34–5 (Bahar va tabestan 1392/Spring and Summer 2013).
185. For a report of this conference, held in 25 April 2011, see Sahand Alijani, "Gozareshi az Hamayeshe Abuzare Ghafghaz" [A report on Abuzar at the Caucasus conference], *Aran: Faslname Tahghighi Motaleati Moaseseye Farhangi*

Aran, Nos. 26–7 (Zemestan 1389-Bahar 1390/Winter-Spring 2011), pp. 207–12.

186. For a report and abstracts of the presentations at the conference held on 12 October 2011, see "Chekide Maghalate "Hamayeshe Gharadade Golestan: Zamine ha va Payamadha" [Abstracts of the conference on the Golestan Treaty: background and consequences], *Aran: Faslname Tahghighi Motaleati Moaseseye Farhangi Aran*, Nos. 28–9 (Tabestan va Paize 1390/Summer and Autumn 2011), pp. 129–57.
187. For a report and abstracts of the presentations at the conference held on 20 February 2012, see "Gozareshe Neshaste Elmi Gharadade Turkamachai dar Daneshgahe Tabriz" [Report on the scientific conference on the Turkamanchai Treaty at Tabriz University], *Aran: Faslname Tahghighi Motaleati Moaseseye Farhangi Aran* 11, Nos. 30–31 (Bahar va Tabestan 1391/Spring and Summer 2012), pp. 171–5.
188. Sayyed Ahmad Nekui va Mir Hadi Musawi Gharalari, "Ta'sire Jonbeshe Gulan Dar Jomhuri Azarbaijan" [The impact of the Gülen Movement in the Azerbaijan Republic], *Azar-Aran: Faslname Tahghighi Motaleati Moaseseye Farhangi Aran*, Nos. 38–9 (Tabestan va Paiz 1393/Summer and Autumn 2014), pp. 9–27; Vali Jabbari, "Jaryane Nowine Eslamgarai dar Jomhuric Azarbaijan: Ba Ta'kid bar Naghshe Doctor Samadof" [The new trend of Islamism in the Azerbaijan Republic: emphasizing the role of Dr Samadov], *Aran: Faslname Tahghighi Motaleati Moaseseye Farhangi Aran*, Nos. 28–9 (Tabestan va Paize 1390/Summer and Autumn 2011), pp. 23–35.
189. See, for example, Kolsum Parcham, "Naghshe Shoaraye Ghafghaz dar E'telaye Zabane Farsi" [Role of the Caucasus poets in promoting the Persian language], *Aran: Faslname Tahghighi Motaleati Moaseseye Farhangi Aran*, Nos. 26–7 (Zemestan 1389-Bahar 1390/Winter-Spring 2011), pp. 171–89; "Haj Aikram Aliyev: Risheye Ma Dar Iran Ast" [Haj Alikram Aliyev: Our roots are in Iran], *Aran: Faslname Tahghighi Motaleati Moaseseye Farhangi Aran*, Nos. 26–7 (Zemestan 1389-Bahar 1390/Winter-Spring 2011), pp. 189–207.
190. See Vali Kuzegare Kaleji, "Bar Resi Didgaha va Mavaze Ahzabe Siasi Armani va Diasporaye Armani dar Ghebal Bohrane Gharabagh" [Views and positions of Armenian political parties and the Armenian diaspora toward the Karabakh conflict], *Azar-Aran: Faslname Tahghighi Motaleati Moaseseye Farhangi Aran*, Nos. 38–9 (Tabestan va Paiz 1393/Summer and Autumn 2014), pp. 75–97.
191. See, for example, Vali Jabbari, "Rosvaiye Dowlate Jomhuri Azerbaijan dar Mosabeghate Eurovision" [The scandal of the government of the Azerbaijan Republic in the Eurovision contest], *Aran: Faslname Tahghighi Motaleati Moaseseye Farhangi Aran* 11, Nos. 30–31 (Bahar va Tabestan 1391/Spring and Summer 2012), pp. 81–95.
192. See Abdolreza faraji rad, Mohammad Darkhor and Seyyed Hadi Sadati, "Bar

Resi Ravabete strategic Israel va Jpmhurie Azerbaijan" [Strategic relations between Israel and the Azerbaijan Republic], *Aran: Faslname Tahghighi Motaleati Moaseseye Farhangi Aran* 11, Nos. 30–31 (Bahar va Tabestan 1391/Spring and Summer 2012), pp. 45–59.

193. See, for example, a critique of the recent visit of Ilham Aliyev to Saudi Arabia, which will lead to the spread of Wahhabism in the Shiite society of the Azerbaijan Republic: Davood Khoshbakht, "Ta'ammoli bar Safare Akhir Rajis Jomhuri Azerbaijan be Arabestan" [Reflecting on the recent trip of the Azerbaijan President to Saudi Arabia], http://fa.arannews.com/?MID=21&Type=News&TypeID=15&id=45458#sthash.FJtMihdy.dpbs
194. *Mahde Azadi*, an old daily paper in Tabriz, had such a policy. See, for example, the series of articles on *Firghe Democrat*: Rahim Shohratifar, "Firghe democrat Dar Sarashibi Soghut" [*Firghe Democrat* in downhill crash], *Mahde Azadi* (Tir-Shahrivar 1380/July–August 2001).
195. See, for example, Servis-e Siasi Tarhe Now, "Pan-Turkism dar Hale Ehtezar" [Pan-Turkism in the process of dying], *Tarhe Now*, No. 138 (20 Mordad 1390/11 August 2011).
196. A lecture given by Ali Shamkhani, secretary of the higher council of national security in Tabriz, *Tarhe Now*, No. 523 (14 Ordibehesht 1394/ 5 May 2015), p. 4.
197. Rasul Ardabili, "Chegoonegi Nofuz va Amalkard Taffakore Zede Eslami Pan-Turkism dar Ghafghaz" [How the anti-Islamic idea of pan-Turkism influences and acts in the Caucasus], *Tarhe Now*, No. 523 (14 Ordibehesht 1394/5 May 2015), p. 5.
198. Leila Masinian, "Rahyafthaye Vahdat Gerayaneh dar tafavot Haye Farhangi va Ghowmi keshvar" [Unitarian approaches to cultural and ethnic differences in the country], *Tarhe Now*, No. 523 (14 Ordibehesht 1394/5 May 2015).
199. One of the only memoirs left of the days of crisis was written by an Azari clergyman, giving important information about the reaction of ordinary Azeris to the Soviets and *Firghe Democrat*. See Ayatollah Mirza Abdullah Mojtahedi, *Bohrane Azarbaijan 1324–25* [Azerbaijan's crisis of 1945–6], ed. Rasul Ja'farian (Tehran: Moasseseye Motaleat-e Tarikhe Moaser, 1381/2002).
200. See *Misaagh*, No. 222 (Mehr 1385/October 2006).
201. Asre Iran, "Dowlate Baku Barnameh Rejeye Hamjensbazan ra Laghv Kard" [Baku government cancelled gay parade program], *Asre Iran* (5 Khordad 1391/26 May 2012).
202. See http://forum.tarikhfa.com/thread1410.html
203. For his remarks, see http://www.aparat.com/v/Q3huH. See also see 8http://sarabnews.blogfa.com/post/985
204. *Misaagh*, No. 213 (26 Khordad 1385/16 June 2006).
205. See *Misaagh*, No. 193 (Khordad 1384/June 2005), p. 2.

206. *Misaagh*, No. 226 (20 Azar 1385/11 December 2006), p. 2.
207. *Misaagh*, No. 224 (Mordad 1385/August 2006).
208. Mansur Haghighat Pour, "Zabane Madarie Azarbaijan Zabane Farsi Pahlavi Ast" [the mother tongue of Azerbaijan is Pahlavi Farsi], *TRT Farsi* (Esfand 1393/22 February 2015), http://www.trt.net.tr/persian/-170290
209. Haghighat Pour, "Ferdowsi Mazhare Moghavemat Irani ha dar barabare Hojume Torkhast" [Fridowsi is the symbol of the resistance of Iranians against the invasions of the Turks], *Azariha* (3 Esfand 1393/22 February 2015), http://www.azariha.org/?lang=fa&muid=53&item=1498
210. Haghighat Pour, "Rah Andazi Farhangestane Zabane Turki Eghdami Siasi Ast" [Establishing the academy of Turkish language is a political action], *Elpress*, 11 February 2015.
211. Some analysts, such as Svante Cornell, point out that Iranian help to Armenia has been in the realm of energy and goods, thus "Iran's support fell short of any military involvement." See Svante Cornell, *Small Nations and Great Powers: A Study of Ethno Political Conflict in the Caucasus* (Richmond: Curzon Press, 2001), p. 318.
212. Vali Zargari Nejad, *Bohrane Gharabagh va Ravabete Iran va Jomhuriye Azerbaijan* [The Karabakh crisis and Iran–Azerbaijan Relations] (MA Diss., Azad Islamic University, Science and Research Branch, 1393/2014).
213. Haghighat Pour has referred to cooperation with a brigade called "Amon" under the leadership of Roshan Javadov, who looked for help from Afghani Shiite volunteers and was successful in bringing 2,000 of them to fight against Armenia. See "Pasokhe Haghighat Pour be Ezharate Mozheke Namayandeye Parlemane Azarbaijan" [Haghighat Pour answers the ridiculous remarks from Azerbaijan's parliament], *Islam Times*, 6 April 2013, http://www.islamtimes.org/fa/doc/news/86
214. Ibid.
215. During my trip to Tabriz in early 2002, one member of the Revolutionary Guard, who had a political position in the office of the governor of Eastern Azerbaijan province, showed me the map of Azerbaijan–Armenia and said that Iranian Revolutionary Guard divisions had warned Armenia about occupying Azerbaijan's territory. According to him, "If we were not there and did not warn Armenians, they were able to go forward and occupy a land strip toward the Caspian and reach the sea."
216. Such trends among Iranian Azeris have been reflected in a few studies done on Iranian Azerbaijan. See, for example, Emil Souleimanov, Kamil Pikal, and Josef Kraus. "The Rise of Nationalism Among Iranian Azerbaijanis: A Step Toward Iran's Disintegration?" *Middle East Review of International Affairs*, Vol. 17, No. 1 (Spring 2013), p. 6, quoting Svante Cornell, "Iranian Azerbaijan: A Brewing Hotspot Presentation to the Symposium on Human Rights and Ethnicity in

Iran," 22 November 2004, organized by the Moderate (conservative) party, Swedish Parliament, Stockholm.

217. Brown, "Observations from Azerbaijan," p. 69.
218. This TV round table is on YouTube; see https://www.youtube.com/watch?v=_b1WnS1FT6c. A short summary of the round table in Farsi is available at http://www.azariha.org/?lang=fa&muid=53&item=1011
219. Ilham Aliyev's lecture in the Azerbaijani parliament, 8 May 2007. See Orhan Gafarli, "Azerbaijan seeks warmer ties with Iran," *Eurasia Daily Monitor* 11, No. 216, p. 2, http://www.jamestown.org/programs/edm/single/?tx_ttnews%5Btt_news%5D=43152&cHash=6b921a9e465289b9f0741d7b66537537#.VVId9vlViko
220. Abdullah Rezai, "Masuliate Tarikhi Azari Haye Iran dar Barabare Aghliat haye Azeri Parakande dar Jahan" [Historical responsibility of Iranian Azeris toward dispersed Azeri minorities around the world], *Vatan: Gahnameye Dakheli Jamiate Vatan*, No. 2 (Khordad 1385/July 2006), p. 15.
221. *Misaagh*, No. 222 (Mehr 1385/October 2006), p. 2.
222. See, for example, Mohsen Sa'adati, "Jonbeshe Aras, Harkati Baraye Laghve Gharadadhaye Golestan va Turkamanchai" [The Aras movement: a move to annul the Golestan and Turkamanchai treaties], *Misaagh*, No. 153 (Day 1382/January 2003), p. 3.
223. For a report and pictures of the demonstrations, see *Misaagh*, No. 225 (16 Azar 1385/7 December 2006), pp. 1, 8.
224. Hossein Shariatmadari, "Nobate Baku" [Baku's turn], *Kayhan Newspaper*, 3 April 2014, http://www.khabaronline.ir/detail/284774/politics/diplomacy
225. Salar Seifoddini, "Irane Shomali Kojast?" [Where is northern Iran?], *Misaagh*, No. 222 (24 Mehr 1385/16 October 2006), p. 3.
226. Akbar Ja'fari, "Irane Shomali, Harkati dar Rastaye Hamgeraai" [Northern Iran, a move toward integration], *Misaagh*, No. 222 (24 Mehr 1385/16 October 2006).
227. In *Misaagh*, No. 225, a report about Shabestari's remarks on the term "northern Iran" was mentioned.
228. "Majalleh Irane Shomali dar Ardabil" [Northern Iran magazine in Ardabil], *Misaagh*, No. 216 (2 Mordad 1385/24 July 2006), p. 2.
229. See, for example, a series of articles printed as "Harkate Azadibakhshe Irane Shomali: Gozashte, Haal va Ayandeye an" [The movement for the liberation of northern Iran: past, present and future], *Misaagh*, Nos. 125–8 (18 Azar-30 Day 1381/9 December–20 January 2002–3).
230. *Misaagh*, No. 128 (30 day 1381/20 January 2003), p. 3. Almost four years later, during the demonstration in protest at the insult of the Prophet of Islam in a Baku-based newspaper, the names of a few members of the movement were reported.
231. http://iranshomali1.blogfa.com/. It bears the following title: Harkate

Azadibakhshe Irane Shomali: Azadi-e Iran-e Shomali va Elhagh-e An be Iran [The movement for the liberation of northern Iran: the liberation of northern Iran and its annexation to the motherland].

232. Bayaniyeh Tahlili Fa'alane Daneshjui va ejtemai Azer Dar Khosuse Eghdamate khasmaney-e Jomhuri-e Baku Alayhe Iran [Analytical declaration by Azeri students and social activists on the hostile actions of the Baku republic against Iran], *Iranboom* (18 Day 1391/8 January 2013), http://www.iranboom.ir/iranshahr/tireh-ha/9013-bayanie-azari-ha-dar-ghebal-siasat-doshmanane-rejim-baku.html
233. http://ruwange.net/NewsDetail.aspx?itemid=635
234. "Vozaraye Defae Iran va Azerbaijan Bar Sare Hamkarihaye Defai va Amniyyati Bayne Tehran va Baku Ta'kid Kardand" [The Iranian and Azerbaijani Defence Ministers emphasised defense and security cooperation between Tehran and Baku], *Payegahe Etela Resanie Dowlat*, 20 April 2015, http://www.dolat.ir/NSite/FullStory/ News/?Serv= 0&Id=261805
235. Mina Muradova, "Azerbaijan and the Iran Agreement," *Central Asia-Caucasus Analyst*, 15 April 2015, http://cacianalyst.org/publications/field-reports/item/13180-azerbaijan-and-the-iran-agreement.html
236. See, for example, "Expert: Baku has unofficially agreed to take part in anti-Iranian coalition," *REGNUM*, 5 May 2015, http://www. regnum.ru/English/641581.html
237. Sabir Rustam Khanli, chair of the WAC, expressed his disappointment at this absence: "Despite our invitation, unfortunately not even one of the members of parliament we had invited attended the congress. They did not even send us a simple congratulation. There was a time when the late Heydar Aliyev sent 60 members of parliament to our congress in Washington. I cannot understand what this insouciance means." See http://modern.az/articles/76368/1/
238. Gevorg G. Avetikyan, "Ethnicity in the Contemporary Islamic Republic of Iran: The Case of 'South Azerbaijan'" (Master of Arts thesis, Central European University, Nationalism Studies Program, Budapest, 2009), p. 43.
239. Hamid Ahmadi, "Political Elites and the Question of Ethnicity and Democracy in Iran."
240. Ervand Abrahamian, "RE: Questions on Iranian Studies," 25 November 2008. See Avetikyan, "Ethnicity in the Contemporary Islamic Republic of Iran," p. 10. ftn. 14.
241. Fereydoun Safizadeh, "On Dilemmas of Identity in the Post-soviet Republic of Azerbaijan," *Caucasian Regional Studies*, Vol. 3, No. 1 (1998), p. 13, http://poli.vub.ac.be/publi/crs/eng/0301
242. In a recent program on GunAz TV (19 November 2014), which academics such as Nasib Nasibli and Dilgham Ahmed attended, the participants lamented the problem of Turkophobia in the Azerbaijan Republic and the fact that most Azeri families prefer to choose Islamic or Persian names for their children rather than

Turkish names. See "Rayejtarin Namha dar Jomhuri Baku, Yousef, Fatimah va Zahra: Gelayeye Nasibli az 'Turk Harasi' Bayne Mardome Baku" [Yousef, Zahra, Fatima, the most common names in the Baku republic: Nasibli complains about Turkopobia among Baku people], http://www.azariha.org/?lang=fa&muid=53&item=1392

243. Hunter, "Azerbaijan: Search for Identity and New Partners."

6. "UN-CIVIL SOCIETY" AND THE SOURCES OF RUSSIAN INFLUENCE IN WEST ASIA: THE SOUTH CAUCASUS

1. "Soft power" of course refers to the full range of non-militarily coercive tools that a state uses to achieve its aims. It may be soft, but it is still power, that is, that which forces another to act in a way s/he would not otherwise do. The definitive discussion of the term remains Joseph S. Nye, *Soft Power: The Means to Success in World Politics* (New York: Public Affairs, 2005). For a more focused discussion on Russian understandings and uses of soft power, see James Sherr, *Hard Diplomacy and Soft Coercion: Russia's Influence Abroad* (London: Chatham House, 2013).
2. For an overview of Russia's "foreign agents" law, see "NGO law Monitor: Russia," International Center for Not-For-Profit Law, 17 February 2015, http://www.icnl.org/research/monitor/russia.html
3. Natalia Burlinova, "Russian Soft Power is just like Western Soft Power, but with a Twist," *Russia Direct*, 7 April 2015, http://www.russia-direct.org/opinion/russian-soft-power-just-western-soft-power-twist
4. For a discussion of the history and usage of the term "uncivil society," see Marlies Glasius, "Uncivil Society," in Helmuth K. Anheier and Stefan Toepler, eds, *International Encyclopedia of Civil Society* (Heidelberg: Springer, 2010), pp. 1583–8. The term is applied specifically to the phenomenon of illiberal NGOs and political parties growing out of Russia's frustration with parliamentary democracy in Andreas Umland, "Post-Soviet 'Uncivil Society' and the Rise of Aleksandr Dugin: A Case Study of the Extraparliamentary Radical Right in Contemporary Russia" (PhD dissertation, University of Cambridge, 2007); and idem, "Toward an Uncivil Society? Contextualizing the Recent Decline of Parties of the Extreme Right Wing in Russia," *Demokratizatsiya*, Vol. 10, No. 3 (2002), pp. 362–91.
5. Dmitry Medvedev, "Interv'yu Dmitriya Medvedeva rossiiskim telekanalam," *The Kremlin*, 31 August 2008, http://kremlin.ru/transcripts/1276
6. For a broader elaboration of this point, see Jeffrey Mankoff, "The Big Caucasus: Between Fragmentation and Integration," Center for Strategic and International Studies, January 2013, https://www.csis.org/analysis/big-caucasus
7. On Nagorno-Karabakh, see in particular Tom de Waal, *Black Garden: Armenia and Azerbaijan through Peace and War* (New York: NYU Press, 2013).
8. See "Russia of Transformations," Defense Ministry of Finland, http://www.defmin.fi/files/2345/Russia_of_Transformations.pdf

9. Other "frozen conflicts" exist in Moldova (Transnistria) and increasingly Ukraine (the Donbas), as well as Georgia (South Ossetia and Abkhazia, discussed below). On these conflicts' historical background and role in Russian foreign policy, see Jeffrey Mankoff, "Russia's Latest Land Grab: How Putin Won Crimea and Lost Ukraine," *Foreign Affairs*, Vol. 93, No. 3 (May/June 2014).
10. David M. Herszenhorn, "Pact Tightens Russian Ties with Abkhazia," *New York Times*, 24 November 2014.
11. The Russian military presence in South Ossetia and Abkhazia, which the international community continues to recognize as part of the Georgian state, in some measure compensates for the 2007 withdrawal of Russian forces from then-united Georgia at the insistence of then-Georgian President Mikheil Saakashvili.
12. Alexander Jackson, "The Military Balance in Nagorno-Karabakh," *Caucasian Review of International Affairs*, No. 18, 19 January 2009.
13. "Soft Power? The Means and Ends of Russian Influence," Chatham House REP Seminar Summary, 31 March 2011, http://www.chathamhouse.org/sites/files/chathamhouse/public/Research/Russia%20and%20Eurasia/310311summary.pdf. See also Agnia Grigas, "Legacies, Coercion, and Soft Power: Russian Influence in the Baltic States," Chatham House, 1 August 2012, http://www.chathamhouse.org/publications/papers/view/185321
14. Russian Ministry of Foreign Affairs, "Plan deyatel'nosti Ministerstva inostrannykh del Rossiiskoi Federatsii na period do 2018 g." (2013). See also Gatis Pelens, ed., *The "Humanitarian Dimension" of Russian Foreign Policy Toward Georgia, Moldova, Ukraine, and the Baltic States* (Riga: Center for East European Policy Studies, 2010); Vladimir Frolov, "Printsipy myagkoi sily," *Vedomosti*, 8 April 2005; Heather A. Conley and Theodore P. Gerber, "Russian Soft Power in the 21st Century: An Examination of Russian Compatriot Policy in Estonia," Center for Strategic and International Studies, August 2011, http://csis.org/files/publication/110826_Conley_RussianSoftPower_Web.pdf
15. Timothy Snyder, "Russia's War, Ukraine's History, and the West's Options" (lecture at the Center for Strategic and International Studies, Washington, 27 October 2014), http://csis.org/event/russias-war-ukraines-history-and-wests-options
16. For an overview of Surkov, see Peter Pomerantsev, "The Hidden Author of Putinism: How Vladislav Surkov invented the new Russia," *The Atlantic*, 7 November 2014.
17. On this shared institutional heritage, see Christopher Marsh and Nicolas K. Gvosdev, "The Persistence of Eurasia," *Policy Innovations* (2009). On the shared political culture, see Kristin Cavoukian, "'Soviet mentality?' The role of shared political culture in relations between the Armenian state and Russia's Armenian diaspora," *Nationalities Papers* (2013), pp. 709–29.
18. Mark Galleotti, "Moscow's Spy Game: Why Russia is Winning the Intelligence War in Ukraine," *Foreign Affairs*, 30 October 2014. See also Sam Jones, "Photos and roses for GRU's 'spetsnaz' casualties," *Financial Times*, 8 August 2014.

19. Although the numbers of migrants from each state given by different sources vary widely, most estimates suggest that several hundred thousand laborers from each of the three South Caucasus states are present in Russia. Using data from the UN, the Migration Policy Institute estimated that 511,000 Armenians, 743,000 Azerbaijanis, and 436,000 Georgians were residing in Russia in 2013. See "International Migrant Population by Country of Origin and Destination," http://www.migrationpolicy.org/programs/data-hub/charts/international-migrant-population-country-origin-and-destination. As of August 2015, the Russian Federal Migration Service gives figures of 366,987 Armenians, 370,025 Azerbaijanis, and 17,787 Georgians (not counting "citizens" of Abkhazia and South Ossetia, which Russia regards as independent states. See "Statisticheskie svedeniya po otnoshenii inostrannykh grazhdan, nakhodyashchikhsya na territorii Rossiiskoi Federatsii," Federal Migration Service, http://www.fms.gov.ru/about/statistics/data/details/54891/
20. "Georgia: Hundreds Left Stranded after Deportations from Russia," *RFE/RL Feature*, 17 October 2006, http://www.rferl.org/content/article/1072088.html
21. On the rise of Putin and its impact on Russian patronage politics, see especially Karen Dawisha, *Putin's Kleptocracy: Who Owns Russia?* (New York: Simon & Schuster, 2015). On Georgia, Ukraine, and Kyrgyzstan, see Melinda Haring and Michael Cecire, "Why the Color Revolutions Failed," *Foreign Policy*, 18 March 2013. As explained below, Georgia's revolution was more successful in overturning the institutional structure inherited from the USSR.
22. Sergei Guriev and Konstantin Sonin, "Dictators and Oligarchs: A Dynamic Theory of Contested Property Rights," *Journal of Public Economics*, Vol. 93, No. 1 (2009), pp. 1–13.
23. Nona Shahnazarian, "Police Reform and Corruption in Georgia, Armenia, and Nagorno-Karabakh," *PONARS Eurasia Policy Memo*, No. 232 (2012), http://www.gwu.edu/~ieresgwu/assets/docs/ponars/pepm_232_Shahnazarian_Sept2012.pdf; George Tarkhan-Mouravi, "The Dramatic Rise and Fall of Mikheil Saakashvili," *Transitions Online*, 18 October 2013.
24. On the Russian understanding of "Eurasia," see especially Dmitri Trenin, *The End of Eurasia: Russia on the Border Between Geopolitics and Globalization* (Washington, DC: Carnegie Endowment, 2002); Evgeny Vinokurov and Alexander Libman, *Eurasian Integration: Challenges of Transcontinental Regionalism* (London: Palgrave Macmillan, 2012); Marlène Laruelle, *Russian Eurasianism: An Ideology of Empire* (Washington, DC: Woodrow Wilson Center, 2005). As Vikokurov and Libman argue, Russian officials' understanding of Eurasia as coterminous with the former Soviet Union is distinct from that of Eurasianist ideologues like Aleksandr Dugin, who see Eurasia in a much wider sense as a counterbalance to the US-led West. The Kremlin's version of Eurasia stops at the old Soviet borders, whereas Dugin's includes states like China, Iran, Mongolia, and possibly even the European

Union. Vinokurov and Libman argue for a third version of Eurasia that is transcontinental, but focused more on economic connectivity and cooperation than on geopolitical balancing. See Vinokurov and Libman, *Eurasian Integration*, pp. 16–29.

25. Anton Barbashin and Hannah Thoburn, "Putin's Brain: Alexander Dugin and the Philosophy Behind Putin's Invasion of Crimea," *Foreign Affairs*, 31 March 2014.
26. Marlène Laruelle, "Eurasia, Eurasianism, Eurasian Union: Terminological Gaps and Overlaps," *PONARS Eurasia Policy Memo*, No. 366 (2015), http://www.ponarseurasia.org/sites/default/files/policy-memos-pdf/Pepm366_Laruelle_July2015.pdf
27. In his 2005 annual address to the Federal Assembly, Putin said Russia "was, is, and always will be a leading European nation." See Vladimir Putin, "Poslanie Federal'nomu Sobraniyu Rossiiskoi Federatsii," 25 April 2005, http://www.kremlin.ru/appears/2005/04/25/1223—type63372type63374type8263487049.shtml
28. Vladimir Putin, "Vladimir Putin Meets with Members of the Valdai Discussion Club," Valdai Discussion Club, 20 September 2013, http://valdaiclub.com/politics/62880.html. See also Timothy Snyder, "Fascism, Russia, and Ukraine," *New York Review of Books*, 20 March 2014.
29. A 2010 poll of Ukrainians, for instance, found that 72 percent of respondents had a negative attitude toward homosexuals. Meanwhile LGBT rights marches in Ukraine, Georgia, and elsewhere have frequently been met with physical violence, even before the start of the Russian propaganda campaign. See Cole Park, "East vs. West? Russia, Ukraine, and the Anti-Gay Wedge," Political Research Associates, 12 December 2013, http://www.politicalresearch.org/2013/12/12/east-vs-west-russia-ukraine-and-the-anti-gay-wedge/#sthash.qhBePhEo.dpbs
30. "Aktsiya za sem'yu i traditsionnye nravstvennye tsennosti sostoyalas' u posol'stva Germanii," Batkyv'skiy Komitet Ukraini/Roditel'skii Komitet Ukrainy, 6 November 2013, http://rodkom.org/2013/4092.html. Dimiter Kenarov, "Dashed Hopes in Gay Ukraine," *Foreign Policy*, 19 January 2015.
31. Andrew Roth, "Crowd Led by Priests Attacks Gay Rights Marchers in Georgia," *New York Times*, 17 May 2013.
32. See Natalya Antelava, "What was Behind Georgia's Anti-Gay Rally?" *New Yorker*, 23 May 2013.
33. "Ruling Party MPs Speak of 'New Pro-Russian Center' Around Ivanishvili," *Civil.ge*, 8 November 2011, http://www.civil.ge/eng/article.php?id=24115; Ellen Barry, "Georgian Leader Emerges as an Enigma," *New York Times*, 8 October 2012; Daniel Halper, "Russian Oligarch Hires Army of DC Lobbyists," *Weekly Standard*, 12 April 2012.
34. "Georgia and Russia: Dreams Deferred," *The Economist*, 6 December 2014.
35. Michael Cecire, "The Kremlin Pulls on Georgia," *Foreign Policy*, 9 March 2015; Svante Cornell, "Georgia—Another Target in Russia's 'Near Abroad,'" *European*

Institute, 1 December 2014, http://www.europeaninstitute.org/index.php/246-european-affairs/december-2014/1961-perspectives-georgia-another-target-in-russia-s-near-abroad

36. "Statement by Serzh Sargsyan at 15th convention of Republican Party of Armenia," *Panorama*, 24 May 2014, http://www.panorama.am/en/current_topics/2014/05/24/serj-sargsyan-hkk/?sw. Both HKK and United Russia are typical post-Soviet "parties of power" that serve more to support the government's policies than to aggregate and represent public opinion.
37. "Tsarukian Meets Russian Ruling Party Members," *RFE/RL* (Azatutyun), 11 February 2015, http://www.azatutyun.am/content/article/26842182.html; Liz Fuller and Richard Giragosian, "Armenian Opposition in Disarray after Prominent Leader Sidelined," *RFE/RL*, 2015, http://www.rferl.org/content/armenia-opposition-disarray-tsarukian-sidelined/26864874.html
38. Vladimir Socor, "Russia's New Moldovan Favorite: Igor Dodon's Socialist Party," Jamestown Foundation, *Eurasia Daily Monitor*, 4 December 2014, p. 216.
39. David M. Herszenhorn, "Moldova Vote Gives Edge to Parties Looking West," *New York Times*, 1 December 2014.
40. Sinikukka Saari, "Russia's Post-Orange Revolution Strategies to Increase its Influence in the Former Soviet Republics: Public Diplomacy po russkii," *Europe-Asia Studies* (2014), pp. 50–66.
41. Ibid. See also Lada L. Roslycky, "Russia's Smart Power in Crimea: Sowing the Seeds of Trust," *Southeastern European and Black Sea Studies* (2011), pp. 299–316.
42. Roslycky, "Russia's Smart Power." Elena Mizrokhi, "Russian 'separatism' in Crimea and NATO: Ukraine's big hope, Russia's grand gamble," Université Laval-Chaire de recherche du Canada sur les conflits identitaires et le terrorisme, August 2009, http://www.psi.ulaval.ca/fileadmin/psi/documents/Documents/Travaux_et_recherches/Crimee.pdf. On the importance of the separatist regions for Russian foreign policy, see Mankoff, "Russia's Latest Land Grab."
43. Fareed Shafee, "Inspired from Abroad: The External Sources of Separatism in Azerbaijan," *Caucasian Review of International Affairs*, Vol. 2, No. 4 (Autumn 2008), pp. 200–11. See also Valery Dzutsev, "Moscow Shows Renewed Interest in the Fate of Ethnic Minorities in Azerbaijan," Jamestown Foundation, *Eurasia Daily Monitor*, 2 July 2012, http://www.jamestown.org/single/?tx_ttnews%5Btt_news%5D=39570#.VUKI_iFVhBc
44. Author's interviews with Azeri scholars and officials, Baku, June 2014.
45. Eduard Abrahamyan, "Current Military and Political Menaces in the South Caucasus," *E-International Relations* (2015), http://www.e-ir.info/2015/02/11/current-military-and-political-menaces-in-the-south-caucasus/
46. Sergei Kapanadze, "Georgia's Vulnerability to Russian Pressure Points," *European Council on Foreign Relations Policy Memo* (2014), http://www.ecfr.eu/publications/summary/georgias_vulnerability_to_russian_pressure_points312; see also

Eka Janashia, "Moscow Distributes Passports in Georgia", *Central Asia-Caucasus Analyst*, 7 May 2014, http://www.cacianalyst.org/publications/fieldreports/item/12966-moscow-distributes-passports-in-georgia.html

47. Aleksei Makarin, "The Russian Orthodox Church: Competing Choices," *Russian Politics and Law*, Vol. 49, No. 1 (2011), pp. 8–23. On Kirill, see "Moscow Using the Orthodox Church to Expand its Influence?" *Stratfor*, 26 July 2011, https://www.stratfor.com/analysis/moscow-using-orthodox-church-expand-its-influence
48. "Osnovy gosudarstvennoi kul'turnoi politiki," The Kremlin, 24 December 2014, http://static.kremlin.ru/media/events/files/41d526a877638a8730eb.pdf. On interpretations of this document, see Leonid Bershidsky, "Putin's Rejection of the West, in Writing," *Bloomberg*, 4 April 2014, http://www.bloombergview.com/articles/2014-04-04/putin-s-rejection-of-the-west-in-writing
49. Irina Papkova, "Russian Orthodox concordat? Church and state under Medvedev," *Nationalities Papers*, Vol. 39, No. 5 (2011), pp. 667–83.
50. Ukraine's religious geography is quite complex. In addition to non-negligible numbers of indigenous Jews and Muslims (mainly Crimean Tatars), Ukraine's Christian population is divided primarily among four churches: Greek Catholic, Ukrainian Orthodox (Moscow Patriarchate), Ukrainian Orthodox (Kiev Patriarchate), and Ukrainian Autocephalous Orthodox. In the far western part of the country, which at one time belonged to the Polish and Austro-Hungarian province of Galicia, a majority of the population belongs to the Greek Catholic Church, which follows the Eastern Rite but acknowledges the authority of the Pope in Rome. The Ukrainian Orthodox Church (Moscow Patriarchate) is a self-governing branch of the Russian Orthodox Church in full communion, via Moscow, with the rest of the Eastern Orthodox world. It is traditionally considered the largest denomination in Ukraine (though the number of its adherents is disputed and recent polling indicates its numbers have declined), with its parishioners concentrated in eastern Ukraine. The Ukrainian Orthodox Church (Kiev Patriarchate) was established in 1992, shortly after Ukraine became independent, and remains unrecognized by Moscow or the wider Orthodox communion. Nevertheless, in recent years it appears to have become the largest denomination in Ukraine, and enjoys support from leading Ukrainian nationalist politicians. The Ukrainian Autocephalous Orthodox Church emerged in the aftermath of the Bolshevik Revolution among Ukrainian nationalists who refused to recognize the authority of the Communist government, which moved to subordinate the Church entirely to its control under Stalin. Heavily persecuted during the Soviet period, its main constituency remains in the Ukrainian diaspora. In 2014, polling by the Razumkov Center found that 17.4% of the Ukrainian population considered itself loyal to the Moscow Patriarchate, 22.4% to the Kiev Patriarchate, and 0.7% to the Ukrainian Autocephalous Orthodox Church. A full 28.1% considered themselves "just Orthodox." See "Ukraine 2014: Socio-Political Conflict and the Church,"

Razumkov Center, 2014, http://www.razumkov.org.ua/upload/1403784774_file.pdf. On the activities of Russian Orthodox clerics in the Donbas fighting, see Andrew Higgins, "Evidence Grows of Russian Orthodox Clergy's Aiding Ukraine Rebels," *New York Times*, 6 September 2014.

51. Author's interview with Georgian scholar, Tbilisi, June 2014.
52. Cecire, "The Kremlin Pulls on Georgia."
53. Author's interview with Georgian scholar, Tbilisi, June 2014.
54. See Tengiz Pkhaladze, "ROC and Independent Georgia," in Tengiz Pkhaladze, ed., *Religion as the Instrument of Russian Foreign Policy toward Neighboring Countries: Georgia, Latvia, Ukraine* (Tbilisi: International Center for Geopolitical Studies, 2012), pp. 37–53. The other states that recognize South Ossetia and/or Abkhazia as independent states include Nicaragua, Venezuela, Nauru, and Vanuatu. Tuvalu also recognized these entities' independence from 2011–14, when it signed an agreement establishing diplomatic relations with Georgia that included withdrawing recognition of South Ossetia and Abkhazia.
55. Vladimir Putin, "Address by President of the Russian Federation," The Kremlin, 18 March 2014, http://en.kremlin.ru/events/president/transcripts/20603
56. Vladimir Putin, "Soveshchanie poslov i postoyannykh predstavitelei Rossii," The Kremlin, 1 July 2014, http://kremlin.ru/events/president/transcripts/46131
57. Anna Kordunsky, "Who are the compatriots Russia strives to protect in Ukraine?" *Christian Science Monitor*, 4 March 2014.
58. Andis Kudors, "'Russian World'—Russia's Soft Power Approach to Compatriots Policy," *Russian Analytical Digest*, No. 81 (16 June 2010).
59. Andy Byford, "The Russian Diaspora in International Relations: 'Compatriots' in Britain," *Europe-Asia Studies*, Vol. 64, No. 4 (June 2012), pp. 715–35.
60. Anton Orekh, "Passport kak batsilla," *Yezhednevnyi Zhurnal*, 9 September 2008.
61. Eka Janashia, "Moscow Distributes Passports in Georgia," *Caucasus-Central Asia Institute Analyst*, 7 May 2014, http://www.cacianalyst.org/publications/field-reports/item/12966-moscow-distributes-passports-in-georgia.html
62. It originated, however, in the 1830s with the man who would later become Tsar Nichols I's notorious Minister of Public Enlightenment, Sergey Uvarov, better known for his doctrine of Official Nationality emphasizing Orthodoxy, autocracy, and nationality [*narodnost'*] as the ideological pillars of Tsarist Russia.
63. Quoted in Vladimir Abarinov and Galina Sidorova, "'Russkii mir', bessmyslennyi i besposhchadnyi," *Radio Svoboda*, 18 February 2015, http://www.svoboda.org/articleprintview/26855650.html
64. Michael Khodarkovsky, "Glory to the 'Russian World,'" *New York Times*, 13 October 2014.
65. See Vladislav Inozemtsev, "Constructing the Russian World," *IP Journal*, 5 December 2014, https://ip-journal.dgap.org/en/ip-journal/topics/constructing-russian-world

66. Kudors, "Russian World."
67. Less than 0.5% of the population in Armenia, around 1.3% in Azerbaijan, and no more than 1.5% in Georgia.
68. Giorgi Lomsadze, "Kremlin Propaganda Chief Asks Armenians to Speak Russian," *Eurasianet*, 12 June 2014, http://www.eurasianet.org/node/68551
69. Mikhail Chernov, "Rossiya vyidet za granitsy Armenii," *Lenta.ru*, 7 November 2014, http://lenta.ru/articles/2014/11/07/russianarm/. See also Andrey Makarychev and Alexandra Yatsyk, "(Non) Russian World, (Non) Soft Power: Putin's Serpentine Policy in the South Caucasus," *Caucasus Analytical Digest* (December 2014), pp. 2–6.
70. Author's interviews with local scholars and analysts, Tbilisi and Almaty, May–June 2014.
71. See especially Thomas Carothers, "The Backlash Against Democracy Promotion," *Foreign Affairs*, Vol. 85, No. 2 (Mar/April 2006), pp. 55–68.

7. TURKEY'S SOFT POWER IN A COMPARATIVE CONTEXT: THE SOUTH CAUCASUS AND THE MIDDLE EAST

1. Joseph S. Nye, *Bound To Lead: The Changing Nature of American Power* (New York: Basic Books, 1991).
2. Joseph S. Nye, *Soft Power: The Means to Success in World Politics* (NY: Public Affairs, 2004), 162–163.
3. D. A. Lake and P. M. Morgan, *Regional Orders: Building Security in a New World* (University Park: Pennsylvania State University Press, 1997); Barry Buzan and Ole Waever, *Regions and Powers: The Structure of International Security* (Cambridge: Cambridge University Press, 2003).
4. Cited in Yee-Kuang Heng, "Mirror, mirror on the wall, who is the softest of them all? Evaluating Japanese and Chinese strategies in the 'soft' power competition era," *International Relations of the Asia-Pacific*, No. 10 (2010), p. 280.
5. Azerbaijan was recognized on 9 November 1991, and Armenia and Georgia, together with the Central Asian republics, were recognized on 16 December 1991. Both Azerbaijan and Turkey worked to make sure that Turkey would become the first state to recognize Azerbaijan.
6. Mustafa Aydın, "1990–2001 Kafkasya ve Orta Asya ile İlişkiler," in Baskın Oran, ed., *Türk Dış Politikası, Kurtuluş Savaşı'ndan Bugüne Olgular, Belgeler, Yorumlar*, vol. 2 (İstanbul: İletişim Yayınları, 2001), pp. 380–81.
7. Ibid., p. 381.
8. Ibid., p. 383.
9. Gareth Winrow, "Turkish Policy in Central Asia," in Alan Makovsky and Sabri Sayarı, eds, *Turkey's New World: Changing Dynamics in Turkish Foreign Policy* (Washington, DC: Washington Institute of Near East Policy, 2000), p. 117.

10. F. Stephan Larrabee and Ian O. Lesser, *Turkish Foreign Policy in an Age of Uncertainty* (Santa Monica, CA: RAND Corporation, 2003), p. 104.
11. Shireen Hunter, "Turkey, Central Asia and the Caucasus: Ten Years after Independence," *Southeast European and Black Sea Studies*, Vol. 1, No. 2 (2001), p. 8.
12. Philip Robins, *Suits and Uniforms: Turkish Foreign Policy since the Cold War* (London: Hurst & Co., 2003), p. 282.
13. Anthony Hyman, "Moving Out of Moscow's Orbit: The Outlook for Central Asia," *International Affairs*, Vol. 69, No. 2 (1993), p. 299.
14. Robins, *Suits and Uniforms*, p. 291.
15. Aydın, "1990–2001 Kafkasya ve Orta Asya ile İlişkiler," p. 384.
16. Lerna K. Yanık, "The Politics of Educational Exchange: Turkish Education in Eurasia," *Europe–Asia Studies*, Vol. 56, No. 2 (2010), p. 294.
17. Pınar Akçalı and Cennet Engin-Demir, "Turkey's Educational Policies in Central Asia and Caucasia: Perceptions of Policy Makers and Experts," *International Journal of Educational Development*, No. 32 (2012), p. 13.
18. Aydın, "1990–2001 Kafkasya ve Orta Asya ile İlişkiler," p. 386.
19. Jerzy Rohozinski, "Azerbaijan and Turkey: The Light and Shade of 'Turkish' brotherhood," in *Turcja after the Start of Negotiations with the European Union—Foreign Relations and the Domestic Situation*, CES Report, (Warsaw, July 2008), p. 15, www.osw.waw.pl/sites/default/files/raport_turcja_ii_ang.pdf
20. For Gülen schools as part of Turkey's soft power, see Bayram Balcı's chapter in this volume.
21. Aydın, "1990–2001 Kafkasya ve Orta Asya ile İlişkiler," p. 244.
22. Ibid., p. 387.
23. Rohozinski, "Azerbaijan and Turkey," p. 14.
24. Ibid., p. 15.
25. Winrow, "Turkish Policy in Central Asia," p. 231; Akçalı and Engin-Demir, "Turkey's Educational Policies in Central Asia and Caucasia," p. 13.
26. Aydın, "1990–2001 Kafkasya ve Orta Asya ile İlişkiler," p. 387.
27. Yasemin Celik, *Contemporary Turkish Foreign Policy* (Westport, CT: Greenwood Publishing, 1999), pp. 127–8.
28. İsmail Cem, *Turkey in the New Century* (Nicosia: Rustem Publishing, 2001), p. 61.
29. Bayram Balcı, "Strengths and Constraints of Turkish Policy in the South Caucasus," *Insight Turkey*, Vol. 16, No. 2 (2014).
30. Aybars Görgülü, "The Litmus Test for Turkey's New Foreign Policy: The Historical Rapprochement with Armenia," in Kerem Öktem et al., eds, *Another Empire? A Decade of Turkey's Foreign Policy Under the Justice and Development Party* (İstanbul: Bilgi University Press, 2012).
31. Akcali and Engin-Demir, "Turkey's Educational Policies in Central Asia and Caucasia," p. 14.

32. Yunus Emre (1238–1320) was one of the greatest Turkish poets, representing the Anatolian Sufi tradition. In 2007, the AKP government established Yunus Emre Centers in several countries to promote Turkey, its culture, and language. There are currently 29 such centers in the world. At the opening ceremony of the London center, then-President Abdullah Gul's speech said that great powers were present not only through their diplomats, but through their cultures as well. See http://www.yunusemreenstitusu.org/icerik_orta.aspx?id=240 (accessed 28 January 2011).
33. Rohozinski, "Azerbaijan and Turkey," p. 15.
34. Turkish Ministry of Foreign Affairs, accessed 8 August 2015, http://www.mfa.gov.tr/azerbaycan-ekonomisi.tr.mfa
35. Turkish Ministry of Foreign Affairs, accessed 8 August 2015, http://www.mfa.gov.tr/gurcistan-ekonomisi.tr.mfa
36. Turkish Ministry of Foreign Affairs, accessed 8 August 2015, http://www.mfa.gov.tr/turkey_s-relations-with-central-asian-republics.en.mfa
37. Rohozinski, "Azerbaijan and Turkey," p. 6.
38. Bayram Balci, "Gülen: Top Issue on the Agenda of Erdogan's Visit to Azerbaijan," Carnegie Moscow Center, 9 April 2014, http://carnegie.ru/eurasiaoutlook/?fa=55290
39. I would like to thank Bayram Balcı for this information.
40. "Georgia: Gülen Schools Flourishing," *Eurasianet.org*, 6 May 2013, http://www.eurasianet.org/node/66929.
41. Speech by Foreign Minister Ahmet Davutoğlu entitled "Principles of Turkish Foreign Policy," at SETA Foundation's Washington DC Branch, 8 December 2009, accessed 10 February 2011, achttp://setadc.org/index.php?option=com_content&view=article&id=202:unofficial-transcript-of-foreign-minister-ahmed-davutoglus-speech&catid=58:text&Itemid=113
42. Yousef Al Sharif and Samir Salha, *Reflections of EU–Turkey Relations in the Muslim World*, Open Society Foundation, Istanbul, 1st printing, July 2009.
43. Ahmet Davutoğlu, "Turkey's Zero-Problems Foreign Policy," *Foreign Policy*, 20 May 2010, accessed 10 August 2015, http://foreignpolicy.com/2010/05/20/turkeys-zero-problems-foreign-policy/
44. Mensur Akgun et al., *Orta Dogu'da Turkiye Algisi* [The perception of Turkey in the Middle East] (Istanbul: TESEV Publications, 2009), http://www.tesev.org.tr/default.asp?PG=DPL00TR01; Mensur Akgun et al., *The Perception of Turkey in the Middle East 2010* (Istanbul: TESEV Publications, 2011).
45. Anthony Shadid, "Resurgent Turkey Flexes its Muscles around Iraq," *New York Times*, 4 January 2011, accessed 10 January 2015, http://www.nytimes.com/2011/01/05/world/middleeast/05turkey.html
46. Michael Kimmelman, "Turks Put Twist in Racy Soaps," *New York Times*, 17 June 2010, accessed 15 January 2015, http://www.nytimes.com/2010/06/18/arts/18abroad.html?_r=0

47. Ibid.
48. "Turkish TV Series Enjoying Increasing Popularity on Arab Stations," *Today's Zaman*, 24 February 2009, accessed 10 August 2015, http://www.todayszaman.com/national_turkish-tv-series-enjoy-increasing-popularity-on-arab-stations_167790.html
49. Marwan M. Kraidy and Omar al-Ghazzi, "Neo-Ottoman Cool: Turkish Popular Culture in the Arab Public Sphere," *Popular Communication: The International Journal of Media and Culture*, Vol. 11, No. 1 (2013), p. 18. A Lebanese viewer summed this up when she said: "*Noor*'s secret is that it's about people who live Western lives, but they are Easterners; they are easy to relate to." Ibrahim Kalin, "Debating Turkey in the Middle East: The Dawn of a New Geo-political Imagination?" *Insight Turkey*, Vol. 11, No. 1 (2009), p. 84.
50. Omar al-Ghazzi and Marwan M. Kraidy, "Neo-Ottoman Cool 2: Turkish Nation Branding and Arabic-Language Transnational Broadcasting," *International Journal of Communication*, No. 2 (2013), p. 2354.
51. Ibid., p. 2348.
52. Seiichi Kondo, "Wielding Soft Power," in Yasushi Watanabe and David L. McConnell, eds, *Soft Power Superpowers* (New York: M. E. Sharpe, 2008).
53. Meliha Benli Altunışık, "Turkey as an 'Emerging Donor' and the Arab Uprisings," *Mediterranean Politics*, Vol. 19, No. 3 (2014).
54. Kemal Kirisci, "Turkey's 'Demonstrative Effect' and the Transformation in the Middle East," *Insight Turkey*, Vol. 13, No. 2 (2011).
55. The first survey was conducted over 24–29 July 2009 by telephone in Egypt, Jordan, the Palestinian territories, Lebanon, Saudi Arabia, and Syria, and face-to-face in Iraq, totaling 2,006 people. The second survey was conducted over 25 August–27 September 2010, this time including Iran with a sample size of 2,267. For the 2009 survey, see Akgun et al., *Orta Dogu'da Turkiye Algisi*; for the 2010 survey, see Akgun et al., *The Perception of Turkey in the Middle East 2010.*
56. Akgun et al., *The Perception of Turkey in the Middle East 2010.*
57. The survey comprised 600 face-to-face interviews in each of Egypt, Jordan, Saudi Arabia; and 400 adults in Morocco, Lebanon, Kuwait, and the UAE. Zogby International (2002), *What Arabs Think: Values, Beliefs, and Concerns* (NY: Zogby International), p. 61; Peter A. Furia and Russell E. Lucas, "Determinants of Arab Public Opinion on Foreign Relations," *International Studies Quarterly*, No. 50 (2006), pp. 585–605.
58. Meliha Benli Altunisik, *Turkey: Arab Perspectives* (Istanbul: TESEV Publications, 2010), http://www.tesev.org.tr/UD_OBJS/PDF/DPT/OD/YYN/ArabPerspectivesRapWeb.pdf
59. Ibid.
60. Kirisci, "Turkey's 'Demonstrative Effect,'" pp. 38–9.
61. Al-Ghazzi and Kraidy, "Neo-Ottoman Cool 2," p. 2349.

62. Kalin, "Debating Turkey in the Middle East," p. 84.
63. European Commission, *Turkey 2010 Progress Report*, COM (2010), 660, pp. 6–36, http://
ec.europa.
eu/enlargement/pdf/key_documents/2010/package/tr_rapport_2010_en.pdf
64. Al-Ghazzi and Kraidy, "Neo-Ottoman Cool 2," pp. 2242–3.
65. Emiliano Alessandro and Meliha Benli Altunisik, "Unfinished Transitions: Challenges and Opportunities of the EU's and Turkey's Responses to the 'Arab Spring,'" in Sanem Aydın-Düzgit et al., eds, *Global Turkey in Europe: Political, Economic and Foreign Policy Dimensions of Turkey's Evolving relations with the EU* (Rome: IAI Research Papers, 2013), p. 234.
66. Ibid.
67. *Global Humanitarian Assistance Report*, 2014, accessed 5 February 2015, http://www.globalhumanitarianassistance.org/countryprofile/turkey
68. Geraldo Zahran and Leonardo Ramos, "From Hegemony to Soft Power: Implications of a Conceptual Change," in Inderjeet Parmar and Michael Cox, eds, *Soft Power and US Foreign Policy: Theoretical, Historical and Contemporary Perspectives* (London: Routledge, 2010), p. 17.
69. Shago Suzuki, "The Myth and Reality of China's 'Soft Power,'" in Parmar and Cox, *Soft Power and US Foreign Policy*, p. 204.
70. Joseph S. Nye, "Responding to My Critics and Concluding Thoughts," in Parmar and Cox, *Soft Power and US Foreign Policy*, p. 218.

8. THE GÜLEN MOVEMENT AND TURKISH SOFT POWER IN THE SOUTH CAUCASUS AND THE MIDDLE EAST

1. Joseph Nye, *Bound to Lead: The Changing Nature of American Power* (New York: Basic Books, 1991).
2. Joseph Nye, *Soft Power, the Means to Success in World Politics* (New York: Public Affairs, 2004), p. 5.
3. Joseph Nye, *The Future of Power* (New York: Public Affairs, 2011), p. 84.
4. Ibrahim Kalın, "Soft Power and Public Diplomacy in Turkey," *Perceptions*, No. 3 (2011), pp. 5–23.
5. Hakan Yavuz, *Toward an Islamic Enlightenment: The Gülen Movement* (Oxford: Oxford University Press, 2013), pp. 25–47.
6. Serif Mardin, *Religion and Social Change in Modern Turkey: The Case of Bediüzzaman Said Nursi* (Ann Arbor: Michigan Publishing, 1989), pp. 183–203.
7. Mustafa Gökçek, "Gülen and Sufism," http://fethullahgulenconference.org/houston/read.php?p=gulen-and-sufism
8. Elisabeth Ozdalga, "Worldly Asceticism in Islamic Casting: Fethullah Gülen's Inspired Piety and Activism," *Critique*, No. 84 (2000), pp. 84–104.

9. Claire Berlinsky, "Who Is Fethullah Gülen?" *The City*, Autumn 2012, http://www.city-journal.org/2012/22_4_fethullah-gulen.html
10. Bayram Balci, "Les écoles néo-nurcu de Fethullah Gülen en Asie centrale: implantation, fonctionnement et nature du message véhiculé par le biais de la coopération educative," *Revue des mondes musulmans et de la Méditerranée*, Nos. 101–2 (2003), http://remmm.revues.org/54
11. Anita Sengupta, *Myth and Rhetoric of the Turkish Model: Exploring Developmental Alternatives* (Kolkata: Springer, 2013), pp. 101–27.
12. Idris Bal, "The Turkish Model and the Turkic Republics," in Vedat Yücel and Salomon Ruysdael, eds, *New Trends in Turkish Foreign Affairs: Bridges and Boundaries* (New York: Writers Club Press, 2002), pp. 211–34.
13. Bayram Balci, "Fethullah Gülen's Missionary Schools in Central Asia and their Role in the Spreading of Turkism and Islam," *Religion, State and Society*, No. 2 (2003).
14. Fiona Hill, Kemal Kirişci, and Andrew Moffatt, "Armenia and Turkey: From normalization to reconciliation," *Turkish Policy*, No. 4 (2015), http://turkishpolicy.com/pdf/Armenia-and-Turkey-From-Normalization-to-Reconciliation-Winter-2015_82b3.pdf
15. Svante Cornell, *Azerbaijan Since Independence* (New York: M. E Sharpe, 2011), pp. 359–91.
16. Bayram Balci, "Between secular education and Islamic philosophy: the approach and achievements of Fethullah Gülen's followers in Azerbaijan," *Caucasus Survey*, No. 1(2013), pp. 107–16.
17. Michael Cecire, "Georgia–Turkey Relations in a Georgian Dream Era," *Caucasus Analytical Digest*, No. 48 (2013), http://www.css.ethz.ch/publications/pdfs/CAD-48-2-4.pdf
18. Justyna Szalanska, "Turkey and Georgia: Strategic Connections," *Bilgesam* (2012), http://www.bilgesam.org/en/incele/452/-turkey-and-georgia—strategic-connections/#.VUEtjCHtmko
19. http://www.ibsu.edu.ge/?lang=en-US
20. Efrat E. Aviv, "Fethullah Gülen's 'Jewish Dialogue,'" *Turkish Policy*, No. 3 (2010), http://turkishpolicy.com/pdf/vol_9-no_3-aviv.pdf
21. Julia Harte, "Turkey Shocks Africa," World Policy Institute, http://www.worldpolicy.org/journal/winter2012/turkey-shocks-africa
22. Jana Jabbour, *La construction d'une diplomatie émergente: le cas de la Turquie au Moyen Orient (2002–2014)*, PhD diss., Sciences Po Paris, forthcoming.
23. http://hizmetnews.com/672/conferences-on-hizmet-movement-in-egypt-attracted-masses/#.VUEu_yHtmko
24. Sophia Pandya, "Hizmet and the Kurdish Question in Southeastern Turkey and Iraq," *Turkish Journal of Politics*, No. 1 (2014), pp. 73–94.
25. Yohanan Benhaim, "Recompositions de l'Etat et coproduction de l'action pub-

lique: Les écoles du mouvement Gülen dans la politique étrangère turque au Kurdistan irakien," *European Journal of Turkish Studies*, No. 21 (2015).

26. Ümit Cizre, "Demythologyzing the National Security Concept: the Case of Turkey," *Middle East Journal*, No. 2 (2003), pp. 13–229.
27. Benhaim, "Recompostions de l'Etat."
28. Robert Hatem and Mark Dohrmann, "Turkey's Fix for the 'Kurdish Problem', Ankara's Challenges", *Middle East Quarterly* (2013), pp. 49–58, http://www.meforum.org/3667/turkey-kurdish-problem
29. Benhaim, "Recompositions de l'Etat."
30. Bill Park, "Turkey–Kurdish Regional Government Relations After the US Withdrawal from Iraq: Putting the Kurds on the Map?", *United States Army War College* (2014), p. 91, http://www.strategicstudiesinstitute.army.mil/pdffiles/pub1190.pdf
31. Bayram Balci, "The Gülen Movement and Turkish Soft Power," Carnegie Endowment for International Peace (2014). http://carnegieendowment.org/2014/02/04/g%C3%BClen-movement-and-turkish-soft-power
32. Heba al Sayed, "Fethullah Gülen's Reforming Thought and Turkey's Relations with its Cultural Neighborhood," in Yasin Aktay, Pakinem El-Sharkawy, and Ahmet Uysal, eds, *Culture and Politics in the New Middle East* (Cairo: Institute of Strategic Thinking and Center for Civilization Studies and Cultures Dialogue, Cairo University, 2012), http://www.atcoss.org/userfiles/file/atcoss1-book-english.pdf
33. Mehmet Kalyoncu, *A Civilian Response to Ethno-Religious Conflict: The Gülen Movement in Southeast Turkey* (New Jersey: The Light, 2008).
34. Nigar Göksel, "Turkey and Georgia: Zero-Problems?", German Marshall Fund (2013), http://www.gmfus.org/file/3054/download
35. Nancy Gallagher, "Hizmet Intercultural Dialogue Trips to Turkey," in Sophia Pandya and Nancy Gallagher, eds, *The Gülen Hizmet Movement and its Transnational Activities: Case Studies of Altruistic Activism in Contemporary Islam* (Boca Raton, FL: Brown Walker Press, 2012), pp. 97–116.
36. Ahmet Kuru, "Globalization and diversification of Islamic movements: three Turkish cases," *Political Science Quarterly*, No. 2 (2005), pp. 253–74.
37. Hakan Yavuz, "Search for a New Social Contract in Turkey: Fethullah Gülen, the Virtue Party and the Kurds," *SAIS Review*, No. 1 (1999), pp. 114–43.
38. Yavuz Baydar, "Erdoğan v Gülen: Zero sum game?", Al Jazeera, December 2013, http://www.aljazeera.com/indepth/opinion/2013/12/erdogan-v-gulen-zero-sum-game-20131228653542676.html
39. Ertan Karpazli, "Erdoğan–Gulen rift began with Mavi Marmara in 2010," *Middle East Monitor*, December 2013, https://www.middleeastmonitor.com/articles/europe/8920-erdogan-gulen-rift-began-with-mavi-marmara-in-2010
40. Shahla Sultanova, "Azerbaijan Backing Turkey's Crackdown on Gülen Movement," *Eurasianet*, April 2014, http://www.eurasianet.org/node/68274

41. Jacques Fairweather, "Erdoğan Seeks to Vanquish Opponent Gülen in Global Fight," *Bloomberg Business*, September 2014.
42. Mina Muradova, "Turkey's Gülen Controversy Spills over to Azerbaijan," *Central Asia Caucasus Analyst*, April 2014, http://www.cacianalyst.org/publications/field-reports/item/12946-turkeys-g%C3%BClen-controversy-spills-over-to-azerbaijan.html

9. THE ARMENIAN IMPERATIVE: CONFRONTING AND CONTAINING OLIGARCHS

1. For more on the birth of specific post-Soviet oligarchs, see Chrystia Freeland, *Sale of the Century: Russia's Wild Ride from Communism to Capitalism* (New York: Crown Business, 2000); and David Hoffman, *The Oligarchs* (New York: Public Affairs, 2002).
2. Anders Aslund, "Comparative Oligarchy: Russia, Ukraine and the United States" (Warsaw: Center for Social and Economic Research (CASE), April 2005).
3. Joel Hellman, "Winners Take All: The Politics of Partial Reform in Post-Communist Transitions," *World Politics*, No. 50 (1998), pp. 203–34.
4. Aslund, "Comparative Oligarchy."
5. Fareed Zakaria, *The Future of Freedom: Illiberal Democracy at Home and Abroad* (New York: W. W. Norton, 2003), p. 75.
6. Richard Giragosian, "Qu'est-ce qu'être « oligarque » au Caucase? Le cas arménien," in Gaïdz Minassian, ed., *Eurasie, au cœur de la sécurité mondial* (Paris: Flammarion, 2011).
7. Richard Giragosian, "Armenia's Crisis for the Non-Democrats," in Michael Emerson and Richard Youngs, eds, *Democracy's Plight in the European Neighbourhood: Struggling Transitions and Proliferating Dynasties* (Brussels: Centre for European Policy Studies (CEPS), October 2009), www.ceps.be/ceps/download/2315
8. Such public displays of wealth are no longer limited to the palatial homes and expansive property of the oligarchs, but now include a much higher degree of public visibility, ranging from status-based special license plates for their vehicles to power displays involving multi-vehicle entourages and groups of bodyguards, often obviously armed.
9. Richard Giragosian, "Networks of Crime and Corruption," *Caucasus Analytical Digest* (CAD), Boell Stiftung, September 2009, http://georgien.boell-net.de/downloads/CaucasusAnalyticalDigest09.pdf
10. Richard Giragosian, "The Shifting Armenian Political Landscape," Radio Free Europe/Radio Liberty (RFE/RL) Endnote, 13 September 2006.
11. Armenia held parliamentary elections in May 2012, followed by a presidential contest in February 2013 and a municipal election in Yerevan in May 2013.

12. For the broader context, see Jennifer Rankin, "Last of the Mohicans. Armenia's President Serzh Sargsyan," *European Voice*, 14 March 2013, www.europeanvoice.com/article/imported/last-of-the-mohicans/76656.aspx
13. In the election held on 25 May 2003, of the 131 seats, 56 were based on the majoritarian system and 75 seats were elected on a national basis using proportional representation.
14. The Kentron TV station was later sold to Gagik Tsarukian, the head of the Prosperous Armenia party; it has been reported that Arsenian was forced to sell the station for a below market price, in a deal that included family members of former President Robert Kocharian as well.

10. UNDERSTANDING VARIATION IN CORRUPTION AND WHITE-COLLAR CRIME: GEORGIA AND ARMENIA

1. Torsten Persson, Gérard Roland, and Guido Tabellini, "Comparative Politics and Public Finance," *Journal of Political Economy*, Vol. 108, No. 6 (2000), pp. 1121–61.
2. Joseph Alois Schumpeter, *The Theory of Economic Development: An Inquiry into Profits, Capital, Credit, Interest, and the Business Cycle*, Vol. 55 (Transaction Publishers, 1934). Also the idea of political competition leading to good governance is an integral point of Washington Consensus.
3. Daniel Treisman, "The Causes of Corruption: A Cross-National Study," *Journal of Public Economics*, Vol. 76 (2000), pp. 399–457.
4. Tatiana Kostadinova, *Political Corruption in Eastern Europe: Politics after Communism* (Boulder, CO: Lynne Rienner Publishers, 2012).
5. In Georgia the willingness to attract more foreign investment was one of the key drivers of anti-corruption reform, rather than more FDI causing greater reform efforts in Georgia vis-à-vis Armenia.
6. According to the 2011 CRRC survey *Caucasus Barometer*, 6 percent of the Armenian respondents report paying bribes over the last 12 months compared to 0 percent in Georgia. The international crime victimization surveys of 2010 and 2011 indicate that Georgia shows one of the best results in Europe: only 0.2 percent of the population mentioned that one or more officials had asked them to pay a bribe in the course of last year, down from 16.8 percent in 2000 and 3.5 in 2004/5. For victimization data, see Jan Van Dijk and Fanny Klerx-Van Mierlo, "Indicators of Corruption: Further Explorations of the Link between Corruption and Implementation Failure in Anti-Trafficking Policies," Working Paper, International Victimology Institute (INTERVICT) (University of Tilburg, Netherlands, 2011).
7. "Doing Business 2007: Georgia is Top Reformer in the Commonwealth of Independent States and Jumps up the Global Rankings," World Bank, 5 September 2006, http://www.doingbusiness.org/press/~/media/FPDKM/Doing%20Business/Documents/Press-Releases06–09/2007/DB07-PR-CIS.pdf

8. Alexander Kupatadze, *Organized Crime, Political Transitions, and State Formation in Post-Soviet Eurasia* (New York, Basingstoke: Palgrave Macmillan, 2012).
9. For full information about the index, see http://info.worldbank.org/governance/wgi/pdf/cc.pdf. The index aims to capture not only perceptions of the extent to which public power is exercised for private gain, including both petty and grand forms of corruption, but also the degree of state capture by elites and private interests. The index aggregates measurements by transparent methodology and it has been widely credited for its reliability.
10. Gia Nodia, "Georgia, Dimensions of Insecurity," in Bruno Coppieters and Robert Legvold, eds, *Statehood and Security. Georgia after the Rose Revolution* (Cambridge, MA: MIT Press, 2006), p. 94.
11. Roy Godson, Dennis Jay Kenney, Margaret Litvin, and Gigi Tevzadze, "Building Societal Support for the Rule of Law in Georgia," *Trends in Organized Crime*, Vol. 8 (2004), pp. 5–27.
12. Georgia profile, CIA, *World Fact Book* 2002, https://www.cia.gov/library/publications/the-world-factbook/
13. Gia Nodia, "Putting the State Back Together in Post-Soviet Georgia," in Mark Beissinger and Crawford Young, eds, *Beyond State Crisis? Postcolonial Africa and Post-Soviet Eurasia in Comparative Perspective* (Baltimore, MD: Johns Hopkins University Press, 2002), p. 420.
14. Christoph Stefes, *Understanding Post-Soviet Transitions: Corruption, Collusion and Clientelism* (New York, Basingstoke: Palgrave Macmillan, 2006), p. 95.
15. Barbara Christophe, "Bringing Culture back into a Concept of Rationality: State–Society Relations and Conflict in Post-Socialist Transcaucasia," in Jan Koehler and Christopli Ziircher (eds), *Potentials of Disorder* (Manchester, UK: Manchester University Press, 2003), p. 203.
16. For instance, Shevardnadze's program for fighting the shadow economy, created in the 1990s, was never executed. As soon as the Ministry of the Economy began implementation, it was sabotaged by the corrupt business–political nexus. See Koba Kikabidze and David Losaberidze, *Institutionalism and Clientelism in Georgia* (Tbilisi: Nekeri, 2000), p. 45.
17. Lincoln A. Mitchell, *Uncertain Democracy: US Foreign Policy and Georgia's Rose Revolution* (University of Pennsylvania Press, 2009).
18. Wheatley Jonathan, "Georgia at a Crossroads: After the Post-War," *Opendemocracy.net*, 22 October 2010; Wilson Andrews, "Work Package: WP3, Corruption and Governance Improvement in Global and Continental Perspective" (Georgia: Country Background Report, 2013).
19. World Bank, *Fighting Corruption in Public Services: Chronicling Georgia's Reforms* (Washington, DC: World Bank, 2012).
20. Zurab Chiaberashvili and Gigi Tevzadze, "Power Elites in Georgia: Old and New," in P. H. Fluri and E. Cole, eds, *Revolution to Reform: Georgia's Struggle with Democratic Institution Building and Security Sector Reform* (GSDRC, 2005).

21. However, this changed as re-privatization proceeded and as the new incumbents developed vested interests. Compared to the 2004 parliament, the UNM faction elected in 2008 had a number of wealthy businessmen. See "Businessmen in Politics and Politicians in Business: Problem of Revolving Door in Georgia" (Tbilisi: Transparency International Georgia, 2013); Andrews, "Work Package."
22. "New Leadership Pledges Fundamental Reforms," *Civil Georgia*, 1 December 2003, http://www.civil.ge/eng/article.php?id=5721&search=
23. Neil Macfarlane. "Post-Revolutionary Georgia on the Edge?" Chatham House briefing paper, March, 2011.
24. "Report on Criminal Justice Statistics," GEOSTAT, July 2011, http://www.geostat.ge/index.php?action=page&p_id=622&lang=geo
25. According to EBRD surveys, in Georgia the percentage of firms indicating corruption as a major constraint decreased from 41.0 percent in 2002, to 23.6 percent in 2005, and to 20.4 percent in 2008. Armenia demonstrates the reverse trend: increasing from 15.3 percent in 2002, to 21.4 percent in 2005, and to 39.6 percent in 2009.
26. Personal communication with the officials of Ministry of Justice, 10 June 2011, Tbilisi, Georgia.
27. Boris Navasardian, *Politics and Governance in South Caucasus—20 Years of Independence* (Berlin: Friedrich Ebert Stiftung, 2012).
28. "Armenia Country Report," BTI, 2012, http://www.bti-project.de/uploads/tx_itao_download/BTI_2012_Armenia.pdf
29. In 2008 the Armenian government mounted pressure, through customs and tax enforcement agencies, on the businesses of Khachatur Sukiassian, supporter of Levon Ter-Petrossian, who ran against Serzh Sargsyan in the presidential elections. Several criminal cases have been raised against Sukiassian, and he was obliged to flee the country.
30. Christoph Stefes, "Governance, the State, and Systemic Corruption: Armenia and Georgia in Comparison," *Caucasian Review of International Affairs*, No. 2 (2008), pp. 73–83; Investment Climate Statement Bureau of Economic and Business Affairs, *US Department of State* (2013), http://www.state.gov/e/eb/rls/othr/ics/2013/204593.htm
31. Security guards and personnel of a restaurant owned by Hayrapetyan attacked and beat Vahe Avetyan, a military doctor, and four others. Avetyan died as a result of his injuries. The investigation did not have any consequences for Hayrapetyan, allegedly because of his political and economic power.
32. US Department of State, "Human Rights Report, Armenia" (2012), http://www.state.gov/documents/organization/204468.pdf
33. Policy Forum Armenia, "Corruption in Armenia" (2013), http://www.pf-armenia.org/document/corruption-armenia
34. The arrests included one high-level official within the Ministry of Environment,

the Chief of Armenian Traffic Police, the former head of State Social Security Service, and the vice governor of Kotyak province. See "Armenia Country Report" and "Nations in Transit—Armenia 2013," Freedom House, http://www.freedomhouse.org/report/nations-transit/2013/armenia#.UvPnDoW2xRw

35. Gayane Mkrtchyan, "Armenia: Scepticism over Police Graft Charges," Institute for War and Peace Reporting (2011), http://iwpr.net/report-news/armenia-scepticism-over-police-graft-charges
36. Human Rights Report, "Armenia 2012."
37. "Armenia: Key Suspect Arrested in Diamond Scandal Linked to PM, Archbishop," *Eurasianet*, 3 February 2014, http://www.eurasianet.org/node/68000
38. "Armenia Country Report."
39. David Petrosyan, "Oligarchy in Armenia," *Caucasus Analytical Digest* (July 2013), pp. 53–4.
40. Bagrat Tunyan, "The Shadow Economy of Armenia: Size, Causes and Consequences," in 3rd Annual AIPRG conference (Washington, DC, 2005); US Commercial Service, *Doing Business in Armenia: 2012 Country Commercial Guide for U.S. Companies* (2012), http://photos.state.gov/libraries/armenia/328666/key_reports/ccg2012.pdf
41. "Armenian Governor Again Accused of Violence," *RFE/RL*, 16 November 2011, http://www.rferl.org/content/armenian_governor_again_accused_of_violence/24392631.html
42. "Georgia: Saakashvili Says Switzerland Will Meet Singapore in Tbilisi," *Eurasianet*, 9 March 2010, http://www.eurasianet.org/departments/news/articles/eav031010.shtml
43. See Paul Rimple, "Who owned Georgia 2003–2012?" (Tbilisi: Transparency International and Open Society Georgia Foundation, 2012). Re-privatization had other negative consequences as well. Since the change of government in October 2012, numerous complaints have been filed. More than 1,000 people claimed that prosecutors had played a central role in the illegal seizure of their property, forcing them to "donate" their real estate to the state. See Thomas Hammarberg, "Georgia in Transition: Report on the Human Rights Dimension: Background, Steps Taken and Remaining Challenges" (European External Action Service, 2013).
44. "Georgia: Tbilisi Lawmakers Try to Define Where Politics Ends and Business Begins," *Eurasianet*, 11 November 2011, http://www.eurasianet.org/node/64535; "Businessmen in Politics and Politicians in Business: Problem of Revolving Door in Georgia."
45. Aleksandr Iskandaryan, "Armenia between Autocracy and Polyarchy," *Russian Politics and Law*, Vol. 50, No. 4 (2012), pp. 23–36.
46. Hrant Mikaelyan, "Civil Society in Armenia," in Mikko Palonkorpi and Alexander Iskandaryan, eds, *Armenia's Foreign and Development Politics: Development Trends* (Yerevan: Caucasus Institute, 2013), pp. 55–69.

47. Aleksandr Khechumyan and Sanja Kutnjak Ivković, "Police Integrity in Armenia," in Sanja Kutnjak Ivković and M.R. Haberfeld, eds, *Measuring Police Integrity Across the World* (New York: Springer, 2015), pp. 37–65.
48. Richard Giragosian, "From Partisan Confrontation to Political Stalemate: The Struggle for Stability in Armenia," in Adam Hug, ed., *Spotlight on Armenia* (London: Foreign Policy Centre, 2011); Navasardian, *Politics and Governance in South Caucasus.*
49. Petrosyan, "Oligarchy in Armenia."
50. "'Hazing' could Subvert Military Reform," *Oxford Analytica—Daily Brief Service*, 3 February 2012.
51. Iskandaryan, "Armenia between Autocracy and Polyarchy."
52. Gevorg Ter-Gabrielyan, "The Internal and the External: Politics, NGOs, Conflict and Peace in Armenia," in Hug, *Spotlight on Armenia.*
53. Walter Kaufmann, "A European Path for Abkhazia: Yesterday's Pipe Dreams?" *Caucasus Analytical Digest*, No. 7, 25 June 2009; Carnegie Endowment for International Peace, "Political Reform in Georgia," Discussion by Thomas De Waal, Ambassador Irakli Alasania, and Cory Welt, 2010, http://carnegieendowment.org/2010/11/16/political-reform-in-georgia/p53
54. The study held in-depth interviews with 36 leaders of political parties.
55. Association for International Relations, *Looking Through the Party Lenses: a comparative study of Georgian political parties' views on foreign and national security policies* (Tbilisi: AIR and Friedrich Ebert Stiftung, 2010).
56. Bokeria, quoted in Thomas De Waal, *Georgia's Choices. Charting a Future in Uncertain Times* (Washington, DC: Carnegie Endowment for International Peace, 2011), p. 33.
57. Lucan A. Way and Steven Levitsky. "Linkage, Leverage, and the Post-Communist Divide," *East European Politics and Societies*, Vol. 21, No. 1 (2007), pp. 48–66.
58. A survey was conducted among 691 respondents: from public servants, members of political parties, NGO activists, members of local governance bodies, student council members, academics/artists/athletes, top business owners and CEOs.
59. AREG, *The Political Elite of Post-Independence Armenia: Characteristics and Patterns of Formation* (Yerevan: Edit Print, 2014).
60. Way and Levitsky, "Linkage, Leverage, and the Post-Communist Divide."
61. Matthew Light, "Police Reforms in the Republic of Georgia: The Convergence of Domestic and Foreign Policy in an Anti-Corruption Drive," *Policing and Society*, Vol. 24, No. 3 (2014), pp. 318–45; Gavin Slade, "Reorganizing Crime: Mafia and Anti-mafia in Post-Soviet Georgia" (Oxford: Oxford University Press, 2014).
62. Mikheil Saakashvili, Remarks at New York State University [online], September 2010,http://www.president.gov.ge/index.php?lang_id"ENG&sec_id"228&info_id"5492
63. Gordadze's address is available at https://www.youtube.com/watch?v=sD5oAXG_nOc, retrieved 13 March 2013.

64. Iskandaryan, "Armenia Between Autocracy and Polyarchy."
65. Stefes, "Governance, the State and Systemic Corruption."
66. Policy Forum Armenia, "Corruption in Armenia."
67. Freedom House, "Nations in Transit—Armenia 2013."
68. *Liberali*, news journal, 23 April 2011, http://www.liberali.ge/ge/liberali/articles/106159/
69. Regional Studies Center. "Strategic Setback: Armenia and Customs Union," Working Paper (Yerevan, October 2013).
70. Richard Giragosian, "Armenian–EU Integration: Missed Opportunities and Strategic Mistakes," 16 January 2014, http://www.ge.boell.org/web/110-1601.html
71. Stephan H. Astourian, "From Ter-Petrosian to Kocharian: Leadership Change in Armenia," Berkeley Program in Soviet and Post-Soviet Studies Working Paper Series, 2000–2001; Gayane Abrahamyan, "Armenia: Diaspora Investors Ready to Move On?" *Eurasianet*, 4 September 2012, http://www.eurasianet.org/node/65860
72. Policy Forum Armenia, "Corruption in Armenia."
73. OECD Economic Surveys, "Baltic States—A Regional Economic Assessment" (Paris: OECD, 2000).
74. Ardo H. Hansson, "The Political Economy of Macroeconomic and Foreign Trade Policy in Estonia," *Trade in the New Independent States* (World Bank, 1994), pp. 133–140.
75. Artis Pabriks and Aldis Purs, *Latvia: The Challenges of Change* (London: Routledge, 2013).
76. Ole Nørgaard and Lars Johannsen, *The Baltic States after Independence* (Cheltenham, UK: Edward Elgar, 1999).

11. BAKU: CREATING A PERSIAN GULF PARADISE ON THE CASPIAN SEA

1. In fact, the oil well drilled in Baku in 1847 was the first industrial oil well drilled in the world.
2. Jamil Hasanli, "The Struggle for Baku Oil at the End of the World War I," *Caspian Crossroads*, Vol. 1 (1997), pp. 12–16.
3. Azerbaijani State Statistics Committee (2011, 2013, 2014), http://www.stat.gov.az.
4. Ibid.
5. Judit Bodnár, *Fin de Millénaire Budapest: Metamorphoses of Urban Life* (Minnesota: University of Minnesota Press, 2000); Kiril Stanilov, *The Post-Socialist City: Urban Form and Space Transformations in Central and Eastern Europe after Socialism* (Ohio: Springer, 2007).
6. Ali Ahmadov, "Construction of Khazar Islands to cost $100 bn," APA News Agency, 27 January 2012.

7. L. Saifutdinova, "Urban restructuring of Baku City Center," *Context*, No. 2 (2010), pp. 26–32.
8. Michael Pacione, "City Profile Dubai," *Cities*, Vol. 22, No. 3 (2005), pp. 255–65.
9. K. F. Gotham, "Theorizing Urban Spectacles," *City*, Vol. 9, No. 2 (2005), pp. 225–46.
10. Kris Olds and Henry Yeung, "Pathways to Global City Formation: A View from the Developmental City-state of Singapore," *Review of International Political Economy*, Vol. 11 (2004), pp. 489–521.
11. Brian Chalkley and Stephen Essex, "Urban Development through Hosting International Events: A History of the Olympic Games," *Planning Perspectives*, Vol. 14 (1999), pp. 369–94.
12. Murad Ismayilov, "State, Identity, and the Politics of Music: Eurovision and Nation-building in Azerbaijan," *Nationalities Papers*, Vol. 40 (2012).
13. Ibid.
14. Ibid.; Anar Valiyev, "The Post-Communist Growth Machine: The Case of Baku, Azerbaijan," *Cities*, Vol. 41 (2012), pp. 45–53.
15. Georgi Gotev, "Minister: After the Baku games, Azerbaijan will be an even more popular destination," Euroactive.com (May 2015), http://www.euractiv.com/sections/baku-2015-european-games/sports-official-after-baku-games-nobody-will-ask-where-azerbaijan
16. "Azerbaijan is to Spend 8 Billion Dollars on Inaugural European Games," *Azadliq Radiosu*, 24 November 2014, http://www.azadliq.org/content/article/26707738.html
17. Ibid.
18. "New Stadium in Baku," Uefa.com (June 2011).
19. "Venues of the Game," Baku European Games Olympic Committee (2015), http://www.baku2015.com.
20. Andrew Jonas and David Wilson, eds, *The Urban Growth Machine* (Albany, NY: State University of New York Press, 1999).
21. "F1: Azerbaijan to host GP from 2016," *Racer*, 25 July 2015, http://www.racer.com/f1/item/106110-azerbaijan-to-host-f1-gp-from-2016
22. Duncan Mackay, "Baku awarded 2017 Islamic Solidarity Games," 26 July 2013, http://www.insidethegames.biz/articles/1015266/baku-awarded-2017-islamic-solidarity-games.
23. Chingiz Huseynzadeh: "Azerbaijan Ready to Accept Islamic Games," *Contact*, 9 June 2015.
24. "Azerbaijan says 2024 Olympic bid possible," *NZ Herald*, 24 June 2015, http://www.nzherald.co.nz/sport/news/article.cfm?c_id=4&objectid=11470128
25. Martin Hvidt, "The Dubai Model: An Outline of Key Development-process Elements in Dubai," *International Journal of Middle East Studies*, Vol. 41 (2009), pp. 397–418.

26. State Statistical Committee of the Republic of Azerbaijan (2011, 2013, 2014).
27. Ibid.
28. Benjamin Jones, "Luxury Brands into Boomtown," *Hotel News Now*, 23 October 2012.
29. Ibid.
30. Ibid.
31. Christine Kessides, "Strategizing for the Future in the Four ECA Cities: Budapest, St Petersburg, Sofia and Split" (paper prepared for ECA Urban Sector Strategy, ECSIN, Washington, DC, 2000).
32. Pirouz Khanlou, "Construction! Destruction?" *Azerbaijan International*, Vol. 13 (2005).
33. Anar Valiyev, "Urban Development in Baku and its perception by citizens," unpublished manuscript.

INDEX